Liquid Pleasures

Drinking has always meant much more than satisfying the thirst. Drinking can be a necessity, a comfort, an indulgence or a social activity.

Liquid Pleasures is an engrossing study of the social history of drinks in Britain from the late seventeenth century to the present. From the first cup of tea at breakfast and mid-morning coffee, to an evening beer and a 'night-cap', John Burnett discusses individual drinks and drinking patterns which have varied not least with personal taste but also with age, gender, region and class. He shows how different ages have viewed the same drink as either demon poison or medicine.

John Burnett traces the history of what has been drunk in Britain from the 'hot beverages revolution' of the late seventeenth century – connecting drinks and related substances such as sugar to empire – right up to the 'cold drinks revolution' of the late twentieth century, examining the factors which have determined these major changes in our dietary habits.

John Burnett is Emeritus Professor of Social History at Brunel University. His many books include *Plenty and Want: A Social History of Food in England* (3rd edn 1989), *Idle Hands* (1994), *Useful Toil* (1994) and *A Social History of Housing* (1986).

Liquid Pleasures

A Social History of Drinks
in Modern Britain

John Burnett

London and New York

First published 1999
by Routledge
11 New Fetter Lane, London EC4P 4EE

Simultaneously published in the USA and Canada
by Routledge
29 West 35th Street, New York, NY 10001

Routledge is an imprint of the Taylor & Francis Group

©1999 John Burnett

Typeset in Baskerville by The Florence Group, Stoodleigh, Devon
Printed and bound in Great Britain by
St Edmundsbury Press, Bury St Edmunds, Suffolk

British Library Cataloguing in Publication Data
A catalogue record for this book is available from the
British Library.

Library of Congress Cataloging in Publication Data
Burnett, John, 1925–
    Liquid pleasures: a social history of drinks in modern Britain /
John Burnett.
        p.   cm.
    Includes bibliographical references and index.
    ISBN 0–415–13181–2 (hardbound). — ISBN 0–415–13182–0
(pbk.)
    1. Beverages—Great Britain—History. 2. Beverages—Social
aspects—Great Britain. I. Title.
    TX815.B87   1999
    641.2′0941—dc21
                                                        98–54588
                                                           CIP

ISBN 0–415–13181–2 (hbk) 0–415–13182–0 (pbk)

Contents

List of figures and tables

Figures

Tables

Introduction

Most people in Britain begin the day with a hot drink, usually tea; at mid-morning coffee is often preferred, while at lunch a soft drink may replace a hot one; tea reappears in the afternoon and coffee in the evening, though this is also the preferred time for alcoholic drinks. Consideration of such commonplaces seems banal: we accept our drinking habits almost unconsciously, as if customary and immutable. Naturally, these patterns vary according to a wide range of determinants – age, gender, social class, region and, not least, personal taste – but nevertheless what the average Briton drinks in the late 1990s can be accurately quantified. Of 8.23 standard cups of liquid consumed daily, tea provides 3.39 cups, coffee 1.65, soft drinks 1.5 and alcoholic drinks 1.37: 75 per cent of people over 10 drink tea daily, 53 per cent coffee, 55 per cent soft drinks and 32 per cent alcohol.[1]

In fact, this pattern is far from unchanging, and drinks now described as 'normal goods' – instant coffee, lager beer, soft drinks, bottled water and table wine – were not in normal use even a generation ago. And three centuries rather than three decades ago, the pattern is almost unrecognizable. The aspiring civil servant, Samuel Pepys, tasted his first cup of tea in 1660 – his usual 'morning draught' was ale or wine, often taken at a tavern; 'Ho-Bryan' (Haut-Brion), the earliest estate-bottled claret, was first experienced in 1663, orange juice (oranges 6d each) in 1669 and champagne in 1677 when he had risen to become Master of Trinity House. By then he kept a considerable cellar of imported wines like Canary, Malaga, Tent (Spanish red), Rhenish and 'Sherris sack' from Jerez, and was fond of sweetened, spiced drinks such as hippocras (flavoured wine) and metheglin (spiced mead). In drawing up a victualling contract for the Navy in 1678 he provided each sailor with a gallon of beer a day or, if sailing south of Lisbon, a quart (2 pints) of wine.[2]

Pepys was living at a turning-point in the history of consumption, at the threshold of the modern world when traditional patterns of eating and drinking as well as of dress, manners, architecture and furnishing were beginning to be transformed by new products and fashions, many of foreign origin. Drinks are not 'givens': they are subject to a range of cultural and social forces, and have changed, adapted or, in some cases, disappeared as the culture at large has diversified and globalized. Historians differ as much over the timing of this first 'consumer revolution' as they do over that of the 'industrial revolution', though most have followed the persuasive lead of McKendrick, Brewer and Plumb in emphasizing the eighteenth century, and especially its third quarter, as the period when a consumer boom attained 'revolutionary proportions'.[3] I wish to show that in the context of drinking habits that revolution was initiated in the mid-seventeenth century and completed before the middle of the next. It was not so much that a consumer revolution accompanied the industrial one as that, in this case, it preceded it, creating new demands on overseas trade as well as on the manufacture of equipment for the new hot drinks tea, coffee and chocolate – especially porcelain, pottery, silverware and furniture. As new worlds were exploited by European powers in the seventeenth and eighteenth centuries, these drinks, together with associated sugar, represented only part of a larger list of new consumables, though a highly significant one: they constituted an ideological expression of a revolution in *mentalité*, of the ways in which the world, and man's place in it, were viewed. It will further be argued that after the lapse of a couple of centuries during which the new drinking habits were so widely established as themselves to become 'traditional', the period from the 1960s onwards is experiencing a new, cold drinks revolution, associated with some decline in the primacy of hot beverages but a remarkably rapid growth in the consumption of chilled drinks. The processes by which in both revolutions drinks that were initially restricted to elite groups in society moved into mass consumption – or, in some instances, remained restricted or actually declined – is a main consideration of this book.

Two things need first to be said about its title and content. 'Modern Britain' is usually taken to mean the period from the later eighteenth century onwards, but for reasons already mentioned the modernization of British drinking habits places our starting-point a century earlier. Similarly, since the history of drinking changes has no finite end, the intention is to follow their course to as near the present as the data allow. Second, the book is concerned with all the main categories of drinks consumed in Britain from water to wine, not only with 'drink', which is often equated with alcohol ('Would you like a drink?', or 'He drinks'). The literature on drink, whether by historians or by temperance writers,[4] has often been restricted in this way to the neglect of the much wider range of available liquids.

There are clearly many ways and discourses by which the subject may be approached. At the basic, physiological level liquids are essential for life, and although humans can survive for some weeks without food, they cannot exist without drink for more than a few days. More than half human body weight consists of water: we eliminate at least 1.7 litres (3 pints) a day, which must be replaced to maintain health. These average requirements may be greatly exceeded for those engaged in heavy labour or energetic activity in warm conditions, and the custom of furnacemen, steelworkers, harvesters and others to drink gallons rather than pints a day was often entirely justified. Many drinks are also important contributors to energy and nutritional needs. At some periods and for some groups milk was as much food as drink, while alcohol was a major source of energy and a significant provider of several minerals and vitamins: it is estimated that alcohol, principally beer, supplied around 400–500 kcal per person per day in the first half of the eighteenth century or one-fifth of energy needs, about 250 kcal in the later nineteenth century and 150 kcal in the 1970s,[5] though considerably larger quantities for adult male drinkers. The 'regular' pub-goer who told a Mass Observation reporter in 1936 that 'beer is food, drink and medicine to me'[6] had some scientific justification.

The physical and psychological effects of the two main categories of drinks, the alcoholic and the caffeine beverages tea, coffee and chocolate, are distinct and, to some degree, opposite. While alcohol in moderate quantity relaxes and tranquillizes, caffeine acts on the brain and the central nervous system to stimulate mental and physical activity – in Louis Lewin's word it is an 'excitant'.[7] The ability of these two substances to alter mood, to relieve stress or to revive, made them seemingly indispensable throughout much of the world. The relationship between drinks and health is a recurring theme of this book since, remarkably, every one of those considered in the following chapters was promoted at some period for its claimed therapeutic benefits: especially in the case of a new product, it was felt necessary to reassure and persuade consumers that it was good for them as well as pleasurable. Throughout the whole period advertisement has been a prominent, and often controversial, characteristic of drinks history.

A history of consumption – and food and drink are the most literal forms of consumption – needs to ask how and when various groups in society became enfranchised to participate. One obvious aspect of this is economic: classes and individuals required purchasing power to become consumers, and historically the 'participation ratio' for new goods generally moved from wealthy, elite groups first to the bourgeoisie and later, though not always, into mass consumption. The place of foods and drinks in family budgets, their types, quantities and costs, is a key element of the ongoing debate about the effects of industrialization on the standard of living, particularly of the working classes; but the case for 'optimism' or 'pessimism' is not resolved by measuring changes in the consumption of an individual product. When, for example, a former luxury like tea became an integral part of the diets of the poor, it may have been at the expense of more desired or nutritionally superior drinks. Economic historians have generally been more interested in questions of supply rather than of consumption. As a major industry, brewing has received considerable scholarly attention, as has the development of overseas trade in Asiatic, American and colonial products, but once these have passed through the hands of producers and intermediaries much less interest has been directed at their ultimate destination.

As recently as 1987 Grant McCracken complained that 'the history of consumption has no history, no community of scholars, no tradition of scholarship'.[8] Although Polanyi and Braudel had begun to explore the key role of consumption in 'the great transformation' from traditional to modern societies,[9] it has fallen principally to social scientists to offer valuable insights into its processes and meanings.[10] Drinking has always meant more than satisfying thirst, and in developed societies very much more. Sociological theories help to explain how consumption defines membership of groups and classes – if we are what we eat, we are also what we drink – and it is now recognized, as McCracken says, that consumption is not merely a reflection of the social changes taking place around it but 'a causal agency in its own right'. Social class and social aspiration have been major influences on drinking behaviour, and theories of conspicuous consumption and diffusion may be useful in showing how possession of goods moved through classes, though we should be cautious in accepting any over-simple, mechanistic view. The well-known 'trickle-down' theory of Gilboy, that 'luxury articles of the rich will seep down through the different social ranks and perhaps end by becoming a necessity for all',[11] does not itself provide an explanation, and the belief that 'fashion' was a principal agent in the diffusion of new products only raises questions about when, why, how and for whom it became influential. Similarly, the question of how consumers acquired the 'taste' for new drinks is highly relevant, though difficult to answer. While accepting that tastes are rarely innate, but culturally shaped and conditioned, Stephen Mennell argues that a purely structuralist approach is too static and has little to offer about how tastes change over time:[12] sociology needs to be informed by history, and vice versa.

Consumers had to learn to like and to want new drinks, some of which were by no means immediately appealing: coffee, for example, has been described as 'innately aversive', a black, bitter liquid that some early drinkers likened to pitch, and many children still have to be accustomed to enjoy tea, often by the addition of quantities of sugar. Those marketing new products well understood that consumers needed to be psychologically sensitized and persuaded, and from the seventeenth century onwards an explosion of information by advertisements, pamphlets, newspapers and, more recently, the mass media has been crucial to the popularization of new drinks. 'Needs' came to be determined not by physiological requirements but in terms of cultural 'wants'.

Drink can be viewed as a factor in cementing the construction of identity as well as a means of bonding social networks. Among the many expressions of cultural want, the festive has been a powerful force, and Mary Douglas suggests that 'the general tenor of the anthropological perspective is that celebration is normal, and that in most cultures alcohol is a normal adjunct to celebration'.[13] The use of wine in the Christian celebration of the Eucharist represents drinking in its most highly symbolical form, but convivial drinking exchanges without alcohol extend to the tea-party, the 'coffee morning', the milk bars of the 1930s and the espresso bars of the 1950s, all social institutions with distinct rituals. The important point is that drinking beyond the needs of thirst is usually a social act, performed with other people at certain times and in certain settings; it becomes, also, a way of ordering the day and defining time – the early morning 'eye-opener', the mid-morning work break, the 'afternoon tea', the evening beer or the late 'night-cap'.

Enough has perhaps been said to indicate that the social history of drink has many dimensions, and that it is complex and under-explored. Mary Douglas recently observed that 'It is difficult to find any survey of all the drinks used in a given population, to say nothing of the relation between them'.[14] That is what this book aims to do. In the following chapters historically based discussions of individual drinks and drinking patterns are elaborated, while the Conspectus reflects on the overall changes in drinks consumption, how and why habits changed and, in so doing, helped to change society.

1 Water: 'The most useful and necessary part of the creation'*

I

Water occupies a central, though ambivalent, position in the history of drinks. Natural philosophers reverenced it as the source of life, the universal element associated with the myths of creation: not only did plants, animals and man need water for life itself, but ablution had magical properties to wash away sin and impurity, a belief transposed from Egyptian and Greek origins into Christian baptism.[1] Water was 'the great purificatory symbol' bringing 'not only physical but ceremonial cleanliness'.[2] Thus, at the Greek 'symposion' (drinking together) wine was normally mixed with water: undiluted wine was 'perilous', but the mixture ensured that the proceedings would be under the influence of both Dionysus and the Nymphs. The Romans adopted similar drinking customs, while at the Catholic Mass a little water was often added to the wine, the correct form at the time of Christ.[3] Pagan wells and springs associated with miraculous cures and the power to confer youth, fertility or rejuvenation were also adopted by the Christian church in many countries.[4]

Yet if strong wine was socially perilous, many waters were known to be dangerous to health, long before any theories of infection were proposed:[5] two kinds of water were always recognized, one pure and life-giving, the other unclean, harmful, even poisonous. In their occupation of Britain the Romans were especially aware of the need for ample supplies of clean water, providing towns and barracks by aqueducts and conduits from springs and streams: pipes of wood, lead or tile fed into settling basins, which deposited suspended sediment before the water passed to public or private fountains.[6] Although much of this sophisticated technology was lost after the occupation, it was partially revived in medieval monasteries and castles where gravity-fed piped supplies were installed, some of which also served local communities. Medieval towns were supplied by springs, wells

*Charles Lucas, *Essay on Waters*, 1756, vol. 1, 81

and rivers – London by the Thames, the Fleet, Walbrook, Langbourn and Oldbourne.[7] For 'sweet, wholesome and clear' waters wells were generally preferred, and some, like St Clement's in London and St Anne's at Buxton, were accorded holy status.[8] But from early times it was recognized that supplies in towns were liable to contamination from refuse of all kinds, the Tudor antiquary John Stow remarking that from the thirteenth century the Thames was becoming unusable for domestic purposes, and that Londoners were already seeking sweet waters at a distance. In 1236 the first patent was granted to bring water in lead pipes from Tyburn to the City – significantly, 'for the poor to drink and for the rich to dress their meat',[9] and by the end of the sixteenth century some twenty conduits had been constructed. Londoners could either fetch water for themselves or pay water carriers for the laborious task of bringing it to their door: the Company of Water Tankard Bearers was reputed to have 4,000 members,[10] not inconceivable when compared with the 2,000 'vile men and raucous women' who hawked water around the streets of Paris.[11] But the growth of London's population required increasingly costly capital works to meet domestic and industrial demands. In 1582 Peter Morrys erected a huge waterwheel under an arch of London Bridge to raise Thames water and convey it to large houses, while in 1609 the Court of Common Council appointed Hugh Myddleton to construct an open conduit from springs at Amwell and Chadwell in Hertfordshire to a Round Pond at Clerkenwell – a major engineering scheme 40 miles long, financed partly by James I and partly by a company of Adventurers (later, the New River Company).[12] These works by individuals and companies for profit suggest an important transformation in the concept of water ownership, which historically had been regarded as a gift of nature, free for the taking. According to the legal authority Blackstone, water flowing in a stream was *publici juris*: no property belonged to an individual, the water was for common use.[13] The justification for charging for water was, no doubt, the cost and maintenance of the equipment involved, but outside London several boroughs took a different course by establishing their own municipal waterworks – Southampton, Plymouth, Hull and Bath in the fifteenth century, Gloucester in the sixteenth, Oxford and Rye in the seventeenth century.[14] These were the exceptions: in almost all towns by the eighteenth century water supply was controlled by individuals or companies for profit.

II

In the Age of Enlightenment water became a commodity to be provided, like any other, for those who could pay. Between 1711 and 1800 fifteen new waterworks were incorporated by statute in Britain and a further thirty-six between 1800 and 1830.[15] London led the way in the scale and complexity of these undertakings, with eight new joint-stock companies serving areas north and south of the Thames:[16] together with the earlier New River Company they became bastions of private enterprise, with a powerful Parliamentary lobby. They provided piped supplies to houses in the wealthier districts where a profitable return could be expected, but ignored poorer areas. Supplies were only 'low service', that is, to ground floors, since wooden pipes could not maintain a sufficient pressure for higher levels.

The comment that the Tyburn conduit was intended for the poor to drink and for the rich to cook their food implies that even in medieval times water was far from being a general drink, and was in fact used only when something better could not be afforded. There were several good reasons for this. Since water had originally been free, it continued to be regarded as the drink of poverty, not greatly valued. Unlike ale or milk, it might quench the thirst, but had no strength, did not satisfy hunger, and encouraged no conviviality or good fellowship. Moreover, many waters were believed to be corrupted by pollution. According to Andrew Boorde in 1542, 'Water is not wholesome, sole by itself, for an Englishman':[17] if used for diluting wine it should be first strained and boiled or flavoured with herbs – no doubt, to disguise any bad taste. Even when water was pure, medical opinion tended not to favour it, being 'cold, slow and slack of digestion'. It was consumed mainly in the form of cooked foods, especially in soups, pottages and porridges, which were mainstays of pre-industrial diets, and in brewed or distilled drinks, all of which involved boiling or strong heating. Typhoid fever, paratyphoid and dysentery were endemic in the seventeenth century as a result of polluted water supplies and defective sanitation,[18] and it did not require modern medical knowledge to avoid waters that looked, smelled or tasted foul.

To the general avoidance of water for drinking an important exception developed from the sixteenth century onwards. At the Reformation in the 1530s holy wells had been suppressed, and subsequently wealthy Catholic recusants began to emigrate to Spa in the Spanish Netherlands (now Belgium) on the pretext of drinking the renowned mineral spring waters there for their health. Concern that they might form a 'fifth column' in preparation for a Spanish invasion led to the lifting of the ban on public drinking of mineral waters, which now received secular rather than religious sanction for their tonic and curative properties. From the mid-sixteenth century 'taking the waters' became a fashionable activity among the English aristocracy and wealthy classes, endorsed by the approval of Elizabeth I, who patronized Bath and had regular consignments of Buxton water sent to Court. Most English spas were for drinking rather than bathing – Tunbridge Wells, Harrogate and a host of local sites such as Hampstead, Wanstead, Astrop, Knaresborough, Epsom and Lichfield. The thirteen spas of 1640 had grown to sixty by 1699, with another thirty-four added in the next fifty years as visits to inland watering places became an important aspect of the commercialization of leisure in the eighteenth century.[19] An extensive trade in bottled mineral waters also ensured that consumers would continue to be supplied at home.[20]

The commercial success of spas depended on the authentication by physicians of the therapeutic qualities of their water and the dissemination of their researches by books, pamphlets and advertisements. Scientific interest in the composition of waters can be dated from Nehemiah Grew's paper of 1679 on the salts of London waters: more extensive analytical work followed in the next century with Charles Lucas (*Essay on Waters*, 1756) and Thomas Percival (*Observations and Experiments on Water*, 1769).[21] Of wider influence than this growing corpus of 'scientific' knowledge, however, were the numerous works on cookery and household economy such as Charlotte Mason's *The Ladies' Assistant*, which devoted several pages to the qualities of different waters. 'A well-known mark of the purity of water is its softness' because hard waters are the cause of kidney-stone and glandular swellings due to their 'acid and nitrous salts'. Spring waters that rise through gravel, sand or porous stone are the best, since they are naturally filtered, but pump water, especially in London, cannot be drunk with impunity, and 'may be the cause of many disorders'. Many people therefore boiled pump water or, if they used water from the Thames, which was often muddy and tasted strongly of weeds, left it to stand in an open vessel or strained it through a sponge.[22]

Many Georgian physicians advised the use of 'medicinal' (spa) waters as part of their dietary regimes in a period of over-indulgence by the wealthy. Saline waters had valuable purgative effects, chalybeate waters containing iron had tonic and restorative properties, sulphur waters were good for the skin and complexion, while others were claimed to cure gout, stone and rheumatism. All were projections of health and beauty to a society greatly concerned with appearance and bodily functions. But even 'simple' waters were a necessary part of the moderate diets that many doctors recommended. The influential George Cheyne (*Essay on Health and Long Life*, 1724) advised daily drinking of water instead of alcohol, Sir John Floyer inveighed against ardent spirits and over-indulgence in tea and coffee, while Joseph Browne also criticized these degenerate imports, advocating spring water and cool drinks made from lemons or cucumbers.[23] Such advice evidently had some influence on contemporary diet, for while some, like Parson Woodforde, continued to eat and drink heavily, others followed the example of the Sussex mercer Thomas Turner (1729–93), who drew up for himself a 'low, moderate rate of diet' as 'conducive to my health, as well as pleasantness and serenity to my mind'. For drink, he took at breakfast water or water gruel, sometimes tea or coffee, for dinner always boiled water with toast in it, or small beer ('but water if I can have it'), and at supper water or small beer 'but never drams or spirituous liquors'.[24] His comment 'if I can have it' may well imply that he drank water when it came from a 'safe' source; otherwise he drank tea or small beer, for which the water was boiled. By the mid-eighteenth century tea was in widespread use, and beer continued to be a staple of men's diets: to drink plain water was either slightly eccentric or an indication of great hardship.[25]

III

Although towns generally experienced the worst standards of water quality, even before the advance of industrialization, it would be a mistake to suppose that country dwellers always enjoyed easy access to pure supplies. Household books advised that well water was best for brewing, rainwater for washing (as it was soft), and freshly drawn spring water for cooking and drinking: even when piped supplies began to appear in some villages before 1914, country people often preferred to take drinking water from clear streams rather than the tap.[26]

Some parts of England were naturally better served than others. Yorkshire generally had ample supplies from springs or swiftly flowing streams; and some villages and small townships had pumps and well-heads, often provided by patronage. Only in the wolds of East Riding, where the rain quickly sank into the chalk, was there a problem: here the villagers collected rainwater in butts with a piece of sacking at the end of the down-pipe to act as a crude filter. Sometimes pond water had to be used, though frequently polluted by cattle, dead cats and dogs and rotting vegetation: it was generally strained through muslin cloth, but one old farmer drank mugs of it by straining through his front teeth.[27] Some country doctors recommended a primitive charcoal filter made from a leaking bucket filled with burnt wood, while for babies it was suggested that distilled water from the inside of the kettle lid should be collected.[28]

Some villages in southern England had excellent water supplies from deep wells, as at Harpenden in Hertfordshire. Here in the 1860s the men drew the water at night, carrying home the heavy buckets to fill large, earthenware pans kept in the 'backhouse' for use next day. Drawing water could be dangerous work in frosty weather when ice covered the flag-stones around the well: local hearsay recalled the case of a woman who slipped into a well but was saved by her hooped dress.[29] But at Headington Quarry on the outskirts of Oxford 'pulling water' was a task often given to girls, especially on washing-day, and here in 1909 a 12-year-old girl was drowned in a well.[30] Unless a cottage had its own well in the garden, carrying home two full buckets suspended from a yoke across the shoulders was heavy work. At George Sturt's Bourne near Farnham, Surrey, this was still done by women in the 1880s, and water was so prized that the cooking water was saved for reuse next day,[31] but in Flora Thompson's village younger wives who had been in 'good service' got their husbands to fetch it – when the village wells dried up in hot weather, this meant a half-mile journey to a farmer's pump.[32] The quality of well water natu-rally varied with the geological formation, its depth and maintenance: the best wells were skilfully lined with brick, and free from contamination by seepage from privies or cowsheds, but this was by no means always the case: over a well that supplied several cottages was a notice, 'This water should be boiled before drinking' – the drainage from some large houses at a higher level filtered into the spring.[33] Problems of water supply in some areas worsened towards the end of the century with the growth of middle-class residence in the countryside, but it long remained uneco-nomic for private companies or municipalities to provide pipes to thinly populated districts, and as late as 1910 only 36 per cent of rural parishes in England and Wales had piped water.[34]

Ample water supplies were a requisite of respectable rural life where women were constantly washing dirty clothes and kitchen floors: the diffi-culty is to know how important water was as a drink. Consumption depended on how safe local supplies were considered to be and what preferred alternatives were economically available to the poorer strata of society: in a wider context, the consumption of liquids of whatever kind was related to the type of diet – the drier the food, the more liquid was needed to make it palatable. At the end of the eighteenth century it was observed that labourers in the north of England and Scotland enjoyed a better standard of living than those in the south because of their more varied, cooked meals:

> In the South of England the poorest labourers are habituated to the unvarying meal of dry bread and cheese from week's end to week's end; and in those families whose finances do not allow them the indul-gence of malt liquor, the deleterious produce of China constitutes their most usual and general beverage.[35]

Frederic Eden contrasted the dry diet of the south with the moist one of the north, where the staples were hasty-pudding (a type of porridge), broths of meat and vegetables, pease-pudding, crowdie and frumenty. 'The cheap-ness of fuel is, perhaps, another reason why the culinary preparations of the Northern peasant are so much diversified, and his table so often supplied with hot dishes.'

Many northern labourers also had the advantage of keeping a cow, and milk was an important constituent of the diet of children and adults. The southern labourer regarded beer as his proper drink, when he could get it, but 'That is not the case in the North where, besides the pure, limpid stream, the general drink of the labouring classes is either whey or milk or, rather, milk and water. . .'.

IV

In most British towns and cities problems of water supply had reached a crisis by the middle of the nineteenth century. Existing provisions had

largely broken down under the impact of greatly increased urban populations and industrial demands: while the population of England and Wales
doubled from 9 million to 18 million between 1801 and 1851, Manchester
grew from 75,000 to 303,000, Birmingham from 71,000 to 233,000, and
Bradford from a mere 13,000 to a phenomenal 104,000.[36] In many of
these centres of unregulated growth existing water supplies from rivers,
streams and wells had become heavily polluted by human and industrial
sewage, unsafe even to a population that did not yet understand the aeti-
ology of water-borne diseases.

Public concern first focused on the problems of London, already the
largest city in the world with a population of 1.6 million in 1821. Little
technical progress had yet been made by the nine London companies,
which drew their supplies mainly from the Thames and the Lea through
screened pipes ('dolphins'): the water then passed into 'settling beds', which
were intended to deposit the grosser sediment. Cast-iron mains, particularly developed by the engineer John Rennie, were beginning to replace
wooden pipes, and were better able to withstand the pressure now developed by steam pumps.[37] The first effective slow sand filter was invented
by James Simpson for the Chelsea Company in 1829 but was only slowly
adopted generally. Meanwhile, the London companies came under public
scrutiny in a series of official inquiries whose Reports express some of
the earliest doubts about the prevailing ideology of *laissez-faire*. In the
1820s the companies supplied only 164,000 people, a tenth of London's
inhabitants: moreover, the quality of water was known to be deteriorat-
ing as water-closets were now coming into wider use and discharging
excrement directly into the Thames. In granting the original franchises
to the companies Parliament had tried to encourage competition by leaving geographical areas ill-defined or even overlapping, so that the same
street might be served by two or three companies. A 'rates war' between
1810 and 1817 ended with the companies agreeing areas of demarcation
and raising their charges in what were now geographical monopolies.
Public protests at these charges led to the formation of an Anti-Water
Monopoly Association in 1819, which successfully petitioned Parliament
for the appointment of a Select Committee on the Supply of Water to
the Metropolis in 1821.

In reply to the public complaints, the companies argued that competition had been wasteful and that increased rates were required by
improvements in technology. Although critical of the companies, the
Report was inconclusive and clearly illustrated the conflict between the
need to control a vital public amenity and the right of investors to pursue
their business affairs without interference. It therefore proposed that there
should be a temporary statutory limit of water rates averaging 25 per cent
above the levels of 1810, but beyond this it could not 'justify an interference of the legislature affecting private property', and decided: 'It is due
to the companies that a liberal construction should be made in their favour

on all doubtful points'.[38] Matters did not rest here, however. In 1827 public anxiety suddenly turned to the question of water quality with the publication of an anonymous pamphlet entitled *The Dolphin: The Grand Junction Nuisance*, which, it has been suggested, marks the emergence of the nineteenth-century public health movement.[39] Its author has been identified as John Wright, the amanuensis of William Cobbett and editor of parliamentary debates for T.C. Hansard.[40] Dedicated to Sir Francis Burdett, the Radical MP for Westminster, it criticized the companies for increased charges well beyond the 25 per cent that Parliament had allowed (it claimed that some residents in Piccadilly who formerly paid £5 a year were now charged £25), but its main attack was directed at the Grand Junction Company, which drew its water from the Thames, opposite the Royal Hospital, Chelsea: the water was drawn through a 'dolphin' (screened pipe) 3 or 4 feet from the outfall of the great Ranelagh Common Sewer. Himself a reluctant customer of the Company, Wright described its water as

> a fluid saturated with the impurities of fifty thousand houses – a dilute solution of animal and vegetable substances in a state of putrefaction – alike offensive to the sight, disgusting to the imagination and destructive to health.

A public petition quickly led to the appointment of a Royal Commission, which reported in 1828 that most of the complaints were fully justified.[41] The Grand Junction Company did not filter its water: only one of the nine London companies cleaned its reservoirs regularly – the rest had not been cleaned for between 1 and 20 years, and contained up to 8 feet of mud. Medical witnesses agreed that the quality of London water had been greatly deteriorated in the last dozen years by the discharges of 145 sewers, and that it was now 'disgusting to the senses and improper to be employed in the preparation of food'.[42] While recommending that all the companies should filter their water, the Report acknowledged that this would not remove soluble matter or chemically combined substances: it therefore concluded with the radical proposal that 'the supply of water to the Metropolis ... ought to be derived from other sources than now resorted to'.[43]

Suggestions for a system of canals from Teddington, above the tidal flow of the Thames, or for deep boreholes that would yield pure, soft water, came to nothing[44] in the face of the companies' powerful vested interests and the strong preference of Parliament for a private solution of any problem. Nor was the sudden epidemic of Asiatic cholera in 1831–2 at this time associated with contaminated water supplies. How unknown the disease was at its outset is suggested by an entry in the diary of Mrs Arbuthnot, a friend of the Duke of Wellington, in October 1831: 'The cholera has arrived at Sunderland. ... Reform is more to be feared' – she died six weeks later of the disease.[45] Altogether, there were 31,474 deaths in Britain and 25,378 in Ireland.[46] Cholera caused widespread panic because of its violence and distressing symptoms of diarrhoea and rapid death from dehydration: contemporaries puzzled over whether there might be a moral explanation for the calamity, and on a day of national fast in 1832 Bishop Blomfield warned his royal congregation that cholera was a sign to the rich 'to increase the comforts and improve the moral character of the masses'. Some support for a moral causation came from doctors who still clung to a 'humoral' theory of disease and believed that cholera was generated in bodies that had been misused by, for example, 'notorious drunkards' and 'worn-out prostitutes', but most scientific opinion was divided between 'miasmatists' and 'contagionists': the former believed that cholera was generated in putrefying animal or vegetable substances and carried in the air, while the latter argued that it was communicated by direct contact with the infected person.[47] The influential doctors Southwood Smith and Neil Arnott, together with the public administrator Edwin Chadwick, were miasmatists who thought that the source of the disease was 'not due to want of food and greater poverty . . . but in the generation of effluvial poisons': the focus of sanitary reform should therefore lie in the removal of all refuse from houses and streets, in thorough cleaning, scouring and sewering.

Chadwick's pioneering *Report on the Sanitary Condition of the Labouring Population of Great Britain* (1842) was the first to fully establish the relationship between environmental factors, disease and death rates, and the central importance of abundant water supplies both for domestic use and for flushing sewers. The Report revealed the deplorable state of water in almost every town. In Manchester the rivers Irwell and Medlock were the receptacles of all kinds of rubbish, and quite unusable: most water for domestic use was taken from shallow wells by pumps, the common practice being for the landlord of a group of cottages to install a pump and let it to one of the tenants, who would keep it locked and charge the rest for use – one poor woman paid 1s a month while the small number of houses served by the Manchester and Salford Waterworks Company paid only 6s a year for a plentiful supply.[48] Matters were little better in Bath, where the Corporation provided a piped supply to some parts of the town, but in the poorer districts drinking water had to be fetched from a pump a quarter of a mile away: 'It is as valuable as strong beer', said a tenant. 'We can't use it for cooking or anything of that sort, but only drinking and tea.' For cooking and washing they took from the river, which was muddy and 'often stinks bad'.[49] Many Scottish towns were equally deficient: Edinburgh had no water company, and inhabitants had to carry heavy pails up five or six storeys; at Stirling it was common to see up to a hundred people queueing at the pumps; while in Dundee people had to take filthy water from the millpond.[50]

Chadwick's argument for improved water supplies was partly sanitary, partly economic and moral. Since sickness and the premature death of breadwinners were main causes of poverty, the costs of poor relief would be reduced if the causes of preventable disease were removed. To his util-itarian mind competition between water companies, sometimes supplying the same area, was wasteful and illogical: such a prime necessity of life required centralized public planning and control. But, Chadwick also believed, lack of abundant water demoralized the character of the people, for the beershop was often nearer than the pump and more comfortable than many workingmen's homes: 'These adverse circumstances tend to produce an adult population short-lived, improvident, reckless and intem-perate, and with habitual avidity for sensual gratifications'. He concluded that better water supplies were 'absolutely essential', and would probably result in extending the lives of the labouring classes by 13 years.[51]

The widespread public concern caused by Chadwick's personal Report led to a Royal Commission in 1843–5 that fully investigated the state of water supplies in fifty large towns.[52] In only six were they considered good, in thirteen indifferent, and in thirty-one bad, deficient in quantity and impure. In Coventry only 300–400 houses out of 7,200 had a piped supply, in Norwich a quarter of the houses, in Newcastle a twelfth, in Birmingham 8,000 houses of 40,000, in Bristol 5,000 out of 120,000; in Liverpool it was reported that there was not one public fountain or pump.[53] These conditions contrasted with the good situation in Nottingham, where 8,000 of the town's 11,000 houses received a constant supply from the Trent Bridge Waterworks for 1d a week.[54] In many other towns house-holders bought water from carriers at prices that varied from ½d to 1½d per bucket of 3 gallons. Weekly charges of 1s were common, but in Leeds some householders paid 2s, a very heavy burden out of wages that varied from 10s to 30s, and comparable with a week's rent. A further difficulty was that the water had then to be stored, sometimes for days, in jugs, pans or butter-tubs, with added risks of infection.[55] The minority of houses having piped supplies were more fortunate, though it was still usually only 'low service' to ground floors and often intermittent, with no service at night or, in the case of the East London Company, on Sundays. Water consumption varied widely with location, cost and available income: in Burton-on-Trent, where water was bought at 1d for three buckets (9 gallons), working-class families bought 27 gallons a week, middle-class families 52 gallons and upper-class families 108 gallons,[56] but even the last fell far short of the good public supply in Nottingham, where labourers' families used 40 gallons a day.[57]

By the time of the second cholera epidemic of 1848–9 little legisla-tive progress had been made towards the improvement of water supplies. The Waterworks Clauses Act (1847) recommended that the London companies should extend their supplies on the constant system, and that their water should be 'pure and wholesome', but it would be another 50 years before either was achieved. Chadwick's dream of a powerful central government body to control all sanitary matters resulted only in an emasculated Public Health Act in 1848, which empowered (but did not compel) local authorities to provide a water supply, except that any existing water company would have to give consent – a clause described as 'a stultifying condition'.[58] One glimmer of future improvement occurred the same year when the Lambeth Company removed its intake to Thames Ditton, above the river's tidal flow and the worst of the capital's sewage, but otherwise no lessons had yet been learned about the causes of cholera. The second epidemic was more severe than the first, spreading to almost every part of Britain and resulting in 60,293 deaths: Glasgow alone suffered 3,800 deaths, the mining town of Merthyr Tydfil 1,400.[59] A step towards understanding the epidemiology of the disease, however, was now possible since the registration of births, marriages and deaths in 1837. It was observed that in poor districts of East London supplied by the Southwark Company, which took its water from below the London bridges, mortality was between five and six times greater than in the West End, which enjoyed relatively safer water from upstream.[60] Such gross differences compelled an explanation.

V

When King Leopold of Belgium was dining with William IV in the early 1830s he gave great offence by requesting water. 'What's that you are drinking, sir?' asked William. 'Water, sir.' 'God damn it, sir, why do you not drink wine?' demanded William. 'I never allow anyone to drink water at my table.'[61] In similar vein, a French visitor to London in the 1840s observed a few simple, iron fountains in the streets equipped with chains and ladles.

> This ladle is the inexpensive cup offered to the poor man by his lord and master. 'Look, water here costs the people nothing. They can drink it in comfort and without having to fetch it from the river.' This is how well-to-do people in London speak, yet they never drink water.[62]

This was almost, but not quite, true in the middle of the nineteenth century. Henry Mayhew reported that residents of Hampstead bought their water from carriers, who used 'the Conduit' or double well, at two pails for 1½d: a carrier told him that it was beautiful for washing or drinking, but 'perhaps it's better with a little drop of spirit for drinking'. One old gentleman used to mix brandy with his two or three glasses at the well, but the carrier had not seen him all last summer: 'His hand trembled like a aspen'.[63]

Water from the Vale of Health supposedly had medicinal properties, but how suspicious people were of the ordinary article is suggested by a comment in *Punch* about the Great Exhibition of 1851, where the contractors had agreed to supply free, pure water on demand: 'The Committee must have forgotten that whoever can produce in London a glass of water fit to drink will contribute the rarest and most universally useful article in the whole Exhibition.'[64] Those who preferred not to take their chance bought lemonade, ginger beer or soda water (no alcoholic drinks were allowed) from Messrs Schweppes, who sold over a million bottles.[65] By mid-century more than fifty soft drinks manufacturers in London alone offered alternatives to water, while bottled mineral waters from thirty-six English spas[66] served a similar purpose: previously taxed as medicines until 1833, these and imported waters from Spa, Pyrmont, Seltzer and elsewhere were now widely available. How much water in its 'natural' state was consumed is impossible to know – Dr Hassall's estimate that 4 pints of river water were drunk daily by Londoners 'in some form or other'[67] would have included tea and coffee and, possibly, brewed drinks also. Many hospitals gave their patients beer rather than water, the boys at Winchester School drank beer with their meals in 1872, and Eton College brewed its own until 1875.[68] The difficulty of discovering whether water was safe to use is suggested by the advice given in a popular book of household hints that if a penknife dipped into the water turned yellow this was evidence of copper, while if a small addition of sulphuric acid turned it black the water was contaminated with animal or vegetable matter.[69] Middle-class ladies drank home-made lemonade, barley water or toast water, all of which involved boiling, and at dinner had glasses of water to mix with their wine or sherry, which also resulted in purification. This probably followed the fashion in France, where according to the Baronne Staffe it was polite to offer a woman water at the same time as wine: a lady never drinks wine neat except at the dessert, but always insists that it be *trempé*.[70]

Patent water filters were in widespread use in better-class houses by mid-century, generally employing granulated charcoal as the purifying agent, which had superseded the graduated gravel of earlier versions. In 1819 Mr James of Knightsbridge was advertising a domestic filter for 12s, which he claimed would last a small family for two years,[71] while the china manufacturers Doultons made a variety of models – earthenware for the kitchen (14s 6d–70s) and marbled china for the dining-room (capacity 6 gallons a day, 30s).[72] Dr Hassall believed that the filters on the market were very imperfect as they removed only larger particles, leaving suspended impurities and the smaller 'animalculae'. Like boiling, they also caused flatness, and it was recommended that for the table water-jug the filtered water should be poured from a height, or transferred back and forth between jugs to aerate it. A little ice in water improved its palatability in warm weather and was used somewhat more extensively in towns after 1844 when the Wenham Lake Ice Company of Massachussetts began to make regular shipments and distributed to all parts of England from their offices in the Strand: Queen Victoria decreed that it should always be available at Court, but, at a yearly cost of £12 to keep the Company's ice-boxes supplied, its sale was restricted to the wealthy.[73]

By such strategies the better-off classes could provide themselves with reasonably palatable water, if at some cost and inconvenience: the problem remained for the working classes, whom, from 1830 onwards, the temperance movement was seeking to dissuade from their habitual attachment to beer and other alcoholic drinks: in advocating water were the 'Waterdrinkers' not directing the poor to a more harmful, perhaps even poisonous, alternative? Even the champion of so many noble causes, Lord Shaftesbury, admitted in 1871 that there was scarcely a pint of water in London that was not distinctly unhealthy, and a great deal that was positively unsafe.[74] The promotion of water as a natural, healthy and, above all, moral drink had passed from the ascetic physicians and Methodist crusaders of the eighteenth century to the temperance reformers of the early nineteenth at a time when its quality was at its worst, though speakers like John B. Gough, 'the high priest of the pump', continued to proclaim the virtues of 'Our beautiful beverage, water, pure water . . . Our beverage is beautiful and pure for God brewed it, not in the distillery, but out of the earth'.[75] Another leading teetotaller, Dr Frederick Lees, argued that water was the general drink at the institution of the Passover, and that the many Biblical references to wine were in fact to unfermented grape juice, but most temperance advocates wisely avoided the water/wine controversy and recommended tea, coffee and, later, cocoa as the best alternatives to alcohol. Several leaders were also prominent in campaigning for improved water supplies and for amenities of 'rational recreation' as alternatives to the public house.

VI

By the close of the nineteenth century it seemed that water had at last been conquered – pumped, piped and purified, brought in abundance to the consumer's own tap, publicly controlled and, in most cases, publicly owned. This represented a major ideological break with the belief in *laissez-faire*, the assumption that free market forces would always provide the best services at lowest cost. As in the case of food adulteration,[76] competition was shown to have failed the public by providing too little water, too low in quality and too high in price. The arguments for public ownership and control were therefore predicated on economic, social and moral grounds – that abundant, pure water was an essential public service, a necessary condition of health and happiness, cleanliness and sobriety, civilized life and national efficiency. The acceptance of these views gradually overcame whatever doubts politicians may have had about 'interventionism' and 'collectivism', for, in the words of Luckin, ' "the salvation of the city" was nothing less than a binding moral duty'.[77]

Even before the third cholera epidemic in 1853–4 public interest in the water question had reached new levels. In 1850 the General Board of Health under Chadwick's direction proposed that 'as early as practicable' the Thames should be abandoned in favour of purer supplies from the Surrey hills, while the following year a government Bill to amalgamate the London companies and enable the Treasury to buy them out passed its second reading but was dropped in the face of strong opposition by the companies. What did emerge from these debates, however, was of great importance. The Metropolis Water Act 1852 was the first significant step in the improvement of London's water, and a major interference with the freedom of sellers to offer the public a potentially harmful substance.[78] It required the London companies within three years to remove their intakes to beyond the tidal flow of the Thames (that is, to above Kingston), to cover all reservoirs within 5 miles of the City, and to filter all water for domestic use unless pumped directly from a well. Although progress was often slower than expected, what has been described as a 'fastidious revolution'[79] was now under way, including the removal of foul cesspits and their replacement by water-closets, the introduction of sewage treatment (first at Leicester in 1853), and the construction of the huge London sewerage scheme by Bazalgette between 1859 and 1865.

The cholera outbreak of 1853–4, before the 1852 Act had come into full operation, concentrated minds on water quality and, for most people at least, confirmed Dr John Snow's theory that cholera was a water-borne disease transmitted by the faeces of infected patients. Snow had already published his first paper *On the Means of Communication of Cholera* in 1849. The second, more widely known edition of 1855 included a map of the notorious Broad Street, Soho, where 500 people died in a small area supplied by a pump contaminated from a cesspool: when the pump was closed the mortality ceased. In fact, it appears that the pump handle was removed after the attack had spent its force, and was a largely symbolic gesture.[80] Neither was Snow the sole originator of the theory of water-borne cholera, for within a month of his paper of 1849 Dr William Budd had published his *Malignant Cholera: Its Mode of Propagation and its Prevention* in which he stated that 'the cause of malignant cholera is a living organism [disseminated] principally in the drinking water of infected places'.[81] The agent of infection was as yet unknown, but by 1867, following the work of Pasteur, Budd was writing of 'the cholera germ': the bacillus was finally isolated by Koch in 1883.

One approach to the problem of improving the quantity and quality of water for the people was a typical example of Victorian philanthropy. In 1859 Samuel Gurney MP founded the Metropolitan Free Drinking Fountain Association to provide public fountains with pure, filtered water. The Association began as a radical movement, challenging the water companies' monopoly and closely allied with temperance, often siting its fountains near flourishing public houses. By 1872 there were 300 fountains in the capital, and the movement had spread to most towns and many villages throughout Britain.[82] The more far-reaching approach to the problem of water supply, however, was municipalization – the ownership of water undertakings by local authorities, which would run them in the public interest on a non-profit basis. While private companies typically adopted short-run, profit maximization policies, municipal enterprises acted as sales maximizers, and were prepared to adopt long-term planning involving large capital outlays.[83] Although there were humanitarian and, often, temperance motives here, too, there was also sound commercial sense: municipalization began in northern industrial towns, free from the stranglehold of the great London companies, partly because hardheaded councillors understood that better water supplies were essential for the needs of industries like textiles, for fire-fighting and for a healthier workforce. Common sense therefore conveniently combined with civic pride and notions of good citizenship.

In 1845 only ten municipalities owned water undertakings, survivors from much earlier enterprises; but between 1846 and 1855 twenty-nine towns obtained local Acts to establish their own.[84] As in other sanitary matters, Liverpool led the way in 1847, obtaining powers to bring water from Rivington, 17½ miles away: Manchester Corporation went for its water to Longdendale in the Pennines in 1855, the same year that Glasgow began to develop reservoirs at Loch Katrine, 34 miles distant. Encouragement for municipalization came from the Public Health Act 1872, which for the first time made it a duty of local authorities to provide a proper water supply, and as urban populations continued to expand in the later nineteenth century cities developed ever more ambitious engineering schemes – Birmingham built 73 miles of conduits and pipes to the Elan Valley in mid-Wales, while Manchester constructed an aqueduct of 106 miles to Thirlmere in the Lake District.[85] London stood out longest, with its statutory companies forming a powerful lobby against public ownership,[86] and only after pressure from the London County Council established in 1889 and two elaborate Royal Commissions (1893–4, 1899–1900) did the companies finally agree to their acquisition at a generous valuation of £46,939,000: the Metropolitan Water Board was established as a public body in 1903.[87] Already by 1897 610 out of a total of 990 municipal boroughs and urban districts were providing water supplies to 87 per cent of the populations of the principal British towns.[88] In the words of William Robson,

> The development of a well-nigh universal system of piped house-to-house supplies is one of the great achievements of the century ... The transformation of the water supply [was] primarily due to the replacement of commercial enterprise ... by municipal undertakings operating on pure public utility principles.[89]

Almost everywhere municipalization generally resulted in the replacement of intermittent by constant supplies and of 'low service' by 'high service' to all floors: water consumption increased, often dramatically – in

Manchester from 4.8 gallons per head per day in 1841 to 32.6 gallons in 1875, and in Leeds from 8.1 gallons in 1851 to 20.5 gallons in 1871. Charges, normally based on rateable values, favoured working-class households, sometimes at the expense of large, under-occupied middle-class houses, but in those towns where water was now brought from upland regions, all classes benefited from softer water, with consequent savings on tea and laundry.

The persistent problem in the later decades of the century was now quality rather than quantity. In the 1850s only a small group of doctors had much concerned themselves with the question – Arthur Hassall, Henry Letheby, Edward Lankester, John Snow, William Budd and Robert Dundas Thomson – of whom Hassall was the most outspoken critic of the dangerous impurity of London water. From microscopical tests he showed that it was 'swarming with living productions' ('animalculae') and heavily contaminated with sewage and excrement: 'wholly unfitted for human consumption'.[90] Michael Faraday also described the Thames in 1855 as 'a fermenting sewer',[91] but when cholera struck for the fourth and last time in 1866, causing 15,000 deaths in East London, the authorities now knew what to do. The infection was quickly traced to the water supplied by the East London Company, which was illegally distributed from an uncovered, contaminated reservoir: strict quarantine, the boiling of water and disposal of patients' excreta prevented another full-scale disaster.[92]

By now it was coming to be recognized that the problems began at source, in the rivers from which the great majority of water was drawn. Royal Commissions on the Pollution of Rivers in 1866–7 and 1870–4 disclosed horrifying accounts of the condition of Britain's rivers as the receptacles for all kinds of rubbish: the Aire and Calder, for instance, were described as 'poisoned, corrupted and clogged by refuse from mines, chemical works, dyeing, scouring of woollen stuffs, skin-cleaning and tanning, slaughter-house garbage and the sewage of towns and houses';[93] the inquiry received a letter from a complainant in Yorkshire stating that it had been written not with ink but with river water. The result of years of investigation, the Rivers Pollution Prevention Act 1876 was a lame measure without adequate powers of enforcement. In theory it made it an offence to discharge 'any solid or liquid sewage matter' into rivers, but its adoption was permissive, and 10 years later only two corporations had fully enforced it: of fifty-six prosecutions brought, nineteen were against sanitary authorities, the very bodies to which its implementation was entrusted.[94] The Act was a compromise between the needs of public health and the interests of manufacturers and sewage disposers who had long regarded rivers as the natural vehicles for their waste, and was rarely invoked.

From 1857 government began to be involved with water quality on a regular basis when Professor Thomson was appointed by the Registrar-General as the semi-official 'government analyst' to carry out monthly tests of London water: he was succeeded in 1866 by Edward Frankland, Professor of Chemistry at the Royal School of Mines, who held the office until his death in 1899. A strong critic of the London companies, Frankland became the leading British authority on water quality, and his monthly reports had great impact through their publication in the press: from 1875 his work was transferred to the Local Government Board, which now had responsibility for public health matters, and in a strange administrative muddle his reports were published alongside those of Frank Bolton, an engineer and former soldier, who was appointed as official Water Examiner to ensure that London's water was 'effectively filtered'.[95]

The Annual Reports of the Local Government Board indicate substantial, though irregular, progress in the supply and quality of London's water in the last quarter of the century. In 1874 only a quarter of all houses received a constant supply, and Frankland noted that there had been a progressive increase in organic impurities since 1871, rendering some water 'eminently noxious'.[96] In 1880 Frankland stated that the Thames had never been so badly polluted with sewage since he took up his appointment: of 142 million gallons of water supplied by the companies, 72 million were sometimes grossly polluted, and only 8.5 million gallons (one-sixteenth) were 'uniformly of excellent quality for drinking'.[97] The problem was that although intakes had now been removed above Kingston, the Thames was polluted from further upstream by such towns as Oxford and Reading, and by drainage from agricultural land; moreover in several places the Rivers Pollution Act was suspended while sewage schemes were still in progress. The greatest improvements in both supply and quality occurred only in the last fifteen years of the century when, by 1898, 92 per cent of houses served by the London companies were now on constant supply at an average of 35 gallons per head per day, and water was reported to be of good quality on 327 days in the year.[98]

These improvements depended on the growth of scientific knowledge – especially the development of bacteriology in the 1880s – the better administration of the sanitary laws, and the energetic work of many local Medical Officers of Health. The death rate from zymotic diseases such as typhoid, typhus, smallpox, scarlet fever and measles fell by almost half between 1860 and 1880, and continued to improve subsequently in what has been described as the 'sanitary revolution'.[99] But as Hamlin has argued, there was no clear relationship between scientific discovery and political and technical actions: the scientific evidence itself was sometimes conflicting and could be manipulated by resisters to change, especially by those who represented the interests of invested capital.[100] Furthermore, attention had been so concentrated on London that some provincial towns had not shared equally in the improvements. In Middlesbrough in the 1890s the ten poorest wards still depended on polluted supplies from the River Tees, and enteric fever was endemic here,[101] while in York in 1898, supplied by a private company, 19 per cent of the working-class houses were without a private service, and in the poorest part of the city there were only thirty taps among 442 houses.[102] Outbreaks of typhoid fever, which recurred in Maidstone in 1897 and in Lincoln in 1905, led to the chlorination of water in these towns, a process pioneered by Dr Sims Woodhead, which was claimed to destroy all bacteria from sewage. Its general adoption was delayed by public concerns about the introduction of 'chemicals' to the water supply, but continuous chlorination became more widespread in the 1920s, and was quietly introduced by the government to all public supplies on the outbreak of war in 1939.[103]

VII

Until recently, 'the quality of our water was one of those things we have forgotten how to worry about'.[104] Water engineers and sanitarians spoke with an easy confidence that the problems of the nineteenth-century dark age had been overcome by a combination of science, technology and administration. By the inter-war years almost all people except those living in some remote places could use as much safe water as they wished (between 20 and 30 gallons per person per day[105]) at low cost and for the trouble of turning a tap. Municipalities, which now supplied 80 per cent of the population, usually charged between 5 per cent and 20 per cent of rate-able values, averaging around 10 per cent, and some regarded water as such a vital public utility that they charged below cost.

Only rarely did concerns about purity resurface when outbreaks of typhoid fever due to contamination occurred in the unlikely environments of Bournemouth, Poole and Christchurch in 1936 and Croydon in 1937. And one new problem emerged at this time in the rapidly growing suburban areas where many new houses were being built: until mains drainage was installed, the usual provision was often cesspools, which the Ministry of Health insisted should be watertight 'deadwells' to prevent any leakage. This sometimes led, as in Norwich, to long disputes over costs, the respon-sibility of householders to empty, and over chlorination, which the Ministry recommended as an additional safeguard.[106] Particularly dry summers between 1933 and 1935 resulted in water restrictions in some areas, and led to calls for better planning of water resources, including the idea of a national grid comparable to that for electricity: it began to appear untidy and inefficient that in 1936 water in England and Wales should be supplied by 833 separate public authorities and 173 statutory companies.[107]

Water was not nationalized by the Labour government of 1945–50: in a sense, it did not need to be since more than three-quarters of the industry was already collectively owned. Instead, some rationalization was carried out by the Water Act 1945, which began to group smaller undertakings into Joint Water Boards, and by the River Boards Act 1948, designed to control the management of rivers from source to mouth and to tighten pollution. By the 1960s a more radical reorganization of what was coming to be regarded as a scarce resource was considered necessary, and in an unusually collectivist measure for a Conservative government the Water Act 1973 effectively nationalized the industry by creating ten Regional Water Authorities with all-purpose responsibilities over supplies, pollution, sewerage, fisheries and navigation. The municipal undertakings, once the proud possessions of Victorian cities, were transferred without compensation, though many of their assets were rapidly becoming liabilities that required heavy investments. As a government responsibility water was now subject to Treasury control: the new Authorities received no rate support and had to cover all costs from current income. Domestic water bills rose sharply, in some areas doubling, while successive Chancellors of the Exchequer substantially reduced the sum available for capital investment.

In effect, the tidying-up of the water industry now made it a relatively easy target for privatization in line with the Conservative policy of 'rolling back the frontiers of the state' and other privatizations. The debate in the late 1980s revived all the concerns about placing a natural monopoly essential for public health in private hands that had been voiced more than a century before, concerns somewhat mitigated by the undertaking that charges – though not profits – would be publicly regulated and quality strictly controlled by an independent Inspectorate: the government would surrender ownership, but not responsibility. In 1989 shares in ten public limited companies were offered on the stock market: widely advertised under the slogan 'You too can be an H_2Owner', they were over-subscribed 2.8 times, and brought the Treasury £5,225 million – for what, critics said, the public already owned.

Public awareness of the cost and quality of water has remained at a high level since privatization, stimulated by greater publicity and by increased domestic charges, which rose from an average £119 a year in 1991 to £218 in 1995. It was noticeable that public attitudes towards the drought and water restrictions in 1995 were less cooperative than in 1976, the worst drought for 250 years, when water was still public property. 'Isn't the buyer entitled to use it as he likes – just like any other commercial product?', asked a newspaper in an area badly suffering from restrictions.[108] Anxieties about quality, however, predated privatization, reappearing in the 1970s as part of wider health and environmental concerns. Derek Cooper's *Beverage Report* complained that 'Nearly 4,000 million gallons of sewage is treated and dumped into our rivers every day; one-sixth of all the water we drink comes from rivers which receive this treated sewage'.[109] Moreover, water mains and sewers installed in Victorian times were beginning to collapse in several cities, with consequent threats of pollution: in 1980 residents in Halifax were having to boil their drinking water, which exceeded WHO limits for several metals, and worm-infested water caused a strike in the mining village of Bircote in Nottinghamshire.[110] The same year, the European Community drew up a Directive on Drinking Water that would become legally binding on member-states in 1985 and set out sixty-eight separate quality tests: at that time the Water Research Centre reported that about half of all British supplies would have failed to meet some part of the Directive, mainly for aesthetic criteria such as colour or taste but also for some potentially harmful substances including lead and nitrates. In 1975 10 per cent of tap water and 20 per cent of first-drawn water was above the EC limit of 50 micrograms per litre for lead, while nitrate levels reached a new height in 1977 when heavy rains after the previous year's drought washed large amounts of accumulated nitrate fertilizers from agricultural land into rivers. Nitrates in water caused particular anxiety since they were associated with the 'blue baby syndrome' (though there were only ten cases of this between 1950 and 1980 and none subsequently) and, possibly, with stomach and bladder cancer in adults. The medical evidence on this is disputed, but a *Report on Nitrates in Food* by the Ministry of Agriculture, Fisheries and Food in 1987 conceded that 'the available evidence does not exclude the possibility of a carcinogenic risk'.[111]

Nevertheless, the Annual Reports of the Drinking Water Inspectorate present a generally reassuring account of the improvements in quality since privatization. In 1995 of 3.2 million tests carried out, 99.5 per cent met the EC standards, leaving 17,500 tests that did not. England and Wales is divided into 2,600 water supply zones, each serving not more than 50,000 people: Table 1.1 shows the proportion of zones that satisfied the standard for the principal criteria.

Given the scale and complexity of the modern water industry – 5,000 reservoirs, 8,000 sewage treatment works, 186,000 miles of mains –

Table 1.1 Percentage of water supply zones satisfying official standards, 1991–5

	1991 (%)	1994 (%)	1995 (%)
Coliforms[1]	95	99.5	99.4
Pesticides	69.4	76.3	79.2
Lead	74.4	80.2	81.3
Nitrate	96.2	98.2	98.9
Iron	68	75.9	75.2
PAH[2]	93	88	87.3
Taste	–	98.7	99.1
Colour	–	99.4	99.8
Odour	–	99.3	99.1

Notes:
[1] Coliforms are bacteria that are not harmful in themselves, but indicate that other, harmful bacteria may be present.
[2] PAH. Policyclic aromatic hydrocarbons are substances present in coal tar. Until the 1970s tar was used to line iron water mains to prevent rusting: this could result in traces of PAH entering drinking water, which in large quantities could be harmful.

Source: Drinking Water Inspectorate. *How Good is Your Drinking Water?* Summary of Reports 1994, 1995

occasional faults are almost inevitable. The Inspectorate claims that 'Drinking water is generally of a very high quality', that it has materially improved since privatization, and that contraventions of the very strict standards are dealt with immediately and without danger to public health. In the area served by Thames Water Utilities, which had a particularly bad reputation for quality in the last century, 1.1 million analyses were made in 1995, of which only 5,168 (0.5 per cent) contravened standards: 70 per cent of the failures were for pesticides (isoproturon, atrazine, simazine), while nitrate levels were exceeded in 15 per cent of samples.[112] Accidents such as that at Camelford in 1988 when 20 tons of aluminium sulphate were mistakenly emptied into a wrong tank at the treatment works and caused many cases of diarrhoea, nausea and rashes[113] receive much media attention, but the great epidemics of water-borne diseases are thankfully things of the past in Britain: between 1937 and 1986 there were twenty-one incidents involving some 10,000 cases of water-borne diseases attributable to public drinking water supplies in the United Kingdom, mostly due to inadequate disinfection.[114]

Water remains the principal liquid drunk in Britain, although this takes a very small proportion of total water usage of 135 litres (30 gallons) per person per day.[115] A survey in 1995 found the daily consumption of liquids of all kinds per person (all ages) to be 1.56 litres (2¾ pints), of which tap water was 1.14 litres (just under 2 pints): only 1 per cent of households had members who never drank tap water, but 30 per cent of households also used bottled water. More than 90 per cent of the tap water went into other drinks, hot or cold. Table 1.2 shows its use for different types of drink.

Hot drinks account for four-fifths of all tap water use. The Survey also asked respondents whether they treated tap water in any way: 11 per cent of households boiled their water, allowing it to cool before use, 9 per cent filtered it by a water-filtering jug, another 2 per cent had a plumbed-in filtering tap, and 10 per cent had a 'Soda Stream' or other sparkling drinks maker.[116] This suggests that a third of households were not satisfied, for

Table 1.2 Types of drink using tap water, 1995

Type of drink	% of all tap water consumption
Tea	49.2
Coffee	29.1
Tap water	9.2 (1/10 litre)
Other cold drinks	7.5
Other hot drinks	3.2
Others	1.8

Source: *Tap Water Consumption in England and Wales*. Findings from the 1995 National Survey. Birmingham. MEL Research, 1996, ii–iv

one reason or another, with their water as it came from the tap, and that more than a fifth treated it for reasons of health. Even so, these results were somewhat more favourable than those of a survey in 1988, which found that 28 per cent of people avoided drinking water straight from the tap, 40 per cent were not happy with its quality, and 45 per cent bought some bottled water.[117]

Concerns about possible health risks of tap water are a main, though not the only, reason for the recent very rapid increase in bottled waters, now the fastest-growing of all food and drink sectors. Bottled spa waters, which had had a limited market since the seventeenth century, were joined in the later nineteenth by more pleasurable, effervescent waters, particularly the German Apollinaris and the French Perrier.[118] Yet in 1970 bottled waters were so insignificant in Britain as to receive no mention in Derek Cooper's *Beverage Report*. Their rise as a popular drink among a broader social spectrum dates from the late 1970s, when they became associated with fitness, jogging and health food shops: subsequently their consumption has been encouraged by campaigns against drink-driving and by the social cachet that attaches to bottled water in restaurants and at dinner-parties.[119] The Chairman of Zenith market research agency recently gave the reasons for rapid growth as 'Wealth, health, travel and concern about tap water': the rise from 25 million litres a year in 1980 to 619 million litres in 1995 has indeed been spectacular, though at 10 litres per person per year this is still only a fraction of consumption in France or Germany. The social profile of bottled water drinkers has moved somewhat down the scale in the last twenty years, partly because of the availability of cheaper supermarket brands, but the heaviest consumers are still non-manual workers aged under 45, especially professional and managerial classes in the south of England and the Midlands,[120] among whom health-consciousness vies with fashion. There is some irony in the fact that enormous cost and labour are involved in ridding tap water of all extraneous substances while increasing numbers of people are willing to pay for 'natural' spring waters, which contain various minerals and live bacteria.

2 Milk: 'No finer investment'?

> There is no finer investment for any community than putting milk into babies.
>
> Winston Churchill, Broadcast, 21 March 1943

I

'Lacte et carne vivant' (they live on milk and meat) wrote Julius Caesar of the British. The milk of various animals was drunk as liquid, eaten in semi-solid form as curds and whey, and made into butter and cheese in Roman Britain,[1] though from the later Middle Ages cows' milk gradually superseded that of ewes, goats and asses. But milk and meat represented distinct dietary patterns, and accounts from the Tudor period suggest that while the wealthier classes generally disdained milk in their preference for flesh, 'white meats' (milk, cheese and eggs) together with bread and pottage constituted the main foods of the poorer, and larger, part of the population. Although cattle were almost universal over Britain, they were more numerous in the pastoral regions of the north, where, by the seventeenth century, areas such as Cheshire in England and Ayrshire in Scotland[2] were already becoming noted for commercial dairying.

At this period many small peasant farmers and copyholders were able to keep a few cows on the still unenclosed common and waste lands. Probate inventories of such small proprietors whose estates were valued at £5–£15 reveal that in the late sixteenth and early seventeenth centuries 87 per cent owned cows in the North of England, 68 per cent in the Midlands, 78 per cent in the East and 55 per cent in the West.[3] Access to some land and possession of a few animals were the peasant's 'commonwealth', and the resultant dairy products a mainstay of his family's diet: Professor J.C. Drummond estimated that his daily ration of 1 pint of milk, 1 pint of whey, 2 ounces of cheese, 2 pounds of maslin bread (mixture of wheat and rye), 2 ounces of pease and 1 ounce of bacon met all present-day nutritional requirements except for some deficiency of vitamin A.[4]

From the late sixteenth century conditions of life for most country people began a slow deterioration under the impact of sharply rising prices, periods of dearth, and the beginnings of enclosures in southern England. Labourers' probate inventories of the late seventeenth century now showed a steep fall in the numbers keeping cows except in the pastoral North, where 80 per cent still did so, but in the Midlands the proportion fell to 31.6 per cent, in the East to 21.9 per cent and in the West to only 4.2 per cent.[5] For the southern labourer the traditional 'white meats' were now dearer and scarcer, and although the total number of cows increased in the seventeenth century more were now kept on large farms, where the milk was turned into butter and cheese for sale in the markets. On these larger estates the age-old problem of winter feeding was beginning to be overcome by the introduction of clover and turnips, followed in the eighteenth century by lucerne, sainfoin, cole and rape, and more regular winter supplies of dairy products could now be assured, though at higher cost. A growing urban market led to the expansion of commercial dairying in the vicinity of towns, especially London, as well as the practice of cow-keeping within the towns themselves. Dairymen were normally both producers and retailers. In London, cows in Tothill Fields, Lincoln's Inn Fields, Islington and elsewhere were milked by milkmaids around 4 or 5 a.m., the milk carried in pails suspended from a yoke and either sold from fixed shops (Nell Gwynn's dairy in the Strand was established in 1666) or hawked through the streets. It was regarded as suitable for young children after weaning, old people and invalids, hardly for healthy adults, though whey was considered very wholesome, and London had several 'whey-houses', which were sufficiently fashionable to be patronized by Pepys: junkets and syllabubs (warm milk frothed over fruit, wine or spices) were also popular. By the end of the seventeenth century milk was being added to the new, costly hot beverages tea, coffee and chocolate: tea was at first drunk, Chinese fashion, without milk, but by 1700 milk or cream (poured in first to prevent cracking the delicate china) was usual, and the bitterness of coffee and chocolate was found to be softened by cream and sugar.

The first two-thirds of the eighteenth century were years of generally improving living standards, good harvests, expanding commercial activity, and increased consumption of the imported luxury drinks and sugar. On enclosed estates opportunities existed for 'improving' landlords to engage in scientific breeding with Durham Shorthorns, Channel Island, Dutch and Flanders cows, and large dairy herds were now found in Middlesex and Surrey, close to the London market, while specialist dairying developed in the Vale of Aylesbury and the Vale of the White Horse.[6] The market for liquid milk in the larger towns was clearly growing rapidly, with an estimated 8,500 cows in London about 1800 (in Hackney 600, in Edgware Road 550, in Mile End 406), while Mr West of Islington was reputed to keep 1,000 cows on neighbouring farms.[7] In Bristol, Edinburgh and other towns considerable quantities of buttermilk were brought in by barrels strapped to the backs of horses: at ½d a quart it was half the price of whole milk, and widely used by the poor.

The relatively good times for the rural labourer began seriously to worsen from the 1760s owing to bad harvests, price inflation, increased taxation and, most of all, the rapid enclosure of common lands and the loss of grazing for animals. Between 1761 and 1801 more than 3 million acres of commons and wastes were enclosed in the name of more efficient land use, mainly in midland and southern England, but the social consequences were often disastrous for the labourer. Arthur Young, who had been one of the strongest advocates of enclosure, later wrote: 'By nineteen out of twenty Enclosure Bills the poor are injured, and some grossly injured. The poor in these parishes may say with truth, "All I know is, I had a cow and an Act of Parliament has taken it from me."'[8]

By the 1790s the diet of the labourer in southern England had been transformed to one essentially of bread and small amounts of bacon, tea and sugar: elsewhere, the older pattern still largely survived, with dairy products, oats and barley in northern England, Wales and Scotland and the recently introduced potato, which was not here scorned as 'the root of poverty'.[9] Moreover the northern diet, with its porridge, soups, hasty-pudding and vegetables,[10] was a warm and moist one, reflecting the greater availability of fuel for cooking, whereas in the South the disappearance of woods and hedgerows forced the poor to buy commercially produced foods – principally white bread, to which tea added a little warmth and stimulation.

Although some contemporaries criticized the labourer for abandoning his wholesome diet for expensive imported luxuries, a few well understood the reasons. In one of the earliest of all social surveys published in 1795 the Revd David Davies of Barkham, Berkshire, collected details of the budgets of his poor parishioners. 'For a long time past', he wrote, 'their condition has been going from bad to worse continually',[11] because their meagre wages had not kept pace with the rise in prices: there was no mention of milk in the Barkham budgets, but 1–1½ oz of tea and ½ lb of sugar per family per week were invariably included. 'Suckling is here so profitable [to furnish veal for London] that the poor can seldom either buy or beg milk'. But replies to a questionnaire sent to fellow clergy and landowners in other parts of Britain indicate that where milk was available it was greatly valued, budgets from Derbyshire, Yorkshire, Durham and Westmorland showing labourers' families spending up to 1s 6d a week on milk out of wages of 7s 7d–10s 2d, while in Wales and Scotland, where some labourers were still able to keep a cow, there was no mention of tea or sugar.[12] In the 119 budgets collected by Davies, the majority of which came from southern England, the average consumption of milk was only 0.5 pints per person per week, but in Sir Frederic Eden's survey of *The State of the Poor* in 1797, where most of the budgets were drawn from northern counties, the average consumption rose to 2.8 pints per week.[13] Overall, the evidence of the late eighteenth century suggests very restricted diets, Professor Oddy calculating that the Davies budgets represented 1,990 kcal and 49 g of protein per day, the Eden budgets 2,170 kcal and 62 g of protein.[14] Allowing for the fact that the principal wage-earner needed, and must have received, more than these low averages, his wife and children would have had correspondingly less: it is estimated that in the south of England 90 per cent and in the north 50 per cent of children and pregnant and lactating women had less than 1 pint of milk a day,[15] and would have been seriously deficient in calcium and several vitamins as well as other nutrients.

II The milk trade, 1800–1914

Supplies

As the population of England and Wales quadrupled between 1801 and 1911 and its distribution changed from one in which 80 per cent of people lived in the countryside to one where 80 per cent were town-dwellers, milk came to be a commercially traded commodity and one of the pillars of the agricultural economy. It was in vain for traditionalists like William Cobbett to mourn the passing of self-provisioning, and a misunderstanding of the collapse of the labourer's economic status to suggest that he should buy a cow for £5 and feed it on a quarter of an acre of land.[16]

Until the later nineteenth century British farmers responded only tardily to the potential demand for dairy products, concentrating, under the protection of the Corn Laws until 1846, on arable cultivation wherever the land was suitable. The considerable interest in improving the quality of stock was concerned more with meat than with milk production – so much so that at the Great Exhibition in 1851 milch cows were outnumbered ten to one by beef cattle.[17] The fact that milk was highly perishable and could not be transported more than about 8 miles on bumpy roads persuaded most dairy farmers remote from towns to turn it into cheese or butter, a constraint that began to be removed from the 1840s by the introduction of railways, which almost from the first started to carry milk. Manchester was the first town to be supplied in 1844, tapping the dairy herds in Cheshire, where farmers began to abandon their traditional cheese-making for the more profitable and less labour-intensive liquid market.[18] In London, where town dairies had been the main source of supply, the Eastern Counties Railway began to carry milk in 1846, but the capital continued to rely heavily on its 24,000 city and suburban cows, whose milk, it was believed, was richer and fresher than that brought by rail. Safest of all was that 'warm from the cow', which could be had from animals driven through the streets and milked at the customer's door, or by visiting St James's Park, where cows were allowed to graze and were milked on the spot to order.[19]

Although disease was endemic in herds at this time, a major outbreak of rinderpest in 1865–7, which caused heavy mortality in town cowsheds, had important effects on milk supplies. Railway milk was now not only needed, but preferred, and improved arrangements for its delivery quickly followed – water-coolers at country stations to prepare the milk for its journey (invented by W.T. Lawrence in 1870), tinned steel plate churns for loading onto special early-morning trains, and large milk depots at the city termini, where the wholesalers' representatives immediately sold it on to retailers.[20] By the late 1860s the Great Western Railway was bringing milk to London from distances up to 100 miles, while the London and North Western gathered supplies from Aylesbury and Rugby.

In place of the producer-retailer, the trade now became increasingly dominated by wholesalers who could control the quantity, price and, to some extent, the quality of milk reaching the market, thus creating a major opportunity for entrepreneurship. The new breed of large wholesaler is well illustrated by the career of the Barham family, who had been dairy farmers in Kent since the seventeenth century. In 1827 Robert Barham settled in London, establishing a farm on fields off the Strand and buying the dairy that had reputedly belonged to Nell Gwynn: his son, George, began a milk round, at first carrying a yoke and two 5-gallon pails. In the 1840s he was the first London dairyman to use the railways regularly, and by the time of the cattle plague was bringing supplies from Derbyshire, 150 miles away, and arranging with the Great Northern Railway to have trains arriving at 4 a.m. each day. By the 1880s the Express Country Milk Supply Company, founded in 1864, was handling around half of London's rail-borne milk, drawing supplies from thirty counties and distributing all over London from Barking to Richmond.[21] Much attention was given to improving the quality and cleanliness of London's milk, with pioneering developments in cooling, bottling (begun in 1884 but not general until the 1920s) and sterilizing in the 1890s.

The increasing dependence on railways spelled the gradual demise of the town cowkeepers, especially when local authorities began to impose sanitary regulations on cowsheds under the Public Health Act 1875. In 1864 there were 1,361 recorded cowkeepers in London, falling to 301 in 1886 and only 80 by 1914.[22] Liverpool had also had large numbers, but Manchester had only 50 cows reported in the city in 1866: almost surrounded by dairying regions, milk here arrived by road or, more smoothly, by canal before the railways.[23] Smaller cities had less need either for town dairies or for railway milk, York at the end of the century being supplied almost entirely from the neighbourhood,[24] Paisley and even Glasgow by dairies within the range of light, horse-drawn vehicles.[25] Some London and suburban dairies survived either by offering high-quality milk at a premium price, like that of Tunks and Tisdall in Holland Park,[26] or, in poor areas, by undercutting the regular price by short measure and/or adulteration.[27] But in 1896 London cowkeepers were described as supplying only 'a drop in the great ocean of milk':[28] by then, many had been driven out by the stricter standards of ventilation, drainage and cleanliness of cowsheds enforced by the London County Council and by the energetic administration of the Food and Drugs Acts (see p. 39).

From the 1870s onwards the dairy industry began to respond to the market opportunities that milk now offered – fixed prices negotiated twice yearly with wholesalers, regular collection by the railway companies, and an expanding urban population with rising standards of living. At the same time, the arable sector of British agriculture began to suffer a long depression when large imports of North American wheat, selling at almost half the price of home-grown, forced many farmers out of cereal growing: in 1872 the UK had 24 million acres under the plough, by 1913 only 19.5 million, much of it having reverted to pasture and rough grazing.[29] Milk production, however, still had the natural protection of distance from foreign competition, both the numbers of milch cows and the milk yield per animal increasing steadily up to 1914.[30] By the end of the century milk was the largest and the fastest-growing sector of British agriculture, and whereas in the 1860s the proportion of milk going to butter and cheese was around 70 per cent, by 1900 it was less than 30 per cent: the volume of liquid milk sold in England increased from 150 million gallons in 1860 to 600 million gallons in 1914,[31] well ahead of the doubling of the population.

The way in which milk reached the consumer also changed significantly from a haphazard service to a highly organized doorstep delivery. By mid-century milkwomen with yokes and open pails had almost disappeared from the London streets, their heavy loads being taken over by men who pushed a wheeled perambulator ('pram') with a large churn from which they ladled milk into the customer's jug: from the 1880s light, horse-drawn floats became common. Larger firms like the 'Express' began to establish regular rounds with door-to-door delivery to the better-class districts of London in the 1860s,[32] providing three deliveries a day at 5–6 a.m., mid-morning (the 'pudding round') and at tea-time. Poorer working-class customers often preferred to buy from a dairy or general shop in small quantities – half or a quarter of a pint – as needs and circumstances dictated. Fixed shops retailing milk in London grew from 1,430 in 1831 to 10,571 in 1901,[33] but the dominant characteristic of the trade in the capital, though to a much less extent elsewhere, was its increasing control by a few large wholesaler-retailers with extensive rounds based on local branches. In 1870 there were eight registered companies in the London trade, and in 1890 twenty-eight, but by 1914 five – Express Dairies, the Dairy Supply Company, the Wiltshire United Dairies, the Great Western and Metropolitan Dairies, and F.W. Gilbert – between them controlled the bulk of London's milk:[34] these had the advantages of cooling stations, cold stores at their London depots, and plants for pasteurization, sterilization and bottling. The milk trade therefore underwent something of a 'retailing revolution' in the late nineteenth century in parallel with similar trends in the grocery trade. Standard prices to the consumer were now usual – 4d a quart in London throughout the year, the summer profit compensating for the higher price paid to farmers in winter,[35] 3d a quart in Manchester[36] and other provincial cities, where shorter journeys were involved and competition between dairymen was keener.

Consumption

Little milk was generally drunk in liquid form by town-dwelling adults in the nineteenth century. Most was used as an addition to hot beverages, especially tea, and to the porridge that was a main article of diet in Scotland and northern English counties; smaller amounts also went into milk puddings and baking, particularly in better-off households. Whole milk was too rich for weaning infants but was often boiled with an equal quantity of water, and some added flour to make what was considered suitable food for babies. Where it was more easily available, for example in dairying regions, milk continued to be important in the diet of adults, Mrs Gaskell describing a Cheshire breakfast in mid-century as consisting of a large platter of porridge in the centre of the table and smaller platters of milk before each person: each then dipped his spoon into the porridge, taking as much or little as they wished to add to the cold milk.[37] In Scotland two meals a day of oatmeal porridge were customary in rural areas, where accounts in the 1860s show labourers drinking milk with or after their food as well as adding it to their porridge.[38]

Table 2.1 summarizes the available data on liquid milk consumption, based either on estimates of total supply or on budgetary surveys and recalculated on a daily basis. This evidence suggests a low and fairly stable consumption over the first two-thirds of the nineteenth century of ⅕–¼ pint followed by a rise from around 1870 to ⅓ pint by 1900. A principal reason for this increase was the improved standard of living of the working classes due to the lower prices of imported foods such as wheat and meat, which released purchasing power for greater consumption of dairy products, tea and sugar: the spectacular rise in tea consumption from 2.3 lb a head a year in 1851–60 to 5.7 lb in 1891–1900 (see Chapter 3) was a main reason for the increased use of milk, as also of sugar, which rose from 24 lb a year in 1849 to 80 lb in 1900. Milk did not share in the price reductions of many other foods from the mid-century onwards, remaining expensive for families with low incomes, where a food budget of around 10s a week often had to provide for four or more children. The budget data from Table 2.1, Nos. 7 and 10, clearly illustrate the effects of income on consumption, and suggest that whereas in working-class homes the main use of milk was as an addition to hot drinks, in middle-class, servant-keeping households the much larger quantities went to children and into cooking also. The very small consumption of English

Table 2.1 Estimates of daily consumption of liquid milk (pints/head), 1829–1913

	Year	Country, place or group	Quantity (pints)
1	1829	London (average consumption)	0.33
2	1841	Manchester and Dukinfield (cotton workers)	0.23
3	1861/2	Lancashire (cotton workers)	0.20
4	1863(a)	United Kingdom (rural labourers)	0.23
	(b)	England (indoor workers)	0.11
5	1865	Britain (average consumption)	0.20
6	1885	Britain (average consumption)	0.25
7	1892(a)	United Kingdom (average consumption)	0.33
	(b)	London, West End	0.75
	(c)	London, East End	0.086
8	1897	Manchester	0.28
9	1902(a)	England (agricultural labourers)	0.107 or 0.21 skimmed
	(b)	Britain (urban workmen)	0.24
10	1904	United Kingdom (average consumption)	0.33
		(labourers)	0.11
		(artisans and mechanics)	0.27
		(lower middle class)	0.55
		(middle class)	0.87
		(upper class)	0.69
11	1913	England (agricultural labourers)	0.11

Sources:

1   Alexander Taylor, *A Farmer's Guide*, 1829, cited Fussell, *English Dairy Farmer*, op. cit., 306
2   William Neild, 'Income and Expenditure of Certain Families of the Working Classes in Manchester and Dukinfield in 1836 and 1841', *Journal of the Statistical Society*, vol. IV, 1841
3   Fifth Report of the Medical Officer of the Committee of Council on Health, PP.XXC, 1863, App.V
4   Sixth Report, ibid., Report by Dr Edward Smith on the Food of the Poorer Labouring Classes, pp. XXVII, 1864
5   J.C. Morton, *Journal of the Royal Agricultural Society of England*, vol. XI, Second Series, 1875
6   J.C. Morton, *The Dairy of the Farm*, 1885
7   R. Henry Rew, 'An Inquiry into the Statistics of the Production and Consumption of Milk and Milk Products in Great Britain', *Journal of the Royal Statistical Society*, vol. LV, 1892
8   W.E. Bear, 'The Food Supply of Manchester', *Journal of the Royal Agricultural Society of England*, vol. VIII, Third Series, 1897
9   Board of Trade, British and Foreign Trade and Industrial Conditions, Cmd.1761, 1903
10 R. Henry Rew, 'Reports on the Production and Consumption of Meat and Milk in the UK', *Journal of the Royal Statistical Society*, Sep. 1904
11 B. Seebohm Rowntree and May Kendall, *How the Labourer Lives: A Study of the Rural Labour Problem*, 1913

agricultural labourers is consistent with the lowest standard of living of all regularly employed workers in the nineteenth century and the major transformation that had overtaken their former dietary pattern.[39]

Averages conceal differences, and the consumption of particular groups or families did not always accord with generalizations. Almost all families, particularly those with young children, seem to have wanted more milk, and some were prepared to sacrifice other foods to buy considerable quantities. In Manchester and Dukinfield in 1841, the lowest-paid of the families surveyed (Table 2.1, No. 2) spent 1s 6d on milk of the wage of 16s a week to help feed a family of seven, and during the 'Cotton Famine' in Lancashire in 1862, when hundreds of mills were closed owing to the blockade of cotton imports during the American Civil War, the unemployed workers continued to buy the same amount of milk (1.4 pints per person per week) as they did when earning moderately good wages, though they cut down on all other foods, including bread and potatoes.[40] When Dr Edward Smith investigated the diets of agricultural workers in all parts of the United Kingdom in 1863 he found that in only eleven English counties did all the families have milk – Devon, Cornwall, Worcestershire, Leicestershire, Nottinghamshire, Derbyshire, Northamptonshire, Yorkshire, Lancashire, Northumberland and Westmorland:[41] the old dietary divide between the North and West and the South and East still persisted.

By the end of the century 'milk' for many poor people had come to mean mainly tinned, condensed milk, which was cheaper, went further, kept longer, and in its popular, sweetened form obviated the need for sugar. A successful process of concentrating milk into a semi-liquid form invented by an American, Borden, was taken up by the Anglo-Swiss Company, later Nestlé, in 1866:[42] several English factories were in operation by the 1880s, but much was imported from Switzerland and America. The cheaper varieties, which could be bought for 1d a tin upwards, used skimmed milk from the butter factories and large amounts of sugar, which helped to inhibit bacterial growth: it was very undesirable as infants' food as it was almost devoid of fat and vitamins A and D, and although infants fed on it tended to grow fat they often developed rickets. Public anxiety about its use, or misuse, was voiced in 1894 in the Select Committee on Food Products Adulteration, and shortly afterwards it was made compulsory for such milk to be labelled as not suitable for feeding infants or young children, though in 1911 it was reported as still widely used for this purpose by the working classes.[43]

Issues about the state of the nation's health took on alarming implications when 34.6 per cent of volunteers for the South African War (1899–1902) were rejected as unfit. The Inter-Departmental Committee on Physical Deterioration (1904) which followed in its wake was particularly concerned at the high rate of infant mortality, which stood at 158 deaths per 1,000 of infants under 12 months in 1895–9, actually higher than the 154/1,000 of 1855–9 despite the medical advances and material improvements of the intervening years. A widely believed cause was a decline of breast-feeding by working-class mothers, especially in areas of high employment for women like Lancashire, though the evidence for a causal connection was, and remains, controversial.[44] What was not disputed was that breast-fed babies were more immune to a variety of diseases than those fed on condensed milk or 'pap' (crumbled bread and diluted cows' milk), and that summer diarrhoea, gastritis and enteritis were reponsible for up to a third of infant deaths. It has been argued that infection of opened tins of condensed milk by flies, attracted by the sugar, was a principal cause of these diseases.[45]

Between the 1890s and 1914 sweetened condensed milk became the main substitute both for fresh milk and for mothers' milk in poorer families. For some ironworkers' families in Middlesbrough 'milk' for a week was one tin, costing 3½d,[46] while in Lambeth, south London, where families were fed on 8s or 9s a week, there was only condensed milk, used in the countless cups of tea and even spread on the children's bread instead of jam.[47] Even in rural England in 1913 only twenty-six of forty-two family budgets investigated included any fresh milk.[48] By then, the stirrings of anxiety about child health had resulted in the establishment of several Infant Welfare Centres and a few Milk Depots, where mothers could obtain bottles of sterilized milk at 2d for a day's supply. Beginning in St Helens in 1899, where the Medical Officer of Health had been greatly impressed by the *goutte de lait* in Normandy, they spread to a dozen other towns and London boroughs, but Deborah Dwork's verdict is that they were not a success: mothers were still too ignorant of the dangers of infected milk, the cost was too high for those who needed them most, while the inconvenience of having to fetch and return bottles was too troublesome.[49]

The quality of milk

Two main factors restricted milk consumption before 1914 – its high price and poor quality. Lack of attention to hygiene characterized milk supply, from the often filthy condition of the cows to the dirty habits of the milkers and retailers: moreover, passed as it was through several hands, there were ample opportunities for adulteration of a liquid that easily lent itself to dilution or worse. Since the 'richness' of milk varied from cow to cow and from season to season, dilution with water was often undetectable even with the lactometer, invented by Dicas of Liverpool about 1800 but not widely used for many years.[50] A naturally 'rich' milk could therefore be allowed to stand for several hours so the valuable cream could be skimmed off, or water could be added to the extent of 25 per cent or more and any resultant thinness or bluish colour disguised with chalk, flour or starch.[51]

The whole subject of adulteration received a scientific exposure, as distinct from hearsay accusation, when Dr Arthur Hill Hassall analysed all the foods and drinks in common use in London for a series of articles in the *Lancet* between 1851 and 1854.[52] Of twenty-six random samples of milk from London dairies eleven were diluted with water from 10 to 50 per cent, Hassall commenting that 'There are but few articles of food more liable to adulteration'.[53] He was also concerned about the insanitary conditions in which most London cows were kept. Fed mainly on grains and distillers' mash, they produced large yields but were often diseased and had a short life: they were closely confined in unventilated, undrained sheds without benefit of light or air.[54] The *Lancet's* revelations about the adulterations of foods and drinks, many with dangerous substances, led with unusual speed to the establishment of a Select Committee in 1855 before which Hassall repeated his earlier findings, adding that anatto was often used to colour diluted milk, and that this was itself adulterated with chalk, flour and turmeric. Dr Alphonse Normandy, who had also studied the subject for several years, stated that milk was 'always watered': he had seen cows being milked in Clerkenwell that were 'in the most disgusting condition . . . full of ulcers, their teats in a most horribly diseased, ulcerated condition and their legs also full of tumours and abscesses': he had not tasted milk for six months afterwards.[55] Even greater alarm was caused by the evidence of Professor J.T. Queckett, who had found calves' brains in milk, apparently used to cause froth,[56] though this was almost certainly an isolated instance. Anxiety was sufficiently aroused for Parliament to pass the first Adulteration of Foods Act in 1860, and the more effective Adulteration of Food, Drink and Drugs Act 1872, by which it became an offence to sell a mixture containing substances for the purpose of adding weight or bulk unless declared to the purchaser.[57] Although the appointment of Public Analysts was not compulsory until 1899, by 1875 150 of 225 local authorities had done so and a Society of Public Analysts had been formed, developing tests and defining limits for adulteration. Milk posed particular problems since its composition was naturally variable, and the Society at first adopted a low standard of 2.5 per cent of fat and 9 per cent of solids-not-fat, changed in 1886 to not less than 3 per cent and 8.5 per cent respectively: up to 1914 milk was their chief object of attention, usually accounting for one-third to a half of all articles analysed and with a higher proportion of adulterated samples than any other (see Table 2.2).

The increasing activity and expertise of the analysts clearly brought improvement by the end of the century, but the experience of different towns varied greatly. London had one of the worst records, with 27.5 per cent adulteration in 1880, while in some boroughs (Marylebone, Paddington, Woolwich) half of all samples were diluted, comparable with Birmingham in that year, where thirty-nine out of eighty-two were adulterated. The maximum penalty of £20 was clearly insufficient to deter persistent offenders, one milkman with eight convictions being fined a total of £90.[58] Even at the end of the century Birmingham, Nottingham,

Table 2.2 Percentage of samples of milk adulterated and of all samples of food and drink adulterated (England and Wales), 1877–1911

Year	Milk adulterated %	All articles adulterated %
1877	24.1	19.2
1879	19.4	14.8
1880	21.4	15.7
1883	20.0	15.0
1884	17.6	14.4
1895	11.1	9.3
1898	9.9	8.7
1902	11.6	8.7
1907	10.0	8.1
1911	10.9	8.7

Source: Annual Reports of the Local Government Board

Liverpool and Portsmouth still had rates of more than 20 per cent, the Report for 1898 suggesting that the explanation might lie in the different practices of the Public Analysts – some condemned milks contained preservatives, others did not.[59] Rail-borne milk over long distances was very subject to souring, and from the 1870s it became common to add preservatives – boric acid, salicylic acid and benzoic acid, formalin or one of several proprietary chemical preparations – which delayed, or at least masked, the souring process: colouring matters such as anatto, aniline dyes and patent products such as 'Cowslip Colouring' were also used to disguise watering and give the yellow appearance that Londoners especially liked. A list of twenty-one patent preservatives was produced in evidence to a Departmental Committee on Preservatives and Colouring Matters in Food in 1901, including some based on hydrogen peroxide, which could contain residual arsenic: colourings and preservatives in milk were eventually prohibited in 1912.[60]

Meanwhile, the new science of microbiology had begun to focus attention on the diseases that could be spread by infected milk, concentrating on the scourge of tuberculosis and its possible association with contaminated milk and meat.[61] It had been long disputed whether bovine tuberculosis, which affected a high proportion of dairy cattle, was the same thing and transferable as human tuberculosis, and at a Congress in London in 1901 the famous Professor Koch argued that the organisms were distinct and not transferable. The controversy continued until 1913, when a Royal Commission concluded that the diseases caused by both strains were identical, and that a considerable proportion of the tuberculosis affecting children was of bovine origin:[62] even so, remedial policies only began seriously in the 1920s.

Tuberculosis was only one of several diseases that could be traced to infected milk supplies. In 1904 Dr George Newman reported that 160 outbreaks of typhoid fever, 70 of scarlet fever and several of diphtheria had been so caused,[63] in addition to the diarrhoea that was responsible for 30,000 infant deaths. Already concerned at milk's poor public image, the British Dairy Farmers Association had established a Dairy Institute in 1886 to research and advise on matters of hygiene, and this was followed in 1912 by the National Institute for Research in Dairying, funded by the Board of Agriculture at Reading University. By then, the larger dairy companies had pasteurizing or sterilizing plants, which destroyed most or all harmful bacteria, but medical controversy surrounded these practices also, Dr Stenhouse Williams, the Director of the National Institute, believing that they destroyed some of the nutritive qualities of milk and undermined the incentive for farmers and distributors to market a clean product without recourse to heat treatment.[64]

By 1914 questions about the price and quality of milk were beginning to take on a political dimension in a wider debate about the role of the state in combating physical deterioration and encouraging national efficiency. In 1906 local authorities were permitted to provide free school meals for 'necessitous' children,[65] and, in the next year, medical inspection of schoolchildren. Should not every town have a municipal milk depot associated with farms under its ownership and control, and should not every child have an entitlement to at least half a pint of pure milk a day at minimum cost, as a Fabian Society Tract of 1905 argued? These could be the first steps towards complete public ownership of the milk supply, 'when the milkman would be on the same footing as the postman'.[66]

III 1914–45

Within 30 years milk consumption in Britain rose from 2½ pints to almost 5 pints per head per week, by far the largest change in its history and one mainly concentrated in the last decade. This was due to a number of reasons – increased purchasing power, expansion of the dairy industry, improvements in the quality and distribution of milk, active promotion by the dairy industry and by nutritionists, and the development of welfare milk services for mothers and children. By the end of the Second World War the factors that had restricted consumption in the past had been overcome, and its greatly increased use was now regarded as a main contribution to improved national health and fitness.

During the First World War milk was not rationed but was price-controlled, rising to 4d a pint retail by 1918,[67] a high level that led some local Food Committees to take over its distribution. Difficulties with labour shortages and imported feedstuffs led to lower output and a fall in consumption of around a quarter,[68] but the milk shortages resulted in a significant social development. In 1917 some local authorities began to provide special nutritional programmes for nursing mothers and young children, and in 1918 the Milk (Mothers and Children) Order formally adopted these practices as part of the developing maternity and child welfare services.[69] Nursing mothers and children under 5 received priority tickets giving them first call on milk supplies, and 'necessitous' mothers could receive milk free or at reduced price.[70] A less popular wartime development occurred in 1915, when the Dairy Supply Company merged with the Great Western and Metropolitan Company and the Wiltshire United to form United Dairies, controlling about half of the capital's wholesale trade.[71] The 'milk combine' was strongly attacked as a semi-monopoly, and the Astor Committee in 1917 recommended that the government should take control of the milk supply in the public interest: the war ended before any decisive action was taken.[72]

The wartime prosperity of British agriculture turned into depression after 1919, and in the next 20 years another 3 million acres went out of cultivation, mainly reverting to pasture: milk prices tended to hold up better than other agricultural products, and a decisive switch to dairying therefore continued, the English dairy herd increasing by 36 per cent between 1913 and 1937.[73] Nevertheless, milk consumption in the 1920s continued to be rationed by cost, remaining at little more than 2 pints per head per week at a standardized retail price of 3d a pint, though improvements in quality now began to give milk a more favourable public image. United Dairies developed tuberculin-tested milk at a premium price, but more important was the extension of bottling and pasteurizing, estimated to cover around 50 per cent of London's milk in the early 1920s.[74]

The promotion of milk began in 1922 with the formation of the National Milk Publicity Council, adopting the slogan 'Drink More Milk' two years later in a campaign to persuade the public that milk was a healthy and nutritious drink, equally good for adults and children, and targeting outdoor and sporting activities. This coincided with the arguments of a number of nutritionists that milk was a near-perfect food, especially valuable for children's health and growth because of its high calcium and vitamin content – the 'accessory food factors' that had only recently been discovered. Dr Gowland Hopkins had shown that a diet might contain ample quantities of calories and proteins and yet fail to maintain health, and that 'protective foods' such as milk, eggs, fruit and fresh vegetables were equally essential: experiments with Scottish schoolchildren in 1925 showed that adding an extra pint of milk to their daily diets increased their growth rates by around 20 per cent as well as improving their general health and vitality.[75] The problem was that the British Medical Association's recommendation in 1933 that children aged 1–5 years should have at least a pint of milk a day (cost 1s 9d), and children 5–10 half a pint, was quite unattainable by the large families of the poor and unemployed.[76] John Boyd Orr's study of the nation's diet, which divided the population into income groups, showed that milk consumption was directly related

Table 2.3 Estimated weekly consumption of milk by income, 1934[a]

Group	Income/week	Expenditure on food	% population	Milk consumption (pints/head)
1	Up to 10s	4s	10	1.8
2	10–15s	6s	20	2.7
3	15–20s	8s	20	3.1
4	20–30s	10s	20	3.6
5	30–45s	12s	20	5.0
6	Over 45s	14s	10	5.5
Average	30s	9s	–	3.1

[a] The quantities are for total milk i.e. liquid milk + the equivalent in condensed and dried milk. Consumption of liquid milk by Group 1 was 1.1 pints/week.

Source: John Boyd Orr, *Food, Health and Income*, London, Macmillan, 1936, 21, 29

to the amount of money available for food (see Table 2.3). Boyd Orr calculated that the income of half the population was inadequate to provide a diet for optimum health, and that Groups 1 and 2 were especially deficient in vitamins and minerals: he further believed that poverty rather than the ignorance or shiftlessness of parents was the main cause, and that it was impossible to feed a child under 14 adequately on 3s a week, the amount allowed under Unemployment Insurance Benefit, when a League of Nations Committee had recommended a minimum diet costing 4s 6d a week for a child aged only 2–3 years.[77]

Anxieties about malnutrition reappeared in the 1930s as they had at the beginning of the century, now supported by the new knowledge of dietary needs, though some viewed the 'Hungry England'[78] debate as left-wing propaganda, and even refused to accept Boyd Orr's scientific findings. It coincided with the depths of the depression in 1931–2 and a collapse of agricultural prices that threatened to ruin the dairying industry, by then the largest sector of British agriculture. Farmers were in a weak position against the powerful dairy companies, who varied prices and quantities at will, while attempts to form farmers' co-operatives to stabilize prices had collapsed through undercutting.[79] Responding to a clamour from protectionists, the government passed Agricultural Marketing Acts in 1931 and 1933 establishing Milk Marketing Boards for England, Wales and Scotland, by which all producers of milk for sale were required to register and sell only through the Boards, which would fix prices and give a guaranteed market to 140,000 producers: the highest prices would be paid for liquid milk, lower prices for surpluses, which would go for the manufacture of butter and cheese. For farmers the Boards 'brought structure to an industry in chaos'; for consumers they increased the output of milk and improved its quality (by encouraging pasteurizing and TT testing), but, according to their critics, at too high a price: the Boards were, in effect, producers' monopolies, whose interest was to keep up margins and prices.[80]

In one respect, at least, the increased milk supplies had important social effects. In 1927 the National Milk Publicity Council had introduced a scheme whereby a third of a pint of milk could be bought in schools for 1d (the full price): in 1934 the MMB took over and greatly expanded it with a government subsidy, enabling elementary schoolchildren to obtain a third of a pint daily for ½d or free to those from the poorest homes.[81] It was a convenient way of disposing of the Board's surplus supplies, but it accorded well with the pressure by nutritionists like Boyd Orr, Dr H.C. Corry Mann and Professor J.C. Drummond for improvements in children's diets. By 1936 83 per cent of elementary schools had adopted the scheme, and 2.5 million children were drinking milk in schools, the proportion rising from 39.6 per cent in the wealthiest socio-economic group to 77.6 per cent in the poorest.[82] Also, in some depressed areas milk was available to mothers and children at 2d a pint, while under the Public Health Act 1936 local authorities could provide free or subsidized milk to expectant and nursing mothers and children under 5.

Apart from these welfare programmes, however, attempts to increase the consumption of milk as a drink were not very successful: most milk continued to go into tea (which reached its maximum consumption in 1931), puddings and the breakfast cereals that now often replaced porridge.[83] Milk bars, which appeared in many towns and seaside resorts after 1935, did something to popularize it among the younger generation, offering fruit-flavoured 'milk shakes' in smart, chromium-plated cafés;[84] around 1,000 ultimately opened. But doubts about the purity of milk continued to haunt the consumer, and even reappeared in 1938 when the British Medical Association objected to the 'Drink More Milk' campaign, arguing that only tuberculin-tested milk was completely safe to drink.[85]

The Second World War provided the opportunity for nutritionists like Professor Drummond, who was appointed Chief Scientific Adviser to the Ministry of Food in 1940, to use the rationing systems to direct food towards groups most in need – in effect, to use rationing as an instrument of social policy. As a home-produced food, now generally accepted as uniquely important for child health, milk was at the centre of the welfare programmes that the war stimulated. Total production was increased from 767 million gallons in 1938–9 to 1,071 million gallons in 1944/5, of which 150 million represented welfare milk, and another 41 million school milk.[86] Retail prices were controlled and subsidized, rising from 3d a pint to 4½d by 1946–7 at a cost to the Treasury of £61.8 million, but rationing in the strict sense was not thought practicable and, instead, priority schemes for particular groups were designed. In June 1940 the National Milk Scheme placed all production under the Ministry of Agriculture and all distribution under the Ministry of Food: expectant mothers and children under 5 were entitled to 1 pint a day at reduced price or free, while mothers with babies under 1 year had a priority allowance of another pint at full price. For schoolchildren, the Milk in

Schools scheme was extended to cover 72 per cent by 1945, 1.25 million receiving two-thirds of a pint a day, 1.75 million one-third (it became free for all in 1946). Children and adolescents between school age and 18 had a priority allowance of half a pint a day: the rest of the population shared the remaining milk, which fell to around 2 pints a week for non-priority groups in winter months.[87]

The official historian of food policy during the war has described the milk scheme as 'a social reform of the first magnitude',[88] while the Chief Medical Officer of the Ministry of Health believed that it had 'probably done more than any other single factor to promote the health of expectant mothers and young children . . . particularly those "underprivileged classes" who before the war could not afford enough milk'.[89] The pre-war average consumption of 2.8 pints a week had risen to 4.4 pints by 1945, and in some formerly depressed areas it was three times higher than in 1935.[90] All the indicators of national health, especially the infant and maternal mortality rates[91] and the heights and weights of children, suggested that the food policies, of which milk was a central feature, had resulted in a remarkable improvement in the nation's fitness.

IV   1945–95

Under the continued encouragement of welfare schemes, subsidies and medical approval milk consumption remained at just under 5 pints per head per week until a major downturn that began in the 1970s. Table 2.4 charts the changes in household consumption, which accounts for approximately 85 per cent of total sales. Average consumption never reached the 'Pinta Milka Day' of the advertising campaign that began in 1958: two years before, the government subsidy had been reduced, resulting in higher prices, but if, as it seemed, total demand had levelled out, it was now much more even across the social classes. In 1950 the wealthiest class A consumed 6.3 pints per person per week, the poorest, class D, 4.4 pints, a range of 42 per cent around the average, whereas before the war the range had been 120 per cent: by 1969 the gap had closed further, with A households consuming 5.4 pints and class D 4.8 pints.[92] Also, households with large numbers of children were not nearly so disadvantaged as

Table 2.4 Household consumption of liquid milk, 1950–95 (pints per head per week)

1950	4.8	1985	3.75
1959	4.76	1989	3.51
1969	4.89	1991	3.31
1970	4.63	1993	3.39
1983	3.92	1995	3.36

Source: Domestic Food Consumption and Expenditure. Annual Reports of the National Food Survey Committee, London, HMSO

formerly because of the provision of welfare and school milk: in 1959, when average consumption stood at 4.76 pints per person, householders with four or more children consumed 4.08 pints per person, made up of 1.99 pints at full price and 2.09 pints of welfare and school milk at either reduced cost or free.[93]

In 1960 Lord Hailsham proudly claimed that 'One of the main reasons, perhaps, for the remarkable improvement in children's health in recent years has been the access of children to reasonable supplies of fresh liquid milk'.[94] By then, 82 per cent of children in schools in England and Wales were drinking free milk, 93.4 per cent in primary schools and 66.2 per cent in secondary schools,[95] but the lower take-up by older pupils provided some justification for a change in policy by the Labour government in 1968, when free milk in secondary schools was withdrawn at a saving of £4.5 million. Three years later Margaret Thatcher, the Conservative Secretary of State for Education, withdrew free milk in primary schools for children over 7 unless they had a medical certificate showing continuing need, saying 'We are not arguing about the nutritional value of milk ... the argument is about how much should be paid by the parents and how much by the taxpayer'.[96] The service could be continued for older pupils if payment was made, but 'the milk in schools scheme was effectively dead'.[97] Although the change produced a political storm, the Report on *Nutrition in Schools* (1975) concluded that the nutrition of children was generally good and that there were no reasons on grounds of health for restoring free school milk to those over 7.[98]

By the mid-1950s the dairy industry had almost doubled its output of milk since 1938–9 and continued to expand into the 1970s, both in numbers of cows and in milk yield per animal,[99] but with consumption beginning to fall, the Milk Marketing Boards faced a problem of over-supply that their energetic advertising did little to stem. Half of all milk was used by children, British adults drinking little as a beverage, as a study in 1958 showed (see Table 2.5). The advertising of milk as a tough, healthy drink for young people engaged in outdoor activities had some effect in stimulating consumption among 16–20-year-olds, but attempts in the late 1960s to revive

Table 2.5 Percentage of people over 16 drinking milk as a beverage, 1958

	In summer		In winter	
	Men %	Women %	Men %	Women %
At breakfast	1	1	0	0
Mid-morning	1	2	1	1
Midday meal	2	3	1	1
Evening meal	1	1	0	0
Supper/snack	6	9	6	9

Source: Geoffrey C. Warren (ed.) *The Foods We Eat*, London, Cassell, 1958, 28, 47, 75, 123, 153

the pre-war milk bars did not catch on. Since almost half of all milk went into tea and coffee, its overall consumption depended critically on these, and from its post-war peak in 1960 tea consumption was falling steadily (see Chapter 3) and not nearly compensated by some increase in coffee-drinking. In 1970 tea accounted for 61 per cent by volume of all beverages and coffee for 16.5 per cent (total 77.5 per cent), while in 1993 tea had fallen to 42.3 per cent and coffee had risen to 21.4 per cent (total 63.7 per cent); milk drunk as a beverage, including flavoured milk drinks, represented only 3.3 per cent of all drinks by volume in 1970 and 2.3 per cent in 1993. The outstanding change in drinks consumption was the increase in soft drinks and alcoholic drinks, which, taken together, represented 16.7 per cent by volume in 1970 but 32.2 per cent in 1993.[100] Less milk was also being used in the home with a reduction in the cooking of cakes and milk puddings and a decline in 'tea' as a family meal: at the now later evening meal, tea was often replaced by other drinks for both adults and children.

These influences were already restricting milk consumption before nutritionists began to point to the fat content of whole milk as a contributory cause of coronary and other diseases. In 1983 the National Advisory Committee on Nutrition Education (NACNE) recommended a reduction of fats in the diet by a quarter and of saturated fats (of which whole milk fats are 60 per cent saturated) by half as a long-term goal: at that time, milk supplied 13 per cent of total fat in the average British diet and 17 per cent of saturated fat.[101] In 1984 the Department of Health and Social Security published the COMA (Committee on Medical Aspects) Report, which also advised a reduction in the fat content of the diet except for infants and children under 5 on the ground that for these groups milk was a valuable source of calcium, vitamins and proteins. This exception was criticized by Geoffrey Cannon and others, who argued that whereas nutritionists had formerly urged the importance of a high protein diet derived from dairy products in response to malnutrition in the 1930s, a switch from animal to vegetable sources of protein was now desirable, and that skimmed milk (0.3 per cent fat) and semi-skimmed (1.5–1.8 per cent fat), which are still rich in calcium, should be preferred to full fat milk at 3.8 per cent fat. The image of milk was further damaged in 1986 by the Chernobyl disaster and concerns about possible irradiation, which caused an 8 per cent fall in milk consumption in some affected areas.

Public attitudes towards milk reached their low point in the late 1980s and subsequently revived somewhat, thanks mainly to the range of different milks that became available. Although a survey in 1988 found that 70 per cent of people greatly overestimated the amount of fat in milk and were very confused about 'saturates' and 'polyunsaturates',[102] the message of the nutritionists was sufficiently understood to have induced a dramatic change in the type of milk consumed in Britain since 1984 when the Milk Marketing Board first made pasteurized semi-skimmed and skimmed milks nationally available. In that year skimmed milk accounted for 5 per cent of household purchases of milk and semi-skimmed for 4.2 per cent: by 1993 semi-skimmed had risen to 41 per cent and skimmed to 12.3 per cent,[103] giving low-fat milks the larger share of the market for the first time. This must rank as a prime example of a knowledge-driven dietary change, a recent survey indicating that perceived obligation to one's family's health is particularly significant in determining attitudes towards different types of milk.[104] What was considered two centuries ago as an inferior, almost waste product used only by the poor has now become most heavily consumed by the wealthiest socio-economic groups (A1 and A2), while consumption of whole milk is highest amongst lowest earners (D) and pensioners. These last two groups are now the largest consumers of all liquid milk, so reversing the historic pattern in which consumption rose with income.[105] The proportion of fat in the household diet provided by milk fell from 13 per cent in 1981 to 10.7 per cent in 1993.

No great change has occurred in the ways milk is used. In 1994 households took 85 per cent of all liquid milk, catering 11 per cent and school milk 1.4 per cent: within the household its main use is still as an addition to hot beverages – tea takes 25.4 per cent and coffee 17.2 per cent – followed by its use with breakfast cereals 21.3 per cent and in cooking 13.3 per cent: 12 per cent of milk is drunk on its own.[106] In some other respects, however, both milk production and retailing are undergoing major restructuring. The doorstep delivery service, unique to Britain for the last 100 years, is rapidly declining in the face of cheaper and often fresher milk in supermarkets and shops:[107] in 1993 it represented 57 per cent of household supplies compared with 81 per cent in 1984. The dairy industry itself has been much affected by Britain's membership of the European Community and the production quota allocations that began in 1984:[108] under the Common Agricultural Policy member-states that exceed their quotas may be fined through the levy system, as may individual farmers, whose own quotas represent a 'property', which may be sold or licensed. The other important structural change was the abolition of the Milk Marketing Boards by the Agriculture Act 1993, and their replacement in England and Wales by Milk Marque Ltd, a voluntary dairy co-operative. This represents a domestic market free from the former constraint under which producers could normally sell only to the Boards: they may now sell wherever they wish, and dairy companies may buy direct from producers rather than through the Marque. The implications of this major change for producers and consumers after half a century of public control are not yet clear. Falling demand, declining doorstep delivery, continued concerns about the nutritional benefits or disbenefits of milk and even about its purity – in 1998 it was claimed that present levels of heat treatment by pasteurization were not always wholly effective – have greatly changed public attitudes towards milk in the last 30 years. The central place that it formerly held in the agricultural industry and in national esteem is now uncertain.

3 Tea: the cup that cheers

Unlike milk, tea, coffee and chocolate were exotic commodities new to Britain in the seventeenth century, imported from great distances and initially restricted to a wealthy clientele that thirsted for luxuries in an age of embryonic consumerism. Tea in particular was to pass into mass consumption to become the national drink of British people of all social classes, having revolutionary effects on their dietary patterns. This chapter explores the processes by which tea acquired this position of primacy among hot beverages and the reasons why, in recent decades, its dominance has been challenged by other drinks.

I

Tea, coffee and chocolate are mild excitants, sometimes classified as 'psychoactive drugs' principally because of their caffeine content, which stimulates the central nervous system and cerebral cortex: in moderation, caffeine can increase mental and muscular activity and relieve the effects of fatigue.[1] Infused in hot water, they have agreeable, warming effects shared by many other vegetable substances used in Britain both before and after the introduction of the new commodities, including mint, sage, camomile, sloe, strawberry and blackcurrant leaves.[2] The tea bush was native to China, where tea was drunk from at least the fifth century, and in Japan in the ninth century; but the fact that in these countries its consumption was mainly limited to elite groups in society meant that tea already carried high social status when appropriated by wealthy Europeans.[3] It was first reported in Europe by the traders and missionaries penetrating into China in the sixteenth century, probably the earliest reference coming from a Venetian traveller, Ramusio, in 1559, who described it as having medicinal properties, good for headaches, stomach ache and pains in the joints.[4] It was important for tea's adoption that almost all early reports made extravagant claims for its therapeutic powers, a description of 1596 remarking that

> They [the Chinese] have also an herb out of which they press a delicate juice which serves them for drink instead of wine: it also preserves

their health and frees them from all those ills that the immoderate use of wine doth breed unto us.[5]

This association of tea with temperance was to become highly significant, especially in Britain.

The precise date of tea's appearance in England is disputed between 1591 and 1612, the latter probably the more likely;[6] at the phenomenal price of £6 10s a pound, the supply came from Holland, where the Dutch East India Company had opened commercial relations with China ahead of its English rival. It was still little known in the first half of the seventeenth century, when coffee and chocolate were already making progress, but its acceptance in aristocratic circles was encouraged by the Restoration of Charles II in 1660 when his Portuguese Queen, Catherine of Braganza, brought her previously acquired taste to the English Court.[7] From the first, tea had strong gender associations. Although it was served in some of the exclusively male coffee-houses that opened in London after 1652 (see Chapter 4) it was not usual in these before the 1690s,[8] and was never the principal drink there. While coffee-drinking began among men in public, the consumption of tea was primarily domestic, beginning in wealthy households where its service was associated with other novel objects of conspicuous display – fine china porcelain teapots, cups and saucers, gilded mahogany tea-tables and matching chairs (as at Ham House in 1683) and silver tea equipages consisting of teapot, tea-kettle, milk or cream jug, sugar bowl and spoon-tray.[9]

The penetration of tea into elite consumption coincided with the euphoria that accompanied the restoration of the monarchy in 1660 after the austerity of the Commonwealth period, and it may be significant that its adoption closely followed periods of dearth in the 1620s and 1630s and the trauma of the Civil Wars in the 1640s.[10] But tea-drinking meant different things to different groups in society. While it quickly became part of the paraphernalia of gentility in the highest circles, it also appealed to and accorded well with the burgeoning commercial and professional classes, for whom it represented values of sobriety, serious purpose, trustworthiness and respectability. If the alcoholic excesses of the aristocracy were tempered by after-dinner tea or coffee, the working patterns of the bourgeoisie (who, like Samuel Pepys, 'did send for a Cupp of Tea' during a busy day at the Navy Office in 1660) benefited from a reviving 'interval drink' that was both refreshing and fashionable, equally acceptable to former Cavaliers and to wine-denying Puritans. The adoption of tea by the middle classes was not simply one of social imitation: rather was it a symbol of revolt against outmoded extravagance and immorality, 'an active process of cultural construction' and 'a demand for respect'[11] by a new, as yet insecure class.

The new drinks were therefore instrumental in the civilizing process experienced by Western Europe in the seventeenth century, especially evident in dietary habits, eating utensils and table manners.[12] For Mintz, the adoption of the new beverages is no less than 'an index . . . for transformation to modernity.[13] Men who drank in the 2,000 or so London coffee-houses were subject to the house rules that prohibited swearing, gambling, quarrelling and profane language: all were regarded as equal, expected to be 'brisk and talk, but not too much'.[14] Alcoholic drinks only appeared in some coffee-houses later in their history, and beyond these restraints they were open institutions where merchants, lawyers and tradespeople could feel at ease in the company of men of letters and gentlemen of leisure. In upper- and middle-class homes the new, hot drinks began to transform the traditional, heavy English breakfast of meats, poultry, fish and ale into a light meal of various breads, cakes, preserves and tea, coffee or chocolate (often a choice of all three in wealthy households), while after the early dinner – still at 1 or 2 p.m. in the late seventeenth century – tea and coffee were served in the (with)drawing room, where the ladies were joined by the men after their port.[15] If men held the stage at dinner, the roles were now reversed: the mistress of the house presided in the drawing-room, making the tea from her tea-caddy, arranging social contacts for her guests, and organizing diversions, which might include music or cards – tea was here the lubricant of conversation and polite behaviour.

From its first appearance tea benefited from the medicinal claims made in the press and by retailers' handbills, some of which promised almost miraculous powers as a cure-all: the sale of leaf tea was at first by apothecaries, who were experienced in handling precious commodities and quite willing to promote its alleged therapeutic properties. Leaf tea was soon also sold by the growing number of glass and chinaware dealers, by silk mercers and milliners (the female clientèles of these are significant), and by the grocers ('grossers') who were emerging from the former pepperers and sometimes now styled themselves 'tea grocers'. Unlike the coffee-houses, ladies could quite properly enter and make their purchases in such premises, a fact of which Thomas Twining, the proprietor of Tom's Coffee House off the Strand, was well aware when he opened the adjacent Golden Lyon shop in 1717.[16]

A luxury article was a natural target for the Revenue, and from 1660 liquid tea sold in the coffee-houses was taxed at 8d a gallon: easily evaded, this was replaced in 1689 by a customs duty of 5s a pound on all imported tea. By then, the still relatively small imports from China were brought by the English East India Company, which had received its royal charter in 1600 to trade with all territories east of the Cape of Good Hope. The adoption of tea, coffee and chocolate by European consumers, like that of sugar and tobacco, was a consequence of the geographical explorations of new lands and the subsequent appropriation of indigenous commodities through colonization or commerce. In the case of tea, Britain had no control over its production before cultivation began in India well into the nineteenth century, and until then all (legal) imports were channelled through the Company's monopoly of trade with China. Commercial imports began in 1669 on an occasional basis until 1685, when the Directors in London noted that 'In regard to Tea, it has grown to be a commodity here', and ordered that in future it should form part of their regular trade: by 1700 imports had reached a sizeable total of 90,000 lb a year, and the tea trade was an established fact.

II

In 1700 tea was still an occasional drink of the wealthy, fashionable few: before the end of the century it was regularly consumed by all social classes, and formed an integral part of the new dietary patterns of the poor. This promotion of tea from restricted to mass consumption was a process rather than an event, and cannot be dated precisely, but when in 1784 William Pitt slashed the customs duty on tea from 119 per cent to 12½ per cent it was a recognition that it was now a normal beverage of the British people, worthy of encouragement, for

> Tea has become an economical substitute in the middle and lower classes of society for malt liquor, the price of which renders it impossible for them to procure the quantity sufficient for them as their only drink.[17]

Well before that, however, tea had found a place in working-class budgets, and its adoption by them and by the bourgeoisie was more a simultaneous process, occurring rapidly in the 1730s and 1740s, than a sequence of assimilation by one class after another. A consumer revolution in the eighteenth century encompassed all groups to some degree, accompanying and stimulating the industrial and commercial revolutions: beneficent harvests and booming overseas trade encouraged 'a convulsion of getting and spending'[18] that democratized consumption of the new beverages as well as a wide variety of goods from silks and cottons to pottery, cutlery, furniture and clocks.

Tea consumption spread westwards and northwards from London, the largest city in Europe, comprising over 10 per cent of the English population and the major dictator of taste: from here, tea-drinking migrated first to fashionable resorts like Bath, next to towns generally, and last to the countryside, a process almost complete within the first half of the century. In Manchester society around 1720 the drink provided at 'afternoon calls' was still home-made wine, but by mid-century tea was the usual offering,[19] while at the Yorkshire spa town of Harrogate in 1763 the ladies gave afternoon tea in turn, 'which, coming but once in four or six weeks, amounted to a trifle'. Lower down the social scale, tea increasingly replaced home-brewed beer, milk and traditional infusions of indigenous plants, which became scarcer as common land and hedgerows disappeared under the impact of enclosures and 'improved' farming. Even in Scotland in 1744 it was noted that 'the Price of Tea [was now] so low that the *meanest* labouring Man could compass the Purchase of it',[20] while in 1767 Jonas Hanway, a fierce critic of the luxury spending of the age, was shocked to find that labourers mending the roads clubbed together to buy tea-making equipment and took time off work for tea-breaks, that cups of tea were sold to haymakers, and that even beggars had been seen drinking tea.[21] This does not necessarily suggest that tea was first associated with work by the working classes rather than with the home, rather that it was used in both contexts. When Parson Woodforde took on a new maid, and agreed that she should have five guineas a year and tea twice a day, it replaced a former custom by which servants received 'beer money' as part of their wage, and in allowing maids from neighbouring houses to take tea with his servants on occasional afternoons he recognized that this had become a normal form of social intercourse at all levels.[22] Although tea's first use was as an interval drink, it was quickly absorbed into meal patterns and drunk either with or after food, especially in labouring families, where it provided warmth and palatability to an increasingly bread-based diet. Pauper inmates at the Nacton almshouse in 1771 petitioned the authorities to replace the usual dinner of pease porridge on two days a week with bread and butter because they were allowed to spend 2d of every shilling they earned as they pleased, and chose to buy tea and sugar to accompany the bread.[23]

Responding to growing demand, the East India Company brought ever-increasing amounts of tea to the Mincing Lane auctions in London. The upward trend was dramatic – from a mere 142,000 lb in 1711 to 890,000 in 1741, then to 2,800,000 lb in 1751, 4,900,000 lb in 1781, and a huge leap to 15,000,000 lb in 1791.[24] These official import statistics are, however, a very inadequate measure of total supplies. As an expensive, highly taxed article, tea was an obvious and relatively easy prey for the smuggler, and with spirits and tobacco was a main part of his trade. The customs duty of 5s a pound remained until 1723, when it was reduced to 4s and, more significantly, to 1s plus 25 per cent of the gross price in 1745, a change that explains the trebling of declared imports between 1741 and 1751, the period in which tea moved into mass consumption. Subsequently, duties were again raised, reaching 119 per cent *ad valorem* by 1784, when the Commutation Act drastically cut them to 12½ per cent in a generally successful attack on smuggling. Much of the trebling of official imports between 1781 and 1791 represented a transfer from illicit to legal trade, and marked a change in sympathy towards smuggling, which had previously been regarded almost as a public service. The volume of smuggled tea must necessarily be conjectural, but it has been suggested that in some years in the first half of the century legal imports may have been little more than 25% of total supplies: Carole Shammas estimates that in 1740–9 legal imports averaging 0.29 lb per person per year (England and Wales) would have been raised to 1.0 lb, in 1770–9 legal imports of 0.70 lb per person would be doubled to 1.40 lb, while by 1790–9, after the Commutation Act, legal imports of 2.0 lb per person were raised only to 2.10 lb.[25] If correct, a figure of around 1 lb a head per year for every man, woman and child by mid-century, or 1½–2 oz a week for an average-sized family, would imply that tea was already in mass consumption.

Two difficult questions arise at this point – why did a new beverage acquire this position of general acceptance, and why tea rather than coffee as in most other European countries? In the early years of the century tea's supremacy over coffee was not certain: in 1700 the official value of coffee imports was £36,000 compared with tea at £14,000, and import values of tea did not regularly exceed those of coffee until the 1730s,[26] though the volume of smuggled trade, which affected coffee little, would present a somewhat different picture of consumption. Tea had certain advantages in that, if necessary, it could be drunk without either milk or sugar, as it was at first in fashionable society, following the Chinese custom: it could be drunk in very dilute form and the leaves reused. Tea 'went further' than coffee, needing only about a third as much to brew; its supply was more reliable, and it was widely advertised and available throughout towns and villages, one estimate suggesting that a quarter of all shops stocked tea in 1760.[27] Tea established its popularity as an economical drink between the 1720s and the 1740s, when the rates of duty were lowered, so that when they were later raised its use was firmly entrenched and was not reversed. The support of medical opinion was also influential, not only because the boiling of water required for tea-making was some guarantee against infected water supplies, but also because many doctors believed that good health depended on a balance of bodily 'humours', and that the bitterness of tea helped to counteract excessive sweetness.[28] Similar claims were made for coffee, but coffee had acquired a predominantly male, public image that did not fit so comfortably into the domestic circle. Furthermore, while countries like France and Holland had direct access to coffee supplies through their colonies in Java and the Antilles, Britain's trade interests in exotic commodities were dominated by the powerful East India Company, with its established China tea connection, and by the rapidly developing sugar trade of the West Indies.[29]

The economic argument that tea possessed a favourable price ratio over coffee may well have been important for some consumers, but does not constitute a wholly convincing explanation. Tea was also the preferred drink of the middle classes, whose incomes did not oblige them to choose cheapness; for them, the associations of tea with respectability, sobriety and a privatized home life in which women's tastes carried authority, were more important. Nor does the 'trickle-down' theory of social imitation – that 'luxury articles of the rich will seep down through the social ranks, and perhaps end by becoming a necessity for all'[30] – explain the processes by which a particular good becomes desired and available. Mere considerations of fashion were scarcely likely to have a major influence on the frail budgets of the poor.

Two other reasons are more important in accounting for the central place that tea came to occupy in working-class diets. Sugar early became associated with the use of tea, adding sweetness, palatability and energy in the form of calories to a drink that otherwise lacked nutritional value. When added sugar became usual is uncertain, but probably within the first two or three decades of the eighteenth century,[31] at the time when black Bohea and Congou teas, stronger and more bitter than green, were becoming popular, especially with working-class consumers. The production and supply of sugar were under British control through her colonies in the West Indies, where plantations had begun in Barbados in around 1640 and were later extended to Jamaica and Antigua. By 1650 there were some fifty sugar refineries in Britain centred in London, Bristol and Liverpool,[32] and imports subsequently grew in close parallel with those of tea: estimated UK sugar consumption rose from 4 lb per person per year in 1700–9 to 8 lb in 1720–9, 11 lb in 1770–9 and 13 lb in 1790–9.[33] Production and consumption were encouraged by a preferential tariff that charged colonial sugar at 4s 10d a hundredweight from 1747–87 compared with foreign sugar at 15s 5d: average retail prices gradually fell from the high level of 16d a pound in the seventeenth century to 8d a pound in the eighteenth and 4d a pound in the nineteenth century.[34]

The complementarity of tea and sugar was especially evident in working-class budgets of the later eighteenth century, where the two commodities were usually listed together as though one depended on the other, so much so that it has been argued that 'the astonishingly rapid assimilation of a new economic product [tea] was directly related to the greater availability of sugar ... and the decline in its cost'.[35] They became incorporated in the working-class diet during a generally favourable economic period when, like white, wheaten bread, they added elements of luxury to the traditional diet of soups, meat, vegetables, dairy products and beer,[36] but from around the 1760s traditional foods came under pressure from rising prices, the loss of common lands and a decline in earnings from cottage industries. In particular, meat and dairy products declined, especially in southern England (see Chapter 2) while tea and sugar – now established and mildly addictive – continued to expand as accompaniments to an increasingly cereal diet. White bread, tea and sugar, formerly the luxuries of the rich, became mainstays of a poverty diet in the late eighteenth century. Two ounces of tea a week for a family, costing 4d, and half a pound of sugar, also at 4d, might seem extravagant items in a labourer's wage of 6–8s a week, as contemporary critics were fond of pointing out, but they gave some palatability and variety to a monotonous diet, warmth to cold meals, and some stimulation to fatigued bodies.

By the end of the century, when bad harvests coincided with high prices and wartime taxation, the new dietary pattern represented a significant reduction in the nutritional status of the labourer. Budgets collected by the Revd David Davies and Sir Frederic Eden in the 1780s and 1790s are estimated to provide only 1,734 calories per person per day (2,109 calories per adult) in southern England, and 2,352 calories (2,823 per adult) in the North,[37] well below energy requirements for manual workers: these labourers spent 10 per cent of their food budgets on tea and sugar in both regions, compared with 12.3 per cent on meat (usually bacon) and only 2.5 per cent on beer.[38]

Increasing dependence on commercial producers and retailers was a characteristic of the new consuming habits – bread from the baker rather than home-baked, beer from the publican-brewer, tea and sugar from the grocer, 30,000 of whom were registered as tea dealers in the 1780s. They sold it either unblended, in a variety of black and green grades, or blended to the customer's order: the principal black teas, in ascending order, were Bohea, Congou and Souchong, the green Hyson, Singlo and Gunpowder. Retail prices reflected seasonal variations in the size and quality of the crop and the wholesale prices paid by dealers at the London auctions, but over the century the trend was substantially downwards as supplies increased and the duties lowered. In the 1720s the leading firm of Twinings was selling teas from 12s a pound for the lowest-quality Bohea Dust to 36s for Finest Hyson, but in 1785, the year following the largest tariff reduction, they offered Bohea for as little as 2s a pound, Congou from 4s to 5s 4d, and Hyson at 6s to 10s: in 1800 Richard Twining wrote to his son, travelling for the firm in Scotland, about the 'roaring trade' the business was doing.[39]

By this time tea or, less commonly, coffee, had generally replaced beer for breakfast; if resources allowed, men drank beer with their supper, but otherwise tea was the family beverage, drunk with and between meals through the day. Arthur Young in 1767 complained of '*men* making tea an article of their food almost as much as women, labourers losing their time to go and come to the tea table',[40] while in 1797 Eden observed that labourers' families in Middlesex and Surrey drank tea three times a day with their meals.

> The poorest labourers are habituated to the unvarying meal of dry bread and cheese, and from week to week's end in these families whose finances do not allow them the indulgence of malt liquor, the deleterious product of China constitutes their most usual and general beverage.[41]

How tea was made in such households at this time is uncertain, but in some it seems that the tea-kettle was kept simmering on the hob throughout the day, more leaves being added as required: in poor homes 'spent' leaves were dried and reused and 'donkey tea' made of burnt crusts was sometimes substituted.[42] Eden noted that at this level tea was often drunk without either milk or sugar, and David Davies, one of the few sympathetic social observers to defend the poor's use of tea, commented

> Spring water, just coloured with the leaves of the lowest-priced tea and sweetened with the brownest sugar is the luxury for which you reprove them. To this they have recourse from mere necessity, and were they now to be deprived of this they would immediately be reduced to bread and water. Tea-drinking is not the cause, but the consequence of the distresses of the poor.[43]

Although the adoption of tea by all classes now seemed irreversible, its place in the nation's diet continued to be controversial. While Samuel Johnson, who described himself as 'a hardened and shameless tea-drinker', might be indulged, and the middle and upper classes who refreshed themselves with tea after substantial meals or took an evening's recreation in a Tea Garden[44] could even be admired for their sobriety, many still thought, like Hanway, that tea-drinking by the poor was 'pernicious to Health, obstructing industry and impoverishing the Nation'. In one respect the critics were right: the new diet was less nutritious than the old, but it was the result of forces of economic change and 'modernization' rather than of choice or extravagance.

III

Between 1800 and 1900 the quantity of tea consumed in the UK increased tenfold – from 23,720,000 lb a year to 224,180,000 lb. However, this disguises the fact that consumption per head actually fell until the decade 1841–50, followed by dramatic increases thereafter (see Table 3.1). In Britain, as opposed to the UK, consumption has been calculated marginally higher – 1.96 lb a year in 1804–6, falling to 1.73 lb in 1824–6, recovering to 1.97 lb in 1834–6 and then beginning a steady rise from 2.14 lb in 1844–6,[45] but the absence of growth until the 1840s is consistent, and remarkable after the increases of the late eighteenth century. Beer consumption is estimated to have fallen by a third between 1800 and

Table 3.1 Tea consumption in the UK, 1800–1900 (lb/head/year)

	lb		lb
1801–10	1.41	1851–60	2.31
1811–20	1.28	1861–70	3.26
1821–30	1.27	1871–80	4.37
1831–40	1.36	1881–90	4.92
1841–50	1.61	1891–1900	5.70

Source: W. Scott Tebb, *Tea and the Effects of Tea Drinking*, Cornell, London, 1905, 7

Table 3.2 Sugar consumption in the UK, 1800–1900 (lb/head/year)

	lb		lb
1801–10	20.15	1851–60	31.19
1811–20	17.37	1861–70	39.93
1821–30	17.96	1871–80	55.21
1831–40	17.20	1881–90	61.17
1841–50	20.45	1891–1900	80.14

Source: Calculated from B.R. Mitchell and Phyllis Deane, *Abstract of British Historical Statistics*, Cambridge University Press, 1962, 355–7

1850 and wine by 41 per cent,[46] while sugar consumption also declined in parallel with tea (see Table 3.2). The fact that tea did not recover its 1800 level of consumption until 1843, sugar until 1850 and tobacco until 1864[47] argues a decline in the purchasing power of many working-class consumers during this period of rapid industrialization.

Consumption of these commodities was restricted by the continued high wartime taxation and by the long depression that began after 1815. The typical working-class family consumption of around 2 ounces of tea a week in the 1790s was still usual half a century later and directly related to income; a survey of Lancashire cotton factory workers in 1841 found that expenditure ranged from 6d to 1s 3d a week between the lowest- and highest-paid earners.[48] These families were not the casualties of industrialization, like the chronically depressed handloom weavers. Describing the diet of the Manchester poor in 1844 as consisting of bread, potatoes and porridge, Engels added:

> As an accompaniment, weak tea, with perhaps a little sugar, milk or spirits, is universally drunk. Tea in England . . . is quite as indispensable as coffee in Germany, and where no tea is used, the bitterest poverty reigns.[49]

In 1813 the cheapest tea sold by Twinings cost 4s 10d a pound, and Congou, the sort more often used by the working classes, was 5s 6d. The duty of 100 per cent was responsible for half these prices, raised further in 1836 when a regressive tax of 2s 1d a pound on all qualities increased the prime cost (before distribution costs and profits) of Congou from 1s 2d to 3s 3d a pound. The decisive change towards lower duties was initiated by Gladstone in 1853. A confirmed tea-drinker and ally of temperance, he proposed to reduce the tax to 1s a pound over three years, a programme interrupted by the Crimean War (1854–6) but achieved in 1863: two years later followed a further major cut to 6d a pound (see Table 3.3). The effect of these changes on prices and demand was dramatic. In Twinings' price list of 1859 Congou was now 3s 2d a pound, and the most expensive tea, Finest Gunpowder Hyson, 7s 6d;[50] by the end of the

Table 3.3 The tea duty, 1815–1914

1815	96% ad valorem	1855	1s 9d lb
1819	100% " "	1857	1s 5d lb
1834	1s 6d–3s 0d lb by quality	1863	1s 0d lb
1836	2s 1d lb, all qualities	1865	6d lb
1840	2s 2d lb, all qualities	1890	4d lb
1853	1s 10d lb	1900	6d lb
1854	1s 6d lb	1906	5d lb

Source: Based on Serena Hardy, *The Tea Book*, Whittet Books, Weybridge, Surrey, 1979, 111

century, when further influences on price had come into play, packet teas of reliable quality were offered by multiple grocers at 1s 6d a pound.

Progressive price reductions confirmed the central position of tea in the working-class diet after the middle of the century. In 1863 Dr Edward Smith believed that tea was now a necessity, 'not from the requirements of the body, but from the acquired habits and tastes of the people';[51] such families were now consuming half a pound a week, estimated to cost £5 4s a year, almost as much as they spent on meat (£6 18s 8d) and half the cost of rent.[52] As well as consumption in the home, workers took tea to be brewed at factory breaks, agricultural labourers boiled a kettle in the fields, and miners took cans of cold tea into the pits. In middle-class homes tea was now more usual than coffee, and only in the wealthiest households did both appear as alternatives at breakfast and after dinner. The later hour of dining in Victorian England – often at 7.30 p.m. or 8 p.m. in the highest circles – created a gap for an additional light meal, 'afternoon tea', at around 4 p.m., a social occasion mainly for ladies and eligible bachelors.[53] Although the English tea ceremony never developed the elaboration of the Japanese, the arts of managing the tea equipment and serving guests were marks of social accomplishment, as was the manner of drinking. Victorian etiquette required the milk or cream (tea-sets always included a 'cream' jug) to be added after the tea, allowing the drinker to decline or limit the amount:[54] to drink from the saucer was no longer acceptable, while a teaspoon laid across the cup indicated that the drinker declined a refill.[55] The polite 'afternoon tea', at which little more than bread and butter or sandwiches were served, was quite different from 'high tea', a substantial meal of cold meats or fish, salads, fruit and cakes that developed in the later nineteenth century, particularly in the north of England and Scotland. In middle-class homes it allowed the servants to attend church on Sunday evening, since no cooking was involved, while in better-off working-class homes it became something of a festive occasion for visitors. Both 'afternoon' and 'high' tea confirmed the central role of the hostess as provider and manager, presiding in her 'separate sphere' of the home. Whether this domestic concentration enlarged or diminished women's social position was debated in the emerging feminist press of the later nineteenth century, where the journal *Kettledrum*, established in 1869, sought to relate tea-drinking to wider social and political issues. While announcing that 'Tea-table talk and tea-table interests will be here discussed, and nothing more', the editorial quickly moved on to 'the rule woman bears over the tea-kettle', stating that the journal would be concerned with such matters as the supply of pure water, short weight, the price of bread, the dilution of milk and the evils of slave-grown sugar.[56]

Until 1833 the East India Company retained the sole right of importing tea, all of which came from China; in Canton the Company's officials, the 'supercargoes', dealt with the guild of Hong merchants, who bought from the country growers through a network of dealers. By the early nineteenth century there was mounting criticism by free traders of the Company's activities, on the grounds that a monopoly inevitably abused its position by overpaying its officials and overcharging the public, a Select Committee claiming that in 1828–9 the Company had charged £1,832,000 more for its teas than similar qualities had fetched in Hamburg, supplied mainly by Holland.[57] Such criticisms were accepted by most contemporaries and later historians,[58] but have recently been challenged by Mui and Mui in a persuasive defence of the Company's conduct of its tea trade.[59] They argue that the market was not under-supplied or over-charged, and that in the end it was the dealers' bids at the London auctions that determined the quantity and price of tea available to the public rather than the Directors of the Company.[60] And while accepting that profits were 'handsome', they show that they were no higher than those of the competitive free traders who entered the market after the abolition of the Company's monopoly in 1833.[61]

In response to constant complaints of Chinese adulteration by English dealers – the mixing of leaves from other shrubs with genuine tea, the addition of used leaves to make up weight, and the 'facing' of inferior leaves with colouring dyes – the Company had appointed a tea inspector in Canton in 1790 to check the goods offered by the Hong. Thereafter the quality of tea was much improved up to 1833, but free trade brought a return of problems, with strong competition between British, Dutch and American merchants, many of whom were inexperienced. Large quantities of plum and ash leaves were now discovered, and almost all green tea was 'glazed' with a mixture of gypsum and indigo or Prussian blue.[62]

Widespread adulteration also occurred in Britain despite laws passed in 1724, 1730 and 1776 that were intended to protect the Revenue rather than the consumer. Leaves from English trees and hedges such as ash, sloe and elder, as well as exhausted tea leaves, were used to make a product known as 'smouch', especially during the period of high taxation in the early decades of the century. In 1820 Frederick Accum, a leading analytical chemist, reported the case of a London grocer who employed agents to collect blackthorn and whitethorn leaves at 2d a pound, which were baked on iron plates, curled, and coloured with logwood, Dutch pink and poisonous verdigris: Accum analysed nineteen samples of green tea bought from London grocers, every one of which contained poisonous copper carbonate.[63] Exposure of adulteration came to a head when Dr Arthur Hassall published the results of his microscopical analysis of foods and drink in the *Lancet* between 1851 and 1854. He found that 'tea' contained leaves of horsechestnut, sycamore and plum as well as a frightening list of colouring or flavouring substances, including black lead, indigo, Prussian blue, Chinese yellow, sulphate of iron, turmeric and catechu.[64] Tea adulteration was overcome in the next 30 years by lower rates of duty, new sources of supply, and the effective enforcement of the Sale of Food and Drugs Act 1875, which established a national system of public analysts and regular sampling: by the 1880s only one or two adulterated samples were reported each year from the hundreds examined.[65]

While the East India Company held a monopoly of the trade with China it took little interest in developing cultivation in India although an indigenous tea shrub had been discovered in Khatmandu in 1816: instead, opium had been cultivated to exchange for Chinese tea. The first tea gardens were laid out in Assam in 1835, and commercial exports began 4 years later.[66] After some over-speculation in the 1860s the Indian tea industry expanded successfully under expert management employing modern technology: by 1900 India produced 100 million lb a year, half Britain's consumption. India concentrated on black teas, which were stronger in flavour than Chinese and were never found to be adulterated. In the 1880s tea cultivation was also developed in Ceylon after the ruin of the coffee industry by disease: in 1900 Ceylon exported 80 million lb a year, and China's contribution had shrunk to 10 per cent (see Table 3.4).

The incursion of these new sources of supply implied a major restructuring of the tea trade from China to the Indian sub-continent, from foreign to colonial sources and from green teas to black. Abundant supplies of cheap, good-quality tea were now available in the later nineteenth century,

Table 3.4 Sources of UK tea supplies, 1866–1903

	India %	*Ceylon* %	*China* %	*Others* %
1866–70	6.6	0	91.4	1.9
1871–5	10.5	0.1	85.6	3.8
1876–80	18.2	0.1	80.2	1.5
1881–5	26.7	1.0	70.7	1.7
1886–90	39.6	10.9	47.1	2.3
1891–5	47.1	29.3	21.0	2.6
1896–1900	50.3	36.3	10.5	2.9
1900–3	58.4	33.0	4.7	3.5

Source: W. Scott Tebb, op. cit., 8

which created the necessary conditions for another fundamental change – a retailing revolution[67] that transformed tea into a branded packaged commodity with nationwide distribution. Tea was first sold in labelled packets by John Horniman in the Isle of Wight in 1826 as a means of guaranteeing weight and purity: his successful business began to distribute nationally when he moved to London in 1852.[68] Another pioneer of packet teas was John Cassell, a Manchester temperance reformer who established the British Hong Kong Tea Company in London in 1843, selling through 700 provincial agents: he later moved into publishing, founding the *Teetotal Times*, which prominently carried his tea advertisements.[69] Underlying these developments in mass marketing lay a moral as well as a commercial purpose – to sell honest, unadulterated tea that would successfully compete with beer and spirits. This was also the purpose of the Central Co-operative Agency, founded in 1850 by a tea merchant, Joseph Woodin, to supply the growing number of local co-operative societies with pure provisions. Despite some early resistance to his unglazed teas they gradually found favour, and the Central Agency was the forerunner of the Co-operative Wholesale Society (1863), which became a leader in the tea trade.[70]

The decisive development towards mass marketing, however, dates from the 1880s, when retailers were able to take advantage of low prices and the new sources of supply. The prototype of the thrusting salesman was Thomas Lipton who, after experience of retailing in the United States, opened his first grocery shop in Glasgow in 1871, adding tea to a limited range of items in 1889. By massive direct purchasing from India and Ceylon and a huge turnover with low profit margins he was able to sell tea from 1s 2d a pound upwards compared with the 3s or 4s of family grocers. By 1900 he had 100 shops in all parts of Britain, and was selling a million packets of tea a week.[71] Lipton's success encouraged the formation of other grocery chains with strong interests in tea – the Home and Colonial Trading Association, the Maypole and Meadow Dairy Companies – which similarly concentrated on a few lines in heavy demand by working-class customers.[72] The fact that real wages rose by almost a third between 1873 and 1896, mainly thanks to lower food prices, provided the basis of the demand side of this retailing revolution, which transformed high street shopping in the late nineteenth century. Specialist tea firms normally distributed through existing grocers' shops – Mazawattee (1884), which marketed a pure Ceylon 'Grannie's Tea', and Ridgways, whose reputation was enhanced by a blend specially made for Queen Victoria: the Queen's garden (tea) parties began in 1868. Brooke Bond and Company, incorporated in 1892, was originated by Arthur Brooke in Manchester in 1869 (there was never a 'Mr Bond', who was added merely for effect), and sold mainly through agents.[73] The Ty·Phoo Tea Company grew out of a Birmingham grocery business founded in 1820: by accident, the founder's son discovered that his sister's indigestion was relieved by tea consisting of very fine particles known in the trade as 'fannings' – essentially rejects from the large leaves generally regarded as superior. Ceylon 'fannings' that had previously been swept up from the warehouse floors, and either burned or used as fertilizer, became the basis of 'Ty·Phoo Tipps' (the double 'p' was a printer's error), launched in 1903. Its claim that it 'cures indigestion' rested on the argument that 'fannings' were the edge of the leaf and devoid of the fibrous stalk, which contained most of the tannin in tea: much was made of doctors' testimonials, and Ty·Phoo had a large outlet in chemists' shops as well as through grocer-agents.[74]

Long before this the battle for the hearts and minds of British drinkers had been won. Tea's last great critic was William Cobbett in the 1820s, who condemned it as 'good for nothing', 'a weaker kind of laudanum . . . an engenderer of effeminacy and laziness'.[75] But thereafter, tea-drinking by the working classes had the general approval of the medical profession provided it did not replace nourishing food, and the powerful support of the temperance movement, which promoted tea as a major ally in its campaign against 'the demon drink'. 'The cup that cheers but not inebriates' would rescue men from the alehouse and women from the gin palace, would preserve the family and restore domestic comfort: by saving what was wasted on alcohol, estimated in 1867 at around a quarter of working class earnings,[76] temperance would raise the standards of the masses to respectability and contentment. Tea was specifically allied with the fight against alcoholic drink from the 1830s onwards at 'temperance teas', a promotional device used by chapels and churches as well as by Chartists and the Anti-Corn Law League.

At the end of the century the still rising consumption of tea seemed insatiable. Usually heavily sweetened with the now cheap sugar,[77] it not only accompanied almost every meal but was an important vehicle for energy, contributing around a sixth of average calorie intake and more than this for working-class women and children.[78] Tea had also moved back into the public sphere with the spread of commercial catering in response to the increased mobility and purchasing power of the population. As refreshment for travellers, Spiers and Pond opened the first railway buffet at Farringdon Station in 1866,[79] but of greater significance was the emergence of the tea-shop, destined to become a uniquely British gastronomic and social institution. Probably the first was that opened in Glasgow in 1875 by Stuart Cranston, a tea dealer whose father, a total abstainer, had established temperance coffee-houses and hotels in the 1840s; Stuart's sister, Kate, promoted the 'artistic' Glasgow tea rooms, providing a restaurant service of lunches and teas appealing to lady shoppers in the city's new department stores.[80] Robert Lockhart's Cocoa Rooms, which also served tea and light refreshments, began around 1879 and spread to a successful chain in the north of England, while in London the Aerated Bread Company opened its first tea-shop in 1884, catering for shoppers and the growing number of women office workers. The best-known of all tea-shops grew out of the enterprise of a tobacconist, Montague Gluckstein, and a relative, Joseph Lyons, providing a refreshment stand at the Newcastle Exhibition in 1887: the first Lyons Tea Shop was opened in 1894 at 213 Piccadilly, and was so successful that by 1914 there were 200 in all parts of Britain.[81]

IV

The thirst for tea continued to be unassuaged in the years before the First World War, UK consumption rising from 6.07 lb per person per year in 1900 to 6.89 lb in 1914: even poorly paid agricultural labourers' families now bought 7½ oz of tea a week, four times as much as a century earlier, while working-class families in London drank as much as 9.9 oz a week.[82] With tea at an average price of 1s 6d a pound, the working classes were the chief beneficiaries of the retailing revolution and intense competition between the packet companies that now supplied half the retail market.

The central place that tea occupied in the nation's diet and psyche was illustrated by its favourable treatment during the food scarcities of the First World War. The government moved very hesitantly towards any form of control until the end of 1916, by which time prices were rising sharply and food queues lengthening: in December 40 per cent of all tea was made subject to a maximum retail price of 2s 4d a pound, followed in October 1917 by price control of 90 per cent. The final stage was reached in February 1918, when almost all tea was 'pooled' into three grades of 'National Control Tea' at a maximum of 2s 8d a pound:[83] most brand names then disappeared with the exception of Ty·Phoo after a deluge of letters to the Tea Controller from doctors and the public claiming its special medicinal properties.[84] Tea was not personally rationed, but customers were required to register with their grocer, who received an allocation of 2 oz per person per week: it seems that most people were able to buy as much as they wished, since many families with large numbers of children did not take up the full allocations.[85]

Between the two world wars tea drinkers benefited from low world prices and low rates of duty. As a war measure, duty had been raised from 5d a pound to 1s in 1915, but was reduced to 8d in 1922, 4d in 1924 and then totally abolished in 1929 for the first time in its history: in 1932, as part of the new policy of Imperial Preference, it crept back to 2d on 'British' and 4d on foreign tea, to be raised again in 1938 to 6d and 8d as Britain prepared for another war. Strong price competition between producing countries developed in the 1920s, which reduced the wholesale price of 'clean common' tea to an all-time low of 7d a pound in 1930. In conditions of world over-supply, producing countries sought to restrict output, finally drawing up an International Tea Agreement in 1933, which reduced production to 85 per cent of the highest output of 1929–31: this had the desired effect of restoring world prices to the pre-1929 level.[86]

The other line of defence was to try to stimulate demand by advertising

Table 3.5 Tea consumption in the UK, 1919–38 (lb/head/year)

1919	8.70	1924	8.81	1929	10.16	1934	9.22
1920	8.44	1925	8.85	1930	9.87	1935	9.42
1921	8.69	1926	8.91	1931	9.67	1936	9.31
1922	8.67	1927	9.03	1932	10.53	1937	9.19
1923	8.68	1928	9.16	1933	9.36	1938	9.09

Source: B.R. Mitchell and Phyllis Deane, *Abstract of British Historical Statistics*, Cambridge University Press 1962, 358

– a difficult task in view of the recognition that tea consumption in Britain was nearing saturation point. A 'Buy British Tea' campaign under Indian auspices began in 1931, which pictured Mr T. Pott (a teapot) proposing to a lady drinker at 11 a.m., 'Now we *must* make this a daily affair'. Advertising escalated as the retail trade became increasingly dominated by a handful of giant firms – Brooke Bond, Ty·Phoo, Lipton, the CWS and Lyons. Many inter-war tea advertisements made health claims for their products, Brooke Bond launching their popular 'Digestive Tea' at 2s 6d a pound in 1932, which echoed the claims of Ty·Phoo.[87] Brooke Bond was, however, overtaken by the Co-operative Wholesale Society, which promoted its 'No. 99' blend, implying 'just what the doctor ordered'. In the 1930s the CWS held 30 per cent of the tea market, the largest share of all.

Table 3.5 shows that consumption continued to rise in the 1920s, reaching all-time peaks of over 10 lb per person per year in 1929 and 1932, the worst years of depression and high unemployment. As it had for many poor people a century earlier, tea still warmed, consoled, and helped to make a monotonous, starchy diet more palatable. On the generally accepted calculation that a pound of tea makes 200 cups, every person in the UK in the 1930s drank rather more than 5 cups a day. By 1932 the average retail price had fallen to 1s 9d a pound compared with 2s 10½d in 1920.[88]

When and how much tea was drunk by the different social classes was revealed by a study of food consumption and meal patterns in Britain undertaken in 1936/7. Tea was found to be 'universally popular. It is drunk from early morning till late at night in all classes of society'.[89] The highest consumption was still in the wealthiest group of the population (AA, incomes over £1,000 p.a.) at 4.5 oz per head per week, and ranged down to 3.4 oz in the poorest (D, incomes under £125 p.a.). Table 3.6 shows the meal occasions at which tea was drunk by the different income groups. Although drinks other than tea were often served at these occasions, such as coffee in the wealthier groups and cocoa in the poorer, the dominant position of tea was very evident, the investigation concluding that 'At all meals covered by the Enquiry – with the possible exception of Supper – tea is by far the most popular beverage'.[90]

Table 3.6 Consumption of tea at mealtimes by social class, 1936–7

	Class AA %	Class A %	Class B %	Class C %	Class D %
Breakfast	85.8	88.6	93.5	97.6	98.3
Morning break	47.8	39.3	35.2	44.0	59.0
Midday meal	15.4	21.7	34.2	49.5	52.6
Tea	94.3	89.9	90.9	92.5	90.2
Evening meal	14.5	23.2	26.0	35.5	39.0

Source: Sir William Crawford and H. Broadley, *The People's Food*, Heinemann, 1938, Tables pp. 41, 46, 54, 63, 73

The 'food front' was better prepared for war in 1939 than it had been in 1914, a Food (Defence Plans) Department having been at work since 1936. The maintenance of adequate tea supplies was accepted as especially important: as the Official History of the Second World War later recorded, 'People could not run a village dance, raise money for Spitfire Funds, get married or maintain morale in air raids without tea',[91] yet all Britain's supplies had to be brought from a great distance, and on arrival at the docks were particularly vulnerable to air attacks. A few days after the declaration of war the Ministry of Food requisitioned all tea stocks and imports, and fixed maximum wholesale and retail prices, from 1941 subsidized to prevent the rapid inflation that had caused public discontent in the previous war. Despite the Japanese threat, India and Ceylon expanded their outputs, and with additional supplies from Kenya and Uganda there was never a serious shortage. From July 1940 tea was rationed at 2 oz a week for all over the age of 5, increased in 1943 to 3 oz for people over 70, and there were additional allowances for merchant seamen, harvesters, blast furnace workers and others. Lord Woolton, the Minister of Food, resisted the idea of a single blend of 'pool' tea, arguing that 'Taste, individual taste, is worth preserving':[92] instead, tea was allocated to the companies in three grades, common, medium and fine, leaving it to the blenders to make the best use and enabling the principal firms to maintain some of their popular brands. Large quantities of tea were also drunk outside the home in canteens and British restaurants and at tea-breaks in factories, strongly encouraged by Ernest Bevin, the Minister of Labour, as an aid to productivity. Consumption per head remained throughout the war at around 9 lb a year, only marginally below that of the late 1930s, while the average price rose only from 2s 10½d a pound in 1942 to 3s 1d in 1945.[93]

Tea continued to be rationed in the period of world shortages after the war, the amount varying from 2 to 2½ oz a week, until a free market was finally restored in October 1952. The immediate effect was to revive consumption to pre-war levels – 9.52 lb a year in 1953 and the high point

Table 3.7 Domestic tea consumption, 1950–96 (oz/head/week)

1950	2.16 (expenditure 5.36 old pence)
1959	2.80
1965	2.61
1970	2.59
1975	2.18
1980	2.05
1985	1.74
1990	1.52 (expenditure 20.09 new pence)
1996	1.38

Source: Household Food Consumption and Expenditure. Annual Reports of the National Food Survey Committee, 1952–97, HMSO

of 9.97 lb in 1956–8, despite sharp price increases after decontrol that raised popular packet teas to around 7s a pound. Public disquiet resulted in a reference to the Monopolies and Restrictive Practices Commission in 1956, which reported that 70 per cent of the trade was now in the hands of the 'Big Four' (Brooke Bond, Lyons, Ty·Phoo and the CWS) but that none held the one-third share required for a 'monopoly': on the contrary, 'keen competition' was held to be the characteristic of the trade.

For a few years after the end of rationing, tea-drinking habits remained unchanged, a survey of the nation's diet in 1958 insisting that 'Compared with tea, coffee, the next most popular drink, holds an insignificant place'.[94] But from the early 1960s tea consumption began a long decline, which was to reduce it to almost half in the next 30 years. Table 3.7 charts this dramatic fall since the peak of 1959. The Annual Reports of the National Food Survey also reveal significant variations in consumption between different groups of the population. Pensioner households are now the heaviest tea-drinkers, in 1991 consuming almost four times as much as the wealthiest social class – 2.75 oz per person a week compared with 0.73 oz:[95] consumption is highest in the oldest age-group, 65–74 (2.7 oz), lowest where the housewife is under 25 (0.9 oz), and is also three times greater in single-adult households than in families of two adults and four or more children.[96] These findings relate to consumption in the home, not including what is drunk in restaurants, canteens and so on, but tea is overwhelmingly a domestic drink, the Tea Council estimating that only 9 per cent of the total supply is drunk outside.[97]

In 1987 the rank order of the 'Big Four' was Brooke Bond, Ty·Phoo, Lyons and Tetley, which had overtaken the CWS when the co-operative stores began to sell other brands but were unable to market their own in the supermarkets. Tetleys built their success largely on the tea-bag, first developed in the United States in the 1920s and introduced to the UK about 1935. After interruption by the war, Tetleys vigorously promoted the tea-bag from the mid-1950s; acceptance was at first slow, it occupying only 10 per cent of the market in 1970,[98] but since then the bag has revolutionized British tea-making to the point when, in 1992, it held 84 per cent of the market.[99] 'Instant' tea, a more recent innovation that requires no milk, then held a mere 2.2 per cent share, while iced tea, a popular American variant, first appeared in Britain in can form in 1994. Leaf tea has now fallen to under 14 per cent of sales: it consists mainly of 'speciality' blends (such as Earl Grey) and high-quality unblended teas (such as Assam and Darjeeling) for those willing to pay premium prices. One important reason for tea's decline is the changes in meal patterns that have taken place over the last two or three decades. Meals have become increasingly polarized towards the beginning and end of the day, with snacks (now 42 per cent of all eating occasions) often replacing lunch and 'tea'. Although drink of some kind is central to a snack, coffee and soft drinks have moved rapidly ahead at these occasions. A recent comment that 'Tea continues serenely to dominate our culture, its rituals pervading every area of our social life'[100] seems more true of the war and immediate post-war years than of the 1990s, when the traditional occasions of 'afternoon tea' and 'high tea' are being replaced by evening meals, and the ritual teapot and cups by mugs and tea-bags. Working wives, small families and greater social informality are not conducive to heavy tea consumption, while public drinking in tea-shops and church meetings is following the fate of temperance societies and Sunday School 'treats'.

Since the 1960s consumers' demand has been for greater variety and choice following rising standards of living after a long period of austerity and restriction. As later chapters show, other drinks – especially coffee, soft drinks and wine – have competed successfully in the drinks market despite their higher costs, and are now conveniently available in wide variety in supermarkets. At an estimated 2p a cup or 47p a week ($3\frac{1}{3}$ cups per person over 10 per day), half of which is the cost of milk,[101] tea is the cheapest drink after tap water, but a drink whose largest consumers are the older and poorer groups of society now has an image that is unhelpful to mass consumption in an affluent society: tea seems to carry connotations of a staid, almost old-fashioned lifestyle, which does not easily fit the pace or leisure habits of contemporary life.

Tea companies have responded to falling demand by co-operative campaigns (such as 'Join the Tea Set' in 1967) and by extensive advertising on commercial television,[102] while the Tea Council, established in 1966, aims to promote public awareness about all aspects of tea: much of its publicity is directed at the 20–34 age-group, which is particularly vulnerable to competition from other drinks. Some nutritionists have recently argued the therapeutic benefits of tea-drinking, echoing in modern terms claims made on tea's first appearance in Britain in the seventeenth century. Research sponsored by the Tea Council suggests that four or five cups of tea a day may have beneficial effects on high blood cholesterol and high blood pressure, two heart disease risk factors, through its content of flavonoids, which have antioxidant effects: these can offer protection against degenerative diseases such as cancer and heart disease. Tea also contains small quantities of useful minerals (manganese, potassium, zinc and magnesium), folic acid, fluoride and B group vitamins.[103] Such benefits, if substantiated by future research, are additional to the long-established psychological effects of tea to change mood – in different situations either to comfort and relax or to revive and stimulate activity.

V

Tea's claim to be the national drink of Britain, crossing regional, class and gender boundaries, has therefore experienced major changes in its history of more than three centuries. Originating as an index of fashion and modernity closely associated with new tastes for all things Oriental, tea passed with remarkable speed from the conspicuous consumption of the wealthy and powerful to use by all classes, changing its role to become a symbol of domesticity, sobriety and respectability. In the process it profoundly influenced the eating habits of both rich and poor, sometimes for the better but for others becoming an integral part of a nutritionally inadequate diet. As prices fell and consumption rose dramatically in the later nineteenth century tea came to carry another set of meanings associated with national pride in Empire, patriotism, Free Trade and the material rewards that Britain's industrial and commercial expansion was now bringing to many people. But in the twentieth century tea was most heavily consumed in periods of crisis rather than of peace and prosperity – during the Depression of the early 1930s and in the Second World War, while more recently tastes in drink have been greatly widened by external influences from the Continent and the United States. Formerly almost the only drink of many people, tea now competes with a growing appetite for coffee, wine and soft drinks, which offer distinctively different satisfactions.

4 Coffee: 'I like coffee, I like tea . . .'*

I

Coffee, like tea, coca, kola, betel and tobacco is an excitant that stimulates the central nervous system, reduces the effects of fatigue, and enhances physical and mental activity: such substances are, in varying degrees, addictive, so that their use has become seemingly indispensable in many parts of the world.[1] But in addition to its physiological effects an important part of coffee's appeal to Western Europe was its exotic, Oriental origin and associations at a time when, in the early seventeenth century, the East still seemed remote and mysterious, and to enjoy its products added a new, glamorizing experience to consumption. The diffusion of a coffee culture to the West from its home in Arabia was a consequence of the expansion of Levantine trade by European nations, of the desire of their citizens to consume a range of new luxuries – whether drinks, sugar, tobacco, fabrics or ceramics – and of the economic ability of their wealthier groups to indulge new tastes. Western Europe in the seventeenth century was 'on the threshold of modernity', one of whose central characteristics was the heightening of individualized wants,[2] especially when these could be demonstrated in conspicuous consumption: the adoption of expensive luxuries proclaimed one's social arrival to a society that increasingly valued material indicators of status rather than the traditional determinants of birth and lineage. The fact that consumption of the new drinks was initially associated with royal courts – coffee with that of Louis XIV of France, tea with that of Charles II of England – gave them added social importance in aristocratic circles and also to aspiring members of the urban bourgeoisie such as public servants, professionals and merchants, for whom participation in the world of fashion was tantamount to a rite of social passage.

The rapid spread of coffee-drinking among these literate groups may partly be explained by the fact that it was the first foodstuff to receive

*The Ink Spots, 1935

wide publicity[3] from travellers, traders, physicians and commercial promoters, and it was significant that much of the early literature on coffee emphasized the supposed therapeutic properties of a drink that was at first classified alongside medicines and spices. Given the impurity of much water at this time, there was sound sense in recommending drinks that required heating to boiling temperature, Dr Andrew Boorde's *Dyetary of Health* (1542) advising that 'Water is not wholesome, sole by itself, for an Englishman' and urging the use of good wine or ale. By the following century moderation in diet and temperance in strong liquors was receiving religious as well as medical sanction, and a characteristic of an increasingly affluent society was a growing concern with the preservation of its health and longevity. For Robert Burton (in 1621) idleness, wealth and an extravagant diet were the causes of social and mental disorders: the rich 'feed liberally, fare well, want exercise, action, employment . . . and thence their bodies become full of gross humours, winds, crudities, their minds disquieted, dull, heavy'.[4] Bryan Turner argues that Burton's work on dietetics was a forerunner of the influential writings of Dr George Cheyne, whose *Essay on Health and Long Life* (1724) and *Essay on Regimen* (1740) advised strict moderation in food and drink, and light exercise for healthy living and mental stability. Cheyne's guidelines of dietary asceticism were disseminated to wider and lower social strata through one of his admirers, John Wesley, who strongly urged moderation and temperance as part of the Methodist discipline:[5] coffee, tea and chocolate therefore fitted squarely into the new dietary regimes as at once fashionable, non-alcoholic and healthful. By the eighteenth century 'the Georgian sick were attending more doctors than ever . . . obtaining mountains of medication, stimulants and sedatives [and] subscribing to a booming health culture'.[6] The promotion of coffee played a significant part in this process by means of books, pamphlets and handbills, not a few of which made exaggerated claims for the drink as a cure-all for a wide variety of ailments: such writings ranged from modest praise of coffee for its 'reviving properties', 'brightening the soul, rousing the mind' and 'being of particular use to persons who make few movements and who cultivate the sciences',[7] to the encomiastic advertisement issued by Pasqua Rosée, the founder of London's first coffee-house in 1652. Following the humoral theory of the day, Rosée stated that 'the quality of this Drink is Cold and Dry' and that it was 'very good to help digestion, and therefore of great use to be taken about 3 or 4 o'clock afternoon [i.e. after the usual dinner time] as well as in the morning'. Moreover, it would relieve coughs, headaches, consumption, dropsy, scurvy and the stone, and was even 'very good to prevent Miscarrying in Child-bearing women'; finally, Rosée claimed, with an eye to his coffee-house patrons, 'It will prevent drowsiness and make one fit for business'.[8] Much of this was doubtless dismissed as legitimate puffing, even by a gullible public, but as an aid to sobriety coffee's virtues were widely accepted, and the support of leading doctors such as Cornelis

Bontekoe and Thomas Tryon, who advised balancing excessive sweetness in the diet with bitter substances such as coffee and tea, was also persuasive.[9] Coffee was admired as an 'eye-opener' in the morning and as an aid to concentration at work breaks:[10] it was the drink of respectability and responsibility, of seriousness and sobriety.

In these respects coffee and tea shared many common characteristics, but in Britain their histories followed very different courses. Coffee tended to be a more public, masculine drink from its early association with the exclusively male coffee-houses: it was primarily a leisure, social drink rather than a domestic family one. It was more often consumed between and after meals than with them, and consequently its overall impact on dietary patterns was less than that of tea. Moreover, its consumption history over three and a half centuries was highly irregular and, to a degree, mysterious. Consumption rose strongly during coffee's initiatory period 1650–1700, remained almost stationary between 1700 and 1800, increased again from 1800 to 1850, declined between 1850 and 1950, then rose again, most rapidly of all, from the 1950s to the present. In terms of household expenditure coffee and tea are today close rivals: more than half British adults drink coffee daily, and average consumption stands at $1\frac{3}{4}$ cups per head per day compared with $3\frac{1}{2}$ cups of tea.[11] This chapter traces the changing place of coffee in the British diet, and seeks to explain why it did not become the predominant non-alcoholic drink as in most other European countries.

II

Coffee arabica was indigenous to Ethiopia, where it grew wild: the roasting and grinding of beans and the infusion of the powder began in the Moslem world, probably in the thirteenth century, and cultivation in the Yemen dates from the same period. The fact that its Arabic name, *qahwah*, was originally a poetic word for wine[12] suggests that it was first thought of as a substitute for this forbidden drink. Coffee-drinking was in general use in the lands of Islam by the mid-fifteenth century, sold in coffee-houses and in the streets in Mecca, Damascus, Aden and Cairo, often close to mosques: it was a favourite drink of pilgrims and of members of the Sufi sect, enabling them to spend nights in religious observance.[13] The first coffee-house in Constantinople was established in 1555,[14] followed shortly by the first reports of European travellers. Reputedly the first Englishman to taste coffee was Sir Anthony Shirley, visiting Aleppo in 1598,[15] but one of the earliest English descriptions was that of a merchant, William Finch, in 1607: 'Their best entertainment is a china dish of Coho, a blacke, bitterish drinke made of a berry like a Bayberry . . . supped off hot, good for the head and stomache'.[16]

Coffee was traded from the port of Mocha, and diffused into Europe from Constantinople by Venetian merchants soon after 1600: by 1616 the

Dutch had also entered the trade, Van den Broecke bringing the first consignment to Holland. Probably the first time coffee-drinking was seen in England was in 1637, when John Evelyn recorded its use by a Greek student, Nathaniel Conopios, at Balliol College, Oxford. The location was significant. By 1650 the first coffee-house in England, and the second in Western Europe, was opened at the Angel Inn, opposite Queen's College, Oxford, by Jacob, a Jew who benefited from Cromwell's toleration of his religion.[17] From its beginning, coffee-drinking was a social activity, associated with lively discourse, debate and the dissemination of news: coffee-houses attracted scholars, men of letters, poets, wits and men of affairs, not the greatest aristocrats and certainly not the labouring poor, but initially a leisured class with common interests in things of the mind. Typical of the early houses was Tillyard's, established by an apothecary in 1655 close to All Soul's College, and patronized by the Fellows and scholars, including the young Christopher Wren. Its discussions of scientific and philosophical subjects formed the basis of the later Royal Society. And when William Harvey, the discoverer of the circulation of the blood, died in 1657 he left 56 lb of coffee to the London College of Physicians with the instruction that his colleagues should meet monthly and drink to commemorate his death.[18]

The emergence of the first English coffee-houses in the 1650s was not accidental. The Civil War had ended with the victory of the Parliamentarians and the execution of Charles I in 1649: for the next 11 years Britain was governed as a Republic against a background of intense political interest and debate. While Oxford had been a Royalist stronghold, London was the Parliamentary base where coffee and Commonwealth quickly became associated. The first coffee-house there was established in 1652 by Pasqua Rosée, the Greek servant of Daniel Edwards who traded in Turkey and had acquired a taste for coffee there. Its immediate success led to a spate of similar establishments, some of which particularly attracted Republicans and radicals: the Turk's Head, opened in Westminster in 1659, operated as a debating club, and is credited with the first use of the ballot box for casting secret votes.[19] After the Restoration of Charles II in 1660 their numbers increased even more rapidly in an atmosphere of confidence and commercial expansion, so much so that in 1663 they were marked down as a source of revenue, required to be licensed and to pay a tax of 4d a gallon on all coffee sold. By then, coffee-houses were already beginning to spread beyond Oxford and London, being reported as far north as York in the 1660s.[20]

Coffee-houses were not greeted with universal approval, however, especially from those with vested interests in other drinks, such as brewers and innkeepers. In 1674 *The Women's Petition Against Coffee* alleged, perhaps only half-seriously, that 'Coffee makes a man as barren as the desert out of which this unlucky berry has been imported; that since its coming the offspring of our mighty forefathers is on the way to disappear': but a defender responded by citing Aristotle to the effect that 'Man is a sociable creature and delights in company', and that 'Discourse is the mind's best diet, and the great whetstone and incentive of ingenuity'.[21] More seriously, the licensing of coffee-houses was seen as a means of public control over institutions that encouraged free political debate and possible intrigue against the Stuarts. In 1672 Charles II requested the judges to consider whether they should be suppressed as centres of disaffection, and three years later issued a Proclamation ordering their closure on the grounds that they wasted men's time, and that 'divers false, malicious and scandalous reports are devised and spread abroad to the Defamation of his Majestie's Government...'.[22] In the face of a huge public outcry the Proclamation was wisely withdrawn a few days later, the patrons of the coffee-houses having successfully asserted their rights to freedom of meeting and speech.

Coffee-drinking appears to have gained from the publicity of the 1670s, for it was reported that more coffee was drunk in London than in any other city in the world, and that in 1708 there were nearly 3,000 coffee-houses in the capital.[23] This was almost certainly a wild exaggeration: their precise number cannot be known, but an early London Directory for 1739 listed 551 houses, 144 within the square mile of the City. In his careful research Bryant Lillywhite has named and located 2,034 London coffee-houses which existed at some time over the much longer period 1650–1850.[24]

In the late seventeenth century coffee-houses were regarded as democratic institutions, open to anyone who could pay the 1d or 2d for a cup: men could stay as long as they wished, meeting friends, talking, reading news-sheets or transacting business. Although their furnishing and decor did not compare with the rich interiors of some Parisian cafés, they were generally clean and orderly, in sharp contrast to most taverns of the time: a set of 'Rules and Orders of the Coffee House' of 1674 required that there should be no swearing, gambling, quarrelling, dice or card-playing, that conversation should be 'Brisk' but 'loud Disputes' forbidden.[25] Initially, only non-alcoholic drinks were served, with tea and chocolate as alternatives to coffee, but the period of total temperance seems to have been quite brief: by the 1690s alcoholic drinks were available in some houses,[26] and by the next century many offered a range of wines, beers and punches. At first the coffee was served black, without milk, cream or sugar, though various additions such as honey, cloves, ginger, cinnamon and spearmint were available at extra cost. But the addition of sugar and/or milk as a sweetener and 'softener' was an instinctive and early response to bitterness, and must have pre-dated the legend that credited Kolschitzky with their introduction to the first coffee-house in Vienna in 1685.[27]

By the last decade of the century coffee was beginning to move into the domestic sphere in aristocratic and wealthy urban households as a drink at breakfast and after dinner, though usually in addition to either chocolate or tea. At breakfast it was becoming part of the new, lighter meal of a variety of breads and preserves that was replacing the heavy repast of meats, fish, ale or wine in fashionable society. The speed of this change should not be exaggerated, however: even the fashion-conscious social climber, Samuel Pepys, still breakfasted on the old pattern in the 1660s, and took ale or wine as his 'morning draught' rather than the new hot beverages. In 1685 powdered coffee for domestic use was being retailed at 3s a pound, raised by customs duties to 4s in 1690 and 6s in 1693: it was still cheaper by weight than tea, though a pound made only around a quarter as much liquid. Thomas Garway, the proprietor of the Sultanese Head, was warning his customers that the powder 'if kept two dayes looseth much of its first Goodness', and advised those living out of London to buy beans, which they could beat in a mortar or grind in a mill 'as they use it'.[28]

III

Although it has been claimed that 'In the year 1730 the English "coffee-mania" vanished as suddenly as it had begun',[29] coffee-houses survived in different forms throughout the eighteenth century, and into the next. It is true, however, that the 'golden age' of the London houses was in decline after the first few decades of the century, and that even during this time their character was changing from the original clienteles of scholars, men of letters and leisure to institutions that combined the pleasures of conversation with the transaction of business. At a time of booming commercial activity the coffee-houses that clustered in the City filled the need for convenient and respectable meeting places for merchants, stockbrokers and insurers, even for lawyers and doctors to see their clients. Some continued to be the favourite haunts of the literati – Addison, Steele, Johnson and others were habitués – and some remained sufficiently fashionable to attract the nobility: for example, Charles Bennet, 2nd Baron Ossulston, with a substantial income of £8,500 p.a. and a town house in St James's Square, usually met his fellow-peers, MPs and lawyers at coffee-houses, his diary recording fifty visits between August 1710 and November 1712.[30] Some were established meeting places for Tory or Whig politicians, while others were venues for lobbies promoting particular commercial interests: the 1,500 London merchants trading with North America in 1700 met in the coffee-houses adjacent to the Royal Exchange – the Carolina, Virginia, Pennsylvania and New York Coffee Houses – where property and slaves were bought and sold, ships' captains brought the latest intelligence, and the members formed lobbies to influence the government on colonial and commercial policy.[31] Coffee-houses were especially important as media of news, taking the latest newspapers and used by the Post Office for collecting letters and packets; business meetings of the East India, Muscovy and Levant Companies were held in them: stockbrokers based their activities at Jonathan's, shippers and insurers at Lloyd's Coffee House, established in 1685, which published its own 'Lloyd's News'.

Coffee-houses played a highly important part in London's literary, political and commercial life, but it is likely that their role in the reformation of manners and the encouragement of sobriety has been exaggerated. Coffee-drinking continued alongside a great increase in the consumption of spirits in the first half of the eighteenth century: as previously noted, many coffee-houses also served alcoholic drinks, and some were barely distinguishable from taverns. Ned Ward in the *London Spy* described a scene of noise, smoke and argument inhabited by a rabble: 'the whole place stank of tobacco like the cabin of a barge', while so many quack medicines were on offer that 'had not my friend told me that he had brought me to a coffee-house, I would have regarded the place as the big booth of a cheap-jack'.[32] In some, cards, dice and other games were played for money, and wagers made – White's Chocolate House was increasingly identified with gaming after a move in 1702 – while some 'low' coffee-houses were reputedly the haunts of thieves and highwaymen or the 'fronts' for prostitution. From around the 1730s many London coffee-houses moved in one of two directions: some became taverns or chop-houses, finding a more profitable market as simple eating places; others changed their open status into subscription clubs for paying members in order to keep out undesirables. This change occurred particularly with the political clubs such as The Cocoa Tree and the Kit-Kat, and with literary clubs like The Tatler's and The Turk's Head.[33]

In the literature of the coffee-house the emphasis has always been on London, but the phenomenon of public drinking was by no means restricted to the capital, and the provincial coffee-houses both persisted longer and had some distinct characteristics. In the first half of the century there were many not only in Bristol (the most numerous after London), Bath, York, Exeter, Warwick, Norwich, Chester, Manchester and Liverpool, but also in less expected towns such as Nottingham, Preston, Sheffield, Yarmouth and Ipswich:[34] they were common in Edinburgh in 1707 and well known in Glasgow, Dublin and Cork. The diffusion of coffee-drinking outside London owed much to those provincial institutions that, in the latter part of the century, drew their clienteles mainly from the 'middling ranks' of society, businessmen, shopkeepers, smaller manufacturers and lower professionals: although they lacked the social cachet of the famous London houses they served a useful purpose as alternatives to the inns and taverns for the expanding bourgeoisie of towns that often lacked established commercial institutions. The increasing popularity of coffee among these groups was evidenced by the fact that from the 1720s many inns and alehouses also began to provide it.[35] Dr Johnson believed that almost every Englishman belonged to a club of some kind – a society, lodge or fraternity – and tradesmen's clubs met both in coffee-houses and in taverns 'for the mutual improvement of their respective business, by dealing with one another'.[36] In 1739 William Maitland noted that although these societies included some of 'the meanest and rudest of the citizens' they were conducted 'in the best order and decorum'. While feasting, drinking and conviviality were central interests of the tavern clubs, those based in coffee-houses had more serious Friendly Society concerns for the protection of members against adversity, and the promotion of charitable and philanthropic objectives. In this respect, they sometimes provided the organizational basis for changes in the wider public interest: for instance, in 1772 a subscription to lower the prices of meat and other foods was opened by the London silk-weavers at the New Lloyd's Coffee House, which was so successful that provincial action followed for the same purpose.[37]

In 1700 legal imports of coffee to England and Wales were valued at £36,000 compared with £14,000 worth of tea. Although yearly imports of both fluctuated widely according to the state of crops and the size of stocks, coffee import values normally exceeded those of (legal)[38] tea until around 1730: thereafter, the disparity rapidly increased as tea established a dominant lead in the second half of the century (see Table 4.1). What this means in terms of average coffee consumption per head is probably less than 1 oz a year in the first half of the century and no more than 2 oz in the later decades, but average consumption is not a meaningful concept for this period, when coffee-drinking was restricted to a small minority of the population; nor is it known what proportion of total supplies went to the coffee-houses rather than for domestic use. In 1700 coffee had scarcely penetrated beyond aristocratic households like that of the Duke of Bedford, who was buying 2–3 lb a month for consumption at Woburn Abbey, a tiny amount for a large establishment that did much entertaining; no doubt it was sometimes offered to guests at breakfast and after dinner as an alternative to tea and chocolate. Domestic consumption spread downwards into the middling ranks of society in the following decades, reflecting their increased purchasing power due partly to a long-term fall in grain prices[39] and also to substantial reductions in the prices of coffee, tea and sugar by mid-century. Before 1700 coffee imports had been geared to the demands of the coffee-houses, but by the early eighteenth century the

Table 4.1 Official values of coffee and tea imports, England and Wales, 1700–1790 (in £ thousands)

	Coffee	*Tea*		*Coffee*	*Tea*
1700	36	14	1750	75	484
1710	23	37	1760	257	969
1720	38	33	1770	218	1,093
1730	64	1,446	1780	146	187
1740	81	151	1790	390	1,777

Source: B.R. Mitchell and Phyllis Deane, *Abstract of British Historical Statistics*, Cambridge University Press, 1962, 285–6

increased supplies brought by the East India Company – nearly 5,000 cwt in 1711, rising to a peak of 28,852 cwt in 1724 – were clearly also moving into domestic consumption: between 1730 and 1740 they fell to a yearly average of 9,000 cwt as tea asserted its superiority.[40] From at least as early as the 1690s the East India Company was also importing large quantities of porcelain coffee, tea and chocolate cups and saucers from China – in 1696 1,273 'small bowles or large Cupps' from the ship *Sarah* – used to line the holds and provide ballast for the precious tea loaded higher up to protect it from sea water.[41] Lorna Weatherill's study of the inventories of the middle ranks of society (ranging from the lesser gentry, professionals and merchants to farmers, yeomen, shopkeepers and craftsmen) indicates the spread of equipment and chinaware associated with the new hot drinks: in the 1670s such goods appeared very rarely, but by the 1730s 15 per cent of inventories recorded the ownership of utensils for hot drinks – 57 per cent of those from London, 15 per cent in east Kent, 12 per cent in Cambridgeshire, but only 3 per cent in north-west England and 2 per cent in Cumbria. On this evidence the diffusion of the new drinks outside London and the south of England was still very slow even at this later date, reflecting differing levels of prosperity in the regions and the numbers of tea and coffee dealers: while in London there was a tea and coffee dealer to every 176 people and in east Kent one to 881, in the North-West there were only 32 dealers, or one to every 1,995 people.[42] If the consumer revolution was very unevenly spread before mid-century this is not to deny its major impact on Britain's foreign trade or its social effects on a sizeable proportion of the population; imports of groceries, of which tea, coffee, sugar, tobacco and chocolate were the principal items, increased from 16.9 per cent of total values in 1700 to 27.6 per cent in 1750 and 34.9 per cent in 1800.[43]

According to the contemporary writer William Massie, in 1760 nearly half of all families in England and Wales drank tea, coffee or chocolate,[44] but by then coffee was a very poor second to its main rival. In the early eighteenth century coffee had enjoyed a distinct price advantage, Thomas Twining in 1715 selling it at 5s 4d to 6s a pound; no different types of coffee were recorded in his ledgers at this time, unlike the tea, which was offered in eighteen different descriptions from the cheapest Bohea at 16–24s a pound to the most expensive Finest Hyson at 36s. By 1742 he was selling three times as much tea as coffee at prices from 6s a pound upwards, and by 1750 cheaper grades of Bohea and Congou could be had for 5s a pound compared with West India coffee at 3s 6d.[45] On the generally accepted calculation that a pound of tea made three or four times the quantity of liquid as a pound of coffee, the price ratio was now much in favour of tea.

When a pound of coffee represented half the weekly wage of an agricultural labourer, it is not surprising that it had made little impact on the diet of the English working classes: in 1795 David Davies's study of the budgets of labourers found no mention of coffee, though most now regularly bought small amounts of tea, especially in southern England.[46] For the gentry and wealthier bourgeoisie coffee fitted well into the fashionable, lighter menus that were spreading from Italy and France, where the coarseness of 'baroque' meals was disdained: fashion now dictated no strong-smelling foods, chicken rather than meat, vegetables, fruits and coffee to end the meal.[47] In England the main effect of the lighter pattern was on breakfast, where a variety of breads, rolls, cakes, butter, preserves and fruit was beginning to replace the former meats, fish and ale, at least in the towns; coffee, tea or chocolate were served as alternatives at this meal according to taste, or, in very grand houses, all three. Coffee then reappeared after dinner, eaten at around 3–4 p.m. in the eighteenth century and, still unreformed, consisting of two large courses, each of many dishes including much roast meat, fish and game. When James Woodforde, the Rector of Weston Longeville in Norfolk, with a comfortable income of £400 a year, had guests to dinner, he served coffee and tea in the drawing-room at around 6 p.m.: tea was his usual breakfast drink, occasionally 'cocoa' (chocolate), but coffee appeared only when he had an important guest like the Archdeacon.[48] Coffee here was evidently for special occasions, not daily use, and within the working class its domestic consumption appears to have been very rare. Although tea played a major role in transforming the working-class diet from cooked soups, porridges and puddings towards dependence on baker's bread, there was no direct equivalent in Britain of the Continental change to a 'coffee-soup' (*Kaffeesuppe* in Germany and Austria, *Kaffe-möcke* in Switzerland) meal consisting of pieces of bread in a bowl of coffee, eaten with a spoon:[49] the *Kaffeekränzchen* or women's coffee circle, however, paralleled the English tea-party, and was the object of similar (male) criticism.[50]

In the early eighteenth century British supplies came almost entirely from the Yemen, through the port of Mocha where the English and Dutch East India Companies traded. Prices varied greatly with crop yields and the monopoly power of the local merchants, which soon persuaded European countries to develop plantations in colonial territories under their own control. The Dutch company had particular success in Java after 1707, and by 1725 was producing 4–5 million lb of coffee a year, probably equal to all European exports from Mocha.[51] France began cultivation in her West Indian possessions, St Dominique, Guadeloupe and Martinique in the 1720s, at the same time as Portugal experimented in Brazil; Britain was somewhat slower to exploit the new possibilities, but began to develop what became very successful coffee estates in Jamaica in 1730. From that decade the West Indies were the main source of world supplies for the rest of the century, and within them the French possessions dominated, producing around three-quarters of world supplies in 1789.[52]

In 1800 coffee still had a very restricted, elite consumption, averaging a mere 0.08 lb (1¼ oz) per head per year while tea had grown to 1.48 lb

(24 oz).[53] There is no satisfactory explanation for this solely in terms of the price of the two drinks. Wholesale prices of coffee in the later eighteenth century were approximately half those of tea (though the previously mentioned liquid disparity has to be considered), benefiting from the development of the new areas of production and from the shorter sea route from the West Indies compared with tea's long haul from China. On the other hand, tea was generally more favoured by the tax system, with reductions in duty in 1745–6 and, especially, by Pitt's Commutation Act in 1784,[54] and it has been argued that the East India Company had such a vested interest in the China trade, and such influence on governments, that it took little interest in coffee and successfully campaigned in the interests of tea.[55] In the British West Indies the powerful sugar interests were more favoured by taxation than coffee, and when world coffee prices slumped in the 1770s this hastened a greater move of planters to sugar: 'foreign' coffee might then have compensated for the shortfall but was virtually excluded by a protectionist tariff that taxed French West Indian coffee 70–84 per cent higher than that from British colonies.[56] Consumption of sugar in Britain rose especially rapidly at this time, from 8 lb per head per year in 1720–9 to 12 lb in 1780–9 and 18 lb in 1800–9.[57]

Other reasons also help to explain why coffee and chocolate remained elite drinks in the eighteenth century while tea moved into mass consumption. Tea 'went further', even when brewed at normal strength; moreover, tea leaves could be used up to three or four times to make a dilute drink (green tea was very pale anyway, so further brews would scarcely be noticeable), but a second brew of coffee had little colour or taste. Tea was palatable without milk and, if necessary, even without sugar, but the lactose and casein in milk were important to soften the bitterness of coffee, and milk was becoming increasingly scarce and expensive to the poor. Coffee was best suited to a concentrated demand in towns where roasting was done regularly and it could be sold in fresh condition, whereas tea, which was not so subject to staling, had a wider distribution in small towns and villages. Taste preference may have been an important factor. It was frequently said that the English did not make good coffee because they would not use sufficient powder, but staleness and adulteration may also have turned off potential consumers. Acts against coffee adulteration were passed in 1718, 1731 and 1803 complaining of the addition of roasted peas, beans and cereals, grease, butter, cocoa nutshells and husks used to add weight. Many other substances were believed to be added – ground roasted roots of dandelion, carrot, parsnip, beet, lupins, rice, acorns, bran and seeds of broom.[58] People who could not afford their own mill, or the higher prices of reputable grocers, ran a serious risk of inferior coffee, which was not only bad value but liable to be harmful to their digestion and health.

IV

For the first half of the nineteenth century coffee and tea consumption exhibited quite different characteristics. In 1815 coffee consumption in the United Kingdom stood at a mere 0.34 lb per head per year, one quarter that of tea at 1.35 lb, but coffee then made steady progress while tea consumption stagnated and, in many years, actually fell: the two came closest in 1840, with coffee at 1.08 lb and tea at 1.22 lb per head per year. Thereafter, tea moved rapidly ahead while coffee began a slow decline to 0.71 lb by 1900, only one-ninth the consumption of tea (see Figure 4.1).[59]

The main cause of this unexpected revival of coffee in the first half of the nineteenth century was the relative prices of the two drinks, determined largely by the levels of duties that gave coffee a distinct temporary advantage. While the tea duty was at its height of 1s 6d–2s 2d a pound in the 1830s and 1840s (see Chapter 3, Table 3.3, p. 59) that on British West Indian coffee, the main source of supply, was progressively reduced from 1s 6d a pound in 1800 to 1s in 1819, 6d in 1825, 4d in 1842 and 3d in 1851. From 1835 coffee from the 'British East Indies', including Ceylon, which had now entered the market, was also charged at these preferential rates, while the Revenue also turned a blind eye to a practice that allowed 'foreign' coffee, for example from Dutch Java and Sumatra, to enter at these low rates provided it had been re-shipped from a colonial port such as Singapore. In 1840 total imports stood at 28.75 million lb, of which 10 million lb came from the West Indies, 4.5 million lb from the British East Indies (Ceylon), and the remaining 14 million lb from foreign sources entered via a British colonial port.[60]

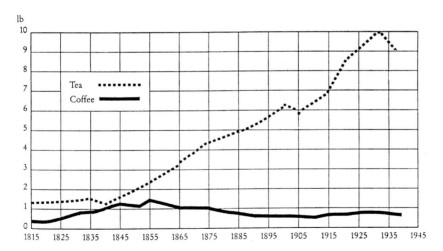

Figure 4.1 Coffee and tea consumption in the UK, 1815–1938 (lb/head/year).

Source: B.R. Mitchell and Phyllis Deane, *Abstract of British Historical Statistics*, Cambridge University Press, 1962, 355–8.

This legalized evasion was particularly beneficial to British consumers at a time when British West Indian coffee production was falling owing to labour shortages and higher prices in Jamaica after the abolition of slavery in 1833: the anomaly was regularized in 1851, when coffee from all sources, including the rapidly developing production of Brazil, was charged at 3d a pound.[61]

In 1813 Twinings were selling 'plantation coffee' (that is, West Indian) at 1s 9d–2s a pound and Java at 3s: by 1859 their prices ran from 1s 4d to 2s for Fine Mocha,[62] while both Ridgways and Fortnum and Mason were making a point of advertising 'pure coffee' at 1s 4d a pound. With Congou tea, the type usually drunk by the working classes, at 3s 6d–4s a pound in mid-century, the two drinks were very competitive, even allowing for the difference in liquid volume. The effect of the reductions in coffee prices was to spread consumption down the social scale into sections of the working classes, as both a domestic and a public drink. In the home, coffee-drinking was particularly adopted in London and northern industrial towns alongside the now firmly established tea: in 1841, for example, cotton factory workers in Manchester and Dukinfield bought 0.8 oz of coffee per head per week and 0.32 oz of tea, the highest-earning families spending equal amounts on each though tea predominated among those with lower incomes.[63] Manchester was well supplied with retail grocers and tea dealers, who also sold coffee, their numbers rising from 134 in 1811 to 235 in 1840 and 335 in 1850, besides the many general food retailers: there were also fourteen specialist coffee roasters in 1850 supplying the shops.[64] In 1841 a skilled London workman earning £1 10s a week and with a wife and five children was buying 2 oz of tea a week at 8d and 7 oz of coffee at 7½d,[65] while even some very poor agricultural labourers in the 1850s were using tiny quantities of both – 4 oz of tea and 2 oz of coffee to last three weeks, as reported from a Northamptonshire village.[66] Writing of Scottish working-class diet at this period, however, Professor Fenton has observed that 'In all of the sources there is scarcely a word about coffee', a survey of 1843 finding that coffee or tea – predominantly tea – was mentioned in only 10 per cent of all Scottish parishes and 20 per cent of town parishes.[67] What is not clear is how the two drinks were used in households that bought both. Coffee was regarded as the superior, stronger beverage, and may well have been reserved mainly for male bread-winners, like much of any 'luxury' food such as meat; women and children tended to prefer the milder-flavoured tea anyway. In some families coffee was for special occasions: even in a well-to-do Edinburgh household with two maids in the 1880s tea was the weekday breakfast drink, but coffee appeared on Sunday morning, the beans ground in the kitchen by a servant and the father making the coffee in the dining-room in a 'Napier' machine.[68] The longer time required for the preparation was clearly a major factor in this, as well as the celebratory nature of the day of rest. Despite the reductions in price, coffee remained the higher social-status drink, Dr Edward Smith's survey of 1863 finding that while almost all the English working classes drank tea, less than half drank coffee. The reason, he believed, was that

> coffee cannot be drunk without milk or sugar, whilst with tea one or both of these adjuncts may be dispensed with. Hence, even in the poorest districts where the less cost of coffee would otherwise give it a preference, it is found practically that the balance lies in favour of the tea.[69]

But although coffee failed to capture a mass domestic market, the lowering of duty to 6d a pound in 1825 resulted in a strong revival of coffee-drinking in public and the emergence of a new type of coffee-house aimed at a different clientele from their eighteenth-century predecessors. Usually described as coffee rooms, the London Directories for 1838 listed 332,[70] but in 1847 the statistician G.R. Porter estimated that there were then 1,500–1,800 in London, and that they were rapidly spreading in other towns. He described them as places 'at which working men are served at a low price', the charge for a good cup of coffee with milk and sugar being between 1d and 3d.[71] One in the Haymarket was open from 5.30 a.m. to 10.30 p.m., and served 1,500 people daily 'of all classes – from hackney coachmen to the most respectable': it also sold tea but no alcoholic drinks, and kept a good range of newspapers and periodicals. The patrons were apparently exclusively male, the early opening hours being intended for men on their way to work, while at lunchtime trades-men and clerks could buy simple fare or bring in their own. In 1852 they were described as 'genuine coffee-shops for the million', 'serious, well-conducted', accommodated in plain rooms divided into stalls by partitions and served by 'neat waitresses'.

> Coffee-houses have effected a great reform . . . I see these strong bands of workingmen, of swart artizans, of burly coalheavers and grimy ballast porters who are content to come straight from the factory, the anvil or the wharf . . . and content themselves with the moderate evening's amusement to be found in cheap periodicals . . . Drinking, they read, and reading, they learn to think, and to wash, and to teach their little children to read, and to think, and to wash'.[72]

The praise may have been over-lavish, but the new coffee rooms certainly played a part in 'the growth of respectable society' among the Victorian working classes, and had the strong support of the temperance move-ment as providing sober alternatives to the taverns and beershops.[73] Not all, however, were as respectable as middle-class reformers may have wished. There were some 'low' coffee rooms, dirty, badly conducted, selling adulterated coffee, and others that, since they were not under the control of licensing magistrates, became venues for radical clubs and societies. In the 1820s a network of ultra-radical coffee-houses developed in London, especially in Bethnal Green, Spitalfields, Soho, Finsbury and Clerkenwell Green where, for instance, the 'British Forum' debating club met at Lunt's Coffee House five times a week to discuss socialism, republicanism, and agrarian and industrial reform: attenders included William Lovett, James Watson, G.J. Harvey and other leaders of the parliamentary reform and Chartist movements.[74]

In 1850 there were also about 300 street coffee-stalls in London, most of which had sprung up since the tariff reduction to 4d a pound in 1842. Mostly situated at the markets and busy street-corners, some appeared as early as 3 or 4 a.m. while others began at midnight 'for the accommodation of "night walkers", "fast gentlemen" and "loose girls"'. The stallholders paid 1s a pound for cheap coffee, adding between 6 and 12 oz of chicory at 6d a pound and selling the 'coffee' for 1d a mug or ½d a half-mug: the chicory added colour and bitterness to what must have been a weak brew, since a stallholder told Henry Mayhew that he used 10 oz of coffee to make 5 gallons (40 pints) of liquid.[75]

Coffee consumption peaked in 1847 at 1.34 lb per head per year before beginning a long decline while tea moved steadily ahead, even before the reductions in duty to 1s 6d a pound in 1854 and 1s in 1863. Two particular circumstances help to explain this reversal of trends in the 1840s. The worst cyclical depressions of the century occurred in 1841–2 and 1847–8, when hundreds of thousands of industrial workers were either unemployed or on short-time earnings: the latter depression immediately followed the distress of the Irish Famine of 1846–7, which also affected parts of Scotland.[76] It would have been entirely natural at a time of crisis to reduce consumption of what was still considered a superior good, and to transfer to the more economical and consoling tea. Once this pattern was established it was subsequently confirmed by the large reductions in the duty and price of tea later in the century. The other explanation concerns the quality of coffee and the wide publicity given to its adulteration in the 1840s and 1850s. How little the existing laws protected the consumer was revealed by the researches of an analytical chemist, John Mitchell, in 1848. He found that pure coffee was practically unobtainable: it almost always contained large amounts of chicory, roasted corn, the roots of various vegetables, and colouring matters such as red ochre: he had even found a substance in coffee that he believed to be baked horses' liver.[77] Chicory root was first used as a cheap coffee substitute in Germany and Holland around 1770, and was widely adopted in France during the Napoleonic Wars when Continental ports were blockaded: in Britain it was grown commercially in Yorkshire and imported in large quantities from Belgium. Until 1840 it was an illegal adulterant, but in that year, influenced by Free Trade arguments, a Treasury Order provided that 'No objections be made on the part of the Revenue to dealers and sellers

Table 4.2 Analyses of coffee by Dr A.H. Hassall, 1851–3

	No. of samples	*No. adulterated*
First Report on ground coffee (a)	34	31
(b)	20	18
Second Report on ground coffee	42	31
Third Report on canister coffee	29	28
Fourth Report on ground coffee	20	19
Fifth Report on ground coffee	34	31
Sixth Report on ground coffee	34	25
Total	213	183

Source: A.H. Hassall, op. cit.

of coffee mixing chicory with coffee'; there was no requirement for labelling or for the proportions of the two to be declared, and for the next dozen years dealers were entirely free to offer whatever mixture they could sell. When Dr Arthur Hassall analysed all the main foods and drinks in common use in London for his weekly articles in the *Lancet* between 1851 and 1854, he paid particular attention to coffee, which he believed was one of the most adulterated of all articles. The results of his six series of analyses are shown in Table 4.2. Reports 5 and 6 were carried out in 1853, when the Treasury Order of 1840 was altered to require that mixtures should be clearly labelled 'Mixture of Chicory and Coffee', but on each of the random purchases only 'coffee' had been asked for: many of the samples had not been labelled, despite a penalty of £100 for each offence. Chicory was always the main adulterant, often up to half and even three-quarters of the weight, but Hassall also found roasted wheat, rye and potato-flour, burnt beans, acorns and mangel-wurzel, while the chicory itself was sometimes adulterated with mahogany sawdust and red oxide of iron derived from the colouring, Venetian red. 'The Shilling Coffee, as vended at the present, is vile and often deleterious rubbish, and we recommend the poor man never to purchase it'.[78]

The *Lancet*'s alarming disclosures about the extent of adulteration received wide publicity, and caused such public concern that in 1855 Parliament appointed a Select Committee to examine the whole question of the purity of foods and drinks. Hassall's findings were fully endorsed by medical and other professional witnesses, one of the most remarkable statements being made by Robert Dundas Thomson, Professor of Chemistry at St Thomas's Hospital, who reported that he had seen a machine invented by a Mr Duckworth of Liverpool for compressing chicory into beans resembling coffee beans: they were 'a very good imitation', and he believed that the apparatus had been patented.[79]

A serious loss of public confidence in coffee at the same time as tea was becoming cheaper and better-quality supplies from India were beginning to be available were principal reasons for the downward turn of coffee consumption after the middle of the century. In 1870 United Kingdom consumers spent £11.76 million on tea and £2.89 million on coffee – one quarter as much; by 1899 tea totalled £18.19 million and coffee £2.32 million – a mere one-eighth;[80] in 1903 average family consumption of coffee stood at only 3.04 lb a year, costing 2s 11d.[81] Widespread suspicion of the quality of ground coffee, the only type normally available to most consumers, continued to deter the public even after the Sale of Food and Drugs Act 1875, which still allowed mixtures provided they were labelled. 'Large classes of the population hardly know the flavour of genuine coffee', declared an expert in 1888; 'Chicory is the chief ingredient in the cheap mixtures because it soon makes hot water black, thick and bitter, and so gives apparent strength to what may contain little of the coffee berry'.[82] At 3d or 4d a pound the admixture of chicory was very profitable, and public analysts appointed under the Act of 1875 continued to find 'French Coffee' containing 40–90 per cent of chicory and 'Turkish Luxury Coffee' with 75 per cent. In 1884 20.3 per cent of all random samples of coffee were found to be adulterated, in one case the 'berries' being ground in the presence of the Inspector, which led him to believe that the former practice of compressing chicory into 'beans' still persisted.[83] By the end of the century energetic sampling had reduced the proportion of adulteration to 10 per cent, but fines as little as 4d plus costs did not deter hardened offenders.[84] Throughout the century the view persisted that coffee in Britain was a very inferior drink to that made on the Continent, either because it was adulterated – too little powder was used – or because it was not made correctly. The leading cookery writer, Eliza Acton, commented:

> We hear constant and well-founded complaints, both from foreigners and English people, of the wretched compounds so commonly served up here under its [coffee's] name, especially in many lodging houses, hotels and railway refreshment rooms . . . Great as the refreshment of it would be to them, especially in night travelling, in cold weather, they reject it as too nauseous to be swallowed.[85]

Many recipes recommended boiling the coffee, one in *Hints for the Table* (1859) suggesting that the powder be mixed to a paste with two eggs and boiled for an hour.[86]

Nevertheless, the coffee-house revival of the 1830s and 1840s persisted through the rest of the century, mainly under the direct or indirect aegis of the temperance movement. Coffee rooms and new types of simple restaurants aimed to provide workingmen with a non-alcoholic alternative to the public house where they could eat and drink cheaply in a respectable environment. The National Temperance League, founded in 1856, established British Workman Public Houses, which provided newspapers, entertainments and sometimes job information and a night's lodging for those in search of work. By 1884 there were 232 limited liability companies under the auspices of the League, owning 667 coffee public houses, besides 646 independent premises.[87] London had more than 100 coffee houses, but some provincial towns were also well supplied – the Liverpool company had sixty-four premises,[88] while Birmingham had handsomely furnished shops in all the main thoroughfares.[89] A similar temperance organization, The People's Cafés, was founded in 1874 under the presidency of the great philanthropist Lord Shaftesbury, while in the 1880s John Pearce progressed from mobile canteens selling coffee and tea to the successful chain of 'Pearce and Plenty' dining-rooms, which rivalled Robert Lockhart's Cocoa Rooms in Scotland and the North of England. The most ambitious attack on the public house, however, came from The People's Refreshment House Ltd, established in 1896 with the aim of acquiring existing licensed premises and reforming them into non-alcoholic places of refreshment: by 1907 it had taken over 233 inns, mainly in small towns and villages.[90] These various endeavours, part-philanthropic and part-commercial, kept alive the habit of coffee-drinking among a section of the 'respectable', male working class, though they did not seriously rival the licensed public house as the Englishman's social centre. They lacked the conviviality that alcohol encouraged, some were poorly managed, and, above all, there was a limit to the number of cups of coffee or cocoa that could be enjoyed in an evening.

V

Between 1900 and 1914 coffee consumption continued its downward trend, from 0.71 lb per person per year to 0.63 lb:[91] with both coffee and tea now averaging 1s 6d a pound,[92] the price advantage was strongly in favour of tea in terms of the liquid yield. When working-class consumers bought 'coffee' it was often a cheap chicory mixture at 1s a pound: in 1900 the United Kingdom consumed 260,000 cwts of coffee and a third as much – 85,000 cwts – of chicory.[93]

The First World War saw a sharp temporary rise of unrationed coffee to 1.11 lb per head by 1918, almost doubling the pre-war figure and suggesting that the public's taste for coffee was highly volatile. The main reason for the increase was use as a substitute for tea, which was in short supply, but it may also be that the stresses of wartime produced the desire for a stronger, caffeine-rich stimulant. Coffee's popularity was also encouraged by the presence in Britain of large numbers of American forces, who were supplied with a recently developed form of soluble coffee.[94] Whatever the reasons, the phenomenon was short-lived. Coffee consumption remained at a low and stable level throughout the inter-war years (see Figure 4.1), returning to 0.76 lb per head in 1919, 0.81 lb (the highest) in 1931 and 0.72 lb in 1938,[95] while tea consumption was ten times greater.

Retail prices of the two drinks were comparable throughout the 1920s and 1930s.[96] Chicory continued to be widely used in mixtures such as 'French Coffee' and in coffee essences, where it composed up to 45 per cent of the contents: the best-known of these, 'Camp Coffee', had been patented by a Glasgow firm, R. Paterson, in the 1890s, and was particularly popular with working-class consumers in the North and Midlands for its convenience of storage and preparation. Coffee dealers had long been anxious to discover means by which the cheap surpluses of Brazil could be stored and marketed in soluble form, and an English chemist, G. Washington, had patented a powdered form of instant coffee in 1909, which was developed in the United States as 'Red E Coffee'.[97] An improved spray-dried process was invented by the Nestlé company in the later 1930s, 'Nescafé' being launched in Britain in 1938, too late to become firmly established before the outbreak of the Second World War interrupted supplies.

Who drank coffee, and on what occasions in the home, was revealed by a survey of the nation's diet in 1936–7, which divided households into five socio-economic groups (see Table 4.3). Coffee-drinking was socially determined, and outside the wealthier classes AA and A was scarcely significant: only once was it the main drink – for class AA (1 per cent of the population) at the evening meal, described here as 'dinner' and eaten at around 8 p.m. The enquiry concluded

> Coffee consumption makes little progress in the British home. No organisation or private interest has made it a duty to educate the public on the merits of coffee and the most appetising ways of making it ... It has been said that London is the centre where the world's best coffee is to be bought and the place where the world's worst coffee is to be drunk ... At the present time there are no signs of any substantial increase in coffee consumption.[98]

During the Second World War, as in the First, consumption rose in response to increased purchasing power at a time when many foods were

Table 4.3 Percentage of coffee-drinking by income groups, 1936–7

	AA (£1,000+ p.a.) %	A (£500– 999) %	B (£250– 499) %	C (£125– 249) %	D (Under £125) %
Breakfast	43.4	17.6	8.1	2.2	1.2
Morning break	22.8	14.6	17.6	9.5	4.9
Midday meal	31.8	31.1	21.7	4.5	2.5
Tea	0.2	–	0.3	0.4	0.3
Evening meal	57.8	37.8	23.8	11.3	5.0

Source: Sir William Crawford and H. Broadley, op. cit., 28, 41, 46, 54, 63, 73

rationed or in short supply. Unlike tea, which was regarded as a basic article of the nations's diet, coffee was not rationed, but dealers received allocations based on pre-war sales and the state of stocks, which benefited somewhat from increased output in Africa (Kenya, Uganda and Tanganyika), and from supplies that had formerly gone to France, now German-occupied.[99] Coffee in no way challenged the supremacy of the great British standby, tea, however: at coffee's unsubsidized price of 32d a pound in 1942, working-class expenditure was a mere 0.2d per person per week compared with 3.8d on tea.[100]

The modern renaissance of coffee-drinking in Britain dates from the early 1950s, and is associated with the appearance of a new type of coffee-house, the espresso bar. It took its name from the espresso machine, a filter under strong pressure, which had been invented by Achille Gaggia in 1946 and marketed here by an Italian dental mechanic, Riservato, but equally important to the success of the espresso bar was the modern image of the new bars – bright, clean, even exotic, with much use of Formica, indoor plants and contemporary furnishing. Like the coffee-houses of the eighteenth century, they were an expression of a new lifestyle but for a younger generation, which discovered in them a 'trendy' social centre that permitted teenagers and young adults to spend an hour or two over a cup of coffee. They chimed with increased disposable income of the young, the growth of foreign holidays, which were already familiarizing people with better coffee, and the democratization of leisure, less determined by class than before the war. The first espresso, the Moka Bar in Frith Street, Soho, was an instant success, serving 1,000 cups a day with its main trade in the evening, and by 1960 there were an estimated 2,000 in Britain, 500 in Greater London and 200 in the West End alone.[101]

In 1958 a second survey of British diet showed that coffee consumption had not yet penetrated far into meal patterns (see Table 4.4). One small indication of change was the increased popularity of coffee at the mid-morning 'work break', whether at home or in offices and factories: in fact, almost twice as many women drank coffee at this time (22 per cent of all) compared with men (13 per cent); at the midday meal it 'ran

Table 4.4 Percentage of adult coffee-drinkers by social class at meals in and out of the home, 1958

	Total %	Upper %	Middle %	Lower %
Breakfast	4	5	6	3
Mid-morning break	17	26	25	14
Midday meal	10	17	13	7
Evening meal	5	12	6	3
Late supper	10	11	12	9

Source: Geoffrey C. Warren (ed.), op. cit.

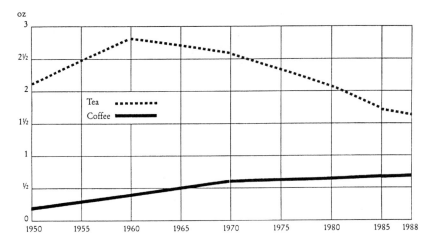

Figure 4.2 Household consumption of coffee and tea, 1950–88 (oz/head/week).
Source: National Food Survey.

a poor second', drunk by 10 per cent of people compared with 57 per cent who preferred tea.[102] Otherwise, although the social grading of consumers was still evident, only 1 in 8 upper-class people ended their evening meal with coffee.

In fact, national coffee consumption had begun to climb steadily from 1950, when it stood at 0.21 oz per person per week: by 1959 it had almost doubled to 0.39 oz, in 1969 it reached 0.58 oz followed by a slow rise to 0.67 oz in 1991 and 0.62 oz in 1993, since when it has remained almost stable. Over 40 years consumption trebled, and in 1993 consumers for the first time spent more on coffee than on tea (20p per person per week compared with 17.8p).[103] Figure 4.2, based on the Annual Reports of the National Food Survey, shows the relative movements of domestic coffee and tea consumption from 1950 to 1988. Consumption is still greater in the higher income groups but highest of all in better-off households of retired people where more time is spent at home. Four times as much coffee is drunk per head in households with adults only as in those with two adults and four or more children, while consumption also varies regionally – the South-West drinks most above the average, Scotland and the North-West least. A statement made in 1968 that Welsh people had 'a pronounced dislike for coffee'[104] apparently still holds some truth. A survey in the late 1960s found that 48 per cent of British people, uniquely in Europe, liked their coffee with at least half milk,[105] but this may have changed with more sophisticated tastes.

Several reasons help to account for the recent revival of coffee-drinking in Britain. Standards of living have risen rapidly since the war, with the result that food and non-alcoholic drink represent only 17.8 per cent of expenditure compared with 26 per cent in 1950: consumers now have a much wider choice and autonomy in food selection, and fewer are constrained to buy the cheapest. In the past, the family was the effective consumer unit and, especially in poorer households, individual tastes were not indulged, but recent demographic trends have greatly reduced the 'traditional' family of two adults and two or three children and increased the proportion of households consisting of only one or two persons to 55 per cent of all. The individual has been enfranchised, and catering for personal preferences has been enlarged. Social imitation has also played a part in the democratization of coffee, aided by extensive television advertising, which has generally presented a middle-class image of the drink, and, given the mildly addictive nature of coffee, the persuasive power of the media to make lasting converts has been more successful than in the promotion of some other products: 'wants' have more easily become 'needs'.

Coffee has also fitted well into the changing meal patterns of recent times, the trend away from formal meals towards snacks and the increasing emphasis on convenience. Meals have become more polarized at the beginning and towards the end of the day, with 'lunch' and 'tea' often replaced by snacks, which now account for 40 per cent of meal occasions. As a stronger, 'richer' stimulant than tea, coffee often accompanies what are little more than work breaks for busy people: it now appears at 33 per cent of British breakfasts, 36 per cent of lunches and 34 per cent of the evening meals that have often replaced the former 'high tea'.[106]

Other changes in British society have also influenced the popularity of coffee. Meals eaten outside the home in restaurants, cafés and canteens, which in 1985 averaged 3.23 meals per person per week, are as often ended with coffee as with tea.[107] Perhaps more important is the fact that some 20 million British people now take holidays abroad each year,[108] and enjoy generally well-made coffee. But probably the most important single reason for the increased use of coffee has been the development of easier and more reliable ways of preparing it, which removed many of the uncertainties for which British coffee was notorious. For ground coffee, domestic espresso and Cona machines became available in the 1950s, and cafetières in the 1970s,[109] but it was principally the mass promotion of 'instant' coffee that converted many Britons to a drink that could be made as simply and quickly as with a tea-bag. The first process, spray-drying, mainly used the cheaper but stronger robusta coffees, but had the disadvantage of driving off many of the volatile constituents that gave flavour, though this was temporarily masked by spraying the powder with coffee oil ('aromatization'). The improved accelerated freeze-drying process, introduced by Nestlé's 'Gold Blend' in 1965, produced soluble granules, a taste and smell closer to 'real' coffee, and allowed the use of better-quality arabica coffees such as Cap Colombie. Both types of 'instant' can be used in dispensing machines, which have considerably increased consumption in offices, factories and other public places. British consumers' demand for convenience has now pushed 'instant' coffee to 90 per cent of the UK coffee market, twice as high as in many European countries.[110]

After the sharp rises in the 1960s and 1970s consumption over the last decade has been almost stable. Further growth may have been inhibited by health concerns about its caffeine content, which averages 80–115 milligrams per 5 oz cup in roast and ground coffee and 65 milligrams in 'instant'.[111] The removal of caffeine from coffee was first achieved by a German chemist, Runge, in 1820, but commercial decaffeination began with the firm of 'Kaffee HAG' in Bremen in 1906. The various processes now in use involve pre-treating the coffee beans with steam, using a solvent to dissolve the caffeine (usually either methylene chloride or a gas, super-critical carbon dioxide), and then removing the caffeine-laden solvent: EC regulations require that not more than 0.3 per cent of caffeine remains. But the fact that decaffeinated coffee currently holds only 4 per cent of the British market suggests that most consumers are not too concerned about what are, in any case, disputed medical effects of caffeine. Indeed, the 'lift' that the caffeine in coffee provides has always been part of its appeal, such that drinkers of decaffeinated versions may feel 'cheated' of one of its principal, proper constituents.

Since 1970 the balance between coffee and tea in the British diet has shifted significantly. In that year total coffee consumption, inside and outside the home, represented 16.5 per cent of all drinks (except tap water) consumed in the UK and tea 61 per cent: in 1993 coffee had risen to 21.4 per cent and tea's share had fallen to 42.3 per cent.[112] Stated another way, the UK population aged over 10 years drinks on average 1.7 cups of coffee a day and 3.5 cups of tea: 57 per cent drink some coffee daily and 79 per cent some tea.[113] The long-established British attachment to tea has been dented but not radically shaken. The majority of consumers now accommodate both caffeine drinks in their diet in different proportions, the relative amounts varying with income, age, class and personal taste. Dramatic changes in the consumption of hot beverages seem unlikely, and it may well be that the transformation of drinking habits that began in the seventeenth century has now run its course to establish a more stable relationship between different cups that cheer.

5 Soft drinks: from cordial waters to Coca-Cola

I

The observation that 'Food has a constant tendency to transform itself into situation'[1] – to become associated with work, leisure, celebration, sport, relaxation – is equally true of drinks in general and of soft drinks in particular. But these also had another important attribute in the promotion of health, and one of the main historical origins of soft drinks lies in the wide range of 'cordials' and 'elixirs' that were principal components of folk medicine in Britain from the Middle Ages until the nineteenth century. Numerous herbals and books of receipts publicized remedies for almost all known ills, either home-made or obtainable from the professional herbalists, who offered an alternative to mainstream medicine, and were patronized by all ranks of society. Influential seventeenth-century works such as those of Nicholas Culpeper taught that herbs or their distilled essences stimulated the natural 'Life Force', so enabling the body successfully to fight disease.[2] Although the influence of self-healing began to wane with the growth of scientific medicine in the Enlightenment, it survived into the nineteenth century in the forms of homeopathy, medical botany and naturopathy, which, for various reasons, commanded support by those who rejected official medicine.[3]

A wide variety of plants, herbs, flowers, berries, fruits and nuts was employed in making 'cordial waters' or draughts, the native sources often supplemented by imported spices. Both in the cottage and in the stately home their making was a recognized part of the housewife's skill, like baking or brewing, though by the eighteenth century many were also available as commercially manufactured, often patented, products. Some cordials were primarily medicinal, some simply pleasantly flavoured drinks, but many had a dual function as both therapeutic and enjoyable: almost all were heavily sweetened with sugar or honey, and many were considered particularly suitable for ladies as aids to digestion or as 'restoratives' for any mild affliction. Spices such as mace, nutmeg, cinnamon and ginger were often added, and some cordials such as Aqua Vitae and Rosa Solis contained distilled spirits of wine, and were similar to liqueurs. But herbs remained the most important constituent, which as well as possessing curative powers were believed to influence the emotions. 'Every appetite, mood, fear, aberration and abnormality has its own appropriate restraining herbs':[4] they could assuage grief, subdue passions, strengthen the memory, stimulate the appetite, aid digestion, and act as aphrodisiacs and rejuvenators. Tudor cordials included Sirrup of Roses, Sirrup of Violets, Sinnamon Water, Rosemary Water and Water of Life,[5] while a receipt book of 1694 suggests a cough cordial of raspberry leaves, honey and lemon, and, less pleasantly, one for pleurisy consisting of aniseed, treacle, liquorice, raisins and horse dung in strong white wine.[6] Treats and treatments were sometimes distinct, sometimes indistinguishable. A popular eighteenth-century cordial, Lovage, was an aromatic drink made from oils of nutmeg, caraway and quassia in spirits of wine, while even more explicit were Eau d'Amour, Eau Divine and Eau Nuptiale, all of which could be respectable subterfuges for alcoholic drinks. The most widely read receipt book of the first half of the eighteenth century, Eliza Smith's *The Compleat Housewife, or Accomplished Gentlewoman's Companion*, included the Great Palsey Water ('of excellent use in all swoonings, weakness of heart and decay of spirits'), Lady Allen's Water, Aqua Mirabilis, King Charles II's Surfeit Water, and the Golden Cordial (containing gold leaf), but also Clary and Orange and Lemon Waters, described as 'fine entertaining waters'.[7]

From the later eighteenth century the growing urbanization of Britain offered fewer opportunities for home-made cordials but more for commercial products having local or regional markets. The two attributes of cordials – the therapeutic and the pleasurable – now tended to separate, some becoming patent medicines or quack nostrums (Olbion Cordial, Daffy's Elixir, Godfrey's Cordial, etc.)[8] while others concentrated on providing a refreshing drink that might have incidental 'health' benefits. Through the nineteenth century, recipe books continued to give directions for homemade cordials, often using ready-prepared essences of fruits and herbs, which were now readily available,[9] but their popularity gradually declined with the rise of carbonated drinks, fruit juices and squashes. Nevertheless, a demand continued for proprietary sweetened cordials such as those made by Stones, distillers and vintners since 1740, whose range included compounds made from peppermint, cloves, cinnamon, caraway and aniseed as well as their widely known Ginger Wine, which sold 240,000 gallons in 1848: some of their traditional cordials such as Lovage, Clary and Peppermint continued to be marketed until the 1960s.[10]

A second source of soft drinks was fruit juices, whose use also dates from at least Tudor times, though at this time they were mainly restricted to native fruits and berries. Citrus fruits were rare luxuries at this period, six silver pennies being paid for a single lemon for a coronation feast for Henry VIII and Anne Boleyn, and still expensive in 1662 when the Earl of Bedford bought oranges at a shilling each and lemons at three shillings a dozen.[11] Raw fruit was generally considered unhealthy by doctors, though apples, pears and soft fruits were appreciated by the poor, especially after the restricted winter diet when many were in a pre-scorbutic condition through lack of vitamin C. Tudor and Stuart herbals recommended spring medicines for 'purifying the blood', which included gooseberries, blackcurrants and strawberry leaves, and as late as the mid-nineteenth century the famous chef Alexis Soyer suggested recipes for Apple Water, a Spring Drink made from rhubarb, and a Summer Drink of redcurrants and raspberries.[12]

The development of citrus fruit drinks, which were to become the mainstay of the soft drinks industry, depended on the expansion of imports of oranges and lemons from Mediterranean countries, the availability of larger and cheaper supplies of sugar from the West Indies, and the emergence of a demand for non-alcoholic drinks that fitted into new patterns of fashionable consumption, prerequisites that first emerged in the seventeenth century but became more pronounced in the eighteenth. Lemonade and orangeade were known at the time of the Restoration,[13] sold in the proliferating coffee-houses of the period, though there was as yet no equivalent of the French *limonadiers* who sold still lemonade in the streets and were granted the monopoly rights of a 'Companie' in 1676.[14] The gradual adoption of citrus drinks in wealthy households marked another important stage in the separation of enjoyable, leisure beverages from medicinal cordials and draughts: they fitted well into the reformed menus of people of taste in the eighteenth century, a change that originated in Italy and France and involved the rejection of heavy, Baroque meals in favour of lightness and moderation. Strong flavours and smells were now unfashionable: chicken was preferred to coarse meat, heavy wines were watered down or replaced by lemonade and orangeade, drunk with 'a botany of the palate' of fruits from Africa, Asia and America. An influential guide to *haute cuisine* of 1807 listed seventy-two non-alcoholic drinks – 'the straightforward fruits and flowers that one serves when the weather is hot . . . infinitely refreshing and quenching . . . like lemonade, the bitter juice of the citron, orangeade, acetous syrup . . . diluted with lots of fresh water or chilled with snow'.[15] In England, where the cooler climate encouraged a preference for the new hot beverages tea, coffee and chocolate, the adoption of citrus drinks was slower, though in summer months they were popular in the eighteenth-century tea gardens and at domestic entertaining occasions.

By then citrus fruits, and in particular lemons, had become recognized as possessing preventive and curative powers for the dreaded disease of scurvy, which caused distressing symptoms of swollen limbs and ulcerated mouths, often resulting in death. On Vasco da Gama's voyage to the East Indies in 1497 100 of his 160 sailors died from it,[16] and scurvy continued to be a main cause of casualties in European navies and armies into the nineteenth century. Its diagnosis and treatment were hampered by the belief that there were two distinct forms of the disease – 'land scurvy' and 'sea scurvy' – which required different remedies. 'Land scurvy' was treated with infusions of fresh plants, especially scurvy-grass, cresses, sorrel and brooklime, although it appears that true cases of scurvy would have been hardly amenable to treatment by scurvy-grass, the principal recommended antidote, which is a comparatively poor source of the necessary vitamin C.[17] The prevailing humoral theory was that 'land scurvy' was 'cold' and required hot antiscorbutic herbs, while 'sea (muriatic) scurvy' was 'hot' and needed 'cooling' medicines. On a voyage to the South Seas in the 1590s Sir Richard Hawkins carried oranges and lemons as a 'certain remedy' for scurvy, and from their first sailings in 1601 the East India Company's ships took citrus fruits on board with good results.

Although the value of lemons as effective antiscorbutics had been practically demonstrated, and they were increasingly advocated by the medical profession,[18] it was not until 1795 that the Royal Navy required a daily dose of lemon juice after six weeks at sea: in Nelson's day it took the form of a pint of 'grog' at noon, consisting of 1 gill of rum to 3 of lemon juice and water, the rum acting as a preservative as well as encouraging take-up.[19] It has been suggested that Nelson's adoption of Lind's principles of diet was as important to his success as his tactical brilliance,[20] but in 1845 the Navy decided, in the interests of economy, to substitute West Indian limes for Mediterranean lemons: only after scurvy reappeared on some long voyages in the 1870s was it realized that lime juice contained only half the quantity of ascorbic acid as lemon juice and therefore required larger doses.[21]

The long-continued debates surrounding scurvy and citrus fruits eventually had important implications for the home market. The fact that, of an adult male population of England and Wales in 1801 of barely more than 2 million, 120,000 served in the Navy during the Napoleonic wars disseminated knowledge and appreciation of these relatively new fruit drinks. Moreover, a direct link can be established between the therapeutic uses of citrus juices at sea and their commercial development as refreshing soft drinks for domestic use. From 1854 onwards, Merchant Shipping Acts required trading vessels likely to be away from port for more than 10 days to carry lime or lemon juice. A firm of ships' chandlers in Leith, Rose's, began supplying ships with West Indian lime juice, establishing their own plantations in Dominica in the 1860s. Lachlan Rose patented a method of preserving the juice without the use of spirits, so establishing Rose's Lime Juice, the first commercially made concentrated fruit drink in Britain, 'delicious, cooling and refreshing ... eminently suitable for family use'.[22]

'Small beers' were another early component of soft drinks, bearing some resemblance to the product of malt and hops but home-made from native plants and herbs or from imported spices.[23] Of the many regional varieties, the commonest were dandelion and burdock, horehound and ginger: in Lancashire nettle beer was popular, in Yorkshire sweet gale (or bog wortle) beer and honey drink ('botchet') made from heather honey from the moors,[24] while other local brews included spruce beer, sarsaparilla, parsnip and sassafras, used in root beer. These were all lightly fermented drinks using yeast and sugar, and as (allegedly) containing less than 2 per cent of alcohol were allowed by the excise authorities to be sold without duty.

By the nineteenth century some of these drinks had passed from the domestic to the commercial stage, with many small businesses supplying a growing urban market. Ginger beer was the most widespread, especially popular in the north of England and Scotland, where more than 1,000 trade names have been recorded.[25] Many small beers were now made of proprietary products that imitated the natural ingredients – ginger beer from ginger tincture, acetic acid and plain syrup, 'Champayne Cyder' (a temperance drink) from butyrate of ethyl, acetate of amyl, acetic acid and sugar colouring: 'At every turn, in all these drinks, are chemicals used'.[26] Home-brewing also continued with the availability of ready-prepared extracts of herbs and flavours, among the best-known and widely advertised Kemp's Compound Essence of Hops and Herbs and Mason's Extracts of ginger, sarsaparilla, horehound and dandelion and burdock, 6d bottles of which would make 8 gallons of liquid. They had particular appeal to Victorian teetotallers as cheap, respectable alternatives to 'the demon drink'. Mason's advertised their products as giving 'herbaceous flavour and a creamy head like bottled ale ... always acceptable at Picnics, in the home ... '.[27] They were strongly encouraged by the temperance movement, the Church of England Temperance Society advertising 'Stokos' (made of oatmeal and lemon), 'Hopkos' (hops and ginger), and 'Cokos' (cocoa and oatmeal):[28] 'Hopkos' was considered especially suitable for the harvest field, where the plentiful provision of free beer or cider was thought to be a cause of early addiction.

Since the Middle Ages certain English springs and wells had been credited with miraculous curative properties, and by the later seventeenth century spas were developing at some of these, providing facilities for 'taking the waters' and bathing as well as accommodation and recreational amenities for visitors.[29] Those who could afford to reside for several weeks at the more fashionable spas such as Bath, Harrogate and Buxton did so partly for their supposed 'cures' of rheumatism or gout or for purging themselves of excessive rich food, partly for purely pleasurable social intercourse and entertainment: lower down the social scale London spas like Islington and Sadlers Wells early became primarily places of amusement for townspeople.[30]

The importance of spas in the history of soft drinks lies in the fact that from an early date their waters began to be commercially supplied to a wider public, who thereby became familiarized with consuming a bottled, labelled drink in their own homes. Elizabeth I had required Buxton waters to be sent to her in London: in the 1660s Pepys was doctored with Epsom waters, while in 1697 Celia Fiennes at Tunbridge Wells noted that the water was not only drunk there but sent up to people's homes in London. By the early eighteenth century 'the movement of people to the spas was matched by the movement of spa waters to the people'.[31]

Of sixty-five English spas at this time nine had their waters bottled and despatched to most parts of the country, either by land carriage or, in the case of Bristol and Scarborough waters, by sea; London merchants also imported the famed Continental waters of Spa (in Belgium), Pyrmont and Seltzer. Mineral waters were retailed in coffee-houses, by apothecaries, grocers, glass-sellers and many others, the tea merchant, Tom Twining, selling large quantities of Spa waters from 1714, importing 7,000 flasks in 1721–2.[32]

At the prices prevailing in London in 1730–40 – Bath and Scarborough waters 7s 6d per dozen (quart) bottles, imported Spa waters 13–15s per dozen (3 pint) flasks[33] – it was still a luxury trade affecting mainly the wealthy and the sick. Spa waters were widely advertised and recommended by medical writers for invalids and for table use as aids to digestion, alternatives to wine and the often-polluted urban water supplies: especially popular were the naturally sparkling waters, which were not available from English spas.

II

Natural mineral waters indirectly bridged the gap between the traditional drinks previously discussed and the modern, science-based soft drinks industry. Through the seventeenth and eighteenth centuries chemists had attempted to analyse the solid constituents of mineral waters, Dr Nehemiah Grew successfully precipitating the magnesium carbonate of Epsom waters in 1697. Robert Boyle, Benjamin Allen and others made progress in the chemistry of spa waters,[34] but particular interest centred on imitating the effervescent Continental waters, which were expensive and difficult to transport. Here the crucial discovery of 'fixed air' (carbon dioxide gas) was made by Joseph Priestley in 1767, possibly preceded by Professor Venee of Montpelier in 1750,[35] but it was certainly Priestley who recognized the importance of using a pump to saturate the water more completely. He believed that his carbonated water possessed medicinal properties superior to those of Pyrmont water, and until at least the end of the century this remained the chief use of what came to be called 'soda water'. Its production on a factory scale was due to Jacob Schweppe, a watchmaker and amateur scientist of Geneva, who began making aerated water in the 1770s, using chalk and sulphuric acid to produce carbonic acid gas, which was passed into water under pressure in a carbonating tank. In 1792, in partnership with an engineer, Nicolas Paul, he established a factory in London, gaining approval for his soda water from Erasmus Darwin and leading figures such as Matthew Boulton and Josiah Wedgwood: it was advertised from 1798 as good for gout, complaints of the bladder, stone and indigestion, and for 'invigorating the system and exalting the spirits'.[36] At 6s 6d a dozen bottles, Schweppe's waters were still expensive, however, partly because until 1840 they were classified as patent medicines and were charged an excise duty of 1½d a bottle.

Aeration was the key process that enabled effervescent waters to be manufactured in quantity and to be charged with syrups of fruit or herbs to produce a range of flavoured drinks. Surprisingly, Schweppes did not market an aerated lemonade until 1835 and their Quinine Tonic Water until 1858, though their reputation as Britain's leading manufacturer was established when they gained the concession for the Great Exhibition in 1851 and sold over a million bottles of soda water there in six months.[37] The commercialization of flavoured aerated drinks, and their promotion from medicinal to purely pleasurable uses, was mainly the work of small, local producers who could set up business on minimal capital. Early in the century inventions by Hamilton and Bramah made it readily possible to compress carbonic acid gas, and in 1813 Charles Plinth patented his 'Portable Fountain', which could be mounted in shops or on a cart for street sale.[38] By the 1830s, in both Britain and America, the manufacture and retailing of carbonated, flavoured drinks were established facts.

London in the 1840s had more than fifty soft drinks manufacturers, by now often using proprietary essences and compounds in a sugar syrup rather than natural juices and flavours. In the home the time and trouble of making such drinks could be avoided by simply diluting such products as 'Robinson's Patent Barley' ('eminently pure and nutritious'), Soyer's 'Orange Citron Lemonade' and 'Nectar', Hooper's 'Sarsaparilla' or Crosse and Blackwell's range of syrups, the advertisements for which always distinguished their 'purity' from the products of nameless, backstreet traders. This lower end of the market was observed by Henry Mayhew, who believed that the street sale of ginger beer had begun in 1822 during a very hot summer. By 1850 there were around 1,500 street-sellers of soft drinks in London during the summer months, some of whom 'brewed' their own beer at home from ginger, lemon-acid, essence of cloves, yeast and sugar: sold at 1d a bottle (up to half froth 'is considered very fair'), the ingredients for seventy-two half-pint bottles cost 1s 7d and yielded 6s. 'Fountains' had appeared in the streets in the 1840s, hired from ginger beer manufacturers at 4–6s a week. Some were very handsome machines of highly polished mahogany and brass costing up to £150; they were fitted with large glass vessels and pumps for injection of the gas, so powerful that no yeast or fermentation was needed. Mayhew was told that some operators added oil of vitriol (sulphuric acid) 'to bring out the sharpness'. The best trade was done at the markets and on fine Sundays on Hampstead Heath, Primrose Hill and Camberwell Green: ginger beer was especially popular on Sunday mornings with men who needed to quench their thirst when the public houses were closed, but children usually preferred lemonade or frothy drinks such as 'Nectar' and 'Persian Sherbet' (essence of lemon, tartaric acid, carbonate of soda and sugar).[39] Twenty years later, the London street trade was described in almost identical terms, with consumption now estimated at 300,000 gallons a year. As well as the usual drinks, some street herbalists were selling false 'sarsaparilla' made from sassafras and burnt sugar: 'If it don't lengthen the life of the buyer, it lengthens the life of the seller. It's about the same thing in the end'.[40]

By the last quarter of the century a number of large-scale manufacturers had emerged in the soft drinks industry, using expensive machinery and either processing their own materials or buying from specialist firms like C.W. Field (established 1870) or Stevenson and Howell (established 1882), who employed trained chemists to produce concentrates, essences and essential oils. One of the biggest manufacturers in 1900, Jewsbury and Brown of Manchester, occupied a large factory with a chemical laboratory, essence laboratory and compounding rooms, and modern machinery for water filtration, carbonation, mixing, bottling and labelling.[41] Technology had also entered into the closure of bottles. In the early nineteenth century they were closed by a wired cork, like champagne bottles, but in 1870 H. Codd invented closure by a glass ball in the bottle neck, which was forced against a rubber washer by gas pressure: the ball was pushed in by hand to release the contents. The more hygienic screw top was patented in 1879, followed in 1888 by W.J. King's lever closure, which survived until recently.[42] All these developments implied that by the end of the century the soft drinks trade was becoming sharply divided between modern, science-based manufacturers, who supplied hotels, restaurants and the better-off domestic market, and small, local businesses, which relied heavily on artificial ingredients and sold their penny bottles at corner sweetshops rather than at reputable family grocers.

In 1841 only 541 persons were recorded as engaged in mineral water manufacture and in 1871 2,555, but by 1891 the number had risen to 6,691: Dorset's single ginger beer and mineral water manufacturer in 1841 had grown to twenty-eight 40 years later, Norwich's three to twenty-four.[43] The mass market of London led the field, with 1,069 employees in 1891: Charles Booth believed that the trade was 'increasing largely', and that although there were still busy and slack seasons there was now more work even in winter.[44] Soft drinks were also popular in Scotland, Glasgow having thirty-seven manufacturers in 1905, Falkirk eleven and Ayr five.[45] This expansion reflected a growing demand, which arose from increased disposable incomes after 1870, especially among the working classes, who were now benefiting from lower prices of bread, meat, tea and sugar. The market was also encouraged by a downturn in liquor consumption (see Chapter 6), by shorter working hours and the growth of holidays, and by increased employment opportunities for women and juveniles. Mineral waters were drunk in the home, in public houses and catering establishments and, less respectably, in the street. Men drank soda water for a 'hangover' or as a 'mixer' for spirits, ginger beer as a thirst-quencher or mixed with light ale ('shandy-gaff'); women and children tended to prefer the sweeter drinks such as lemonade, orangeade, sherbet or kali, while in Robert Roberts' Salford the taste was for dandelion and burdock, herb beer and unspecified 'pop' – no 'real' man would touch any of the stuff.[46]

In middle-class homes the soda-siphon was standard dining-room equipment, the contents drunk with whisky or as an alternative to the bottled spring waters that continued to be available. But compared with later years, the choice was still quite narrow, as Mrs J.E. Panton complained in 1888: 'If some genius would invent something cheap, healthy, palatable and without alcohol in it, I for one will patronize him largely and give him honourable mention'.[47]

'Where is the Temperance Allsopp?' G.J. Holyoake asked, and the extent to which soft drinks benefited from the growth of the temperance movement should not be exaggerated. The principal alternatives to alcohol advocated by reformers were tea and, to a lesser extent, coffee and cocoa, warm drinks that could be enjoyed at all seasons by all ages. Nevertheless, soft drinks were regularly advertised by the temperance magazines, of which *The British Workman and Friend of the Sons of Toil*, founded by Thomas Bywater Smithies in 1855, reached a remarkable circulation of 250,000 in 1862.[48] The first temperance hotel opened in London in 1836, and by 1865 there were some 200 in England, many of a rather primitive standard of comfort and convenience: in 1872 a new company, Temperance Hotels Ltd, was launched with the aim of establishing a chain of better-class premises that would appeal to middle-class lady and gentlemen travellers. More important were the efforts to tempt working men out of the public house by providing similar but non-alcoholic institutions for their leisure time – the 'British Workman Public Houses Without the Drink' – which originated in Dundee in 1853: they were followed by 'The People's Café Co.' (1874), 'The Coffee Public House Association' (1877) and 'The People's Refreshment Houses Association' (1896).[49] Although these attempted to replicate the environment of pubs, with bar counters, games and newspapers, they did not achieve the conviviality of licensed premises or the turnover for long-term profitability, and it was significant that the non-alcoholic working men's clubs founded by Henry Solly (The Club and Institute Union, 1862) were selling beer by the 1890s. Some men who had 'taken the pledge' still preferred to use the pub as their social centre, and one effect of the growth of temperance was that publicans increasingly stocked soft drinks in order to retain their teetotal customers: it was noted in the 1860s that such clients were now welcomed whereas 20 years previously they had been scorned.[50]

The expansion of soft drinks production depended importantly on the increased availability and lower costs of raw materials, above all fruit and sugar. United Kingdom sugar consumption rose dramatically in the second half of the century from an average of 25 lb per head per year in 1850 to 85 lb in 1900:[51] previously heavily taxed, the duty of 14s a hundredweight in 1854 was totally abolished in 1874, halving the price of raw sugar from 21s 6d a hundredweight to 11s 3d by 1900.[52] Increased supplies of fruit were especially marked from the 1870s onwards, greatly expanding the limited range available earlier in the century. This resulted partly from the commercial development of tropical and sub-tropical regions, and partly from a major shift in British agriculture towards fruit-growing in response to the depression in cereal and meat prices in the 1870s and 1880s: between 1873 and 1904 the acreage of English land under orchards increased by 63.9 per cent, and between 1888 and 1904 that devoted to soft fruit grew by 111 per cent. It is estimated that total domestic production of fruit doubled between 1870 and 1908, while imports increased tenfold to 13 million hundredweight, more than half of which were citrus fruits.[53]

Estimates of production and consumption of soft drinks at the end of the nineteenth century must be uncertain in view of the continued existence of many very small manufacturers who were probably unrecorded. Official statistics from the Census of Production indicate a consumption of 87.9 million gallons in 1900 and 80.5 million gallons in 1913,[54] perhaps suggesting the effects of an increase in average price from 2.55d to 2.85d a pint at a time when the purchasing power of wages fell by around 12 per cent. The available statistics suggest an average consumption in 1900 of about 2 gallons (16 pints) a head per year at a total cost of £7.5 million (compared with beer at £114.9 million).[55] No statistical data are available before 1900, and the estimate of Prest and Adams that in 1870 total consumption stood at 66.7 million gallons admits to a 'very large' margin of error.[56]

By 1914 the British consumer was becoming familiar with a range of branded soft drinks, which were widely advertised and available either nationally or regionally. The precedent for this stage in the commercial development of the industry came largely from the United States, where sixty-four manufacturing plants in 1850 had already grown to 387 in 1870.[57] Because of their medicinal associations many drinks were made by herbalists and sold in drug stores from soda fountains, even in the 1850s described as 'Temples resplendent in crystal, marble and silver' and dispensing up to 300 flavours.[58] America in the late nineteenth century was a land of proprietary nostrums, appealing to a nation experiencing the strains of rapid transformation from scattered farming communities to an urban, competitive society. What Mark Pendergrast has characterized as 'a nation of neurotics' was besieged by mass advertising, six patent medicine makers each spending $100,000 on publicity in 1885. The other major influence on American soft drinks was the temperance movement, which originated there in 1829 and had powerful support from organized religion and women's groups. 'Hires Root Beer' was patented in 1876 as 'The Nation's Temperance Drink': made from sixteen wild roots and berries, it claimed to purify the blood and make rosy cheeks;[59] Dr A.C. Ayer's 'Sarsaparilla' promised to 'dislodge and expel any lurking taint of Scrofula from the system',[60] while Dr Pepper's cherry soda drink of 1885 'aids digestion and restores vim, vigor and vitality'. The direct antecedent of Coca-Cola, however, was a French drink of 1863, 'Vin Mariani', a combination of wine and coca leaves that was fiercely promoted in Europe and America with alleged testimonials from Queen Victoria, Sarah Bernhardt, President McKinley and three Popes. Coca had been used in Peru and Bolivia for at least 2,000 years as a stimulant, aid to digestion, hunger-suppressant and aphrodisiac – to the Incas it was the 'Divine Plant'. In the 1870s and 1880s Europe and America experienced almost a coca mania, as its principal alkaloid, cocaine, was approved by many doctors and described by Freud in 1884 as a 'magical substance'. In 1885 Dr John S. Pemberton of Atlanta, Georgia, added his own imitation of 'Vin Mariani', 'Pemberton's French Wine Coca', to his range of cough and headache cures, but also included the West African kola nut, which had similar properties to coca.[61] The same year, Atlanta adopted Prohibition, and Pemberton, who was himself a teetotaller, dropped the wine from his formula, experimented with other herbs, fruits and essential oils, and in 1886 launched 'Coca-Cola' as a temperance drink and 'brain tonic', refreshing and medicinal. The first advertisement recommended

> Coca-Cola Syrup and Extract for Soda Water and other Carbonated Beverages. This Intellectual Beverage and Temperance Drink contains the valuable Tonic and Nerve Stimulant properties of the Coca plant and Cola (or Kola) nuts, and makes not only a delicious, exhilarating, refreshing and invigorating Beverage ... but a valuable Brain Tonic and a cure for all nervous affections – Sick Head-Ache, Neuralgia, Hysteria, Melancholy, etc. The peculiar flavor of Coca-Cola delights every palate.[62]

Asa Candler, who acquired Coca-Cola on Pemberton's death in 1889, began a vigorous advertising campaign, gradually emphasizing the enjoyable rather than the therapeutic claims of the drink. When public concern over the contents of patent medicines resulted in the Pure Food and Drugs Act 1906, he removed the trace of cocaine from the product: advertising in future presented Coca-Cola as a leisure drink enjoyed by opera stars, middle class theatre patrons, sportsmen and young, female models. 'These girls drank Coca-Cola. By drinking Coca-Cola – for only a nickel a bottle – Americans could associate themselves ... with the world in which winsome girls such as these seemed to dwell'.[63]

The combination of health with pleasure in a cheap, massively promoted drink that was widely available was an American phenomenon, but it also influenced the development and marketing of new products in Britain. Coca-Cola itself first appeared here in 1900 when Asa's son Howard Candler brought a gallon of syrup to London and discovered an American operating one of the new soda fountains: regular shipments began in 1901, though on a very small scale. Schweppes had produced a kola drink in 1885, though it did not appear regularly in their price lists before 1916.[64] More significantly, two new British proprietary drinks appeared in the first decade of the century whose advertising bore some resemblance to the promotional methods of Coca-Cola. In 1901 Robert Barr, a mineral water manufacturer of Falkirk, launched 'Iron Brew' as a stimulating tonic, restorative and hangover cure: made from a secret recipe of fruit extracts and iron salts, it was vigorously advertised to become 'Scotland's second national drink', outselling Coca-Cola in the 1980s by three to one.[65] 'Vimto' (originally 'Vimtonic') was the creation of a Manchester druggist and herb importer, John Joel Nichols: at a propitious time in 1908 when a Licensing Act further restricted opening hours of public houses, he marketed 'Vimto' as a temperance drink and health tonic, registered in the 'medicines' category. It contained twenty-nine ingredients, including grape, blackcurrant and raspberry juices, vanilla, capsicum, horehound and others known only to two people (like Coca-Cola). Originally intended to supply temperance bars, hotels and cafés, it was promoted as a healthful leisure drink, 'Invigorating, Refreshing', with the advantage of being served either cold or hot and thereby overcoming the winter downturn of most soft drinks. Before 1914 its sales were mainly in the north of England, though they have subsequently become international.[66]

'Iron Brew', 'Vimto' and 'Tizer' ('The Appetizer'), another new product of this period, were strongly flavoured drinks that bore some resemblance to the home-made herb beers that had been traditional in the Midlands and North. The mass production of fruit juices also developed at this time, with Stower's Lime Juice rivalling that of Rose's, and 'Idris' and 'Kia-Ora' (established 1911) setting new standards of quality for citrus drinks: instead of artificial flavours Kia-Ora established hygienic extraction plants in Messina and Valencia to use local fruits at their peak of ripeness.[67]

III

The First World War interrupted the growth of soft drinks by restrictions on the use of sugar and imported fruits and by the imposition of a wartime duty of 1d a pint in May 1916, which contributed to a rise in average prices from 2.85d in 1914 to 5.13d by 1918.[68] Some manufacturers like Schweppes who insisted on maintaining high standards suffered a major reduction in output,[69] but by 1918 total UK soft drinks production was an estimated 81.7 million gallons, slightly above the 1914 figure. Remarkably, however, total production after the war fell to a low point of 44.8 million gallons in 1922, thereafter recovering slowly to 75.9 million in 1932, then increasing rapidly to 110.2 million gallons by 1938, 2.5 times the volume of the early 1920s and equivalent to almost 20 pints per head per year.[70] These statistics suggest that disposable income for what was still a luxury good was restricted in the 1920s by the high prices of soft drinks (1920 average 6.6d per pint, 1930 4.6d), but quickly increased in the somewhat more favourable economic climate after 1932, aided by a large fall in sugar costs, which reduced average soft drinks prices to 3.6d a pint by 1938.[71]

While in the United States the consumption of soft drinks was boosted by the general adoption of Prohibition until 1933, there was no similar encouragement in Britain, and the penetration of American drinks here was insignificant. In 1924 when the Coca-Cola Company sent Colonel Hamilton Horsey to make a long-term market assessment he reported that although prospects were quite good, the drab weather generally favoured a taste for hot drinks: no immediate action followed.[72] He might have added that there was no equivalent in Britain of the drug store, a major social centre for American youth in which Coca-Cola was already inspiring a slang vocabulary of courtship – a 'Coke Date' and a 'Coke Frame' (a girl shaped like a Coke bottle).[73] In Britain between the wars soft drinks for consumption on the premises were mainly available in public houses, where they were often over-priced and alien to the environment, in cafés, sweetshops (some of which provided a table and chairs for customers) and in herbalists' shops and temperance bars, which were especially found in Midland and Northern towns. Some of these, like Elliott's Blue Lion Temperance Bar in Sheffield and Whalley's in Manchester, were popular with sporting groups since 'the Temp.' had no restrictions on age, and 'herb shops' were among the few places where children (and their pocket-money) were welcome. Cinemas and dance halls provided further outlets, the latter generally regarded as places where it was not respectable to breathe alcohol on one's partner. In these and other ways, the growth of soft drinks consumption in the 1930s was related to the development of mass leisure, which resulted from rising standards of living, shorter working hours and longer holidays – especially holidays with pay, which by 1937 covered between 4 and 5 million workers.[74] Mass attendance at sporting events, the growth of personal mobility by bicycles, cars and motor coaches, camping, hiking and the exploration of the countryside through organizations like the Youth Hostels Association, all provided opportunities for 'rational recreation', to which soft drinks were natural adjuncts. Whether 'temperance' in its earlier sense now played a significant part is doubtful in view of the sharp decline in church attendance, though some soft drinks continued to be so advertised as a guarantee of their respectability and suitability for family use. More often stressed were broad health claims in the form of generalized 'tonic' values, 'Vimto', for example, stating that 'You will feel the benefit from the very first glass', 'Vimto eliminates that out-of-sorts feeling', and 'When Hubby's Fed Up ... She knows how to manage things'[75] (with 'Vimto'). Soft drinks were for treats and special occasions, not for everyday use in the home. In their survey of the nation's meal patterns in 1936/7 Crawford and Broadley found no mention of the use of fruit juices at breakfast: at the mid-morning break at home only 3–4 per cent of people had a soft drink, while with the evening meal the highest consumption, even in the wealthiest group of the population, was a mere 2.4 per cent.[76] At 'tea', the main family evening meal, there were no soft drinks.

The Second World War had both negative and positive effects on consumption. Under the wide powers of the Ministry of Food the whole industry, which was a heavy user of sugar and imported materials, was controlled and rationalized into the Soft Drinks Industry (War Time) Association: all supplies were rationed and sugar gradually reduced to 20 per cent of the pre-war level. Brand names were disallowed, except that manufacturers who specialized in a local drink and had sufficient stocks of materials could sell a 'Speciality Flavour Cordial'; otherwise, all drinks were sold at fixed prices under one SDI (Soft Drinks Industry) label. Many small firms disappeared after 1942, though they were compensated from the profits of the survivors. By contrast, on America's entry to the war the Coca-Cola Company's President, Robert Woodruff, promised that every US serving man or woman would be able to buy Coca-Cola at 5 cents a bottle anywhere in the world and regardless of the cost. Bottling plants accompanied the American forces to Britain, North Africa, Europe and the Far East, spreading Coca-Cola virtually around the world and stimulating an appetite for soft drinks in both host and occupied countries.[77] Lord Woolton, the Minister of Food, recognized the importance of soft drinks as an aid to morale, and made priority allocations to the services and works canteens, but, more directly related to nutritional needs, fruit juices were allocated to pregnant mothers, infants and children under 5. Blackcurrant and rosehip syrup were replaced after 1941 by 'lease-lend' supplies of concentrated orange juice,[78] familiarizing people in lower income groups with the benefit and enjoyment of fruit drinks.

Expansion of the industry resumed after the SDI Association was wound up in 1948 and, more particularly, after the ending of sugar rationing in 1952, but the industrial concentration that the war had encouraged quickened in the increasingly competitive conditions of mass production, distribution and advertising in the post-war market, the estimated 1,000 firms of 1960 falling to around 500 ten years later.[79] With full employment and rising real wages in the 1950s and 1960s the youth market was now particularly targeted by the mass media, including the new commercial television, as a distinct sector experiencing surplus income, leisure time and the persuasive influence of fashion. In the home, however, soft drinks were only just beginning to appear in 1958 when another survey of the nation's diet was made: at breakfast in summer 7 per cent of women and 4 per cent of men drank fruit juice, but at no other meal in the home, including the mid-morning break, was a soft drink consumed by more than 3 per cent of people over the age of 16.[80] The government's National Food Survey, which measured total domestic consumption by all members of the household, showed a similar picture. In 1959 fruit juices were drunk by 7 per cent of households and welfare orange juice by 2 per cent:[81] families spent an average of 1s 11d a week out of a food budget of £5 0s 3d (2 per cent),[82] and in 1965 still only 2s 2d.[83]

By then, however, Britain was beginning to experience a cultural revolution, which included a major transformation in drinking habits. In 1970, when estimated consumption of soft drinks had grown to 500 million gallons (around 80 pints a head per year), Derek Cooper remarked that

> No kitchen is complete now without a bottle of Squash, and whereas before the war, in the 'Age of Want', if a child was thirsty it went to the tap, it now automatically pours out a 'drink', usually orange in colour and flavour if not in content.[84]

Mothers who had reared their children on subsidized orange juice acquiesced in the belief that they were providing a 'health' beverage, now publicly endorsed by the Food and Drugs Act 1955 and the Soft Drinks Regulations 1964. The principal ingredients of soft drinks were, of course, water and sugar, comprising 99 per cent in the case of Coca-Cola. The two broad divisions of the industry were concentrates for dilution (squashes and cordials), which were permitted up to five times as much preservatives since they would not be consumed at one time, and unconcentrated, usually carbonated drinks, for which bottles were charged with a measured quantity of syrup (the 'throw') and then filled with aerated water. Saccharin was widely used as a cheaper and stronger sweetener than sugar and, at this time, cyclamates, which did not leave the bitter after-taste of saccharin: when it was shown that they could cause bladder cancer in animals, their use was prohibited in the US in 1968 and subsequently in the UK.[85] A wide range of acids was (and is) in use, including citric, tartaric, phosphoric, lactic and acetic; permitted preservatives included sulphur dioxide and benzoic acid, while many artificial colours were employed, mainly derivatives of coal tar dyes.[86] One of these, rhodamine B, was prohibited in the 1960s when it was found to cause allergies in some people and hyperactivity in some children. The legal descriptions of soft drinks could also be confusing to consumers. 'Orangeade' or 'orange flavoured drink' need not contain any orange: a 'juice' must be the undiluted juice of the fruit (plus permitted sugar); a 'squash' must contain 25 per cent of juice but a 'crush' only 5 per cent.[87] It is highly likely that many consumers were unaware of these pitfalls.

In 1970 soft drinks accounted for 6.4 per cent of all drinks (except tap water) consumed by the UK population over the age of 10: this was half as much as alcoholic drinks and a third as much as coffee. By 1985 the proportion of soft drinks to total liquid consumption had doubled to 12 per cent, and in 1995 stood at 20 per cent, greater than alcohol (15 per cent) and the same volume as coffee. In 1995 57.7 per cent of people drank soft drinks daily, compared with 77 per cent who drank tea and 31.8 per cent who drank alcohol.[88] This ranks as the greatest change in British drinking habits in modern times, following a trend first established in the US, though still lagging behind consumption in some other European countries – the UK's 145 litres per person per year (5 pints per week) is exceeded by Germany's 230 litres, Italy's 200 and France's 185.[89]

Nevertheless, the scale of the British industry is immense. In 1995 it produced 9.6 billion litres valued at £6.4 billion, and spent £89 million on advertising, replacing lager as the most heavily promoted drink.[90]

The reasons why in the last 25 years soft drinks have moved into mass consumption – from luxuries to near-necessities – are complex and under-explored. Consumption is ultimately influenced by the state of the economy and the extent of personal disposable income, and despite recessions and the return of high levels of unemployment, the majority of British families have enjoyed larger spending power, often dependent on the additional earnings of working wives. Food and non-alcoholic drink now takes less than 20 per cent of household income, almost half as much as in the 1950s, releasing more income for leisure, holidays and luxuries as well as for housing and transport. Income still has a determining influence on consumption, however: in 1995 average family expenditure on soft drinks was £1.78 a week, but the wealthiest 10 per cent spent £3.45 compared with only 63p by the poorest.[91] Around three-quarters of all soft drinks purchases are now brought home,[92] suggesting that they are now integrated into the increasingly informal, individualized, consumption patterns of today. Snacks now account for 40 per cent of meal occasions in Britain and a cold drink appears at 30 per cent of these, while already in 1988 a soft drink was drunk at 19 per cent of breakfasts and 22 per cent of evening meals.[93] A bottle or can also fits very conveniently into a packed school lunch, now brought from home by 40 per cent of children,[94] while of the 46 per cent who eat a school canteen lunch one in three children buys a soft drink compared with 11 per cent who drink milk.[95]

Robert Goizueta, Chairman of Coca-Cola, recently described his product's phenomenal success as due to 'The Three As' – 'Availability, Affordability and Acceptability': Coca-Cola satisfies 'enduring realities' by meeting 'the fundamental, recurring human need for refreshment'.[96] Availability has greatly increased in Britain in recent years, with sales in supermarkets, newsagents, garage forecourts and by vending machines. But soft drinks are to do with much more than the mere satisfaction of thirst. Part of their psychological appeal is that they can equally be associated with activity and relaxation, with resting or doing, since their high sugar content provides around 80 calories of quick energy per bottle or can: advertising associates soft drinks with pleasure, enjoyment, gratification and reward, with sports, holidays, escape from work and routine. Their acceptability has also gained because of distrust about the purity of tap water, and because of public disapproval of drink-driving; around 12 per cent of British adults are now estimated to be non-drinkers of alcohol. Although advertising has traditionally targeted young consumers, who are particularly vulnerable to fashion and peer pressure, soft drinks are now increasingly promoted to adults as alternatives to alcohol and, in 'diet' form, for slimming.[97] By confirmed teetotallers soft drinks (including 'Ribena' and 'Vimto') are used in some churches instead of communion

wine, conveying 'meanings' of celebration well beyond any material attributes, but even in the predominantly secular world of today they can carry
symbolic meanings of reassurance, familiarity, home and love, attributes
well represented when US forces in the Gulf War celebrated Christmas
1990 with Coca-Cola. (Coca-Cola first used Father Christmas in their
advertising in the 1930s.)

In Britain carbonated drinks comprise 49 per cent of the total soft drinks
market; within this group colas are 46 per cent, having increased their
share from 29 per cent in 1980. Next in order are squashes (33 per cent),
fruit juices (12 per cent) and bottled water (5 per cent).[98] Coca-Cola and
Pepsi dominate the cola market, with 60 per cent and 20 per cent respectively, but in 1994 a 'cola war' erupted with the launch of cheaper
supermarket brands by Sainsbury, Safeway, Virgin and others. Fierce
competition characterizes the trade, but 'brand loyalty' is a powerful force,
as Coca-Cola discovered in 1985 when they changed their formula in
order to compete with Pepsi, but quickly reverted to the original in the
face of a storm of protest. Bottled water, though still a small sector in
Britain, is the fastest-growing one, reaching 619 million litres in 1995 from
a mere 25 million in 1980.[99] The current prediction is that total soft drinks
production will continue to rise to 10 billion litres by the year 2000, though
there are concerns that demographic trends may not be so favourable in
the long term. Table 5.1 shows consumption of soft drinks by age. Regarded
as the 'core consumers', the 15–24 age group is estimated to decline by
33 per cent between 1990 and 2000, only partially compensated by an
increase of the 10–14 group by 13 per cent. Manufacturers are now active
in designing soft drinks with greater appeal to older consumers – caffeine-
free and 'diet' versions of existing drinks and a range of 'Adult Soft Drinks',
many of which focus on 'energy' or 'sports' attributes. In some respects
the new products represent a return to the earlier 'health' associations of
soft drinks though endowed with exotic names conveying 'sophistication'
– 'Kiri', 'Gini', 'Kisqua', 'Royal Mystic', 'Oasis', 'Aqua Libra' and many

Table 5.1 Age distribution of soft drinks
consumers, 1995

Years of age	% of all soft drinks
2–4	10
5–9	15
10–14	18
15–24	20
25–34	14
55–64	4
Over 65	5

Source: Britvic Soft Drinks Industry Report,
1996, 9

others.[100] Intended partly as alternatives to alcohol, many 'New Age' drinks are mixtures of fruit juices and herbs having therapeutic claims: Aqua Libra 'helps to restore alkaline balance', Oasis 'calms and rejuvenates', 'Duchy Originals' are substitutes for red and white wines, while 'Purdeys' and 'Norfolk Punch' contain up to thirty herbal extracts including ginseng, gentian, gurana, thistle, centaury, schizandra, feverfew, alehoof and prickly ash bark:[101] at £1.95–£2.99 a bottle some cost as much as cheap wine. Another new category that appeared in 1995 was alcoholic 'soft' drinks ('alcopops') containing 4–5.5 per cent of alcohol (more than most beers) derived from a shot of spirits, but, unlike beer, sweet and fizzy. One of the best-selling of more than 30 brands, 'Hooper's Hooch' (brewed by Bass) is aimed at the 18–24-year-old group, but their sweetness makes them appealing to younger drinkers who, according to Alcohol Concern, may become 'hooked' at an early age.[102]

Health issues have again become important in the promotion of soft drinks, including the 'psycho-active' claims of some 'New Age' elixirs for enlarging mental activity and verbal fluency. On the other hand, there has been strong criticism in some medical quarters of the wide variety of artificial ingredients currently permitted,[103] and especially of the danger to children's health of large quantities of mildly addictive sugars. The increased use of soft drinks has contributed to raising sugar consumption in Britain to around 100 lb per person per year, twice the amount recommended by most nutritionists: Coca-Cola contains the equivalent of seven teaspoons of sugar per bottle, a glass of blackcurrant cordial or bitter lemon five, tonic water four and orange squash two.[104] A recent survey of the diets of children aged $1\frac{1}{2}$–$4\frac{1}{2}$ years showed that in 1992/3 86 per cent consumed non-diet soft drinks at an average of 2,092 grams per week compared with 83 per cent who drank whole milk at 1,872 grams: half of those who drank soft drinks consumed 1.5 litres a week, but citrus fruits were eaten by only a quarter of the children.[105] The danger is that a heavy consumption of sugars may inhibit the appetite for more nutritious foods as well as having particularly harmful effects on teeth. A third of the children aged $1\frac{1}{2}$–$2\frac{1}{2}$ years were using bottles every night, a quarter of which consisted of carbonated drinks, squashes or flavoured milks, and 30 per cent of those aged $3\frac{1}{2}$–$4\frac{1}{2}$ years had experienced dental decay.[106]

Within a remarkably short space of 25 years soft drinks have come to occupy a central place in British diet. They represent a classic instance of the power of advertising to shape demand, particularly of younger consumers who were influenced by fashions in popular culture, and possessed more spending power than previous generations. Tastes acquired in youth passed into adulthood and into the home, and Britain did not experience the political objections to 'Coca-colonization' which, for a time, restricted consumption in Italy, France and communist countries. A 'soft drinks revolution' may now be considered an accomplished fact, comparable with that of the hot drinks revolution that Britain experienced two centuries earlier.

6   Beer: 'A moral species of beverage'*

Beer occupies a different position in the repertoire of drinks from those so far discussed. As an alcoholic beverage it has the power to change consciousness, to promote a sense of well-being and lubricate social relations, as well as satisfying thirst and providing nourishment. It was already a normal drink of British people for many centuries before receiving official recognition as the second necessity of life in the Assize of Bread and Ale in 1267, and only under the influence of the Temperance Movement in the nineteenth century did some people come to condemn it as a poisonous drug, a main cause of poverty, disease and a litany of social ills. From a household drink accompanying all meals and festivities beer slowly acquired a primarily recreational role: unlike the new hot beverages, which moved from elite to mass consumption, beer followed an opposite course from being the drink of all social classes to becoming one whose heaviest consumers were among the poorer strata of society. And while it continued to hold a special place in the nation's psyche, evoking nostalgic images of good fellowship in farmhouse and tavern, its history has been one of overall decline, particularly rapid in the twentieth century.

Beer's importance to the national diet and economy has attracted a large literature. Much of the writing in the Victorian period was either romantic anecdotage or critical denunciation by teetotal campaigners, but in recent times the history of the brewing industry has received scholarly attention[1] as well as that of the Temperance Movement.[2] Instead, this chapter focuses on the consumption of beer – its quantity and quality, its place in the diet and the domestic budget, the places and occasions of drinking and the reasons for changes in the patterns of usage.

*Lord Brougham, 1830

I

Beer was probably the first drink deliberately made by man. It was brewed from fermented barley by the Bronze Age civilizations of Mesopotamia and Egypt in the third millennium BC, where some 40 per cent of the total grain yield went for this purpose: temple workmen received a ration of two pints a day, senior dignitaries as much as eight pints. Beer was made of varying strengths up to a 'barley wine' of around 12 per cent alcohol and flavoured with a wide variety of herbs and plants.[3] Its production became widespread in temperate Europe in the Celtic Iron Age on the edges of the wine-growing regions; strong ale was an elite drink among wealthy Britons in the third and fourth centuries[4] and, as spiced and sweetened 'bragot', among Welsh princes.[5] One great advantage was that it could be made from materials widely available,[6] another that, at different strengths, it was both an everyday drink and a prized, potent beverage for celebratory, even ritual occasions. For winter festivals like New Year 'wassail' was drunk in Saxon times, a hot, spiced ale passed round in a communal bowl ('was-hal' – 'be of health', 'good health'),[7] while special brews were associated with many local events – 'bride-ale' (for weddings), 'Church ale' (for fund-raising), 'Tithe ale' (for the annual collection of tithes), 'scot-ale' (at which the participants shared the expense) – as well as church festivals such as Easter and Whitsuntide.

The central role of beer to English diet and social life was recognized by the national Assize of Ale (1267), which established a maximum price per gallon according to a sliding scale of corn prices:[8] the intention was to ensure a reasonable profit to the brewer and a fair price to the consumer, while quality was controlled by 'ale-conners', who were expected to attend all public brewings. Administered by the local magistrates the Assize appears to have worked with some success for the next three centuries or so. Its enactment indicates that brewing was already a commercial activity in the early Norman period, but much beer was also brewed and sold at home by 'ale-wives', who were not subject to guild regulation, and by manors, monasteries, colleges and, probably, the majority of private households above the level of peasant. Like baking, brewing was a normal activity of the housewife, though requiring more initial outlay in equipment and subsequent materials; it was usually done monthly but for special, keeping brews in March and October.

So far, the terms 'beer' and 'ale' have been used indiscriminately, as they appear to have been before the fifteenth century: 'ale' was the Danish word, 'beer' the Anglo-Saxon,[9] but it was an unhopped drink, sweet, heavy and dark-coloured. The use of hops as bitter flavourings and preservatives may have begun in Bohemia and Bavaria in the ninth century, and they were widely used in Flanders by the fourteenth; they were introduced to England by Flemish brewers early in the fifteenth century, and the new, hopped 'beer' was made subject to the Assize in 1441.[10] Thereafter, until the seventeenth century at least, 'ale' meant the traditional, unhopped drink, while 'beer' made progress in London and the South but only slowly elsewhere.[11]

In the absence of recorded statistics of production before 1684 it is only possible to speculate that consumption in these early centuries was high by subsequent standards. The peasant's diet of bread, pottage, vegetables, and some cheese and salt fish, was bulky and monotonous, made more palatable by ale at breakfast, dinner and supper. That it was also a recreational drink is indicated by the Church's frequent attempts to suppress drunkenness in alehouses, and by a statute of Edward I requiring London taverns to close at curfew. Under the Tudors, increased fears of social and political unrest led to the first general Licensing Act (1552), giving magistrates power to grant, control and limit licences. Drunkenness and 'tippling' were blamed, rightly or wrongly, on the experience of English soldiers in the Low Countries, though the line between satisfaction of thirst and over-indulgence was difficult to draw: since no precise measurement of alcoholic content was possible at this time, beer was liable to be brewed at a strength that caused rapid intoxication, a foreign visitor to England in 1598 commenting that 'Beer is the general drink and excellently well tasted, but strong and what soon fuddles'.[12] In private households it was often brewed in great quantities – William Harrison's wife and maidservants made around 200 gallons each month for a modest establishment[13] – since water was often unsafe to drink and tea and coffee not yet available. Beer was therefore consumed at every meal and, in stronger forms, in the evening and for entertaining, and was not despised by the royal court and aristocracy. Elizabeth I normally drank beer at breakfast, while the Earl of Northumberland's Household Book of 1512 specified for his and his lady's breakfast a quart (2 pints) of beer and of wine; their two young sons were allowed 2 quarts of beer but no wine, while two children still in the nursery received 1 quart. Such allowances seem generous, yet Lady Lucy, a Maid of Honour in Henry VIII's court, received a gallon (8 pints) of ale at breakfast, dinner and supper each day.[14] Though it is unlikely that such quantities were actually consumed, beer was considered a very healthy and nutritious drink, the eminent Dr Andrew Boorde writing in his *Dyetary of Helth* (1542)

> I myself, which am a physician, cannot away with water, wherefore I do leave all water and do take myself to good ale, and otherwise for ale I do take good Gascon wine, but I will not drink strong wines.

That domestic brewing was very widespread is evidenced by a study of Tudor inventories from the Midland counties of England. Of people who left fairly modest estates worth £20 upwards 41 per cent in towns and 28.4 per cent in rural areas possessed brewing equipment: of those with estates worth less than £20 only 8.5 per cent and 1.3 per cent

respectively owned such equipment.[15] The urban figures were swollen by
the numbers of small innkeeper-brewers who sold to the public, but a
significant feature of the sixteenth and seventeenth centuries was the growth
of larger wholesale Common Brewers who supplied inns, establishments,
provisioned ships and also exported beer. By 1699 there were 194 Common
Brewers in London, responsible for the majority of beer brewed in the
capital.[16] Commercial brewing on this larger scale developed partly because
the use of hops now produced a more stable product with better keeping
qualities, and partly because the growing urban populations offered a mass
market for a bulky product that could not be economically transported
by land more than about 4 or 5 miles. Commercial brewing therefore
developed first in London, the largest market, in Edinburgh and in particular towns that established reputations for high-quality beers, such as
Burton, Derby, York, Chester, Hull and Nottingham.[17]

Despite these developments, private brewing accounted for around 65
per cent of total beer production in the 1690s.[18] An indication of what
was considered normal consumption at this period is suggested by the
allowances in public institutions: for example, at Christ's Hospital thirty
barrels, each 36 gallons, were drunk each week by 407 children, an average
of 3 pints a head a day, and St Bartholomew's Hospital in 1687 gave the
same, but a sailor's diet of 1615 allowed a gallon a day to each man to
accompany his dry ration of biscuit, bacon and cheese.[19] An analysis of
Scottish diets between 1639 and 1743 (hospitals, orphanages, estate servants
and military) yields a rather less generous allowance of 2.1 pints a day[20]
– General Monk's Scottish troops in London in 1659 who, observed Pepys,
'are most of them drunk all day', must have been supplementing their
rations in the numerous alehouses. Wartime expenditure brought the first
national taxation of beer in 1643 (2s a barrel on strong, 6d on small beer),
which by 1690 had risen to 6s 6d and 1s 6d respectively,[21] a levy that
doubled the price of strong beer. From 1684 the annual output of Common
Brewers and Brewing Victuallers in the United Kingdom was recorded,
which, together with estimates for private brewing, yield a total production in that year of 18,582,000 barrels, an average of 832 pints a year for
every man, woman and child, or 2.3 pints a day. This would have provided
a major contribution to the energy value of the diet – around 400–500
kcal (about a fifth of average requirements) and substantial amounts of
calcium, magnesium, riboflavin and nicotinic acid.[22] Since men drank
considerably more than women and children, the value to their diets would
have been even greater: 4 pints a day, by no means unusual, would have
yielded around 1,000 kcal, at least a quarter of the energy needs of a
working man, as well as making a largely cereal diet more palatable.

It is likely that these high consumption levels of the late seventeenth
century represent a peak never subsequently regained. Tea and coffee
were not yet serious competitors to beer, especially among the working
classes, while, for the better-off, wine consumption was adversely affected

by the Navigation Act (1651) and the imposition of a heavy duty of £4 a tun in 1688. But beer output was now itself sensitive to changes in the level of taxation, the high production of 23,056,000 barrels in 1689 falling steadily to 18,679,000 in 1691 and 14,637,000 in 1700 after the trebling of duty in 1690. Although private brewing was exempt from tax, this increase clearly affected Common Brewers and Brewing Victuallers, who would have had to pass on the costs to the consumer in higher prices, reduced strength, or both.

II

The eighteenth century marked important changes in both the production and the consumption of beer. The share of private brewing gradually fell from around two-thirds of the total in 1700 to half by the last decade,[23] while that of public brewing increased proportionately, but the strong survival of private brewing by households and institutions is evidence of the central place of beer in the national diet despite the growing competition of spirits and of tea. The comment of César de Saussure, a French visitor to England in the 1720s, that 'In this country . . . beer . . . is what everyone drinks when thirsty', ceased to be true only in the later eighteenth century as prices rose and the standard of living of the labourer collapsed in the pauperized parishes of the south. In mid-century 'The large landowners, the country squires and parsons, the Oxford colleges, the public schools – in short, all who had large establishments or any connection with the country as opposed to town, brewed their own beer'.[24] This was certainly true of Parson Woodforde in Norfolk, who regularly brewed both strong and table beer and from his annual income of around £400 paid his maltster £22 18s 6d in 1790 compared with his butcher's bill for the year of £46 5s 0d.[25] But in the poor agricultural parish of Barkham, Berkshire, in the 1780s home brewing had practically died out, and beer was only for special occasions. Brewing was mentioned in only two of the labourers' budgets collected by the Revd David Davies, one by a married man earning 9s a week: 'The wife, having an infant at the breast and fancying *very* small beer better than mere water, brews a peck of malt once a month which costs 1s 4d, hops ¼lb 4d: this is, per week, 5d'. A peck of malt (a quarter of a bushel) would have made about 7 gallons, some 2 pints a day. But, significantly, this family also bought ¼lb of tea a month for 9d and a pound of sugar costing 8d.[26] In another family, where the wage was only 7s a week, 'they seldom brew except against a lying-in or a christening', though here the man was 'given' small beer during the day by the farmer, reckoned at another 1s a week.[27] What little these families spent on tea, Davies commented, would not nearly supply them with beer since the price of malt had doubled from 3s–3s 6d a bushel in 1750 to 5s 3d–6s 6d in 1794 without any corresponding increase in wages.

Time was when small beer was reckoned one of the necessaries of life, even in poor families . . . Were the poor able to afford themselves this wholesome beverage, it would well enough compensate for the scarcity of milk. But on account of the dearness of malt . . . small beer has been these many years beyond their ability to use . . . [28]

Home brewing survived more widely in the Midlands and North, partly because wages were higher here, and partly because fuel for the long firing process was more available from unenclosed woods and wastes or from nearby coal-pits. The tradition was particularly strong in Yorkshire, where hops were often replaced by locally gathered bitter herbs such as alehoof, ground ivy and coltsfoot. Strong celebratory ales, which were served hot in winter (mulled ale, posset and wassail), were a feature of weddings, christenings, funerals and of seasonal thanksgivings like Church Supper (a predecessor of Harvest Festival) and Back End Supper (at the end of winter ploughing).

These were ritual occasions for special brews, unlike the small beer supplied to men at harvest, haymaking, ploughing and other laborious tasks as encouragement and reward. The heaviest drinkers, however, were forgemen and foundrymen, who worked in temperatures from 90 to 140°F and could lose 20 lb a day in sweat: to replace this they drank from 8 to 24 pints of weak home-brew per shift,[29] but agricultural labourers could reach the lower level of this. Sir Frederic Eden reported that Midlands labourers in the 1790s generally received a gallon a day at harvest, and some farmers allowed this quantity all the year round: 'Each man has his gallon bottle filled in the morning, and what he does not drink he takes home to his family'. Living-in servants in farmhouses expected 'drink' with every meal, and Eden noted that some men served with a 2 quart copper can 'will see the bottom single-handed'.[30] Such allowances provided substantial amounts of energy: it is estimated that servants employed at Gordon Castle in 1739 derived 62 per cent of their nutrition from bread and oatmeal, and only 11 per cent from meat, but 19 per cent from ale.[31]

But the characteristic of eighteenth-century brewing history was the growth in the output of Common Brewers (wholesalers) and Brewing Victuallers (retailers). There existed a wide spectrum of size, from small publicans who brewed in their backyards and sold in their kitchen taprooms up to some very large, highly capitalized businesses, especially among the 'great brewers' of London. In 1748 the twelve largest of these already accounted for 41.9 per cent of London's output, and by 1800 77.7 per cent. Calverts were the first to brew more than 50,000 barrels a year in 1748, Whitbreads first with 200,000 in 1796, and Barclays first with 300,000 in 1815.[32] This was industrialized brewing on a revolutionary scale, factory methods, technology and managerial skills applied to meet the demands of a mass market. Outside London, only a handful of pale ale brewers in Burton, Derby and Nottingham reached an output of 20,000 barrels a year, while 23,690 licensed victuallers each brewed a mere 251 barrels a year.[33] In Scotland there was a similar trend towards larger-scale brewing in response to population growth and urbanization: brewers like Archibald Campbell (1710), Hugh and Robert Tennent (1740), William Younger (1749) and George Younger (1762) established reputations for strong ales, some of which found markets in England, the Low Countries and North America.

The dominance in the London trade achieved by the twelve great brewers depended importantly on their promotion of a new beer product, 'porter', which was particularly suitable for large-scale production. Before this, three types of beer had been generally available in towns – the sweet, heavy ale; a lighter, more hopped beer; and a weak table beer often drunk with meals. In public houses it was usual to order a mixture of two or three of these – 'half-and-half' or 'three threads'.

> Thus, the publican had the trouble to go to three casks and turn three cocks for a pint of liquor. To avoid this inconvenience and waste, a brewer of the name of Harwood conceived the idea of making a liquor which should partake of the same united flavour; he did so, and succeeded, calling it 'entire' or 'entire butt' . . . and as it was a very hearty and nourishing liquor and supposed to be very suitable for porters and other working people, it obtained the name of porter.[34]

This was in 1722. Ralph Harwood was a partner in the Bell Brewhouse in Shoreditch, not one of the great breweries, but his process was quickly taken up by them so that porter became their main line by mid-century. It was a thick, black beer, bitter, and with a distinctive flavour from high-dried malt, and needed to be matured for up to 18 months to produce the desired 'hardness'. The soft London waters of the Thames and the Lea were particularly suitable for porter-brewing, and it did not need malts and hops of such high quality as those used for pale ale. Above all, the London firms had the great advantages of economies of scale and a local mass market: they employed the latest technology, including Boulton and Watt's steam engines, thermometers, hydrometers, saccharometers and attemperators. These enabled them to produce a stable beer of reliable quality and also, by finely adjusting the gravity, to keep prices down during the inflation of the later eighteenth century. In 1710 the retail price of standard beer was 2½d a quart, 4d for pale ale ('twopenny', i.e. 2d per pint). From the 1720s to 1761 London porter was fixed at 3d a quart until the beer duty was raised from 5s to 8s a barrel during the Seven Years War; thereafter it remained at 3½d a quart until the end of the century, mainly by lowering gravity.[35]

According to Henry Jackson in 1758, 'Beer, commonly call'd Porter, is almost become the universal Cordial of the Populace', a reference not only to its popularity but also to its supposed health benefits. Nevertheless, during the century total beer production remained at a substantially lower level than the high point of 1689, when an estimated 23 million barrels had been brewed; average production now ranged around 15 million barrels a year, with a low of 13 million in 1786 and a high of 18.2 million in 1732.[36] Yearly variations in output mainly reflected the size of the grain harvest, and Britain experienced many years of crop failure during the later century – 1756–7, 1764–74, 1782–4, 1789, 1795 and 1799–1800.[37] When set against the growth of Britain's population from around 6.5 million in 1700 to 10.5 million in 1800, the statistics suggest substantial falls in consumption per head from around 600 gallons a year in 1700 to 500 in 1750 and 400 (8 pints per person per week) by 1800.[38] This fall in overall consumption by a third in little more than 100 years is remarkable, and raises questions about changes in the standard of living at this time. Part of the explanation lies in the increased consumption of spirits in the first half of the century (see Chapter 8) and of tea in the second half (see Chapter 3), but whether the switch to tea-drinking was a preferred change or caused by increasing pressure on domestic budgets is debatable – David Davies was clear that the latter was the case. Those who, like Parson Woodforde, could afford to take advantage of the wider range of drinks now available did so liberally, drinking not only home-brewed beer and London porter, but also cider, wine, gin and punch, as well as tea, coffee and, occasionally, chocolate. At a lower social level, artisans earning good wages continued to drink large quantities of beer as a normal part of their diet, Benjamin Franklin in the 1720s expressing surprise that his fellow printers in London each consumed 6 pints of strong beer a day with and between meals.[39] Even late in the century inmates of poorhouses and workhouses were still often served with beer, at least in the South of England and the Midlands: a pint of small beer at supper was usual, and in some institutions the same at breakfast and dinner, but further north milk with the porridge or hasty-pudding was the usual liquid supplied.[40] Frederic Eden believed that the southern labourer 'takes more liquids into his stomach than the Cumberland or the Yorkshire man',[41] which may well have been true since the southern bread diet would have needed more liquids than the moist northern one with more abundant milk.

Institutions tended to reflect the kind of diet eaten by labourers a generation earlier rather than contemporary changes. By the end of the century beer's role was changing from a universal drink to that of the somewhat better-off, and from a domestic drink to one increasingly consumed outside the home for pleasure. Of the 193 family budgets collected by Davies and Eden between 1787 and 1796, 90 per cent of which were of agricultural labourers, purchased beer accounted for only 2.5 per cent of food expenditure in the south and 2.4 per cent in the north.[42] But in the towns alehouses had multiplied under a lax licensing system, S. and B. Webb believing that an estimate of 40,000 premises in 1773 should have been nearer 100,000.[43] Only from the mid-1780s was the laissez-faire licensing policy tightened in a concerted attempt to suppress vice and reform the morals of the working classes. Supported by the Crown, evangelical clergy, ratepayers and many industrialists, the new policy resulted in many areas in fixing closing hours (usually 10 p.m. in summer, 9 p.m. in winter), Sunday closing before noon, the suppression of redundant licences, and closer control over the quantity of new ones. The new strictness was applied vigorously until about 1800 and rather less so down to 1815, and appears to have been particularly successful in the manufacturing districts of Lancashire and the West Riding, where comparatively high wages had been an inducement to heavy drinking and brutal sports. Once regarded as legitimate meeting places for all social classes for a wide variety of purposes, public houses had become suspect by the late eighteenth century as the foci of dissent, disrespect and crime. 'It is not the fashion for gentlemen and people of rank to frequent alehouses', noted Eden in 1797.[44] Now, in the wake of the American and French Revolutions, they were viewed as potential centres of radicalism and sedition:[45] although beer was still a widely approved beverage, excessive indulgence was not condoned in the new climate of public morality.

III

Domestic brewing, formerly the major contributor to total beer production, declined rapidly in the first half of the nineteenth century to near insignificance. For the rural working classes this was one aspect of the collapse of their economic position and the reduction of many to a subsistence level, often dependent on poor relief. Brewing required resources beyond the daily struggle for existence – equipment that Cobbett valued at around £10, and spare cash to buy heavily taxed malt and hops at regular intervals. In the depressed state of agriculture after 1815 farmers petitioned for the abolition of the malt duty, which, said a Hampshire magistrate, 'would empower the poor labourer to brew his own beer . . . his poor wife and children would partake of his beverage instead of a dreadful compound of tea'.[46] No relief was forthcoming, and even if it had been, there remained the obstacle of fuel now that so many common lands had been enclosed. 'Where fuel is scarce and dear, poor people find it cheaper to buy their bread of the baker than to bake for themselves', Davies had noted in 1795,[47] and what was true of baking was even more true of the longer firing needed for brewing. By 1815 brewing by the cottager had all but died out in the south of England; it survived better in the north, though even in Yorkshire few labourers brewed by the 1840s[48] or in Wales after the 1870s.[49] In total, it is estimated that private brewing represented about one-fifth of beer output in 1830, one-eighth in 1851–5 and a mere one-fortieth by 1866–70.[50]

By contrast, in 1815 the twelve great brewers of London produced around 2 million barrels a year, a fifth of national output. Thereafter, the

Table 6.1   Numbers of brewers in England and Wales, 1839, 1880 and 1914

	1839	*1880*	*1914*
Common Brewers (wholesalers)	2,349	2,507	1,236
Beer retailer brewers	18,017	6,157	880
Publican brewers	27,554	12,336	1,477
Total	47,920	21,000	3,593

Source: George B. Wilson, *Alcohol and the Nation*, 48–9

history of the industry was one of ever-increasing concentration as small brewers were squeezed out by larger firms, which 'tied' public houses to guarantee themselves assured outlets. In 1817 it was reported that almost half the licensed houses in London were 'tied', and that 'this system is very prejudicial to the interests of the community at large,[51] but public concern that such monopolies inevitably raised prices and deteriorated quality did not halt the process. Outside London a similar trend towards fewer, larger units of production was characteristic of the second half of the century, when railway construction opened up regional and even national markets for beer – for example, the Burton pale ale brewers, Bass, expanded their output eightfold between 1853 and 1876. By 1914 concentration of the industry was even greater than Table 6.1 suggests, as 45 per cent of all beer was now produced by forty-seven Common Brewers and 25 per cent by the ten largest. Beginning with the Irish firm of Guinness in 1886, several of these formed themselves into limited liability companies, and in the face of a declining consumption of beer an intense 'brewers' war' developed to buy up more licensed premises: by 1899 75 per cent of all licences were 'tied' to brewers, and in many towns monopoly was almost complete.[52]

Already in the early nineteenth century the power of the great brewers to dominate the market, especially in London, and of unelected magistrates to grant, refuse and withdraw licences was coming to be regarded as unacceptable by legislators who had imbibed the gospel of Free Trade. The principle that 'the demand for goods ought to regulate the number of vendors' was, it was felt, particularly true of the second necessity of life – to what Lord Brougham described as 'a moral species of beverage', whose consumption ought to be encouraged as a healthy alternative to gin. In 1830 the Beerhouse Act allowed any householder assessed to the poor rate to open his house as a beershop free from magistrate's licence on payment of 2 guineas (£2 2s) to the local Excise office: the only restriction was that they should sell only beer or cider, and should open from 4 a.m. to 10 p.m. as against the often unlimited hours in licensed houses. The intention was that competition with the existing inns and alehouses would bring lower prices and improved quality, and to the same end the duty on beer was abolished, leaving only that on malt and hops.

The effects of free trade in beer were immediate and spectacular. Within six months 26,342 new beershops had opened, and by 1838 45,717:[53] in Liverpool fifty beershops opened every day for several weeks, while in villages where there had formerly been a single public house there were sometimes now half a dozen, and 'the labourer had to run the gauntlet through the beershops'.[54] Very few proprietors of the small 'Jerry shops'[55] brewed their own beer: many immediately became 'tied' to brewers, and the intense competition that developed between them, and between the beershops and the licensed alehouses, often resulted in poor-quality, adulterated beer. Similarly, the hope that customers would be 'introduced to houses of better order' was unfulfilled, as the unregulated beershops easily became haunts of criminals and prostitutes.[56] Beer consumption rose temporarily, as well it might, but had levelled off by 1840. The one benefit that could be claimed was that its price fell by 1d a quart in London and up to 2d elsewhere from the previous 4½d–6d a quart.

Public anxiety about the effects of the Act began early, though it was not until 1854 that a Select Committee unequivocally concluded that 'the beershop system has proved a failure'.[57] By then the temperance movement, which began in 1829, had turned from its acceptance of beer as a desirable alternative to spirits to a general condemnation of all alcohol – teetotallism. From 1855 a series of statutes began to restrict opening hours, first on Sundays and later on weekdays: by 1874, and continuing up to 1914, weekday opening hours were limited to between 5 a.m. and midnight in London and from 6 a.m. to 11 p.m. in other towns.

For around a century and a half after its introduction in the 1720s porter, and its stronger version, stout, were the most popular beers in London and many provincial towns. Its dark appearance, distinctive flavour and supposed nourishing qualities seemed to fit well with the earlier stages of industrialization, when much energy was needed for outdoor work and long factory hours. In the Midlands and the North porter's primacy was challenged by paler, brighter ales like those brewed in Burton, where hard waters containing calcium sulphate produced a more sparkling drink. Approved by many doctors, Bass's bottled India Pale Ale achieved large home and export sales, and at its premium price was regarded by the middle classes as a thoroughly respectable table drink. The trend towards lighter, paler beers in the later century reflected changes in the nature of work and the growth of non-manual occupations, and was stimulated by the abolition of the excise duty on glass in 1845 and the gradual substitution of glass in public houses for pewter and earthenware pots. Science and technology also played an important part in this shaping of new tastes. Brewing of fresher, 'running beers' was made possible by Baudelot's refrigerator (1859), and by the application of Pasteur's researches on fermentation to the development of pure yeasts. The age of scientific brewing dawned with the appointment of Horace T. Brown to Worthingtons in 1865 and Cornelius O'Sullivan, later founder of the influential 'Bacterium

Club', to Bass in 1866.[58] In the 1870s some restaurants began to stock imported lager, first brewed on a large scale in Munich and Pilsen in the 1840s and later in the Netherlands (Heineken) and Denmark (Carlsberg); Tennent of Glasgow began brewing lager in 1885, though consumption was insignificant for many years.[59]

The beer that was drunk in the nineteenth century was, however, often very different from that which left respectable breweries because of the wide extent of adulteration.[60] Although there were occasional complaints about this in earlier centuries,[61] there is no evidence of widespread sophistication until the 1790s, when the high prices of grain during the French Wars tempted smaller brewers and publicans to dilute beer and restore 'strength' by the use of drugs. Officially, no ingredients other than malt and hops were allowed by the Excise, but when a leading analytical chemist, Fredrick Accum, published his *Treatise on Adulterations of Food and Culinary Poisons* in 1820 he disclosed a range of illegal substances used as substitutes – cocculus Indicus ('India berry', a poisonous picrotoxin), copperas, quassia, capsicum, hartshorn shavings, 'multum', 'mixed drugs' and many others. Between 1813 and 1819 there were nearly a hundred convictions of brewers, publicans and 'brewers' druggists' for defrauding the Revenue, though the effects on health of narcotics such as cocculus Indicus and grains of paradise were not considered. Accum found that the strength of porter at Barclay's, Hanbury's and other leading brewers averaged 5.25 per cent alcohol, but at public houses the same beer reached only 4.5 per cent,[62] clearly indicating that publicans 'stretched' their barrels by diluting with small beer or water; he also found that, to avoid the expense of long storage, sulphuric acid was sometimes used to 'harden' new beer. In fairness to the great brewers, however, only Thomas Meux was successfully prosecuted for using salts of tartar to give a frothy head to his porter (a 'cauliflower head' was regarded as an indication of strength). Adulteration was principally practised by small brewers, publicans and, after 1830, the new beershop keepers, who were struggling to compete by underselling the standard price by 1d or more a quart. These patronized 'beer doctors' who offered cheap substitutes and 'nostrums', or used the numerous 'Guides', 'Friends' or Vade Mecums available to the trade. One of the best-known, Samuel Child's *Every Man his own Brewer*, recommended for porter cocculus Indicus, capsicum, salts of tartar, liquorice, treacle, linseed, ginger, 'colour' and 'heading'.[63] 'Malt, to produce intoxication, must be used in such large quantities as would very much diminish, if not totally exclude, the brewer's profits'.

By mid-century the proliferation of beershops and the tying of public houses to brewers, often on unfavourable terms to the tenant, had brought adulteration to a head. In 1855 George Phillips, Chief Chemical Officer of the Excise Department, reported that of forty samples of hops examined thirty-five had contained one or more of quassia, cocculus Indicus, grains of paradise and tobacco,[64] while another chemist, John Mitchell, who had analysed 200 samples of beer over the previous 9 years, had not found one unadulterated except when taken direct from a brewery.[65] While the commonest adulteration was simple dilution – the publican turned a barrel of beer (36 gallons) into 48 gallons by adding 'liquor' (water), sugar, salt and iron sulphate for a frothy 'head' – the use of harmful drugs was a serious health hazard, not restricted to London: the Chief Constable of Wolverhampton reported that he had made many convictions for narcotics in beer, and believed that much apparent drunkenness was due to them rather than malt.[66]

Public alarm about the contents of beer resulted in some voluntary reform by the trade, for example the establishment in 1851 of the Metropolitan Brewing Company 'to supply the public with Genuine Beer', but general improvement had to wait on the passing of legislation, first the Adulteration of Foods Act 1860 and, more effectively, the Adulteration of Food, Drink and Drugs Act 1872. In many areas the newly appointed Public Analysts began to examine random samples and prosecute offenders: in 1873 the PA for North Staffordshire found twenty-six out of eighty-nine random samples of beer adulterated, six with poisonous cocculus Indicus.[67] When the Inland Revenue Act 1880 restored the duty on beer, the Excise Department became more active in testing for adulteration by publicans, and in effect a concordat developed by which the Excise concentrated on dilution and the public analysts on other additions. By the 1880s narcotics had all but disappeared, partly because of greater inspectorial vigilance and partly because of the change in taste towards lighter, less stupefying beers. Consequently, the proportion of samples reported by Public Analysts as adulterated was comparatively small – 9.3 per cent in 1877 but falling quickly to between 2 per cent and 5 per cent up to 1914, though with occasional high variations (1892 16.8 per cent, 1900 8.8 per cent):[68] the main addition was salt, used to disguise dilution and encourage thirst. The results of the Excise tests for added water were very different, however – 78 per cent in 1880, 29 per cent in 1890 and still 15 per cent at the end of the century:[69] the persistent rumours in late Victorian England that the workers' beer was watered had real foundation.

Some believed that much worse than water was used, that there was now widespread 'legalized adulteration' since the duties on hops and malt had been abolished (1862 and 1880 respectively) and brewers were allowed to use any materials that were not injurious to health. By the 1880s brewers were taking advantage of 'the free mash-tun' to use maize, rice and sugar, preservatives, colourings, primings and bitter substitutes, many of which were formerly illegal. Against these developments a 'Pure Beer' campaign emerged with the aim of restoring only the traditional ingredients of malt and hops: in 1886 William Quilter MP introduced a bill 'for better securing the Purity of Beer', which required notices to be displayed at points of sale of any beers not made exclusively from barley-malt and hops. Having passed Second Reading, the Bill was lost in the following parliamentary dissolution, but continuing public pressure resulted in a Departmental Committee on Beer Materials, 1896–9, in which leading chemists disagreed over whether harmful substances were now being used. A Minority Report particularly objected to the use of sulphuric acid for inverting sugar and to salicylic acid as a preservative, which had been banned in several European countries; it also argued that the modern drink lacked the nutritional value of malt beer, which had been important in working-class diet.[70] In the face of an uncritical Majority Report, however, no action followed until in 1900 the fears of the reformers were unexpectedly and dramatically realized. A mysterious disease, variously described as 'alcoholism' and 'peripheral neuritis', broke out in Manchester and spread to the Midlands: by the end of the year 6,000 cases were reported and 3,000 deaths had occurred, mainly among heavy drinkers. The disease was eventually traced to arsenical poisoning derived from a firm of brewing sugar manufacturers who made glucose by a process involving sulphuric acid, which was itself made from arsenical iron pyrites. A hastily convened Royal Commission recommended that not more than one-hundredth of a grain of arsenic per gallon of liquid or pound of solids should in future be allowed: up to 4 grains of arsenic per pound of brewing sugar had been detected.[71]

How far the widespread publicity that beer adulteration received, especially in the mid-nineteenth century, affected consumption is difficult to assess. Probably the literate middle classes were more influenced than others, and it is noticeable that sales of bottled beers with sealed tops increased at this time, partly because they guaranteed that the contents were as they had left the brewery. Beer in moderate quantities continued to be generally approved by the medical profession until at least the 1870s, being served in hospitals, public schools, and to the sick in workhouses, even after the introduction of the deterrent New Poor Law in 1834. On the land, the long-established custom of farmers supplying labourers with beer continued even after the Truck Act of 1887 made it illegal to pay part of the wage in drink; thereafter, there was nothing to prevent it being 'given' as an encouragement to hard work. At harvest and haymaking in Cambridgeshire it was usual to give the men a pint of strong beer at each of the four meal-breaks,[72] while in Bedfordshire sheep-shearing also called for four or five pints a day.[73] In the later century these allowances came under attack from temperance reformers for encouraging excess and introducing young labourers to alcoholic drink, and the practice developed of giving 'beer money' as an alternative – £1 for men and 10s for lads in Oxfordshire,[74] £1 5s for the four weeks of harvest in Essex.[75] But apart from occasional celebrations, the labourer spent little on drink from his meagre wages. In North Oxfordshire in the 1880s, where the wage was 10s a week, the men's wives allowed them 1s a week for pocket-money: the men slowly sipped half a pint of beer (1d) each evening in the village inn, and argued that this saved coal in their cottages as their wives and children went early to bed.[76] The inn was as much their home as their cottage: only half a dozen men who 'had religion' did not drink, but no-one got drunk. At Quarry, in North Oxford, some men grew vegetables and flowers to exchange for drink, and at the Mason's Arms, the most plebeian of the four village inns, those who could not afford to pay were allowed to sip from a communal quart pot.[77]

Heavy drinking was much more characteristic of the towns and of workers in communities such as mining. In 1900 Rowntree spelled out the predisposing conditions to drink under which many still lived:

> Housed for the most part in sordid streets, frequently under over-crowded and unhealthy conditions, compelled very often to earn their bread by monotonous and laborious work and unable, partly through limited education and partly through . . . physical exhaustion, to enjoy intellectual recreation, what wonder that many of these people fall a ready prey to the publican . . . ?[78]

For such people beer did much more than quench thirst, or dull fatigue and the pangs of hunger. It was associated with manliness and virility, and in its principal locus, the public house, with conviviality, good fellowship, class and occupational identity. The intensification and routinization of work that industrialization brought caused psychological strains on people whose former work patterns had often been irregular, governed by the seasons or by their own choice. In domestic industries the 'Saint Monday' holiday had long been observed – for some an opportunity to extend the weekend's drinking or to recover from it – but the custom spread into London factory trades in the 1830s,[79] and survived for much of the century in workshops with craft traditions. Heavy drinking had been rife on 'Cobbler's Monday',[80] and was still common among engineers in the 1860s,[81] though soon after then reductions in working hours and the growth of the Saturday half-day were beginning to end the custom; it seems to have persisted longest in the furniture trades, where Charles Booth was told in 1902 that the men 'worked a ghost' (an extra shift) on Friday nights in order to keep 'Saint Monday'.[82] By then many trade customs that involved beer-drinking were also in decline. In 1839 John Dunlop, a Greenwich magistrate, had recorded 300 drinking usages in 98 trades, some of the commonest being payments for 'footings' on apprenticeship, ending apprenticeship, changing jobs, marriage, birth of children, learning a new skill or completing contract work: almost every trade had its elaborate code for extracting beer-money against which it was almost impossible to resist, and Dunlop thought it 'wonderful that there are any sober men in the mechanic class at all when such perpetual drinking domineers over them'.[83]

The consumption history of beer between 1800 and 1914 falls into three distinct periods: 1800–1860, 1860–1880, and 1880–1914. Table 6.2 gives

Table 6.2   Beer consumption, England and Wales, 1800–1914
(gallons/head/year)

1800–1804	33.9	1840–44	30.5	1880–84	33.6
1805–9	32.8	1845–49	29.2	1885–89	32.5
1810–14	30.2	1850–54	29.5	1890–94	33.4
1815–19	28.0	1855–59	29.3	1895–99	34.5
1820–24	29.0	1860–64	31.6	1900–1904	34.3
1825–29	28.4	1865–69	35.9	1905–9	30.9
1830–34	33.8	1870–74	38.2	1910–13	29.4
1835–39	35.4	1875–79	40.5		

Source: T.R. Gourvish and R.G. Wilson, *The British Brewing Industry, 1830–1980*, 1994,
Table 2.3, 30.

per capita consumption (men, women and children) per year for England
and Wales, omitting Scotland and Ireland which were not mainly beer-
drinking countries.[84] For the first 30 years of the century consumption was
falling, until the Beerhouse Act gave a temporary boost in the 1830s,
followed by a further decline in the 1840s and 1850s. As consumption of
beer's competitor, tea, was also falling in this period, these trends add
some support to the pessimists' case for a reduction in working-class standards of living: at least, they suggest that the alternative view based on
rising real wages applies only to the minority of workers who had fixed
earnings, and excludes the many who were self-employed, casually
employed or unemployed.[85] Consumption declined in this period because
home brewing was ceasing in many areas, and because the high prices of
the war years (porter rose to 6d a quart in 1804 and 1813) had changed
the role of beer from an everyday drink towards a recreational one for
surplus income. In the post-war depression and unemployment after 1815
fewer people had such a surplus, while the duties on beer (10s a barrel
on strong and 2s on small beer) remained at their wartime level until
1830. What is remarkable is that their abolition in that year did not have
a more dramatic effect on consumption. Although tea was now regularly
consumed by the working classes, it in no way substituted for the social
attractions of beer, nor was the temperance movement yet having a major
impact on drinking habits. The conclusion must be that low and irregular
earnings, periodical cyclical depressions in factory industries (1831–2,
1841–2, 1848, 1853–4), and the painful death of formerly prosperous
domestic trades like handloom weaving, restricted purchasing power for
what was ceasing to be regarded as the second necessity of life.

Between 1860 and 1880 consumption revived, to peak at 42 gallons
per head per year in 1875–6. This coincided with a period of rising
real wages for many workers as the economy moved into sustained growth
and the benefits of industrialization began to be shared. More workers had
more surplus income, while as yet there were relatively few counter-
attractions to the traditional leisure pursuit of drink. Contemporaries

believed that the working classes consumed 75 per cent of all the beer brewed, but individual levels of consumption varied greatly. In 1899 Joseph Rowntree and Arthur Sherwell estimated that while 56 per cent of the whole population drank alcohol in some form, children under 15 did not drink, that women drank only half as much as men, and that 3 million adults were total abstainers.[86] Projecting these calculations backward in time, Gourvish and Wilson suggest that male drinkers in 1844 consumed 72 gallons a year and in the peak year, 1876, 103 gallons[87] (16 pints a week): this seems quite credible as a rough, general average, though some men in heavy occupations could comfortably consume 16 pints in a couple of days.

From 1880 to 1914 consumption declined, though not evenly, falling particularly from 1880 to 1887 and from 1900 onwards: by 1914 consumption per head in England and Wales was no higher than in the 1840s. This new pattern presents something of a puzzle, since although real wages continued to rise until around 1896, mainly because of lower food prices, for the first time greater spending power did not go on alcohol. The main reason was not so much the success of the temperance movement or stricter licensing policies as changes in the role of beer in working-class life. By the late nineteenth century tea had become the domestic drink and beer mainly an extra-mural, non-family, recreational indulgence for men, but surplus income was now courted by a range of new consumer goods and services – not only new imported and manufactured food products, factory-made clothing, furniture, metalware and toys, but also popular newspapers, music-halls, sports, travel and holidays. Many working-class families were moving closer to the norms and life-styles of the lower middle classes, and in this sense non-institutionalized 'temperance' was a powerful influence on drinking habits. Heavy drinking and drunkenness were not now 'respectable' but characteristic only of the lower strata of the class, the outcasts and slum-dwellers untouched by the forces of social progress. The fundamental change was in leisure habits and the ways in which most people now spent their time and money. A clergyman told Charles Booth that what was needed to curb the still heavy drinking of some workers was 'a different sort of stimulus. With clerks, the greatest preventive of drink has been the bicycle'.[88] Social reformers observed with satisfaction the growth of thrift among the working classes through membership of savings banks, co-operative and building societies, while others welcomed the development of 'counter-attractions' to drink – gardens and allotments, parks and playing fields (115 controlled by the London County Council in 1910), sports, both participant and spectator, libraries, museums and travel – all forms of 'rational recreation' that offered physically and mentally improving alternatives to the public house. Commenting on the declining consumption of alcohol in his Budget speech of 1905, Sir Austen Chamberlain said:

> The fact seems to be that we are witnessing a change in the habits of our people of which we shall have to take account in any consideration

Table 6.3 Estimated annual expenditure per head on alcoholic drinks in the UK, 1820–1913

	£	s	d		£	s	d		£	s	d
1820	2	8	6	1855	2	14	6	1885	3	18	4
1825	2	19	5	1860	2	18	6	1890	4	5	1
1830	2	16	5	1865	3	11	3	1895	4	3	4
1835	3	3	0	1870	3	16	1	1900	4	10	4
1840	2	18	10	1875	4	7	3	1905	3	15	11
1845	2	12	11	1880	3	10	11	1909	3	8	11
1850	2	18	10	1884	3	10	9	1910	3	9	3
								1913	3	12	5

Source: Based on G.B. Wilson, *Alcohol and the Nation*, 223–5, 423. From 1820 to 1884 the estimates are by William Hoyle, from 1886 to 1909 by Dawson Burns, and from 1910 onwards by Wilson.

of our financial system. I think the mass of our people are beginning to find other ways of expending some portion of the time and money which used previously to be spent in the public house. No change has been more remarkable in the habits of the people than the growing attendance in the last fifteen years at outdoor games and sports and large places of public entertainment like theatres, music-halls and so forth which, though not conducted on strictly temperance lines, do not lend themselves to the consumption of drink or offer it as their chief attraction. Again, the extension of cheap railway fares and the enormous growth in cheap excursions absorb a further portion of the money which used formerly to be spent on drink'.[89]

Social reformers, however, were still greatly concerned at the effects which high expenditure on drink had on family budgets, especially on those of the poorer classes. Table 6.3 shows annual expenditure on alcoholic drink. For a family of five people the annual cost in 1850 would be around £15, in 1875 £22 and in 1913 £18. In 1881 the British Association calculated that wage-earners spent an average of 9.6d a day on all food and drink, of which beer took 1.4d (14.5 per cent) and spirits 0.75d: spending on beer was the same as that on bread (1.41d), almost as high as that on meat (1.87d), and almost five times greater than that on tea (0.29d).[90]

Charles Booth believed that in London it was common for a quarter of working-class earnings to go on drink (4–6s a week out of a wage of 24s), while Rowntree in York put the fraction at a minimum of one-sixth of earnings;[91] a recent estimate is somewhat lower than these – 15 per cent of total consumer expenditure in 1876, falling to 12–13 per cent in 1900.[92] But averages conceal individuals: actual consumption varied with occupation, region, custom and, not least, personal taste. Some ironworkers in Middlesbrough spent half their wages on drink,[93] and Rowntree and

Table 6.4   Average weekly expenditure on alcoholic drinks by trades, 1899

	s	d		s	d.
Charcoal makers	1	0½	Coal miners	4	1¼
Cocoa factories	1	6	Builders	4	2¼
Cotton mills	2	0	Engineering trades	4	4¼
Cutlery and file-makers	2	8½	Saw mills	5	0¼
Cabinet-makers	3	5½	Painters	6	1½
Chemical works	3	7½	Dock workers	8	4½

Source: Joseph Rowntree and Arthur Sherwell, *The Temperance Problem and Social Reform*, 1899, 438

Sherwell cited the case of a feltmaker and his wife earning 25s a week who drank five pints of beer each weekday and ten pints on Saturdays and Sundays (15s).[94] An analysis of expenditure on drink by different trades does not disclose a very consistent pattern except that those in strenuous occupations, like miners and dockers, were among the heaviest consumers and indoor factory workers generally among the lightest, but heavy drinking also continued to characterize some skilled craft-workers like engineers and painters (see Table 6.4).

Charles Booth also believed that 'a steady artisan' drank two quarts of beer a day (4s 8d a week), but what worried reformers was that some of the heaviest drinking was done by those who could afford it least – that 'the people drink enough to keep them poor'.[95] The relationship between drink and pauperism provided a rich field for social statisticians, who reached widely differing conclusions: in 1869 the Convention of Canterbury, after enquiring of Masters of Workhouses, stated that at least 75 per cent of those receiving poor relief owed their condition 'directly or indirectly' to drunkenness, though Booth put the figure much lower at 21–25 per cent, less important as a cause of pauperism than old age or ill-health.[96] The precise connection between drink and crime was similarly disputed, Lord Chief Justice Coleridge in 1891 going so far as to say that 'if England could be made sober, three-fourths of her gaols might be closed'.[97] The prevailing view was that heavy drinking was a voluntary act, the result of moral failure and weakness of character or, as some teetotallers believed, of sin. In the early nineteenth century a few doctors like Thomas Trotter and Thomas Sutton began to recognize alcoholism as a disease,[98] but only from the 1870s was a campaign launched by the British Medical Association and the National Association for the Promotion of Social Science for the treatment of alcoholics: eventually in 1898 the Inebriates Act sanctioned the establishment of government reformatories, though only for the compulsory treatment of criminal inebriates.[99]

If alcohol was sinful, so also were the places where the innocent were tempted and corrupted, and from 1834 onwards a stream of official committees of inquiry debated how access to drink should be controlled and limited. Particular criticism was directed at the 'gin palaces' that began to appear from 1815 but multiplied after 1830 in competition with the new beershops. Gin palaces broke completely from the domestic character of alehouses, where the taproom had been the family's kitchen: now customers were separated from servers by bars, rooms were provided for different classes of customers – public bars, parlours, 'snugs' and so on – and some had discreet side entrances where women could enter unobserved. Always the characteristic was ornament and display, much use of mirrors, engraved glass, bright gas-lamps and highly polished woodwork: 'The domesticity of the old pub gave way to the commercial glamour of the new people's palaces, gaudy compensations for the meanness of everyday life.'[100] Some had 'long rooms' that could accommodate up to 300 people; others had 'singing saloons' for 'free-and-easies', very popular on Sunday evenings. In many areas public houses were the only places with rooms sufficiently large to hold meetings, and they therefore served as the clubhouses of trade unions and the 'lodges' of Friendly Societies: again, some acted as banks for changing notes into coin (with the expectation that drink would be bought for the service), and in Wales some mining employers owned their own pubs, in which 'truck' tickets could be exchanged for beer.[101] In dock work publicans were intimately associated with employment, and in the Port of London most of the 'undertakers' who organized the unloading of coal were publicans, and the necessary qualification for a 'constant man' was that he should be a heavy drinker.[102]

In these and many other ways the public house was, as Booth put it, 'the primordial cell of British social life', but by mid-century whatever claims it may once have had to be a common meeting-place of all social classes was long past. The public house of the later nineteenth century was socially and, to an extent, sexually segregated: it was the working man's 'home from home' but not his wife's if she valued her respectability. Only in the poorest, slum district of York in 1900 were women found in considerable numbers in the thirty-nine local pubs, and three-quarters of them stayed for less than 15 minutes – they came for a quick nip rather than for social drinking like the men. In a pub in a respectable district of York used mainly by artisans and clerks, only 9 per cent of drinkers were women.[103]

Nevertheless, the issue of 'women and drink' was much debated towards the end of the century in a new context. Although there was no empirical evidence to support the view, some observers believed that there was now more female drinking, and that this was 'one of the unexpected results of the emancipation of women'. Such 'emancipation' may well have progressed further in London than in more puritanical York, for Charles Booth thought that

> On the one hand, she has become more independent of man, industrially and financially, and on the other more of a comrade than

before, and in neither capacity does she feel any shame at entering a public-house.[104]

According to the same source, women treated each other to drinks as much as men, and some drank to excess – 'we like to have a little fuddle on Monday' (? after washday). Contemporaries also believed that there was more drinking at home by wives, both working class and middle class: bored by life in the suburbs, with husbands out at work and children in school, they made use of 'grocers' licences' to buy drink on the household account and imbibe in secret.[105]

Female intemperance came to be widely discussed at the end of the century by politicians, the medical profession and eugenicists as part of the debate about 'physical deterioration' and Britain's supposed economic and imperial decline. 'A drink-sodden population is not the true basis of a prosperous Empire',[106] according to Lord Rosebery in 1902. The effects of drink on the mothers of the race and their children were debated by the Inter-Departmental Committee on Physical Deterioration (1904) following the revelations of Britain's unfitness during the South African War, when 34.6 per cent of volunteers were rejected on medical grounds. Mothers should take greater responsibility for the welfare of their children, wives for that of their husbands. Some women were 'tainted with incurable laziness and distaste for the obligations of domestic life':[107] they produced unpalatable, half-cooked meals that drove their husbands out to seek warmth and cheer in the public house.

If the public house could not be abolished – and total prohibition of the liquor trade was never a serious possibility in Britain – perhaps it could be reformed into decency and cleanliness, a place where good beer, non-alcoholic drinks and food would be served, newspapers and games provided – a respectable social centre to which families could resort without fear or shame. Such changes would require structural alterations and refurbishments to existing premises and, reformers believed, publicans who had no financial interest in pushing the sales of intoxicants but were paid fixed salaries – what came to be known as 'disinterested management'. These ideas were first proposed by the Revd Sidney Godolphin Osborne in 1852 and adopted in a few rural parishes in Dorset, Oxfordshire and Hertfordshire, usually on the initiative of clergy or paternalistic landowners.[108] In Birmingham the radical Mayor, Joseph Chamberlain, proposed an alternative scheme for municipal ownership of public houses, an extension of what had already been done with gas and water undertakings, and based on the 'Gothenburg system' in Sweden. Pubs would be strictly controlled by managers, their numbers reduced, and profits used for civic improvements: his scheme was accepted by the Corporation but rejected by Parliament in 1877. What happened in Birmingham and some other cities in the 1880s and 1890s was a major rebuilding of pubs by brewers experiencing a decline in sales and strong competition for custom: magnificent new premises appeared, often in Gothic and Renaissance styles, with elaborate interiors and comfortable seating to discourage 'perpendicular drinking' at the bar.[109] The most successful of the 'disinterested management' schemes was the People's Refreshment Houses Association, sponsored by Dr Jayne, the Bishop of Chester, in 1896 to acquire existing licensed premises and reform them by providing temperance drinks and food as well as beer: they would then be managed as public 'trusts'. By 1907 the PRHA and associated trusts had acquired 233 premises, mainly in small towns and villages,[110] and it seemed possible that a successful alternative to the brewers' tied house system had been found.

IV

By 1914 the moralistic case for liquor control was already losing ground to 'national efficiency' arguments. During the First World War these became paramount, and the measures that governments took to curb drinking, though conceived as temporary, in fact mark a turning-point in the history of liquor consumption. As Henry Carter, one of the architects of the policies, wrote in 1919,

> It used to be stated that men could not be made sober by Act of Parliament . . . This view cannot now be sustained. Recent measures have proved an effective remedy for much that was undesirable and detrimental to national efficiency.[111]

What was remarkable during the war was that although wages, particularly of semi-skilled and unskilled workers, rose rapidly and there was practically full employment, beer consumption fell by almost half and convictions for drunkenness (England and Wales) from 190,000 in 1913 to 29,000 by 1918. 'A profound change in the drinking habits of large classes of the population has been initiated.'[112]

Temperance had long been a strong influence in the Liberal Party, but the strategic reasons for liquor control were food shortages, especially of grain and sugar, and the effects that heavy drinking was having in the early months of the war on industrial output, particularly in shipyards and munition factories. In a much-quoted speech in 1915 Lloyd George said, 'Drink is doing more damage in the war than all the German submarines put together'; in some munitions areas it was reported that not only 'Saint Monday' was regularly observed, but 'Saint Tuesday' and even 'Saint Wednesday'. Government acquisition of the entire liquor trade was seriously considered, but rejected in favour of ever-tightening controls, beginning with closing of public houses at 10 p.m. and greatly increased beer duties.[113] In 1915 the Defence of the Realm (Amendment) Act established a Central Control Board (Liquor Traffic) with powers to take complete state control in any area producing war materials: in these, opening hours were reduced from 19½ to 5½ hours a day, and the sale of alcohol on credit and 'treating' were prohibited. Nationally, the output of beer was reduced from 33 million 'standard' barrels (that is, at 1055° gravity) to 13.8 million by 1918, though because the strength was gradually lowered to 1030° by 1918 the 'bulk' barrelage (that is, actual quantity of liquid) was 19 million barrels; this still represented a fall in consumption approaching half, and of a considerably weaker beer.[114]

Social engineering was carried furthest in a few, highly sensitive areas, Enfield Lock, the Cromarty Firth and, most importantly, the Gretna and Carlisle districts. In 1915 a site surrounding Gretna was chosen by the Ministry of Munitions for the largest of its new National Factories. Its building involved virtually the creation of a new town by more than 10,000 navvies earning high wages: drunkenness threatened a breakdown of public order and serious delays in the work. In 1916 the Control Board took over the drink trade in the area, acquiring 119 licensed premises and four breweries in Carlisle and 134 premises in Maryport and district. About half the public houses were closed as 'redundant', the remainder placed under salaried managers and strict controls, including complete Sunday closure, a 'spirit-less Saturday' and no sale of alcohol to people under 18. There were, however, some constructive measures along the lines of the 'improved public house': some served meals, some provided pianos, billiard tables and newspapers, some seated all customers at tables to which waiters brought their orders.

The Carlisle experiment undoubtedly achieved its main object of greatly reducing drunkenness and disorder in the area'.[115] Nationally, there was some public resentment at the doubling in price of beer, its reduced strength and the limited opening hours, but organized labour generally accepted these restrictions as a necessary sacrifice, and temperance reformers applauded them. For alcohol, government control went further in a dirigiste direction than in any other aspect of food policies, which did not include any direct rationing until the beginning of 1918; with drink, moral and national efficiency considerations combined powerfully to 'make people sober'.

Any expectation that beer-drinking would return to pre-war levels was quickly unrealized. Between 1919 and 1939 consumption remained at historically low levels, though with variations reflecting the state of the economy and employment: it rose in the brief post-war boom until 1920, fell from 1920 to 1922 and from 1929 to 1932, with some recovery from 1922 to 1924 and from 1932 to 1937. Nevertheless, the average annual consumption of 13 gallons per head in the 1930s was only half that of 1900 (see Table 6.5).

Such a dramatic fall is surprising, since although the inter-war years were marked by high unemployment, the majority of people enjoyed a rise in real wages of around 35 per cent over the 20 years. Unemployment was certainly an influence on the downturn in consumption in the early 1930s, and it fell particularly on beer-drinking occupations like mining,

Table 6.5 Beer consumption in the UK, excluding Eire, 1919–38 (gallons/head/year, based on standard barrels)[a]

1919	19.34	1926	16.57	1933	12.42
1920	20.66	1927	16.68	1934	12.84
1921	18.05	1928	15.92	1935	13.44
1922	14.87	1929	16.28	1936	13.74
1923	16.99	1930	15.47	1937	14.37
1924	17.82	1931	12.93	1938	14.32
1925	17.78	1932	10.73	1939	14.6

Source: Gourvish and Wilson, Table VIII, 618.

Note

[a]   These statistics are based on standard barrels of 1055° gravity. Because most beer was brewed well below this at *c.* 1040°, the actual quantity of beer as drunk, the 'bulk' barrelage, was approximately a third greater.

shipbuilding and the steel industry, but at its height of 3.25 million in 1931–2 it affected only a fifth of the total workforce; the rest, with increased disposable income, would hardly have been deterred by tax changes that raised the average price of a pint of draught beer from 6d to 7d in the early 1920s and to 7d again between 1931 and 1933.[116] It is more likely that the low consumption levels of the war years were perpetuated by continued stricter licensing and, more importantly, new leisure patterns, which replaced the former centrality of the pub in working-class life. Under the Licensing Act 1921, public houses were not allowed to open before 11 a.m., had to close for at least two hours in the afternoon and at 11 p.m. in London and 10 p.m. elsewhere: total opening hours – nine in London and eight elsewhere – were only half those of 1914.[117] There is no clear evidence that the proportion of total abstainers increased significantly between the wars, an estimate suggesting that 10 per cent of men and 20 per cent of women were non-drinkers in 1935;[118] what happened is that those who formerly drank continued to do so, but drank less. In 1891 beer consumption in London had been 46 standard gallons per head per year, in 1928 it was 23 gallons, exactly half; in 1914 the poorest Londoners had spent around a quarter of their earnings on drink, in 1928 15 per cent was the average for all employed London workers. A further change since the 1890s was that the average age of drinkers in public houses was about 10 years higher, and there were now relatively fewer drinkers under 25.[119] A similar picture emerged from Seebohm Rowntree's second social survey of York in 1936. Here the average working-class family expenditure on drink was 7s a week or 10 per cent of earnings, considerably less than the 16.6 per cent of 1900, and buying only half as much beer. Although there was still some heavy drinking in York, it was mainly confined to older men, and no new group of heavy drinkers had appeared.[120] Traditional drinking patterns survived more strongly in industrial towns of the Midlands and the North than in London and the South. Mass Observation's study of drinking in 'Worktown' (Bolton, Lancashire) in 1938 found that 90 per cent of pub-goers were over 25 and only 16 per cent were women: the usual drink of men was mild beer at 5d a pint, of women bottled Guinness, stout or brown ale. About 60 per cent of the drinkers were 'regulars', using the same pub almost every night, known by their first names and served with their usual drink without ordering: they averaged 3.16 pints on weeknights, 4.57 pints on Sundays. Asked why they drank, 53 per cent said for health or beneficial physical effects – 'nourishing', 'tonic', energy, laxative, sleep-inducing, 'lead in my pencil', 'it is food, drink and medicine to me'. The other main reason, given by 35 per cent of respondents, was for social/companionship purposes: several men said that they did not much like the taste of beer, but used the pub for friendship.[121]

The principal reason for the decline in consumption was a remarkable growth of counter-attractions requiring time and money that might otherwise have been spent in the public house. A restructuring of the lifestyles of many working-class people was bringing them closer to middle-class norms of behaviour and consumption, a transformation that resulted from rising real incomes, smaller family size and changes in occupational structure as traditional manual work declined and more supervisory, clerical and minor professional employments opened up. The movement of population out of old city centres was also an important factor: in the new council and speculatively built suburban estates, the pride of possessing modern homes with more space, gardens and amenities absorbed more time, cost and interest than life in small, terraced houses or two or three rooms.[122] Here there was encouragement for a more privatized family life as well as space for friends and entertainments: in 1935 nine out of ten homes had a wireless set; many had gramophones and pianos bought on hire-purchase. With shorter working hours, gardening and the cultivation of allotments (936,000 in 1934) became popular leisure activities, while outside the home new forms of mass entertainment were especially attractive to younger people: in 1935 there were 4,400 cinemas with a weekly attendance of 18 million as well as many more dance halls, theatres, music-halls, social and sporting clubs, cafés, teashops and restaurants. More people were now taking an annual holiday and enjoying a new mobility by excursion trains, coaches, motor-cycles and cars (1.7 million cars in 1936).[123] Such changes constituted new freedoms for many working people, including a greater emancipation from drink than the temperance movement had ever achieved.

The response of the trade to falling demand and increasing competition was to try to make beer more attractive. This took two main forms, advertising and public house improvements. From 1933 the Brewers' Society organized a co-operative advertising campaign with the all-embracing slogan 'Beer is Best', associated with images of sport, recreation and relaxation (the temperance movement responded with 'Beer is Best left Alone'), while individual brewers projected similar 'health' messages –

'Bass gives an edge to your appetite and promotes good digestion', Younger's beer is 'Just What the Doctor Ordered', and, best known of all, 'Guinness is Good for You'. The fact that demand for beer picked up somewhat after 1933 may have been partly due to the effects of advertising – many of the respondents to the Mass Observation survey of 1938 stressed the 'healthfulness' of the drink – or to recovery from the worst of the depression, or to both.

The other line of defence was to try to improve the image of the public house by making it brighter, cleaner, more comfortable and attractive to a wider clientele including the middle classes, women and younger drinkers. In a speech to the trade the Director of the Brewers' Society, Sir Edgar Sanders, said: 'We want to get the beer-drinking habit instilled into thousands, almost millions, of young men who do not at present know the taste of beer'.[124] Improvements to pubs usually involved opening up small, dark bars, 'saloons' and 'snugs' to more space, light and air, providing comfortable seating and a wider range of drinks including lighter beers, soft drinks and cocktails. The aim was to destroy the sordid 'spit-and-sawdust' image of many old Victorian pubs, and to attract more respectable, discerning customers, who would enjoy a social evening in pleasant surroundings. Such changes were officially approved by the Royal Commission on Licensing (1929–32), which rejected demands for greater licensing restrictions although it recommended 'a further test' of the Carlisle public ownership scheme.[125] Brewers had their best opportunity to create improved public houses when they built new premises in suburban housing estates and on arterial roads to cater for the motorized customer: some were large and lavish, with 'cocktail lounges', conservatories, games rooms, even swimming pools and tennis courts, while in the suburbs of York some had concert rooms and permanent orchestras. 'Poetry in Pubs' was begun by 'The Taverners' in 1937, and some brewery companies sponsored 'Tavern Concerts' of classical music.[126] Although architectural aesthetes had fun with 'Brewers' Tudor', 'Plywood Jacobean' and 'Neo-Georgian County Grammar School' styles,[127] most people liked them; they no longer wanted a 'home from home', but an environment that, like the cinema, represented ambitions and dreams – 'the portals to the world of fantasy'.

The history of beer during the Second World War was very different from that in the First, both output and consumption continuing the rise that had begun in the later 1930s. National efficiency was not now threatened by drunkenness and industrial unrest, and in these circumstances government could regard reasonable supplies of beer (as of tea) to civilians and the forces as an aid to national morale at a time when many foods were rationed. Brewing materials were strictly controlled, and the United Kingdom was divided into eighty-eight zones, each to supply its own needs as far as possible: public houses were required to take from the nearest brewery, even if this meant breaking a tied house agreement.[128] The main public complaints were about prices, which rose from an average

Table 6.6 Beer consumption in the UK, 1945–95 (gallons/head/year, based on bulk barrelage)

1945	22.3	1960	18.9	1980	26.0
1950	18.4	1965	20.1	1985	24.2
1955	17.8	1970	22.6	1990	24.3
1958	17.1	1975	25.5	1993	22.4
		1979	27.1	1995	21.9

Sources: 1945–90, Gourvish and Wilson, Tables VIII and XI, 1990–5, Customs and Excise Reports, Brewers and Licensed Retailers Association Statistical Handbook

of 5d a pint for draught beer in 1939 to 1s by 1945, and strength, which was reduced by 15 per cent. At this lower gravity, bulk barrelage increased from 24.7 million in 1938 to 31.3 million in 1944 and consumption from 20.3 gallons a head per year to 25.6 gallons.

From 1945 consumption followed an erratic course, though with three distinguishable periods – a fall from 1945 to 1958, a rise from then until 1979, followed by another decline which has persisted to the present (see Table 6.6). Consumption per head in 1995 was almost exactly where it had stood at the end of the war: for those aged over 15 it was 27.1 gallons a year, or 4.1 pints a week. In the immediate post-war years the continuation of 'austerity' controls over raw materials restricted any expansion by brewers, while the duty on beer was raised even higher than in wartime: labour and transport difficulties sometimes resulted in 'No Beer' notices in public houses. When food was derationed between 1950 and 1954 consumers were at last able to indulge their tastes for meat, butter, sugar and other previously scarce items as well as resume spending on clothes, housing, furniture, motoring and holidays. Rising living standards in the 1950s did not therefore result in increased beer consumption. Leisure activities became more family-centred and home-based, often around the new television set, and while more people were learning to drink wine on the Costas, fewer were drinking beer in public houses.

The downward trend was, however, reversed in 1958, and for the next 20 years a revival raised consumption by 60 per cent by 1979. During this period beer shared in a general rise in alcohol consumption, its annual increase being 2.4 per cent while that of wine was 7.4 per cent and of spirits 5.2 per cent.[129] There appear to be two main reasons for this change. In these relatively affluent years before the return of high levels of unemployment, more people had disposable income for consumer goods, new leisure activities and for drink. Second, the beer market itself underwent a restructuring with the growth in popularity of lager, which until the 1960s had been mainly available as a high-priced, bottled import: lager then began to be brewed under licence by British brewers and available on draught. It appealed to a wider social spectrum than 'mild' or 'bitter', especially to younger drinkers and women, and the youth market in the

1960s and 1970s was both larger and more affluent than formerly. Also important was the development of 'keg' draught beers, which were carbonated and pasteurized, and had some of the brightness and sparkle of bottled pale ales: they also had good keeping qualities and could be served by less skilled bar staff. Both lagers and keg beers were very suitable for canning, and supermarket sales for home consumption were another significant aspect of the growth in demand at this time.

Public houses, too, underwent change as they began to adapt to the booming leisure industry in which customers required comfort, good service and, often, a choice of cooked meals well beyond the limited range of traditional bar food. The microwave oven made it possible to serve pre-prepared dishes quickly, enabling pubs to compete successfully with cafés and restaurants, especially at lunchtime. By 1972 the pub had been so far civilized and sanitized that the Erroll Committee recommended later opening hours, the abolition of the afternoon closure period, and the admission of children under certain conditions: all-day opening for up to 12 hours was allowed by the Licensing Act 1988.

At 27.1 gallons per head, 1979 was the peak year of post-war beer consumption. Its subsequent decline to 21.9 gallons in 1995 is not easily explained, though it seems that the state of the economy again reasserted itself as a significant influence on demand. Beginning with the recession of 1979–81, unemployment rose to more than 3 million by 1986 (11.2 per cent), declined in the late 1980s, but again returned to over 3 million in 1993: the loss of jobs in mining and manufacturing industry was particularly heavy, directly affecting the incomes of traditional beer-drinkers. At the same time, increases in duty and VAT contributed to a trebling in the price of beer between 1980 and 1995. Yet economic constraints did not prevent an increase in wine consumption of 58 per cent between 1979 and 1990, and major growth in the soft drinks market (see Chapter 5). This suggests that the beer market was still critically dependent on manual workers, and that the favourable image of lager became tarnished in the 1980s by publicity about under-age drinking and 'lager louts'.

Since the last war both food and drink have absorbed much smaller proportions of household expenditure than during the nineteenth century. In 1960 food accounted for 30.5 per cent, alcoholic drink for 3.2 per cent; in 1975 the proportions were 24.8 per cent and 5.1 per cent (the peak year) and in 1994/5 17.8 per cent and 4.3 per cent respectively. In this last year household spending on alcoholic drinks averaged £12.33 a week, of which beer and lager were £7.05, just under 60 per cent.[130] Men were much heavier consumers of alcohol than women – an average of 13.9 units a week compared with 4.2 units – but although semi-skilled and unskilled men still drink most of all (15.6 units) they are now closely followed by managerial and junior professional workers.[131] A major change since the war, however, is that beer consumption now declines with the increasing age of drinkers, a reversal of the former pattern: in 1995 the heaviest regular consumers were males aged 18–24 (12.6 pints per week), the lowest those aged over 50 (8 pints per week).[132]

The structure of the market has changed radically in recent years. Lager has emerged as the clear favourite (54.8 per cent of all beer in 1995), while 'mild' beer, formerly very popular, has shrunk to 2.8 per cent of the market for draught. Much more beer is now sold in packaged, particularly canned, form, which first appeared in the 1960s: in 1995 packaged beers represented 34.6 per cent of the market, enjoying competitive pricing in supermarkets and convenience for home consumption. Drinking in public houses has fallen correspondingly, although no new institution has challenged their primacy as social centres, and 29 per cent of British adults still visit a pub at least once a week.[133] Almost all now serve food, of varying choice and quality, and many are restaurants in all but name: pubs are now 40 per cent of all catering outlets in Britain, and catering accounts for 25 per cent of pub turnover. However, the idea of pubs as 'continental-type cafés' where whole families could enjoy food, drink and amusement, has not yet been realized; Children's Certificates were legalized in England and Wales early in 1995, but by June 1996 only 2,750 had been issued, mainly, it seems, because of the structural alterations required and restrictions imposed by licensing magistrates. Although a few traditionalists mourn the passing of the old pub, there is little danger now that children would be exposed to sights and sounds of drunkenness, swearing and brutality. Drinking by children is, however, a social problem that has caused recent concern: in 1995 it was estimated that 6 per cent of boys and 5 per cent of girls aged 11–15 drank more than the recommended adult limits (21 units a week for men, 14 for women: ½ pint of beer = 1 unit), and that for 16–19-year-olds the proportions rose to 15 per cent and 8 per cent respectively.[134]

A different sort of concern is voiced by some serious beer-drinkers who campaign for a more traditionally made product and a greater variety of local brews, which were available before the concentration of the industry into a handful of large companies. Some reaction has recently arisen against carbonated, 'characterless' keg beers in favour of cask-conditioned products brewed by small, independent firms, which produce beers of individual flavour and strength. The movement began in 1963 with the Society for the Preservation of Beers from the Wood, and, more actively, in 1971 with the formation of CAMRA (the Campaign for Real Ale). With their encouragement there are now around 150 publican-brewers and 'microbreweries' making a small dent in the domination of the large, brand-name brewers who, in 1995, spent £102 million on advertising. These complaints of 'traditional' beer-drinkers of the present day echo the concerns of nineteenth-century consumers about the monopolistic development of the brewing industry and its hold over 'tied' houses. Yet beer has proved to be remarkably resilient to all the changes in British drinking habits that have occurred over the last three centuries. Britain still drinks half as much as at the height of Victorian consumption in the 1870s and more than between the two World Wars: most is now lighter, paler, fizzier than formerly, some of it barely alcoholic, and the alleged British preference for warm mild beer has yielded to one for sharper, cold lagers. In one respect there has been some return to the much older pattern of consumption in the home and as an accompaniment to meals. The convenience of the can and supermarket shopping has resulted in an increasing proportion of beer being bought, often by women, for home consumption: like the weak table beer of the past, it is drunk for refreshment, not for intoxication. The overall trend has been towards moderation, and even those who drink beer every day averaged only 10.1 pints per week in 1995,[135] not much more than some heavy drinkers in Victorian England would have consumed in a day.

7 Wine: 'Use a little wine . . .'

Drink no longer water, but use a little wine
for thy stomach's sake and thine often infirmities.
I Timothy, v. 23

In the context of British drinking habits wine holds an ambiguous place, since until very recent times its consumption was so small and socially restricted that its importance in the lives of most people could almost be dismissed as negligible. Yet wine has been consumed in Britain since pre-Roman times, and its secular and religious significance has greatly exceeded any statistical measurement. The pleasure of the serious wine-lover, according to Robert Capon, lies in

> drinking in all the natural delectabilities of wine, taste, color, bouquet, its manifold graces, the way it complements food and enhances conversation, and its sovereign power to turn evenings into occasions, to lift eating beyond nourishment to conviviality.[1]

The romantic discourse of wine, a constant theme since Hellenic times, has tended to obscure its more practical uses – as a thirst-quencher and coolant, as an anaesthetic and disinfectant, and as a medicine used in a wide range of treatments: it is also a valuable article of diet, the estimated consumption of an adult male in the Roman period of a litre a day contributing around a quarter of his caloric needs.[2] But beyond any such material benefits, wine has carried symbolic meanings unlike any other drink. It has always been a social lubricant, an essential component of celebrations and festivities for those whose means allowed: it was an elite drink, a status symbol associated with costly vessels of silver and glass, often with elaborate rituals of toasting and pledging, which honoured guests and confirmed fellowship.[3] For Roland Barthes wine is 'above all, a converting substance, capable of reversing situations and states . . . for instance, making a weak man strong or a silent one talkative. Hence its old alchemical heredity, its philosophical power to transmute'.[4]

This power of wine to transmute was central to the Eucharist in the Christian Church, especially in the Roman Catholic formulary, where it became 'the blood of Christ' – hence the use of red wine as a metaphor for the sacrificial blood.[5] In fact, the ritual use of wine long pre-dated Christianity, libations to the gods being central in the Jewish tradition as well as in Egyptian, Greek and Roman cultures, but for two millennia it was specifically sanctioned in the Christianized West while in other societies it was a forbidden narcotic. This religious approval of wine posed difficulties for nineteenth-century teetotallers, who attempted to redraft some 500 Biblical references into non-alcoholic forms, usually unfermented grape juice.[6] The significance of the controversy was that in temperance and puritanical circles it fostered a distrust of wine as 'foreign', 'Papist' and alien, if not positively sinful.

I

The origins of wine – the fermented juice derived from many fruits, berries and plants – are traceable to at least the fourth millennium BC in the eastern Mediterranean and Mesopotamia. The earliest wine was probably made from the date palm,[7] but vines were cultivated in the Aegean in the third millennium, and grape wine was traded from Israel to Egypt.[8] Viticulture spread easily to Greece, where wine was specifically ordained in the cult of Dionysus with symbolic associations of well-being, warmth, blood and virility.

The traditional account that in Britain wine was unknown before the Roman occupation[9] has now been challenged by evidence that England was already importing Italian wine in the second century BC.[10] Nevertheless, viticulture followed rapidly on the heels of Roman conquests in north-western Europe, many vineyards being established in southern England:[11] subsequently, cultivation accompanied the spread of Christianity since wine was required for the Eucharist, and many monastic estates developed vineyards at least as far north as York. The Domesday survey of 1086 identified 130 English vineyards, 78 lay and 52 ecclesiastical.

Through the medieval period consumption of wine was relatively high by later standards, but it never rivalled beer as the drink of the masses. It was drunk by those who possessed or desired status – kings, courtiers, nobles, senior clerics and wealthier townspeople, especially holders of public office: a banquet or hospitality was incomplete without wine. Consumption expanded after the marriage of Henry II to Eleanor of Aquitaine in 1152, which brought the important wine-producing districts of Gascony under the English Crown and fostered what became a major taste for claret: an estimated wine consumption of 8 pints per head per year in the mid-fourteenth century was not reached again until 1966.[12] The drinking habits of the English people were profoundly influenced by political and economic factors as, for example, in 1353 when a trade agreement with Lisbon and Oporto brought quantities of Iberian table wines in return for fishing rights. Sir Charles Petrie went so far as to suggest that 'Changes of taste are mainly imposed from without, and are the result of legislation, taxation and wars; they are forced upon, rather than demanded by, the average palate'.[13]

One early exception to this theory, however, was the strong taste for sweetened and spiced wines, which developed in the later Middle Ages. Sweetness was already characteristic of English ale and mead, and the highly seasoned food required strongly flavoured drinks to accompany it and to counteract the saltiness of preserved meat and fish. Honey and, later, sugar were therefore added to many wines,[14] while those from southern Europe and the Levant that were naturally sweet, such as Malmsey, Malaga and Madeira, were much prized. Made drinks like hippocras (red wine, honey or sugar, cinnamon, ginger, nutmeg, grains of paradise, cloves and galingale) were also popular, and regarded as therapeutic as well as pleasurable.[15] The appropriation of these new commodities, sugar and spices, depended on the development of trade routes with the East, mainly through Venice, but was primarily a result of taste and fashion rather than political constraint.

The popularity of wine increased in the Tudor period with the growth of wealth and foreign trade: in a competitive age when 'men gaped for gain', wine demonstrated status and success, whether drunk at home or in the growing number of inns and taverns, which were socially distinct from alehouses.[16] The contemporary commentator, William Harrison, in 1577 believed that some eighty kinds of wine were imported from France, Spain, Italy, Germany, Greece and the Levant, while a new wine, 'sherris sack' (like an Oloroso sherry, but often sweetened), was shipped from Jerez under agreement with the Duke of Medina Sidonia.[17] Wine prices continued to be controlled in the reign of Henry VIII – Gascony wine 8d a gallon, Malmsey, sack and sweet wines 12d[18] – considerably more than beer at 1½–3d the gallon according to strength, and clearly indicating that wine was a privileged drink. Although medical opinion generally approved it – Dr Andrew Boorde (in 1542) particularly commended claret to accompany meat – excessive indulgence was not encouraged, and some contemporaries regarded all wine as dangerous. For Walter Raleigh 'it transformeth a man into a beast, decayeth health, poisoneth the breath, destroyeth natural heat . . . maketh a man contemptible, soon old, and despised of all wise and worthy men'.[19]

Puritan strictures against excess appear to have contributed to a reduction in wine consumption in the early seventeenth century, as did Charles I's own example of moderation – he drank only one glass of wine at dinner, which he diluted with water. However, Charles Petrie's argument about the effects of politics on consumption was shortly to be realized.

In 1642 a treaty was made with the newly independent Portugal that established privileges for English merchants in Oporto and Lisbon: these began to establish a major export in what was to become a preferred English wine, 'port'.[20] Then in 1651 Cromwell's Navigation Act prohibited entry to English ports of ships carrying goods other than those of the exporting country. Aimed at England's rivals, the Dutch, it precipitated war and dealt a serious blow at the wine trade, as almost all wines from the Rhine and Moselle and a substantial proportion of French wines had been carried by Dutch vessels. Finally, the Wine Act of 1688 imposed a heavy duty of £4 the tun (252 gallons) on imported wines, setting a maximum retail price for claret at 8s a gallon and 4s for Portuguese and Spanish wines.[21] The pattern of wine consumption was thereby profoundly changed: French wines became increasingly restricted to the most wealthy, while Iberian wines were greatly encouraged. The most expensive of the French wines was a new, sparkling variety, champagne, enjoyed by Charles II in exile and popularized in his Restoration court after 1660.[22] As yet an extremely restricted drink, there is no mention of champagne in the Diary (1659–69) of the up-and-coming Samuel Pepys. He normally drank ale as his 'morning draught', often in a tavern: in cold weather he liked 'purl' (ale sweetened, spiced and heated). His favourite wine was sack, but for the entertainment of guests he kept a cellar of Claret, Canary, Malaga and Tent (Spanish red). In 1663 he noted with approval his first taste of 'Ho Bryan' (Haut-Brion), probably the earliest claret sold under its estate name.[23]

II

The extent of wine consumption in the eighteenth century must be uncertain, since the official Customs statistics of imports cannot take account of the unknown volume of illicit trade. As a heavily taxed article, there was a good market for smuggled wines, especially better-quality French clarets, and an extensive trade along the south and east coasts, which inefficient, and sometimes corrupt, officers were powerless to control.[24] The fact that officially declared imports leapt after 1786, when Pitt reduced the duty on French wines by half,[25] suggests that the earlier figures need to be multiplied by a large factor, in some years possibly doubled (see Table 7.1).

The absence of any sustained growth until the last decades of the century is remarkable, particularly when set against the population increase (1740 c. 6 million, 1800 9 million)[26] and the increasing wealth of England from agriculture, industry and commerce. Assuming that the extent of the illicit trade was more or less constant, a fall in per-head wine consumption in Georgian England is indicated – on the official statistics from around a gallon a year in 1700 to only half a gallon in 1740–80, with a return to a gallon thereafter. Such statistics are of course of little meaning for an

Table 7.1 Wines officially imported into England, 1700–1800 (thousands of Imperial gallons)

1700	4,935	1735	5,127	1770	3,512
1705	2,535	1740	3,192	1775	3,725
1710	3,333	1745	3,367	1780	4,308
1715	4,568	1750	3,246	1785	3,110
1720	4,020	1755	3,474	1790	7,331
1725	5,150	1760	3,240	1795	9,945
1730	4,163	1765	3,808	1800	7,472

Source: G.B. Wilson, *Alcohol and the Nation*, 1940, 359–61

article whose consumption was very largely restricted to the wealthy. Ralph Davis suggests that on the basis of the statistician Gregory King's contemporary estimate of the distribution of social classes in 1688 there would have been less than 200,000 regular wine-drinkers,[27] giving then an annual consumption of about 20 gallons, or 3 pints a week. A hundred years later, when the number of potential wine-drinkers would have been swollen by population growth and greater national wealth, the consumption of regular drinkers would have been considerably less than 3 pints a week.

The explanation for this decline lies in two main factors: tastes and tariffs. In 1700 tea and coffee were not yet in mass consumption; by 1800 the repertoire of drinks had been greatly extended – tea was now drunk across the social divides, and the new type of beer, porter, was widely popular, as were spirits such as gin, rum and brandy. Wine was therefore in competition with other alcoholic drinks and with the sober alternatives of hot beverages, which commended themselves to those influenced by the movement for the reformation of manners; the particularly low levels of consumption in mid-century coincided with both the heyday of cheap gin and the general adoption of tea. But old tastes were also changed, and new ones formed, partly by changes in tariffs, with the need of governments to raise revenue for the long series of wars and to secure allies and trading partners by preferential duties. None had greater effects on English wine-drinking habits than the Methuen Treaty with Portugal (1703), by which tariffs on Portuguese wines would not exceed two-thirds of those on French, in return for the removal of restrictions on the import of English cloth.[28] Under these terms, and subsequent even higher duties on French imports, French wines were practically squeezed out of the legal market, while 'port' came to dominate English wine-drinking habits: in 1770 champagne cost 6s a bottle, claret 4s 6d, red or white port, Lisbon and sherry 1s 6d. Over the whole period 1704–85 legally imported Portuguese wines accounted for 65.4 per cent of the total, Spanish for 29.3 per cent and French for a mere 3.6 per cent.[29]

The port of the early eighteenth century, however, was not the same as that which later generations came to revere, and the Methuen Treaty itself was not responsible for changing tastes from lighter to heavier, fortified wines.[30] The port drunk in Portugal and first imported was a fairly light, sweet table wine: the practice of strengthening it with brandy, which Cyrus Redding, the Victorian authority on wine, dated from 1715 but other authorities not till mid-century, was primarily an innovation by English merchants in Oporto responding to a demand for a strong, sweet wine that travelled and kept well. The addition of spirit checked fermentation, allowing natural sweetness to develop slowly as well as increasing the alcoholic content: expert English factors also learned how to blend and mature port, by the later century for up to 10 or 15 years. The taste was not forced down unwilling throats, which had favoured sweetness in wine for centuries past and which, by the eighteenth century, had also developed a strong appetite for ardent spirits. The adoption of fortified port therefore neatly combined an appetite for sweetness and strength in a new, socially fashionable drink.

Port was drunk with, between and after meals – therefore, both as a table and as a recreational wine. Previously, wine had usually been drunk fresh from the cask, and even claret was drunk from the current year's growth; only the development of efficient corks (and corkscrews) allowed wines like port to be bottled and stored.[31] The port bottle normally held five-sixths of a pint, and port was sipped from small glasses over dinner, now at three or four in the afternoon, and by men after the end of the meal, sometimes until the small hours. There is no reason to doubt the contemporary references to three- and four-bottle men whose drinking sessions extended over several hours. Dr Johnson, who was not a heavy drinker, managed three bottles of port at a dinner in University College, Oxford in 1778, apparently with no ill effects.[32] James Boswell often drank to oblivion in bouts of 'spree drinking',[33] while many peers, politicians, judges, poets and authors were heavy imbibers. Until late in the century drinking to excess was not considered disgraceful: on the contrary it was manly and convivial, an aid to wit, good humour and fellowship.

Eighteenth-century wine was not always what it seemed, however, and was sometimes distinctly unwholesome. As early as the fifteenth century the Vintners' Company appointed inspectors to 'prove and assay wines', and subsequently many recipes were published for 'improving' thin or sour wines and passing off inferior qualities at a higher price. Poor wines were coloured with sloes and blackberries, extra flavour added by ginger, cloves, orris root, grains of paradise and elderberries, while in 1696 a receipt for Artificial Claret consisted of cider, clary juice, raisins and blackberries.[34] The would-be adulterator could also easily acquire information from household cookery books, which offered recipes for home-made wines and cordials, a long-established art of the stillroom. Eliza Smith's popular *Compleat Houswife* included sixteen varieties of 'Made Wines' from apricots, cowslips, oranges, raspberries and other fruits, as well as 'English Champagne' and 'English Sack'.[35] These were at least innocuous, consisting of fermented fruit juices with quantities of sugar and raisins, but professional adulterators were less concerned about effects on health. The most dangerous addition, sugar of lead (litharge), was sometimes used to sweeten sour wines, and has been suggested as a major cause of the gout so prevalent in Georgian England.[36] Deliberate adulteration increased at the end of the century when duties were raised during the French Wars, and almost all descriptions of wine – port, claret, Rhenish, Malaga and others – were faked by unscrupulous merchants, druggists and tavern-keepers. From a basis of spirit of wine made from fermenting molasses, colour was provided by burnt sugar, logwood and cochineal, flavour by orange peel and *terra japonica*, astringency by hops or oak chips, while sourness was corrected by plaster of Paris and chalk.[37] The precise extent of these frauds cannot be gauged, but the large literature on the subject and the volume of public complaints at this period suggest that it was extremely widespread.

III

Surprisingly, the growth of wealth in the nineteenth century and the increased size of the middle classes did not result in greater wine consumption. On the contrary, the average consumption in the United Kingdom of 0.46 gallons per head per year in 1800 fell to a mere 0.23 gallons in 1851, recovered somewhat to a peak of 0.56 gallons in 1876, and then remained at between 0.37 and 0.40 gallons until the end of the century.[38] Despite lower levels of duty and positive efforts of governments to encourage wine, the British people were not dissuaded from their attachment to beer and spirits, which in 1898 stood at 31.4 and 1.04 gallons per year respectively.[39]

There was also little change in the types of wines consumed until after 1860, Table 7.2 indicating the continued popularity of the strong, sweet wines, port and sherry, before a modest recovery of French imports in the later decades. In 1830 Spanish and Portuguese wines held 77 per cent of imports: until 1850 port was the largest single import, after which time Spanish sherry held the field until 1873, when French wines moved into first place. Nevertheless, by 1913 Portuguese imports again exceeded French, and together with Spanish made up half the total trade.

The domination of Iberian wines was all the more remarkable since in 1831 the Methuen Treaty was abrogated and all wine duties were equalized at a lower rate of 5s 6d a gallon[40] except for imports from the Cape of Good Hope, which were admitted at half duty – the first 'Empire' wines. Total wine imports rose in the next two decades (see Table 7.2), though the rapid increase of the population (England and Wales 1831 13.9 million, 1851 17.9 million) prevented any substantial change in per head consumption. Wine-drinking had not spread downwards from the narrow circle of the wealthy, and although William IV still drank two bottles of claret at dinner, many men now drank a good deal less than

Table 7.2 Wines officially imported into the UK, 1800–1910 (thousands of Imperial gallons)

	French	Portuguese	Spanish	Total all imports
1800	482	4,814	1,915	7,472
1810	873	6,450	2,358	10,819
1820	240	2,457	979	5,170
1830	352	2,603	2,505	6,880
1840	570	2,980	4,022	9,311
1850	600	3,563	3,827	9,304
1860	2,445	2,536	5,326	12,475
1870	4,779	3,458	7,434	17,775
1880	6,996	3,145	5,395	17,385
1890	6,263	3,991	4,007	16,194
1900	5,383	3,862	4,574	16,804
1910	3,966	3,795	3,262	13,735

Source: George B. Wilson, *Alcohol and the Nation*, 1940, 361–3.

The other, minor contributors to the total were Germany, the Cape of Good Hope, Madeira, the Azores and Canaries

their grandfathers had done. This was mainly due to a growth of 'temperance' in a broad sense – not the absolute abstinence from alcohol of the teetotallers, but a greater refinement of manners and behaviour in which drinking to excess was no longer acceptable in fashionable society. At Court Queen Victoria refused to sit in the drawing-room after dinner until the gentlemen joined the ladies 15 minutes or so later, and at Osborne House, built to Prince Albert's design, the billiard-room, formerly male territory for further drinking, was open-plan to the drawing-room. These social changes accompanied a gradual decline in taste for strong port and its replacement by lighter sherries and Rhenish wines, a natural choice for a German Court.

It is also likely that wine consumption in the first half of the century was restricted by the wide publicity given to adulteration. Many recipe books continued to be available to merchants and innkeepers for faking 'English Claret' and 'English Port', mainly from cider and British spirits,[41] but the public became much more aware of such frauds after the appearance of Fredrick Accum's *Treatise on Adulterations of Food and Culinary Poisons* in 1820. Accum, a leading analytical chemist, claimed that few commodities in England were more adulterated than wine. He described the use of alum, Brazil wood and bilberries to heighten the colour of port, gypsum to rectify cloudy white wines, and oak sawdust to give astringency to immature reds. Much spoiled cider was converted into 'port', the bottles and corks of which were treated with supertartrate of potash to imitate the 'crusting' of old vintages, and, most dangerous to health, preparations of lead were used to prevent acidity and 'recover' ropy wines.[42] Not all this falsification was domestic, however. Until well after mid-century counterfeit sherry made at Cette in the Mediterranean was notorious, as was 'Hambro Sherry' from Hamburg, made from poor-quality German wines and potato spirit.[43] A Select Committee on the Wine Duties in 1852 believed that around a fifth of all wine was faked in some way, probably an underestimate. The problem was that wine was easy and profitable to adulterate, especially port, which because of its strong flavour and deep colour could readily conceal cheap additions like Cape wine. Cyrus Redding claimed in 1851 that port-drinking had declined in recent years because its quality had fallen off so badly.[44]

While beer and spirit consumption was increasing in the 1850s, that of light wines was stagnating, although opinion was beginning to regard them as desirable 'temperance' alternatives to stronger alcohol. The Free Trader, G.R. Porter, argued that 'to the working man wine is altogether denied' by high taxation, and that without duty good French wine could be sold at 6d a bottle and still show a profit: it would be 'a great addition to the innocent enjoyments of the people'.[45] The Chancellor of the Exchequer, William Gladstone, who liked to drink a quart of champagne to his dinner, agreed. He believed that 'It is idle to talk of the taste for port or sherry and the highly brandied wines as fixed and unchangeable', that France had a great capacity to produce wines 'fitted for the taste of the middle and lower classes of this country', and that lower duties would prevent the 'masses of evil . . . fraud and adulteration' that the present system caused.[46] Gladstone's policies neatly combined moral and commercial dimensions when, in 1860, he began a major restructuring of the wine duties and of the accessibility of wine to the public. First, duty on all wines was reduced to 3s a gallon, so ending the former preference to Cape imports. In 1861, however, he gave a preference to light wines (less than 16° alcohol content, later raised to 26°) of only 1s a gallon, while the heavier ports and sherries paid 2s 6d.[47] By the Refreshment Houses Act (1860) restaurants and other 'eating houses' could take out an Excise licence for the sale of wine on their premises, in order, as Gladstone argued, to encourage sobriety by linking drinking with eating. Finally, in 1861, any grocer or other shopkeeper was allowed to take out a 50s licence for the 'off' sale of bottles of wine.[48] 'Gladstone's Claret' could now be bought almost anywhere.

One result of the changes was to open the way for the mass-marketing of cheap wines aimed at a new class of drinker, essentially the lower middle class and better-paid workers. In 1857 the brothers Walter and Albert Gilbey had established a London business selling Cape wines, then enjoying the 50 per cent tariff preference. When Gladstone removed this discount they quickly began offering Bordeaux clarets at 18s a dozen bottles, selling through off-licence agents, mainly grocers, who were now allowed to trade in wine. From 1865 they began to deal directly with French growers, and a little later with growers in Spain, Portugal and central Europe, introducing many new wines to the English market: by 1894, when Gladstone praised Gilbeys as 'the openers of the wine trade', they stocked 192 brands and claimed that one in every seventeen bottles of wine drunk in the United Kingdom bore their label.[49] The Victoria Wine Company, the creation of William Winch Hughes in 1865, worked on the different principle of direct retailing in its own shops – sixty-three by 1879, ninety-eight by the time of Hughes' death in 1886. At this period the firm concentrated on strong Spanish and Portuguese wines at 11d a bottle, 3d for a quarter of a pint in the customer's own jug. Like other pioneers of the retailing revolution, Victoria Wine advertised widely, aiming at the respectable, lower-income consumer who might be persuaded that a glass of wine at Sunday dinner was 'a more genteel thing than drinking a glass of beer': especially 'genteel' was their Saumur 'champagne' at 25s for a dozen bottles.[50] Yet another approach to the mass-marketing of wine was taken by Simon and Peter Yates, who, from 1881, began to acquire existing licensed premises and convert them into 'Wine Lodges'. These consisted typically of one large 'Open Room' with simple benches and scrubbed board floors – the very opposite of the Victorian gin palace – so that customers could be closely supervised. Peter Yates believed that he had a mission to educate the working man and his wife to appreciate good wine and food, and supplied his 'Wine Lodges' and 'Tea-Total Taverns' with quality products from his own farms, butchers' shops and wholemeal flour mill – prime beef sandwiches and pork pies were among the specialities.[51]

In 1880 Gladstone observed that 'the character of the [wine] trade has been fundamentally changed', and that cheap wines had now practically cut the ground from under the feet of the adulterator. The Reports of Public Analysts after 1875 show that wine as imported was almost always sound, and that domestic adulteration, though not unknown, was now rare: in 1884 two samples of 'Fine Old Port' and 'Fine Old Sherry' bought in Salford were declared to be 'innocent of the juice of the grape' and in 1890 the analyst reported of some 'Scotch Port' that 'It is not clear what beverage the purchaser would expect to buy under that name'.[52] But any hope Gladstone may have had of persuading the British to become a nation of wine-drinkers was not fulfilled. By 1880 French imports had almost trebled since 1860 (see Table 7.2), exceeding Portuguese in 1867 and Spanish in 1876. Total imports peaked in 1873 at 21.7 million gallons (1860 12.5 million) but subsequently fell back steadily to 12.3 million gallons by 1913, almost exactly where they had stood 50 years earlier for consumption by a much smaller population: by then both Portuguese and Spanish imports each again exceeded French. One reason was the spread of the vine disease phylloxera to most French vineyards after 1875,[53] causing a rise in prices and scarcity of good-quality wines, but more fundamentally, wine had not commended itself to most British people after a brief flirtation in the 1860s and 1870s. In 1882 a Committee of the British Association estimated that the working classes spent a mere £900,000 a year on wine (£30 million on spirits and £56 million on beer), only 10 per cent of the total of £9 million.[54] The strong support of Gladstone's policies by doctors like Robert Druitt, who recommended light wines as a tonic for nursing mothers, seamstresses, governesses and even children, seemingly had little influence.[55] Mr Pooter, the fictional suburban clerk with social pretensions, might entertain his guests with 'Jackson-Frères' champagne at 3s 6d a bottle, and had port and sherry (1s 3d) on his sideboard, but the working man had not been tempted to exchange three or four pints of beer at his convivial local pub for a shilling bottle of claret at home. Charles Booth noted that many young working people did their courting in public houses because they were ashamed of their homes, and that 'the young men treat the girls to a glass of wine':[56] this was almost certainly port or sherry, or port and lemon, a favourite women's drink, since other wines were rarely available outside the few Wine Lodges.

The general trend in wine-drinking over the century was towards lighter varieties: port was overtaken by sherry in mid-century, and sherry itself by unfortified wines after the 1870s, but port and sherry together still had half the total wine market up to 1914. Both had been drunk as table wines, and in traditional circles like Oxbridge colleges this continued until late in the century: at Queen's College, Oxford, the 'common stock' of the cellar up to 1868 consisted only of fortified wines, mainly port, with some sherry and madeira.[57] Numerous guides to fashionable dining suggested appropriate wines for the various courses: Thomas Walker's *Art of Dining* (1835) recommended punch with turtle soup, champagne with whitebait, and claret with grouse, while the famous chef Francatelli advised Chablis with oysters, sherry or madeira with soup, dry white wines with fish, and Burgundy with the entrées.[58] The gradual introduction in fashionable dinners from the 1860s of *service à la Russe*, in which each course was served separately by waiters, made for a profusion of different wines, but for less formal occasions it remained a matter of choice, the older Forsytes in the 1880s seemingly drinking nothing but champagne through dinner. Normally by this period champagne accompanied the earlier courses, followed by claret with the roasts and ending with port or brandy. But by the 1890s ladies were objecting to men 'soaking' after dinner, and it was said that the Prince of Wales's initiation of smoking cigars in the dining-room dulled the appreciation of delicate clarets and even crusted port. The Edwardian dinner now usually concluded with a fairly brief brandy before the gentlemen joined the ladies for coffee or tea. Some idea of the annual wine budget of an upper middle class family with an income of £800 a year is provided by the estimate of G. Colmore in 1901:

		£	s	d
Claret,	9 doz. bottles at 1s 3d	6	15	0
Port,	1½ doz. at 3s 6d	3	3	0
Sherry,	1 doz. at 2s 8d	1	12	0
Whisky,	4½ doz. at 3s	8	2	0
Brandy,	2 bottles at 5s		10	0
	Total	£20	2	0

There was also £35 a year allowed for 'entertaining', which would have included champagne and other drinks.[59]

During the First World War consumption of wine continued its long-term decline. Unlike beer and spirits, there was no attempt to impose government controls, but supplies from France were badly affected, and total wine imports fell from 11.4 million gallons in 1913 to 7.1 million in 1917, returning to 11.3 million the following year. In 1916 and 1917 port again accounted for almost half of total imports, maintaining the long-established British taste for fortified wine. For a brief period in 1919 the post-war boom and euphoria raised imports to 19.2 million gallons,[60] but as Table 7.3 indicates, they quickly fell back to historically low levels in the inter-war years. The statistics also show that French imports, the main source of table wines, fell dramatically, while Portuguese and Spanish ports and sherries continued their hold on the market. 'Other countries' (Germany, Italy and central Europe) contributed little, but two new sources of wine became significant by 1938. In 1927 Winston Churchill, as Chancellor of the Exchequer, reintroduced a tariff preference for Empire wines (light 2s a gallon, heavy 4s, compared with 3s and 8s respectively on foreign), which considerably encouraged Australian and South African imports: by 1938 these approached a quarter of total imports, Gilbeys and other mass merchants promoting them strongly in this period of depression. The other new feature was the rapid growth of 'British wines' (or 'sweets'), which by 1938 accounted for nearly a third of the market. Some

Table 7.3 Estimated UK wine consumption, 1920–38 (millions of gallons)

	1920	1931	1938
French	3.7	2.1	1.9
Portuguese	5.4	4.7	4.0
Spanish	2.9	2.6	3.4
South African	–	0.6	1.4
Australian	0.5	2.4	3.2
Other countries	0.9	1.2	1.4
British wines	1.6	2.8	6.3
Totals	15.0	16.4	21.6

Source: Richard Stone, *The Measurement of Consumers' Expenditure and Behaviour in the UK, 1920–1938*, Cambridge University Press, 1954, vol. 1, Table 68, 188

Table 7.4 Number of bottles of wine consumed per year by income groups, 1913–14 and 1923–4

1913–14		1923–24	
Income/year £	*Bottles/year*	*Income/year £*	*Bottles/year*
50–100	4	100–150	None
100–150	8	150–200	6
150–200	16	200–250	12
250–500	30		

Source: The Colwyn Report. Report of the Committee on National Debt and Taxation, App. X (1926)

were derived from native fruits, berries and herbs, and had been manu-factured on a commercial scale by firms like Stones for more than 100 years, but by the early twentieth century a main source of materials became imported 'must' of grape-juice, raisins and grape-sugar.[61] British wines were free of customs duties, and paid only a small excise tax: in 1938 at an average price of 1.6s a pint they were less than half the cost of imported wines at 3.9s,[62] and represented one of the cheapest forms of alcohol avail-able. Even with their contribution, however, wine consumption remained stubbornly low – 0.42 gallons per head per year at the peak of 1919–20, 0.34 gallons in 1925, 0.30 in 1930 and 0.31 in 1935.

In 1926 the Colwyn Committee surveyed drinking patterns in Britain, comparing the present with the situation before the war. It found that there was now rather more wine-drinking at home than formerly, partic-ularly of Empire and 'medicated' ('tonic') wines, which were popular with women. Wine consumption was directly related to income, as Table 7.4 suggests.[63] Similarly, Crawford and Broadley's survey of the national diet in 1938 found that wine was drunk with the evening meal by only a minority of the wealthiest classes – 13.7 per cent of the AA class (incomes over £1,000 a year) and 3.4 per cent of class A (incomes £500–£999 a year).[64] For the majority of people between the wars 'wine' meant port or sherry. When drunk at home, it was for celebratory occasions like weddings or Christmas, and mainly for women, while in the pubs of 'Worktown' it meant the same – sherry or port, usually served with lemon, 3d the glass.[65]

Unlike beer, wine was not considered of national importance during the Second World War, and received no preferential treatment in scarce ship-ping space: in any event, many of the wine-producing regions of Europe were under German occupation. What little was available was also taxed much more heavily, the pre-war duties of 4s a gallon on foreign table wines and 8s on fortified rising to 25s and 50s respectively by 1948.[66] Total imports fell from 21 million gallons in 1940 to a mere 4.4 million by 1945, with consumption per head following the same downward trend – 3.7 pints a year in 1937, 1.6 pints in 1942 and 0.7 pints in 1944. After the war it slowly climbed back to 2.2 pints in 1953, 3.0 pints in 1957 and

Table 7.5 Wine-drinking patterns in 1950: (a) men and women over 16 who drink, (b) frequency of drinking, in percentages

(a)			
Wine only	4.6		
Wine and beer	3.1		
Wine and spirits	8.0		
All three	25.3		
(b)			
Wine every day	0.7	⎫	
More than once/week	1.7	⎬	'Regular' wine-drinkers 5.2%
Once/week	2.8	⎭	
Less than once/week	36	⎫	Rarely or never
Never	58.8	⎭	94.8%

Source: B. Seebohm Rowntree and G.R. Lavers, *English Life and Leisure: A Social Study*, London, Longmans, Green, 1951, 164–5

3.6 pints in 1960, returning to the pre-war level.[67] In 1950 another survey indicated how little wine-drinking habits had changed (see Table 7.5). In 1959 the average expenditure of households in the United Kingdom on wines and spirits (they were not then separated) was only 2s 8d a week, rising to 20s ½d in the wealthiest social class. This compared with an average spending on beer of 6s 8d a week and on tobacco of 18s 10½d.[68]

An unprecedented and unpredicted rise in wine consumption began from 1960, when it doubled in the decade and continued to grow strongly subsequently. Table 7.6 shows per head consumption of the whole population for 1960–75 and, more realistically, for those aged over 15 for 1980–95. The present consumption of around 4 gallons a head a year is four times greater than any previously recorded figure, and represents a major new direction in drinking habits, 100 years after Gladstone had hoped to convert Britain to a wine-drinking nation.

The reasons involve a wide range of factors to do with changes in taste, fashion, occupations, leisure and relations between the sexes as well as

Table 7.6 Consumption of wine in the UK, 1960–95 (pints/head/year)

1960	3.6	1980 (aged over 15)	17.9
1964	5.0	1982	19.1
1968	6.5	1985	23.5
1971	7.0	1987	25.9
1972	7.9	1990	27.5
1973	9.3	1993	30.2
1975	11.3	1995	32.1

Sources: 1960–75: Williams and Brake, Table 111.3, 383; 1980–95: *The Drink Pocket Book*, Henley-on-Thames, NTC Publications, 1996, 81

others concerning availability and accessibility. As Britain moved out of austerity after the mid-1950s, rising standards of living provided the economic basis for a revolution in spending and leisure habits. While expenditure on food – historically the largest item in household budgets – took an ever-declining proportion (1960 30.5 per cent of spending, 1995 17.8 per cent),[69] millions of people began to take packaged Continental holidays, to cook Mediterranean-type dishes at home, and to eat out in restaurants in which wine was often a natural accompaniment. Although from the 1970s many heavy industries were in decline, the proportion of people in non-manual occupations increased, contributing to an em-bourgeoisement of society in which many more people now defined themselves as 'middle class'. The democratization of wine-drinking is a symbol of this change for people who before the war would not have contemplated wine with a meal. The growth of wine consumption survived the return of high levels of unemployment in the early 1980s and 1990s because many, though not all, of those affected were still outside the regular wine-consumers.

The initial post-war boost to consumption was provided by Stafford Cripps' reduction of the duty on table wines from 23s a gallon to 13s in 1949, and was followed by further reductions in 1973 when Britain joined the European Community and in 1984 after an EC ruling that wine duties should be harmonized. The fact that they have been raised almost every year since, to stand at £1.30 a bottle in 1997, may have contributed to some slackening in the rate of growth in the most recent years.

Another major stimulus to consumption has been the much greater accessibility and choice of wines since the 1960s. In public houses light wines by the glass became generally available from this time, while the advent of the Wine Bar, a more sophisticated version of the Wine Lodge, provided an attractive alternative to the pub, especially for women. But the most important development was the introduction of wines by super-markets, where bottles could conveniently be added to the shopping without encountering the possible embarrassment of the traditional 'off-licence'. Sainsburys acquired a licence in 1962, quickly followed by the other major stores including even the Co-operative Societies, while in 1966 the abolition of resale price maintenance on alcoholic drinks led to cut-price competition between supermarkets, discount houses and high street wine chains. It was noted in the 1970s that women were now drinking more light wines, aperitifs and champagne than men, and some advert-isers switched from television promotions to women's magazines.[70] In 1997 84 per cent of all wine in Britain was sold by off-licences, and 61 per cent by supermarkets alone. The comfort of modern homes, the attractions of home entertainment, and the penalties for drink-driving have combined with convenience foods and the interest in home cooking to achieve what Gladstone had hoped – to associate wine with meals in the home.

Wine has passed from a drink of privilege to one of mass consumption, and Britain has been at least partially converted to a Europeanization of taste. An estimated 30,450,000 people in the United Kingdom now drink wine, a third of them more than three bottles a month: the largest consumers are in social grades A and B and in the age-group 35–49 years, followed by younger drinkers aged 25–34. But port now accounts for only 0.9 per cent of the wine market and sherry for 3.1 per cent: fortified wines, again as Gladstone hoped, have given way to light table wines at 76 per cent of the market in 1995.[71]

Wine has always carried meanings beyond the mere satisfaction of thirst. In Britain, where it was for centuries a privileged drink, its recent rise is still associated with a degree of sophistication, with celebration, entertaining and special occasions rather than the habitual consumption of southern European countries. To some older, puritanical Britons it can even evoke feelings of guilt associated with a xenophobic distrust of the foreign and Latin, although teetotalism no longer has the significant force it had a century ago. Wine-drinking in Britain still seems to require sanction, and it may be that this is now being provided by new medical evidence about the possible health benefits of moderate consumption. Particular claims have been made for the value of phenols, which can destroy pathogenic bacteria and give some protection to a high cholesterol diet, yeasts which aid digestion, vitamins (B and C) and tannins present in the skins and pips of grapes used mainly for red wines.[72] The lower levels of heart disease in wine-drinking countries like France and Italy compared with Britain and the United States have been particularly associated with the tannins in red wine, which, it is claimed, can inhibit the thickening and clogging of arteries, a main cause of coronary attacks. St Paul's advice to 'use a little wine for . . . thine often infirmities' may have found medical justification.

IV   Vinetum Britannicum, or a Treatise of Cider

(J. Worlidge, 1676)

In several areas of England, especially but not only the western and south-western counties,[73] the alternative to beer was home-produced cider made from fermented apple juice. Although Celtic origins of cider-making have been suggested, it is generally accepted that it was introduced to England from Normandy in the twelfth century,[74] and that production on any scale dates from the thirteenth, when new varieties of bitter apples began to be cultivated, and cider-making spread on manors and monastic estates. Two types of drink were made – 'cyder', made entirely of apple juice, as strong as much imported French claret and regarded as 'the English wine', and 'cider', which was either cyder 'stretched' with water or the product of a second or third pressing of the same apples to produce a much less alcoholic drink for labourers. True 'cyder' was highly esteemed, drunk in royal and noble households and sipped like wine: many writers in the sixteenth and seventeenth centuries extolled its virtues and health benefits while criticizing cider as thin, sour stuff, fit only for the poor.[75]

Major developments occurred in the seventeenth century, when 'improving' landlords in the West Country planted orchards of the Redstreak apple as a cash crop, much improving both the quantity and quality of cider. From ports in the South-West it was taken on board ships as, when matured, it would keep well and was considered by Lind and other doctors to have valuable antiscorbutic properties. It also began to develop a commercial market outside the region, being shipped down the Thames from Lechlade to 'cider houses' in Oxford, London and elsewhere where fine 'cyder' was sold at much the same price as wine. Some of this was bottled, a process developed by Andrew Yarranton around 1670, which allowed a longer fermentation and produced a sparkling drink at the same time as champagne was first entering the market: the fact that French and German imports were restricted by the Navigation Act 1651 and the Wine Act 1688 gave cyder a distinct advantage at this period. In its home territory it was the universal drink, Daniel Defoe in Herefordshire in the 1720s noting that 'for twenty miles together we could get no Beer or Ale in their Public Houses, only cider, and that so very good, so fine and cheap, that we never found fault with the exchange'.

Cider-making also benefited from technical improvements in the later seventeenth century such as the invention of a horse-driven apple mill in 1664 and an improved portable hand-mill, the 'Ingenio', introduced by John Worlidge in the 1670s. Although these undoubtedly increased the scale of output, total cider production cannot be measured since the Excise duty introduced in 1643 applied only to cider for sale, not that made on hundreds of farms, large and small, for household consumption and 'given' to servants and labourers as part of the wage. An estimate that in the decade 1756–65 national consumption ranged between 2½ and 5 pints per person per year[76] gives little idea of how much was drunk in the cider counties – in Herefordshire in the eighteenth century the allowance to farm labourers was around 6 pints a day, and up to 24 pints a day in the harvest field.[77] This was clearly very different from the strong cyder drunk in gentry households, where 'a huge tankard was always placed at each end of the table',[78] or that offered by Parson Woodforde to guests in Norfolk, costing from 6d to 1s a bottle.[79]

The significance of cider in the countryside is illustrated by the development of cults that took curious forms – wassailing the apple trees at Twelfth Night, beating or howling at the trees, burning the bush, burying cake and cider in the orchards, and blessing the apples on Midsummer Eve[80] – fertility rituals intended to ensure the size and quality of the crop. But by the nineteenth century the part-payment of labourers in cider was under attack both by temperance reformers and by philanthropists like Canon Girdlestone in north Devon, who was indignant that labourers' wages in the 1870s were only 8s or 9s a week, plus 3 or 4 pints of cider daily, 'very washy and sour ... valued at 2s a week, but much over-valued'.[81] By the Truck Act 1887, such part-payment of wages was, in theory, made illegal, and some farmers began to offer tea to their men.

This was the crucial decade in the development of the modern cider industry, when in 1887 H.P. Bulmer, son of the Rector of Credenhill, Herefordshire, began making cider with the intention of creating a national market. Travelling round the country, he found that in most towns the response was 'What's cider? We've never heard of it', but gradually won acceptance by advertising and competing at agricultural shows. Bulmer mechanized production by installing steam-driven presses and hydraulic pumps, and was a pioneer of scientific cider-making, installing a labora-tory in 1905.[82] Together with Gaymers and Whiteways in the 1890s (Coates not until 1925) this was the beginning of factory production, with research and marketing aided by the National Association of Cider Makers estab-lished in 1893 by the MP for Hereford, Radcliffe Cooke. Total cider output, estimated at around 20 million gallons in 1870, rose to 33 million in the mid-1880s but then fell to 25 million in 1900 and back to 20 million in 1914. In 1900 two-thirds of production still went to farm consumption, but by 1914 half the output was for retail sale, and at an average price of 3d a pint was very comparable to beer.[83] The decline after the 1880s follows that of alcoholic drinks generally, but with the added effects of heavy rural migration at this time and the reduction of truck payments.

Between the two World Wars total production continued to slide to 16 million gallons in 1938, but the proportion of factory-made output increased from 5 to 13 million, most rapidly after 1932. This suggests that the urban market for commercial cider was now accelerating, with screw-top bottles making it more accessible for home consumption.[84] Manufacturers struggled to raise its image, which still tended to carry asso-ciations of rural unsophistication and poverty.

The emergence of cider into mass consumption dates only from the 1960s, when it began to be widely advertised on television as a drink for young adults: in this respect it paralleled the promotion of soft drinks, with similar associations of sport and activity. Cider also gained from the growing popularity of wine among consumers, who found that dry, slightly carbonated cider was often an acceptable substitute at a favourable price. Most of the cider-makers were acquired by brewery companies, especially Allied Breweries, who were now keen to promote draught, keg cider in their public houses. Consumption rose from 18 million gallons in 1963 to 34 million in 1973, to 49 million in 1980 and then, dramatically, to 123 million in 1995. The annual consumption of the UK population over the age of 15 is now 20 pints a year (wine 32 pints), and has been growing faster than wine. Women are slightly larger consumers than men (52 per cent of cider drinkers), while 55 per cent of drinkers are in the 18–34 age group: significantly, however, three-fifths of cider is drunk in the home and usually integrated into meal patterns.[85] Now in a variety of strengths, flavours and packaging, cider is an established part of the repertoire of modern drinks and can reasonably lay claim to being 'the English wine'.

8 Spirits: 'Water of Life'

I

Spirits were a later addition to the repertoire of alcoholic drinks than beer or wine, although the process of heating a liquid into vapour and then condensing this into a pure essence was a fairly simple one, which could be performed in a primitive still. It was possibly known to the Chinese around 1,000 BC,[1] and it has been suggested that at the time of Christ gnostic sects used 'burning water' on the heads of converts at baptismal ceremonies (literally, baptism by fire):[2] subsequently, the requisite knowledge was brought to the West either by the Cathars or by returning Crusaders, who had seen distillation practised by Arab alchemists. A coded recipe for 'aqua ardens' appeared in a French monastic tract about 1190 alongside one for artificial gold,[3] and through the medieval world spirits were regarded as mysterious, even magical, substances, used only medicinally for their stimulating, reviving qualities. English records of 'aqua vitae' distilled from wine appear in the fourteenth century, when it was made by monks and apothecaries, and became more widely known during the Black Death (1348–9) as a warming prophylactic. Spirits were also redistilled with herbs and flowers from the physic gardens of monasteries to make a variety of liqueurs with therapeutic properties, while in private households spirit-based 'cordials' were recommended for the treatment of palsey, the plague, smallpox, apoplexy, ague and other diseases.[4] But the line between such medicines and pleasurable drinks was a thin one: 'treatments' could easily become 'treats' or a ladies' subterfuge for an alcoholic 'restorative'.

By the sixteenth century aqua vitae was becoming well-known in England, its production encouraged by dispossessed monks, who established themselves as apothecaries. Spirits were beginning to be served together with sweetmeats at the end of banquets as pleasurable, stimulating aids to digestion,[5] so neatly combining the dual functions. In Scotland by this time usquebaugh (whisky) made from malted barley was well-established in the Highlands, having been introduced, like Christianity, from Ireland, and as early as 1505 the first of many attempts to control the trade was made by placing it under the authority of the Royal College of Surgeons in Edinburgh.[6] The popularity of another, foreign, spirit – gin – was promoted by the experience of English soldiers in the Netherlands after 1570. This spirit, redistilled over juniper berries, is credited to Professor Sylvius of Leyden University in the mid-sixteenth century: known in French as 'eau de genièvre' (juniper), it was corrupted in English into 'geneva' and, later, 'gin'. It began to be manufactured on a commercial scale by Lucas Bols at Schiedam in 1575, and small quantities exported to England. Almost from its introduction, gin began to change the role of spirit-drinking from medical towards more purely pleasurable purposes, and by late Tudor times there were already complaints that the power of ardent spirits was leading to a new habit of drinking to intoxication, with consequent threats to public order and social stability.

In 1621 there were reported to be 200 distillers in London making 'Aqua Vitae, Aqua Composita and other strong and hott waters',[7] and a petition to Parliament by these supposedly reputable traders complained that what was being sold as 'British Brandy' was often made from beer dregs, wine lees, rotten fruit and almost any fermentable material. Genuine French brandy dates from this decade, when acid grapes from the Charente region (of which Cognac was the capital) were treated with a second distillation, the liquid matured in casks to produce a strong spirit. In 1646 England imported around 380,000 gallons, by 1689 2 million gallons,[8] and brandy had become a highly esteemed drink by the wealthier classes. Both the imports of Dutch gin ('Hollands') and British distilling benefited from the interruption of wine supplies from France and Germany at this time, and in 1638 the Company of Distillers was established, with a monopoly of producing spirits in London and within a radius of 21 miles. This was an attempt to control a growing trade by self-government and to suppress dishonest practices, though in the absence of any agreed definition of spirits or their proper constituents this was a virtual impossibility. During the century patents were sought for distilling spirits from buckwheat, turnips, parsnips and carrots, 'which are much cheaper and better than any distilled from corne'.[9]

The major development in British distilling occurred in the last decade of the seventeenth century with the accession of William III, the establishment of a Dutch alliance, and heavy duties imposed on French wines and brandy. In what appears to have been a deliberate policy of steering British tastes towards spirits, duties on strong beer were also doubled in 1690 from 3s 6d to 6s 6d the barrel and on small beer from 9d to 1s 6d.[10] These charges coincided with a period of good grain harvests, when landowners were happy to encourage a new market for corn at a time when beer production was falling.[11] Spirits, more strongly alcoholic than drinks formerly known in Britain, found a niche in liquid appetites as the traditional dependence on ale and beer began to yield to the new, non-alcoholic hot beverages, tea and coffee. Brandy, whisky and gin complemented these better than long draughts of cold beer: they were drunk as 'whets' at any time of day, after meals as 'digestives', added to tea and coffee for extra flavour, and extensively used as a main ingredient of another new drink, 'punch', imported by East India merchants. By the late seventeenth century punch was also being made from another new spirit, rum, distilled from West Indian molasses following Britain's capture of Jamaica in 1655. Apart from its use in the Navy, where its better keeping qualities made it more suitable than beer in tropical waters, rum was much valued for its sweetness and aroma. In addition to these imports of brandy, rum and 'Geneva', British-made spirits contributed substantially to total consumption by the end of the century, the officially recorded statistics for England and Wales rising from 527,000 gallons in 1684 to 948,000 in 1693 and 1,223,000 gallons in 1700.[12]

II

The 'gin mania' that followed from the encouragement of distilling in the 1690s excited huge contemporary concern and debate, and subsequently became part of popular historical mythology. In 1879 the famous historian William Lecky wrote:

> If we consider all the consequences that have flowed from it [it was] the most momentous in that of the eighteenth century, incomparably more so than any event in the purely political or military annals of the country . . . The grand jury of Middlesex declared that much the greater part of the poverty, the murders, the robberies of London might be traced to this single cause.[13]

Or, in the words of Dorothy George in 1925, 'It would hardly be possible to exaggerate the cumulatively disastrous effects of the orgy of spirit-drinking between 1720 and 1751'.[14] In fact, the phenomenon was exaggerated, lasted relatively briefly, and was mainly confined to the capital, though this does not deny that for a generation many of the poorer inhabitants of London were reduced to a state of degradation, or that the attempts of government to remedy a situation that they had created were inept to the point of ludicrous.

The immediate causes of the epidemic were the ease of manufacture by hundreds of small distillers,[15] the low duty of 2d a gallon, and the absence of any requirement for a retail licence. In 1725 there were a reported 6,187 premises selling spirits in London, excluding the City and Southwark, and in Westminster and St Giles one in every four houses were said to be dram-shops. Underlying this easy accessibility was a range of favourable economic and political circumstances. Between 1715 and 1745 there were only three bad harvests (1727, 1728, 1739–40): in most years corn crops were abundant, with prices low and surpluses that farmers were keen to sell for distilling. In the opinion of many like Daniel Defoe, distilling was desirable because it encouraged trade, gave employment, reduced foreign imports, and was 'one of the most essential things to support the landed interest'. A Parliament in which landowners predominated naturally concurred. Imports of brandy and wine from England's enemy, France, were prohibitively taxed, and in the words of André Simon, 'At no other period in history did the masses respond more enthusiastically to the call of patriotism as when they were called upon to be patriotically drunk'.[16] The good years for farmers were good for the population generally – full employment, low prices and a rising standard of living:[17] if excessive spirit-drinking sometimes resulted in destitution, it did not originate from poverty so much as from an experience of surplus spending power, much of which was disposed of in the traditional form of alcoholic drink as well as in the new hot beverages. People could afford both spirits and tea, often combining them in one drink. Fashion and social imitation also played a part in a growing taste for stronger liquors. In the courts of William III and Queen Anne gin and brandy were drunk, while port, fortified with brandy, became the favourite drink of the better-off, replacing the weaker French clarets, but a craving for sweetness as well as strength is evident in the large consumption both of Iberian wines and of gin, which at this period was heavily sugared and flavoured. For these reasons gin appealed to women who were already familiar with 'medicinal' cordials: between a quarter and a third of spirit-sellers were women, many more than among licensed victuallers, and contemporaries were convinced that 'servant-maids and labouring men's wives' who had never entered alehouses patronized dram-shops.[18] The description 'Mother Gin' ('Mother's Ruin' was a nineteenth-century, temperance version) clearly implies that the drink acquired approving, feminine associations.

Table 8.1 shows the consumption of British spirits 1684–1760. These are the officially recorded statistics, which relate only to spirits on which duty was paid. In 1729, following a campaign for restriction led by the Middlesex magistrates, a licence fee of £20 for retailing spirits was imposed, and the spirit duty was raised from 2d to 5s a gallon. Thereafter, the recorded statistics need to be supplemented by those for the illicit trade, which in some years probably doubled the total. In fact, the Act of 1729

Table 8.1 British spirits charged for consumption in England and Wales, 1684–1760 (thousands of gallons)

1684	527	1735	6,440
1700	1,223	1741	7,439
1710	2,201	1743	8,203 (peak)
1720	2,483	1750	6,603
1730	3,778	1755	5,051
		1760	1,819

Source: B.R. Mitchell and Phyllis Deane, *Abstract of British Historical Statistics*, 1962, 254–5

was found to be unworkable, was repealed in 1733, and was followed by another wave of drunkenness and disorder, which precipitated the even more draconian 'Gin Act' of 1736 requiring a £50 licence for retailing. Widespread opposition from the trade and the London public resulted in rioting, an explosion in Westminster Hall, and threats on the life of the Master of the Rolls, Joseph Jekyll, the chief initiator of the Act:[19] public processions for the burial of effigies of 'Mother Gin' and 'Madame Geneva' were only mock-serious expressions of loss. The Gin Act was fairly easily evaded by disguising gin with some addition such as wine and selling it under another name – 'Parliamentary Brandy', 'Sangree', 'Colic Water' and so on – and the Act was quietly dropped in 1739. The sordid story was then repeated. Official consumption climbed to a peak of 8.2 million gallons in 1743, though contemporaries believed that the true figure was nearer 19 million: renewed outcries about the debauching of London's population included the essay by Henry Fielding, the senior Bow Street magistrate, on *The Causes of the late Increase of Robberies* (1751) and Hogarth's widely published caricature of 'Gin Lane', depicting the depths of degradation to which a gin-soaked people had sunk. These marked the final fling of the propagandists. Yet another Act in 1751 at last found a level of public acceptance, with distillers forbidden to retail and a moderate retail licence fee of £2 annually renewable. External events were equally important in the suppression of the 'gin mania'. The run of abundant corn harvests ended in the late 1750s, and in 1757, 1759 and 1760 distilling was temporarily prohibited to conserve stocks for bread: higher spirit prices turned public tastes back to beer, especially the new variety, porter (see Chapter 6, pp. 117–18), which the London brewers were actively promoting through an expansion of 'tied' public houses.

The official statistics yield a consumption of more than a gallon a year for every man, woman and child in England and Wales in the 1740s, but gin-drinking was very largely a London phenomenon, with minor outposts in Bristol, Norwich and Manchester. In the capital legal gin consumption may therefore have been around 10 gallons a head, more than this for adults, and very much more again when illicit distilling is included. After 1760 production fell to 2–2.5 million gallons a year until at the end of the century it climbed to around 4 million gallons. By then gin was a much better-quality product not despised by the wealthier classes, very different from the raw alcohol, redistilled several times for extra strength, and 'flavoured' with coriander, grains of paradise, orris, even oil of turpentine and sulphuric acid, that had been hawked about the streets in the earlier decades. In the quantities that some people drank, this would have been highly injurious, but the belief that it was a main cause of the excess of deaths over births in London was an alarmist exaggeration. Between 1730 and 1749 74.5 per cent of children baptized in London died before the age of 5,[20] but young children were not main gin-drinkers, and adult death rates remained broadly stationary. The principal causes of child mortality were infectious diseases resulting from severe overcrowding, lack of sanitation, polluted water supplies and inadequate nutrition, in which lack of care by alcoholic parents doubtless played some part, though an incalculable one.

The taste for strong spirits continued throughout the eighteenth century, with the diminished British contribution supplemented by imports of French brandy and Dutch 'Geneva', estimated in 1782 at 2.5 million gallons,[21] not including the unknown quantities smuggled. A large increase in the import of West Indian rum from 1 million gallons in mid-century to 3 million by the end[22] is also notable. Like gin, this was much improved from the fiery 'Killdevil' spirit of the early century by rectification and the introduction of warehouse bonding by the Board of Customs in 1736, which ensured that most rum was matured before sale. Rum remained suspect by many doctors, however, as a cause of colic, 'dry gripes' and gout due to lead poisoning derived from the pewter 'worms' used in the distilling apparatus.[23]

By contrast, whisky was scarcely known in England in the eighteenth century, and only just beginning to be a commercial product in Scotland. Simple, pot-still distilling was a family affair in the Highlands, a useful way of converting surplus barley into a drink to moisten the bannocks or to take as 'drams' to keep out the cold and wet. Although after the Act of Union in 1707 Scotland in theory became subject to the English Excise laws, it was not in the economic interests of landowners and magistrates to enforce them strictly: as a Ross-shire minister explained in 1796, 'Distilling is almost the only method of converting our victual [barley] into cash for the payment of rent and servants, and whisky may, in fact, be called our staple commodity'.[24] Whisky crossed the social boundaries, and was as popular among Scottish aristocrats as among the poor:[25] the offer of a dram was a customary ritual of hospitality, and Elizabeth Grant must have been one of the very few at the end of the century to disapprove of it.

> At every house it was offered, at every house it must be tasted or offence would be given, so we were taught to believe . . . Whisky was and is the bane of that country; from early morning till late at night it went on. Decent gentlewomen began the day with a dram . . . In the pantry [of our house] a bottle of whisky was the allowance per day [for the servants].[26]

What the production and, therefore, consumption of whisky was from many hundreds of small pot-stills is impossible to know – there were supposed to be around 200 in the Glenlivet area alone. Private distilling for the household did not require a licence until 1781, and even after that enforcement was practically impossible in the remote Highlands. An important development is traceable from the 1730s, when distilling on a larger, commercial scale began to spread into the Lowlands, encouraged by the

Gin Act of 1736, which exempted aqua vitae from duty. By the end of the century Lowland distilling was becoming dominated by the two related families of John Haig and Robert Stein, who were developing markets in the Scottish industrial towns and exporting to England. The recorded statistics of production are dubious and irregular – 776,000 gallons in 1750, only 55,000 in 1760, but 1,670,000 gallons in 1800 and 4,350,000 by 1825, when for the first time production of whisky equalled the output of British spirits (mainly gin).[27]

III

The consumption of spirits in the nineteenth century was determined by three principal factors. In 1850 Britain was becoming an urban society, where half the population lived in towns, and by 1900 three-quarters. Most of the new workers had greater spending power than the impoverished agricultural labourers: many were exposed to heavy manual labour in the open, while factory workers experienced long hours of monotonous labour causing psychological as well as physical strains. Spirits helped to relieve the pains of adaptation to unfamiliar work routines and squalid living conditions in towns that lacked recreational provisions beyond the public house. However, these encouragements to drink were challenged by the rise of the temperance movement, which began in 1828 as an anti-spirits campaign, only later turning into an attack on alcohol generally. Nevertheless, the strongest condemnation was always reserved for ardent spirits, seen as the cause of rapid intoxication and all the evils of crime, disease and poverty that supposedly flowed from it. The third factor influencing consumption was, naturally, the price of spirits, which was largely determined by the level of duty. Here, Victorian governments faced a conflict between the need to raise public revenue, of which Customs and Excise duties on alcohol provided between 30 per cent and 40 per cent, and political pressures, which argued in different ways at different times: while in the earlier decades of the century Free Traders pressed for the removal of controls and a general reduction in tax burdens, later, and especially in the Liberal Party, opinion turned to attacking the social problems of drink by reducing the number of licensed premises, shortening their opening hours and making spirits less accessible by raising duties.

Several trends are indicated in Table 8.2. Low levels of consumption accompanied the economic depression after the end of the French Wars in 1815, but were temporarily relieved by a reduction in the whisky duty in Scotland (from 6s 2d to 2s 4d a gallon) in 1823 and on spirits generally in England (from 11s 8¼d to 7s a gallon) in 1825. These changes were intended mainly to suppress illicit distilling and smuggling, and resulted in a doubling of the quantities of spirits charged for duty from 9.4 million gallons in 1820 to 18.2 million in 1826.[28] Somewhat lower levels then returned between the 1840s and the 1860s, due primarily to

Table 8.2 Consumption of spirits per head per year in the UK, 1800–1914 (proof gallons)

	Home	Imported	Total		Home	Imported	Total
1800–1804	0.49	0.31	0.80	1860–64	0.68	0.19	0.87
1805–9	0.60	0.25	0.85	1865–9	0.71	0.26	0.97
1810–14	0.61	0.23	0.84	1870–74	0.84	0.30	1.14
1815–19	0.52	0.17	0.69	1875–9	0.89	0.32	1.21
1820–24	0.51	0.17	0.68	1880–84	0.81	0.24	1.05
1825–9	0.90	0.20	1.10	1885–9	0.72	0.22	0.94
1830–34	0.91	0.20	1.11	1890–94	0.79	0.21	1.00
1835–9	0.99	0.18	1.17	1895–9	0.82	0.21	1.03
1840–44	0.74	0.13	0.87	1900–04	0.84	0.20	1.04
1845–9	0.81	0.15	0.96	1905–9	0.71	0.15	0.86
1850–54	0.90	0.18	1.08	1910–14	0.55	0.12	0.67
1855–9	0.82	0.17	0.99				

Source: George B. Wilson, *Alcohol and the Nation*, 1940, Table 2, 335

duty increases to 8s a gallon in 1855 and 10s in 1860. As Chancellor of the Exchequer, Gladstone in 1860 was encouraging the consumption of light wine as a drink of 'temperance' (see Chapter 7, pp. 149–50), while believing that ardent spirits were 'not only evils in themselves, but fruitful parents of crime'. Despite this discouragement, spirit consumption revived from the later 1860s to reach its nineteenth-century peak of 1.30 gallons per head a year in 1875, having grown since 1870 by no less than 28.8 per cent, a faster rate of increase even than that of beer at 20.3 per cent. This sharp rise reflected increased spending power of the working classes in this 'golden age' of Victorian prosperity when, as yet, surplus income still tended to go largely on the traditional leisure outlet of drink. While beer was a daily necessity for many workers, spirits were more of an occasional indulgence, and in the 1870s they could be indulged in more often than ever before. By the 1880s, however, the demand for spirits began to slacken, partly because of higher levels of unemployment but also because there were new, attractive ways of spending – a wider range of imported foodstuffs, factory-made clothing and furniture, new leisure activities and recreational goods such as cigarettes.[29] The working classes, who, it was estimated, consumed three-quarters of all spirits in the United Kingdom,[30] were also beginning to consume a wider variety of goods and services, ranging from frozen meat and canned tropical fruits to bicycles, holidays and music-halls. By 1887 spirit consumption had fallen to 0.93 gallons per head a year: it revived to a minor peak of 1.12 gallons during the South African War in 1900 but then resumed a decline sharpened by a fall in real wages and by increases in the spirit duty in 1907 and 1910 – an unpopular measure in Lloyd George's 'People's Budget' was to raise the level from 10s to 14s 9d a gallon. By then, consumption stood at 0.65 gallons a head a year, only half that of 35 years earlier.

These statistics of the average consumption of every man, woman and child do not, of course, represent that of those who actually drank spirits. In 1898 it was estimated that there were 3 million total abstainers from alcohol in the UK, that 14 million children under 15 did not drink, and that women drank only half as much as men: these calculations would suggest a male consumption of 2.37 gallons a head a year and of females 1.19 gallons.[31] The assumption that women drank only half as much spirits as men is, however, open to doubt. Charles Booth believed that while men, at least in London, drank mainly beer, women more often drank spirits, and that the habit of 'nipping' had increased since public houses were more comfortable and attractive than formerly: even 'respectable' women were now seen in them, particularly those that had ladies' saloons. A police officer reported that heavy drinking among women was not common until after marriage: 'It is not till they get older that women take to gin and ale and become regular soakers'.[32]

Gin remained the most popular spirit until late in the century, experiencing a revival after 1830 with the creation of glamorous gin palaces. Numerous descriptions of gin were offered by alluring names, bottles and decorative casks – 'Best Cordial Gin', 'Cream of the Valley', 'Old Tom', 'The Celebrated Butter Gin', 'Out and Out' and many more, mostly heavily flavoured and sweetened. It was usually sold at 3d a quarter-pint, the price of a quart of beer, and gin palaces often kept their own speciality to attract 'bingo-boys' (heavy drinkers) making a 'gin crawl'.[33] Gin was also the basis of many cordials, some of which were medically prescribed for colds or dyspepsia – 'Ginger-Gin', 'Gin and Cloves', 'Gin and Peppermint', and so on, while Dickens served gin punch and 'Gin Sling' to guests at Gadshill. By mid-century 'mixed drinks', many of which were of American origin and commonly included gin, were becoming known in England. 'Mint Julep' was described by Eliza Acton in 1845, and Alexis Soyer, the famous chef of the Reform Club, opened an American Bar serving forty different drinks in 1851 as an attraction to visitors to the Great Exhibition. 'Mixed drinks' contributed to the popularization of gin among the middle and upper classes, but even more important was the development of improved quality, drier 'London Gin' by distillers like Booths (established 1740) and Gordons (1769). 'Dry Gin', dating from the 1870s, was particularly suitable for use with quinine tonic waters, first drunk by servants of the Empire in tropical climes: naval officers usually preferred gin with angostura ('pink gin'). The quantity of British spirits distilled in England – practically all gin – rose steadily from 6.1 million gallons in 1851 to 9.8 million in 1881 and 13.9 million in 1914.[34]

By contrast, rum remained a mainly working-class spirit in the nineteenth century apart from some use in punch and other mixed drinks. Sweet, heavy and pungent, its consumption was much influenced by the weather, rising materially in cold, wet conditions when outdoor workers took comfort in a glass of rum and warm milk. Its familiarity among sailors in the form of 'grog' (see p. 96) also extended to workers in ports, docks and harbours. As a colonial product it enjoyed a substantial tariff preference, and in 1831, while imported brandy was taxed at 22s 10d a gallon (almost 3s a pint), the duty on rum was lowered to 9s a gallon.[35] Consumption doubled from 2.5 million gallons in 1840 to a peak of 5.4 million in 1875 but then declined in line with other alcoholic drinks to 3.6 million gallons in 1914.[36] The variety of spirit consumed was socially determined. Brandy, apart from what was medically prescribed, was for the wealthy of Victorian England. It was sometimes drunk as a preliminary to a meal – a 'whet-cup' in the North or a 'coupe d'avant' elsewhere, in order to 'crisp the stomach' – but more often at the end of dinner by men instead of port. The brandy of mid-century was dark and heavy, paralleling the taste for fortified wines, but in later decades lighter brandies like VSOP (Very Special Old Pale) were preferred.[37] No precise consumption statistics are available for an article that was extensively smuggled because of its high level of duty, but the officially recorded imports show a modest rise from 3.4 million gallons in 1840 to a maximum of 4.5 million in 1876: thereafter, cognac suffered from the disastrous effects of the phylloxera disease, making imports scarce and even more expensive. By 1900 consumption had almost halved to 2.6 million gallons, and continued its downward trend to 1.5 million in 1914.

The other major reason for the decline of brandy was the rise of a competitor, whisky, which was to become the dominant British spirit. Scarcely known in England in the early nineteenth century, it was the national drink of Scotland, made in thousands of small pot-stills, licit and illicit: in 1822 alone 6,000 prosecutions were reported[38] out of an estimated 14,000 illegal stills. But this decade marked the beginning of the commercialization and commodification of Scotch whisky. In 1820 the Duke of Gordon, whose estates included the distilling region of Glenlivet, offered to suppress the illicit trade in return for substantial reductions in duty, an offer accepted in 1823 when the distilling licence was set at £10 and the Excise duty lowered from 6s 2d to 2s 4½d a gallon. George Smith of Glenlivet took out the first licence in 1825 and quickly built up the largest commercial distillery in Scotland: by about 1840 illegal distilling had greatly declined owing to stricter enforcement of the law and the growing availability of capital to establish larger units of production.[39] This process was greatly aided by the invention of the patent Coffey still in 1830, which gradually industrialized the manufacture of whisky. Until then, pot-stills could produce only small quantities of spirit: they were labour-intensive, requiring frequent refilling, and could only use a mash exclusively of malted barley. The patent still invented by Aeneas Coffey was a continuous process, producing greater output at lower cost from cheaper, unmalted grain and yielding a strong spirit of 86–96° alcohol. Progress was limited by the large capital required, so that in 1860 there were only twelve patent distilleries in Scotland compared with 111 pot-stills[40] producing the traditional malt whiskies. The recorded consumption of whisky in Scotland between 1830 and 1850 averaged 6.1 million gallons a year for a population of around 2.5 million, a quantity that stimulated the formation of the first anti-spirits campaign in 1828. Archibald Geike believed that Highlanders drank steadily but could hold their drink, while Lowlanders in the cities aimed to get intoxicated as quickly as possible: 'To many wretched beings it offers a transient escape from the miseries of life, and brings the only moments of comparative happiness which they ever enjoy'.[41]

In England in mid-century whisky was only just beginning to be known, was expensive and not to all tastes. Queen Victoria drank it when at Balmoral and gave the Royal Warrant to a local distiller, Beggs, while its popularity south of the border began to be enhanced by the interest in all things Scottish – from Sir Walter Scott's novels to tweeds and tartans. Until the 1860s 'Scotch' was either single malt, produced in pot-stills and smoky from peat firing, or patent still spirit that was practically pure, tasteless alcohol. The important development which established the modern whisky industry was the blending of the two distillates to produce a lighter, cheaper, but well-flavoured spirit, which appealed to urban Lowlanders and English consumers. The innovator was Andrew Usher in 1853, but the development of blended whiskies was led from the 1860s by firms like James Buchanan, John Walker, William Teacher and John Dewar, the last of whom introduced the first famous bottled brand. Blended whiskies proved to be a successful alternative to brandy during the scarcity caused by phylloxera, and were marketed on a mass scale by the wine merchants Gilbeys, who bought the Glen Spey distillery in 1887, and by the Victoria Wine Company, who in 1896 were offering fourteen blended whiskies from 2s 9d a bottle upwards.[42] By the end of the century whisky was the most popular spirit in England, heavily promoted by advertisements and labels that were becoming household names. Single malts were still needed for the connoisseur, but were more important now for blending, and the number of pot-stills actually increased to 142 in 1908: the patent stills by then generally used imported maize, around 30 per cent cheaper than barley and with a higher extraction rate.[43] Because of its later entry into mass consumption whisky did not follow the general decline in spirits after the mid-1870s: on the contrary, supplies of Scotch whisky to England grew from 2.1 million gallons in 1876 to 7.2 million in 1900 (supplies of Irish whiskey grew from 1.6 to 4.3 million). Hit by the duty increase in 1909 from 11s to 14s 9d a gallon, supplies then fell to 5.1 and 2.1 million gallons respectively by 1913.[44]

By the late nineteenth century the quality of spirits drunk in England had generally much improved. R. Shannon's *Practical Treatise on Distilling and Rectification*, which remained a standard work for many years after its first publication in 1805, included a recipe for English Gin, which required small quantities of oil of vitriol, oil of turpentine and oil of cloves to be added to a base of clear spirit and water – either rainwater or Thames water. Fredrick Accum in 1820 believed that brandy and rum were much adulterated, dilution with water being followed by the addition of molasses, sugar and 'Spirit Flavour' obtainable from brewers' druggists. 'Oak sawdust and a spirituous tincture of raisin stones are likewise used to impart to new brandy and rum a ripe taste resembling brandy or rum being kept in oaken casks.'[45] An Act of 1818 required proof spirit to contain not less than 49.28 per cent of pure alcohol, but, Accum noted, most imported brandies contained more than this and would admit of a pint of 'liquor' (water) being added to a gallon.[46] If the dilution caused turbidity, this could be corrected by adding alum, subcarbonate of potash or (poisonous) acetate of lead. Brandy was especially tempting to the adulterator because of its heavy taxation, and the invention of the patent Coffey still in 1830, which could produce large quantities of almost pure alcohol, facilitated the manufacture of 'Patent Brandy' – grain spirit mixed with some genuine cognac or flavoured with fruit juices. In his analyses carried out for the *Lancet* between 1851 and 1854 Dr Hassall found that the alcoholic content of gin in London ranged from only 22.35 per cent upwards, so that some samples were less than half the legal strength: besides water, cayenne pepper was the most common addition,[47] but another leading analytical chemist, Dr Alphonse Normandy, reported to the Select Committee on Adulteration in 1855 that he had a copy of a brewers' druggists' list of substances available for the adulteration of spirits that included subcarbonate of potash, oil of vitriol (sulphuric acid), grains of paradise and cocculus Indicus, a poisonous picrotoxin that had caused the death of a man in 1829 when used in rum. 'The object is to sell water for spirits . . . and then the ingenuity of the publican comes into action to restore the intoxicating quality.'[48]

Dangerous adulterants of this kind did not generally survive the publicity of the 1850s, but Public Analysts appointed under the Adulteration Acts of 1872 and 1875 continued to find a higher proportion of spirits adulterated than any other food or drink. In 1878 47 per cent of samples of gin and 46.4 per cent of other spirits were reported against, and temperance reformers may have been pleased to learn that a good deal of gin contained little more than 20 per cent of alcohol. In any case, retailers found a legal loophole in the decisions in *Sandys* v. *Small* (1878) and *Gage* v. *Elsay* (1883) that no offence was committed by selling spirits below the legal standard provided the vendor had given reasonable notice of dilution to the purchaser: the words displayed in a bar that 'All spirits sold here are mixed', was held to be adequate 'constructive notice' even if not read or understood by the customer. Many publicans refused – or failed – to take advantage of this, and as late as 1890 18.1 per cent of all samples of spirits were reported as adulterated, and 284 cases were brought to court.[49] Middle- and upper-class consumers who generally bought their spirits in sealed bottles of reputable brands enjoyed a considerable measure of protection from such frauds.

It is not likely that medical opinion exerted much influence on the consumption of spirits since doctors were divided as to their benefits or harmful effects: except for a small minority of temperance doctors, many continued to prescribe the moderate use of brandy or, less often, whisky, for a variety of maladies, and as general stimulants, restoratives and pain-killers. Excessive consumption resulting in alcoholism began to be identified as a disease early in the century by doctors such as Trotter, Black and Thomson,[50] but drunkenness – especially of the poor – was generally viewed as a moral and social problem, a self-inflicted cause of crime, brutality and family breakdown for which weakness of character was primarily responsible. Nevertheless, attitudes towards the health implications of drink, especially of strong drink, began to change significantly at the end of the century, fuelled by the anxiety over national fitness, which the rejection of 34.6 per cent of volunteers for the army on medical grounds appeared to demonstrate.[51] Although the medical witnesses who gave evidence to the Inter-Departmental Committee on Physical Deterioration in 1904 differed as to whether inadequate diet, slum housing, the employment of mothers of young children or other economic and environmental factors were the main causes of ill-health, many laid the blame on drink, and believed that drinking by women was on the increase: 'If the mother as well as the father is given to drink, the progeny will deteriorate in every way, and the future of the race is imperilled'. Ten years later such fears seemed to be confirmed when only one man in every three was graded A1 and fully fit for military service.

IV

In retrospect it is clear that the decisive turning-point in spirit consumption in Britain was the First World War (1914–18), when severe restrictions were imposed in the name of national efficiency, and drinking habits were fundamentally changed, never to return to their pre-war level. This was all the more remarkable in that the working classes enjoyed more disposable income as a result of full employment and rising real wages and, given the traumas of war and the scarcities of many foods and luxuries, would have increased their liquor consumption had it been available. This was, indeed, the case during the first year of war, when spirit consumption in the UK rose from 31.6 million gallons in 1914 to 35 million in 1915,[52] and increased drunkenness and absenteeism from work threatened war production in shipyards and munitions factories. Lloyd George considered both a total ban on alcohol and a 'half-way' prohibition of spirits, but rejected this alternative as 'unfair to local tastes' (in Scotland) and because of fear that it would add to unrest in Ireland. Instead, his Budget of April 1915 proposed to double the duty on spirits from 14s 9d to 29s 6d a gallon, and to dilute whisky, brandy and rum from 25° to 35° under proof. These encountered such violent opposition, especially from trade interests, that they were withdrawn except for a clause providing that spirits would not be sold until they had been warehoused for at least three years.[53] By June 1915, however, a Central Control Board (Liquor Traffic) was beginning to restrict public access to alcohol – opening hours of public houses were greatly reduced (from 19½ hours a day in the metropolis and 16 hours elsewhere to 5½ hours), dilution of spirits to 30° under proof was made mandatory and up to 50° under proof permissible, 'treating' was made illegal, and off-licences were forbidden to sell spirits in less quantity than quarts (to discourage the use of pocket flasks). Finally, the spirit duty was raised in stages to 30s a gallon by 1918 and 50s in 1919.[54] In the areas taken under Direct Control, such as Carlisle and Gretna, restrictions went even further. All public houses were closed on Sundays and no spirits were allowed to be sold on Saturdays (the 'spirit-less Saturday', February 1917); no person under 18 was to be served with spirits, the ordering of a pint of beer and a measure of spirits (as a 'chaser') at the same time was prohibited, and all grocers' licences for the sale of alcohol were abolished. Whisky distillers, who were heavily dependent on imported grain, suffered especially, and at the height of the German U-boat attacks in 1917 pot-still production was prohibited and patent still output limited to 50 per cent that of the previous year.

However unpopular with the public and the trade, the activities of the Central Control Board were, in their own terms, highly successful. Consumption of spirits in the UK fell from 35 million gallons in 1915 to 15 million in 1918, or from 0.76 gallons a head a year to 0.33 gallons: proceedings for drunkenness declined from 157,000 to 32,000 (England and Wales) and from 48,000 to 11,600 in Scotland.[55] In 1919 Lord D'Abernon, the Chairman of the Board, wrote with pride that 'A profound change in the drinking habits of large classes of the population has been initiated', and hoped that 'the nation does not relapse to the level of alcoholic excess which prevailed before the War'.[56] In this respect it seems that there was little public demand to return to pre-war 'normalcy', for a new Licensing Act in 1921 retained the afternoon closure of public houses and limited opening hours to nine a day in London and eight elsewhere,[57] only half those of 1914. Moreover, after a brief period of post-war euphoria, when spirit consumption rose to 0.49 gallons per head a year in 1919, the rest of the inter-war years were marked by major falls – to 0.39 gallons in 1921, 0.28 in 1926, 0.22 in 1931 and 0.19 in 1935, less than half that of 1920 and a mere one-sixth of that of 1900. This dramatic change cannot be simply explained as a result of the economic depression and the high levels of unemployment, although this clearly affected workers in some industries like shipbuilding, who had traditionally been spirit-drinkers. Overall, average real wages rose by a third between the wars, and at its height in 1931–2 unemployment affected 22 per cent of the labour force: the majority of the working classes were better off than before but chose to drink less for reasons previously discussed (see Chapter 6, pp. 133–5).

Spirits were, however, relatively more expensive than formerly since their price remained stable[58] while retail prices generally fell by 37 per cent over the period: increases in duty brought the average price of a bottle of whisky to 12s 6d (compared with 3s 6d before the war), a price that in the 1930s represented a quarter or a fifth of many weekly wages. Whisky was now easily the most popular spirit, accounting for 66 per cent of the spirits market in 1939, but despite heavy brand advertising the distilling industry suffered badly owing to the fall in home demand and the loss of exports to the United States during the years of Prohibition, 1920–33. In 1923 the pot-still makers of malt whisky had produced 13.2 million proof gallons; in 1927 they distilled only 5.6 million and in 1932–3 none at all in a deliberate, but vain, attempt to persuade the government to grant tax reliefs.[59]

The reality of falling spirits consumption and depression in the distilling industries seems at variance with the popular images of the 1920s, when the 'bright young things' imbibed freely at cocktail parties and nightclubs. Their much-publicized excesses related to a very small and unrepresentative section of the population, but nevertheless the domestic cocktail party became quite characteristic of middle-class, suburban life at this time. In 1938 £34.2 million was spent on spirits in off-licences for home consumption, more than half the total spirits expenditure of £63.4 million.[60] The cocktail party was a convenient way of entertaining at a time when the scarcity and cost of domestic servants were restricting the size and frequency of formal dinner-parties. An American innovation,[61] though related to the earlier 'cups' and 'punches', cocktails were shorter mixed drinks usually based on gin, brandy, rum, liqueurs and fruit juices, and bearing exotic names. The first English cocktail party has been credited to the painter C.R.W. Nevinson in 1924, who was finding little entertainment in London between tea and dinner.[62] Limited as its influence was, the cocktail party did something to restore the popularity and respectability of gin: gin and whisky dominated the inter-war spirits market, in 1938 accounting for 8.6 million gallons of consumption compared with only 552,000 gallons of rum and 406,000 of brandy.[63]

Contemporaries believed that the greatest fall in consumption was among the working classes. Before the war 'spirits entered into the normal drinking habits of the very poorest families', but in 1935, according to *The New Survey of London Life and Labour*, they had virtually disappeared except for special occasions.[64] This appeared to be confirmed by an estimate of the consumption of a husband and wife according to income groups before and after the war (see Table 8.3). Higher prices of spirits and the widened range of consumer goods and leisure activities had greatly restricted consumption in the working class, and in 'Worktown' (Bolton, Lancashire) in 1938 four out of every seven public houses sold no spirits at all. 'For the ordinary Worktowner drink equals beer', and 'the drinking of spirits by ordinary pubgoers is very small'. A landlord observed that those who did order spirits

Table 8.3 Estimated consumption of spirits and wine by husband and wife, 1913–14 and 1923–24

	Income/year £	Spirits Bottles/year	Wine Bottles/year
1913–14	50–100	9	4
	100–150	15	8
	150–200	18	16
	200–500	22	30
1923–24	100–150	None	None
	150–200	5½	6
	200–500	7½	12

Source: Report of the Committee on National Debt and Taxation (the Colwyn Report), 1926, App. X, 58, 61

were usually either suffering from some illness, or businessmen hard pressed by work or financial problems. In the lounge of the best hotel in town, however, frequented by middle-class men and their ladies, drinking patterns were very different: 'shorts' were the normal order – cocktails at 10d, whisky, gin and 'It' (Italian vermouth), gin and lime, and sherry.[65]

During the Second World War (1939–45) drunkenness and absenteeism no longer posed the threats to productivity that they had in the First, but problems of supplies were just as great. In 1940 a Government Committee on Brewing and Distilling was established to control materials, much priority being given to whisky for export to the United States in exchange for food and armaments. Supplies of grain were so critical in 1942 that all Scottish distilleries were temporarily closed, and despite Churchill's plea to the Minister of Food in 1945 – 'On no account reduce the amount of barley for whisky . . . this characteristic of British ascendancy'[66] – output that year was limited to three-sevenths that of 1939.[67] Gin suffered a similar fate, quickly disappearing from public houses and off-licences, and there were even some black market substitutes like 'Edgware Road Gin',[68] reminiscent of nineteenth-century adulteration. Further pain to spirit-drinkers was caused by sharp increases in duty – from 72s 6d a gallon to 97s 6d in 1940, 137s 6d in 1942, 157s 6d in 1943 and 190s 10d in 1947. The combined effects of scarcity and high prices resulted in a fall in spirits consumption of a quarter, less than production statistics would indicate because of greater releases from bond: the average consumption of 2.4 pints per person per year fell to 1.9 pints in 1945, remaining around this level into the early 1950s.[69]

The wartime and post-war years of scarcity cast a long shadow over the spirit trades, and it was not until 1955 that distillers were finally free to import grain and produce as much as the market would bear. In 1948 a market research survey had estimated that 31.6 per cent of the population aged over 16 drank no alcohol, far higher than the 12 per cent estimated at the beginning of the century: the survey also calculated the frequency of

Table 8.4 Frequency of drinking spirits, 1948 (percentages of men and women over 16)

Every day	1.5	⎫	'Regular' drinkers
More than once/week	3.3	⎬	9.6%
Once/week	4.8	⎭	
Less than once/week	31.9		Occasional drinkers
Never	58.5		Non-drinkers

Source: B. Seebohm Rowntree and G.R. Lavers, *English Life and Leisure: A Social Study*, Longmans, Green, 1951, 164

spirit-drinking as shown in Table 8.4. On this evidence six out of ten Britons never drank spirits, and it seemed that austerity and high prices (5s to 8s for a large whisky and soda) had habituated consumers of alcohol to low-gravity wartime beer, of which 30.3 per cent of the population were estimated to be regular drinkers and a further 21.9 per cent occasional. All this was to change dramatically after 1953, with a trebling of spirit consumption between then and 1990: the rise was particularly rapid in the 1970s, reaching a peak of 7.36 pints a head a year in 1979, a level not seen since the early years of the century. After another minor peak of 6.8 pints a year in 1988, consumption has stabilized or fallen somewhat most recently to 5.3 pints in 1996 (see Table 8.5).

The British consumer had not been permanently dissuaded from his taste for strong drink by the untypical experiences of World Wars and inter-war depression. Nor was this a case of substitution of one form of alcohol for another, since wine consumption rose equally rapidly and that of beer fell only slightly.[70] A principal reason is the rise in disposable income, which, for the majority of the population, survived the return of high levels of unemployment in the 1980s: in 1979, the peak year of spirit consumption at 7.36 pints a year, unemployment officially stood at 5.4 per cent, then rose steadily to its peak of 11.2 per cent (3.1 million) in 1986 by which time spirits had fallen to 6.5 pints. The long-established relationship between alcohol consumption and economic activity still existed, though not nearly as strongly as in the past. Drink now occupies a fundamentally different place in household budgets from that of a century ago, when it took one-sixth of working-class income.[71] In 1994–5 alco-

Table 8.5 Consumption of spirits in the UK, 1955–95 (pints/head/year of all persons, 1955–74 and of persons over 15, 1975–95)

1955–59	2.7	1975–79	6.4
1960–64	3.3	1980–84	6.3
1965–69	3.7	1985–89	6.6
1970–74	4.7	1990–95	5.9

Sources: 1955–74, Williams and Brake, Table III 3, 383; 1975–95, *NTC Drink Pocket Book*, 1997, 113

holic drink averaged £12.32 per household per week but only 4.3 per cent of expenditure (food and non-alcoholic drinks £50.43, or 17.8 per cent of total expenditure). Within the alcohol total, spirits took £2.13 a week, wine £2.63 and beer £7.38. This does not imply that income does not still exert a strong influence on spirit consumption and expenditure, the weekly amount rising from £0.78 per household in the poorest tenth of the population to £4.18 in the wealthiest.[72]

Another important factor has been the greater ease of availability of spirits in supermarkets and the increased proportion sold for home consumption. While the traditional off-licence is mainly male territory, the supermarket is female, where women customers can conveniently and anonymously add bottles to the household shopping. Of the average expenditure on spirits of £2.13 a week, £1.27 (60 per cent) was spent in off-licences,[73] predominantly supermarkets and discount stores, which particularly benefited from the ending of resale price maintenance in 1966. An increase in spirit-drinking among women may be associated with this greater ease of access as well as with women's earnings and independence: there is now a higher proportion of 'regular' (that is, weekly) women drinkers of gin, vodka and white rum than men, who predominate in the consumption of whisky and dark rum. Consumption of most spirits increases with age, though there are significant proportions of young drinkers, 18–24 years, for vodka (28 per cent of regular drinkers) and white rum (19 per cent).[74] Vodka has been the major innovation in the spirits market since the 1960s, now holding an 18.5 per cent share, greater than gin (12 per cent) and second only to whisky (41.5 per cent): white rum (5.7 per cent market share) also became popular from the 1960s and, in the form of Bacardi and Coke, neatly combined alcohol with an established taste.

Other factors that have influenced spirit consumption in recent years have included the growth of mass leisure and the association of advertising with sporting events, the expansion of restaurant eating, and the phenomenal growth of foreign travel and holidays. Drinkers have become familiar with a much wider range of spirits than formerly, which now include Greek ouzo, Mexican tequila and Italian grappa as well as a great variety of liqueurs. The choice of spirits is still to an extent socially determined, though while brandy has the largest proportion of regular drinkers in the wealthier social grades A and B, it has now been joined here by gin; whisky drinkers are almost equally distributed across the social grades, while vodka has its largest proportion of regular drinkers in C1 (lower middle-class) and rum in D and E grades (semi-skilled and unskilled workers).

Conspectus

At the close of the Middle Ages in Britain the available drinks were almost confined to water, milk, ale and wine: spirits were just beginning to be known, but confined to medicinal uses. Three of these four main drinks were indigenous: only wine was imported, and its consumption was strictly limited by wealth and rank. Previous chapters have shown that the repertoire of drinks in modern Britain has been vastly extended as new products became commercialized and commodified to reach mass markets, giving rise to new industries and new means of distribution. Although these changes have been continuous, I have argued that they have been particularly concentrated in two great periods of transformation when the adoption of new drinks acquired revolutionary scale – the mid-seventeenth to the mid-eighteenth century, and that from the 1960s onwards. This Conspectus first addresses the overall changes in the consumption of drinks and, second, offers explanations of the causes of change.

I

New drinks did not necessarily displace existing ones, but widened the choice of what was available. Nevertheless, for most people there were limits to the quantity of liquids consumed, either physiological, financial or cultural, so that sometimes a substitution effect reduced the consumption of a traditional drink to make space for a new one. During the first drinks revolution the adoption of tea, coffee and chocolate contributed to a substantial fall in the output of beer from its peak of 23 million barrels in 1689 to 18.3 million in 1720 and 16.1 million in 1750.[1] The estimated consumption in 1689 of 832 pints per head per year, or 2.3 pints a day for every man, woman and child,[2] represents the highest recorded figure of what had been the everyday drink of all classes. Caffeine drinks were then still restricted to small, elite groups, but as tea moved into mass consumption in the 1720s and 1730s a long-term decline in beer becomes evident. Tea began to replace beer as the breakfast drink, at work-breaks and in the home at any time, particularly for women and children, while beer gradually became more of a recreational drink and, in the new form of 'porter', used mainly by men.

By the mid-eighteenth century beer consumption had fallen to around 500 pints per head per year, but its decline coincided with a major rise in spirits during the 'gin mania' and with a sharp increase in the consumption of strong wines following the commercial treaty with Portugal in 1703. The growth of caffeine drinks did not, in the short term, diminish the taste for alcohol but, rather, moved it into different forms. Tea could be drunk in quantity, as a 'long' drink like beer, while wine and spirits were normally sipped, and spirits were often added to tea and coffee. Also, both port and gin were heavily sweetened at this period, helping to compensate for the natural bitterness in the caffeine drinks. What is here being suggested is that the trajectory of one drink cannot be viewed in isolation from others, that drinks are not only complementary to food (as discussed later) but to each other. In this first period of transition the quantity of alcohol in the British diet did not fall substantially since at their peak in the 1730s and 1740s spirits were contributing around 30 per cent of the total. Any suggestion that the introduction of caffeine drinks had a major impact on sobriety before 1750 is questionable.

By then a new package of drinks had therefore emerged, the tea and coffee compensated by stronger forms of alcohol than previously known. In Britain, unlike much of Continental Europe, tea quickly became the leading caffeine beverage: coffee had a public presence in the coffee-houses of London and provincial towns, but in the home it was mainly restricted to wealthy groups as a breakfast or after-dinner drink. Coffee occupied particular niches in the day for particular classes, and did not become a universal, anytime drink.

This was even more true of the other new, hot beverage, chocolate, which has so far received little mention. A bitter, spiced drink of the Maya and Aztecs, chocolate was brought to Spain by Cortès in 1528 and first used as a medicine and restorative since it provided a rapidly assimilable source of energy.[3] Spanish clergy accepted that it was a drink rather than a food, and therefore did not break the fast. For around 100 years it remained a Spanish monopoly, and was particularly associated with the Catholic world of southern Europe, where it became a fashionable breakfast drink. Introduced to France in 1615, its use subsequently spread to Germany, the Netherlands and England where, like coffee and tea, it was first sold in coffee-houses in the 1650s: some of these, like 'The Cocoa Tree' and 'White's', specialized in the drink. Until well into the nineteenth century chocolate was a thick, viscous liquid from its content of butter-fat, which needed frequent stirring in specially designed chocolate pots: it was long supposed to have aphrodisiac powers, and was often served with added wine.

Between 1650 and 1750 the two big growth areas of consumption were groceries – especially caffeine drinks, sugar and tobacco – and semi-durables such as pottery, glass and textiles, many of which were tableware objects associated with the new drinks: by the latter date, the popularity of tea was evidenced by the estimate that one in every four shops in England had a licence to sell it.[4] Over this period there were substantial reductions in the initially very high prices of tea, coffee and sugar, at the same time as a long-term fall in grain prices, which further added to purchasing power. But from the 1750s to the end of the century drinking patterns changed in a period of poor harvests and rising prices.[5] What had been a generally rising standard of living now began to deteriorate, especially for wage-earners whose incomes lagged behind price rises as a rapidly expanding population pressed on the means of subsistence. Changed economic conditions had direct effects on the consumption of drinks. Beer production after its fall in the first half of the century now remained almost level – 16.1 million barrels in 1750, 15.9 in 1775 and 16.5 in 1799 – but for the population of England and Wales, which grew from around 6 million to 9 million, this represented a substantial fall in consumption per head. Again, from its official peak of 8.25 million gallons during the gin mania in 1743, a figure which contemporaries believed the illicit trade at least doubled, consumption of British spirits fell to 1.8 million gallons in 1760 and remained at around 2–2.5 million until a modest revival to 4 million at the end of the century. Lower levels of alcohol consumption therefore accompanied the early stages of the Industrial Revolution despite the generation of greater national wealth. Milk also became scarcer and dearer in the later eighteenth century, especially in southern England; the one drink that increased spectacularly at this time was tea, the official import of which grew from 2.3 million lb in 1750 to 14.7 million lb in 1788.[6] By then it was a universal drink, though, for the United Kingdom at an average consumption of around 1¼ lb per head per year, well below ½ oz a week, the quantity was still limited. Although the budgets of poor families now regularly included 1–2 oz a week, this was small compensation for the reduction in more nutritious drinks, and represented a decline in the living standards of many at this time.

The evidence from drinks history further suggests that disposable income for many of the working classes continued to decline in the first half of the nineteenth century. Beer consumption in England and Wales fell from 34 to 29 gallons per head per year, only briefly revived by the Beerhouse Act of 1830; it returned to its 1800 level after 1865. After its large increase at the end of the eighteenth century, tea consumption also declined until 1844, the beginning of a sustained growth, and sugar consumption, by now closely linked to that of tea, followed the same downward course until 1850. Even the consumption of wine, mainly a middle- and upper-class drink, also showed a sharp fall from 0.46 gallons per head per year in 1800 to 0.23 gallons in 1850.[7] The only drink that moved in the opposite direction was coffee, benefiting from tariff reductions in the 1820s and increasing from 0.34 lb per head per year in 1815 to 1.35 lb in 1854, its peak before beginning a long-term fall:[8] reductions in its price revived public drinking in a new type of Coffee Rooms, and also brought coffee into some urban working-class budgets. With this exception, the drinks considered were all 'normal goods' established in the previous century, and their decline in the first half of the nineteenth argues a fall in living standards for large sections of the population. Historians who dispute the appropriateness of the description 'the hungry forties' may be more willing to accept 'the thirsty thirties.'[9]

Conversely, there is strong evidence for a rise in disposable income in the third quarter of the century. Beer, spirits and wine in the United Kingdom all reached nineteenth-century peaks within a year of each other – spirits in 1875 at 1.30 gallons a year, beer at 34.4 gallons (England and Wales 40.5 gallons in 1875–9), and wine at 0.56 gallons in 1876.[10] Also between 1850 and 1875 tea consumption rose 2½ times, and sugar consumption more than doubled, while milk supplies improved as a result of rail transport and better distribution methods. In this period, therefore, there was no substitution of one drink for another: consumers were drinking both more alcoholic and non-alcoholic drinks, and the large increase in tea consumption did not displace the demand for beer and spirits, which traditionally rose in times of favourable economic conditions.

Between 1876 and 1914 a different pattern began to emerge in which all alcoholic drinks now declined despite a continued rise in real wages in the first 20 years of this period: beer consumption fell from 34.4 gallons per head per year to 26.7 in 1914, spirits from 1.30 to 0.69, and wine from 0.56 to 0.23 gallons. Reasons for this major change have been suggested in previous chapters (see particularly Chapter 6,), where it is argued that the development of new spending patterns and recreational opportunities was at last beginning to break the hold of alcohol on consumers' time and income. Tea, on the other hand, continued its upward progress from 4.4 lb per head per year to 6.9 lb in 1914, while the category of other non-alcoholic drinks also expanded in this period. Cocoa – formerly 'chocolate' – moved into mass consumption in the late nineteenth century as a result of technological developments and factory production by a handful of large firms. The key invention was that of a Dutch chemist, Conrad van Houten, who in 1828 developed a press that extracted most of the fat content of the bean, or cocoa-butter: this left the defatted powder for use as a smoother, more soluble drink, while the cocoa-butter was combined with sugar and flavourings for solid chocolate. The van Houten process was not used widely in Britain until the last third of the century, Frys, Cadburys and other manufacturers continuing to make the old form of cocoa, to which starch (arrowroot, sago, tapioca or powdered lentils) was added to counteract the fat, and some consumers preferred this thicker drink, which they believed was more nutritious. Advertising stressed the medicinal benefits of 'Dietetic', 'Homeopathic' and 'Pulmonic' brands for invalids and children, but it was only from the 1870s when pure cocoas were widely marketed that consumption rose rapidly – the 0.2 lb per head per year of 1870 rose to 0.54 lb in 1890 and 1.18 lb in 1910. This represented a sixfold growth in 40 years, and by 1910 cocoa consumption was almost double that of coffee.[11]

Also in this period appeared a group of beverages that were explicitly promoted as 'health' or 'food' drinks. Liquid diets had long been recommended for certain categories of invalids and patients, and most cookery books included recipes for drinks based on meat, cereals, eggs or milk, or combinations of these.[12] Nineteenth-century chemists experimented with ways of extracting and concentrating the essences of these substances, the first commercially successful process being that of Justus von Liebig in 1847 for his liquid extract of beef, 'Extractum Carnis'. Production expanded to Britain in 1865, and the extract was renamed 'Oxo' in 1900: formed into 1d cubes, it became instantly convenient and affordable. Another meat extract, 'Bovril' (from Bo = ox and Vrilya, Bulwer Lytton's 'life force' in *The Coming Race*), was the creation of an emigré Scot in Canada, John Lawson Johnston, in 1871: on return to England in 1884 he vigorously promoted it by advertisements and free tastings. Another emigré to America, James Horlick, patented his 'Malted Milk' in 1883, first intended as an infant food: it was later renamed 'Horlicks', and a large factory was built for its English production at Slough between 1906 and 1908. 'Ovaltine', made from malt extract, eggs and milk, was developed by a Swiss chemist, Dr George Wander, in 1904: it was first imported from Switzerland, but an English factory and farm was opened at King's Langley in 1913. These products, together with the growth of milk supplies and soft and temperance drinks, reflected a growing concern about health issues in the middle classes in the years before 1914 and, especially, the improved nutrition of children.

Consumption of alcohol continued to fall between the two World Wars despite a rise in real wages of around a third. Beer output declined from 37.1 million barrels in 1899–1900 to 17.9 million in 1932–3 and at a considerably weaker strength,[13] while spirits followed a similar course from 0.47 proof gallons per head per year in 1920 to 0.32 gallons in 1938 (1900 1.12 gallons).[14] The effect of these changes was to greatly reduce the total quantity of absolute alcohol consumed from about 83 million gallons in 1871–5 to 40 million in 1931–5:[15] consequently, the average contribution of alcohol to energy needs fell from around 250 kcal a day to only about 100 kcal in the 1930s.[16] Tea, on the other hand, climbed to its all-time peak of 10.5 lb per head per year in 1932, equivalent to an average of five cups per person per day: tea comforted during the years of depression, though it provided no calories apart from added milk and sugar.

Through the Second World War and the post-war years of austerity it seemed that the moderation of British drinking habits had become a permanent trend, that 'temperance' had at last prevailed, not in the form of total abstinence but as generally well-controlled, harmless enjoyment: in 1957 consumption of beer and spirits was almost exactly the same as it had been 20 years earlier, while that of wine was considerably less. All this was to change from the late 1950s onwards. While tea consumption has diminished, that of coffee has grown to the point where household expenditure on it is now greater. Soft drinks have shown spectacular increases, but the previous trend towards reduced alcohol consumption has not been maintained: beer grew from 151.6 pints per head per year in 1960 to 175.1 in 1995 (peak 217.1 in 1979), cider from 2.9 pints to 15.3, wine from 4 pints to 25.5, and spirits (at 100 per cent alcohol) from 1.25 pints to 2.25. The outstanding growth in wine and cider has mainly contributed to a marked increase in total consumption of absolute alcohol from 8.25 pints per head per year in 1965 to 12.6 pints in 1995 (esti-mated consumption in the peak year 1876, 19.6 pints).[17]

These increases in wine, cider and coffee suggest some Europeanization of British drinking habits. They have not been made at the expense of beer and spirits, though it is also significant that lager, formerly a European import, now accounts for more than half of the beer market. Again, while British milk consumption, previously one of the highest in Europe, has fallen, that of soft drinks and bottled water has much increased. Yet in the context of world drinking habits the United Kingdom has remained a relatively sober nation, mainly because of its continued adherence to tea as the principal liquid consumed: in the league of alcohol-consuming coun-tries the United Kingdom stands nineteenth in the world with 7.5 litres of absolute alcohol per person per year, well behind France (11.4 litres), Germany (10.3) and even Switzerland (9.7), though ahead of the United States (6.6 litres) or Norway (3.7).[18] In the most recent years growth rates for most drinks have slackened or levelled off, and it may well be that consumers are now adjusting to an equilibrium that includes a much wider variety of both alcoholic and non-alcoholic drinks than ever before.

II

In explaining how and why these changes in drinking behaviour occurred two broad sets of reasons have to be considered, material and non-material. In the first place, a drink had to be available in regular, predictable supply for it to become established as a normal good. As we have seen, beer was already a commercial commodity in the Middle Ages as well as a domestic product: the brewing industry responded to the growth of demand from an increasing population by adopting advanced technological processes at an early stage in highly capitalized plants, and by concentrating produc-tion in large, efficient units. It had the advantage of existing retail outlets in the form of public houses, many of which became 'tied' to breweries to create semi-monopolies. The supply of non-indigenous drinks presented greater difficulties. The long history of imported European wines often depended on political or commercial alliances, and was made possible by relatively short sea-routes, but the appropriation of Asian and New World products such as tea, coffee, sugar and rum required elaborate organization and heavy investment in long-haul shipping. Many European countries moved from dependence on irregular and allegedly overpriced local sources to establishing plantations in colonies under their direct control, using native or imported slave labour: colonialization, which often followed on the heels of missionaries and traders, was therefore a key element in the provision of new drinks, whether coffee or rum from the West Indies or cocoa from West Africa. Acquisition of the source of supply was not, however, inevitable, the outstanding exception being tea, where, for nearly 200 years, the East India Company traded with China before British-controlled estates were developed in India.

It was equally important that consumers should be able to buy these goods conveniently at no great distance from home: wealthier customers in the countryside could send their orders to the nearest market town or even to London for delivery, but most people in the eighteenth and earlier nineteenth centuries relied on local shops, pedlars and occasional visits to markets. One reason why tea rather than coffee moved into mass consumption at this time was its wider availability in shops of many kinds, including the small village shop. Convenient packaging was also important, whether packeted tea or cocoa, bottled beer or milk. In the late nineteenth century the development of multiple grocery chains and co-operative stores heralded a retailing revolution that further increased availability while lowering prices: today's supermarkets are a logical extension of the principles of bulk purchase, high turnover and relatively low profit margins.

It is obvious that drinks had to be affordable by sufficiently large groups for market supply forces to operate. Britain's prosperity during the first half of the eighteenth century allowed new commodities to be quickly appropriated not only by the middling classes but also by many wage-earners in town and country, and once established as integral parts of the dietary pattern they survived when economic conditions deteriorated. However, levels of consumption normally varied in line with trade cycles, so that in bad times poorer consumers tended to reduce purchases of more expensive foods and drinks, but not to omit them completely. Tea, established in working-class diets in the first half of the century, survived through the second half despite rising prices and falling real wages because it had passed from luxury to necessity: labouring families buying one ounce of tea a week out of miserably low wages were behaving rationally, despite contemporary criticism, because no drink other than water would have cost less.

As caffeine drinks became the principal family beverages, the role of alcohol gradually changed towards more recreational use and was more sensitive to movements in disposable income. Consumption of spirits had greatly increased in the earlier years of the eighteenth century but became a natural target for economy when prices and levels of taxation rose later. The downward trend of all alcoholic drinks continued during the first half of the nineteenth century but, remarkably, they were now joined by tea and sugar: we have argued that this strongly suggests a reduction in disposable income of many of the working classes, lending support to the 'pessimist' case in the standard-of-living debate. Paul Glennie has observed that 'When incomes rose, working-class consumption decisions stemmed from consumption cultures formed within low-income contexts':[19] thus, in the period of rising real wages 1850–75, consumers bought more of all drinks, alcoholic and non-alcoholic, which they had previously had to restrict. As yet, alternative outlets for spare income were still limited, but by the last quarter of the century new goods and recreational amenities were successfully competing with traditional patterns of working-class spending to cause a long-term fall in alcohol consumption.

The same holds for the inter-war years, when improved standards of living for the majority coincided with a continued reduction in alcohol consumption. Better housing, food and dress, more holidays and new forms of entertainment made greater calls on income: it was not that most consumers could not afford more alcohol (there were, of course, exceptions among the unemployed), but that their wants had changed. What is unique about the period from the 1960s onwards is that not only has a taste for new forms of alcohol emerged alongside that for coffee and soft drinks, but spending on housing, durable goods, transport, holidays and entertainment has also risen sharply – the volume of disposable income has allowed both. Food, historically the largest item in household budgets, now takes a much smaller proportion than formerly – 17.8 per cent in 1994–5, including beverages, compared with 30.5 per cent in 1960: alcoholic drinks at the later date took 4.3 per cent of family expenditure compared with 3.2 per cent.[20] Many families now have dual earners, and most have many fewer dependent children than in the past: consequently, consumers' choice of food and drink is less constrained by income than at any earlier time.

Availability and affordability are key components of choice, but the physical environment in which drinks are consumed is also important. The new hot beverages adopted after 1650 fitted existing usage in which people of all classes were familiar with warm drinks – heated ale, possets, caudels, toddies and punches – especially in cold weather. They were appreciated in ill-heated houses and outdoor work before the age of factories and offices. Labourers who brewed tea while working on the roads or in the fields welcomed its warmth and stimulation, while their social superiors were woken to the comfort of tea in bed. But caffeine beverages were not merely additions to the existing range of hot drinks: their greater significance was in contributing to a revolutionary change in the system of nutrition among the poorer classes even more than among the wealthy. Until the eighteenth century the food of working people had included more meat, dairy products and vegetables in addition to cereals, often prepared in the form of soups, broths, pottage and, in the North and Scotland, porridge: it therefore consisted of meals that were warm and moist. In the unfavourable economic climate of the later eighteenth century bread increasingly replaced this former variety as meat, milk, cheese and butter became more expensive.[21] As free fuel from woods and wastes disappeared under the advance of enclosures, home cooking became more restricted: traditional domestic skills like baking and brewing declined while dependence on shop-bought bread and groceries and commercially brewed beer increased. Thus, by an apparently strange inversion, white bread and tea, once the luxuries of the rich, became hallmarks of a poverty-line diet. Tea provided warmth and fluid to meals that often consisted only of bread with some occasional cheese or bacon, giving the semblance of a hot meal to a cold, dry one: as one of the few defenders of the use of tea by the poor, the Revd David Davies pointed out, without it their diet would be reduced to bread and water.[22] In fact, the bread-and-tea diet was a rational choice for restricted incomes: white wheaten bread was more palatable than coarse wholemeal and provided 384 calories per penny in the 1790s, twice as many as meat or sugar though considerably fewer than the oatmeal and potatoes more widely used in the North and in Scotland.[23] These, in any case, required cooking: the tea-and-bread diet was quick and convenient, an instant, anytime meal. For the poor of the nineteenth century, whether in country or town, it became all but universal, and while any superior foods such as meat were reserved for male breadwinners, it was said that women and children 'lived on bread and tea', just as in Vienna in the 1890s a survey reported that working-class women lived on *Kaffeesuppe*[24] (coffee with pieces of bread).

The trend towards cold drinks in contemporary Britain may also be explained partly by environmental factors. It would not be an exaggeration to say that Britain has experienced a heating revolution since the 1950s in which homes and offices, shops, cars and public transport are warmed as never before: it may also be that average temperatures have risen as a result of global warming and that winters, in particular, are milder than previously. Bodies that in the past needed heavy clothes and hot beverages now wear lighter dress and take their milk and soft drinks, lager, cider and white wine from the domestic refrigerator. Iced coffee and tea have not yet progressed far compared with the United States, where in 1947 a survey reported that 40 per cent of Americans drank iced tea but never hot,[25] and iced water is not automatically served in restaurants, but a transatlantic influence appears to be playing some part in a general trend towards cold drinks, which fit better with lighter meals, salads and continental dishes than do hot tea or warm beer.

The role of the state in influencing the consumption of drinks is difficult to assess. Fundamental was its policy of taxing drinks as a reasonably convenient source of revenue: thus, beer was taxed from 1654, tea from 1660, spirits from 1684, the rates of duty usually reflecting the needs of war or foreign policy. Previous chapters have noted, for example, the effects of the Methuen Treaty with Portugal in 1703 on Iberian wine consumption, the reduction of the coffee duty in the 1820s, and the gradual lowering of the tea duty in the later nineteenth century: by contrast, tea consumption in the first half of that century was restricted by penal duties, and that of beer and spirits by heavy taxation during the two World Wars. Taxation policy steered an erratic course between Free Trade ideology, which underlaid the Beerhouse Act of 1830 and Gladstone's attempt to popularize light wines in 1860, and pressure by the temperance movement to make alcohol less accessible by increasing its cost and restricting retail access. Throughout the first half of the nineteenth century taxes on alcohol and liquor licences contributed over 30 per cent of total tax revenue, rising to 43.4 per cent (the peak) in 1879–80, but falling to 14.2 per cent in 1935–6 as consumption fell and other forms of taxation became more important.[26]

Beyond its inconsistent incursions into taxation and licensing the modern state had little to do with any health aspects of drinks. Early attempts to suppress the adulteration of beer and spirits, tea and coffee, were more concerned to protect the revenue against loss than to protect the consumer against deleterious substances, though with the appointment of Public Analysts after 1872 the safety of foods and drinks received greater attention. Before that, the condition of water supplies had become of public concern following the outbreaks of cholera, and from 1852 legislation, though not effective for many years, was intended to ensure that water was 'pure and wholesome'. The outstanding instance of consumption deliberately induced by government policy was that of milk, publicly subsidized for infants, children and expectant mothers from the 1930s. Though supported by dairy interests and the Milk Marketing Boards, it was primarily due to the influence of nutritionists like John Boyd Orr that the value of milk, particularly for under-nourished children, was recognized.[27] Subsidized supplies raised average milk consumption from 3 pints per person per week to 5 pints during the war and until the 1970s when universal public provision was felt to be no longer justified.

But, as Ben Fine has observed, 'consumption is dependent upon a continuous and shifting relationship between the physical and the social properties of commodities'.[28] Drinks are consumed not only, or even mainly, because they are available and affordable: they have to be desired and enjoyed. Alcoholic drinks had always contributed to conviviality, celebration and festivity, and through their varying rituals confirmed membership and fellowship within groups: beer and wine represented differences in social status but shared the common element of sociability, 'the framework and introduction for conversation and conviviality'.[29] While alcohol in moderation liberated the drinker from mundane restraints and anxieties, the adoption of the caffeine drinks depended on a different set of social attributes. It was initially important that they were expensive novelties, which thereby defined the social superiority of users: they announced status publicly, and were 'in the fashion' as markers of modernity at a time of new thought in art, science and politics. It was probably not so important in the first place that these drinks were immediately enjoyed as that they were seen to be consumed. The reasons why caffeine drinks were adopted by the bourgeoisie were somewhat different. Social emulation was doubtless important for some people, but tea and coffee for this class carried other meanings, of sobriety and seriousness, increasing mental activity without the impairing effects of alcohol. In the Age of Enlightenment it was a rational use of time for men to drink these beverages, for women part of 'the civilizing process' that was bringing more polite manners and gentler relationships into domestic life. Louis Lewin believed that caffeine could 'sterilize nature and extinguish carnal desires': certainly, it did not stimulate sexual virility or physical passion.[30] As tea later moved into mass consumption it lost its original associations with novelty and luxury to become, above all, the drink of morality and respectability, firmly linked with the religious revival and the temperance movement and, more generally, with Victorian values of work, thrift and sobriety.

Part of the appeal of the new, hot beverages was that they could so easily be sweetened: sugar was added to tea, coffee and chocolate almost from their first appearance, and by the early eighteenth century was all but universal, the demand for one reinforcing that for the other. Consumers had long been familiar with sweet ale, mead, naturally sweet Mediterranean wines and the addition of honey to warm drinks, so that sweetening the bitterness of caffeine was a natural extension of existing custom. Like spices, sugar also enjoyed a generally favourable medical opinion as a drug that could alter the humoral balance of the body,[31] and although the fact that it added calories to the food of the poor was not yet known, it was appreciated that it helped to relieve the monotony of cereal-based diets. It may further be argued, as does Sidney Mintz, that part of the hidden appeal of sugar lay in the meanings of affection, love and even sex that it conveyed, gratifying both donor and receiver.[32] The craving for sweetness was, of course, evident in many spirits, cordials and fortified wines, while the great popularity of soft drinks among younger consumers is also directly associated with their sweetness. A recent survey found that only 30 per cent of British people over 10 now take sugar in their tea,[33] suggesting that contemporary tastes may have changed under the influence of dietary concerns, although any reduction here is more than compensated by the high quantities of sugar in modern manufactured foods: in industrialized societies total sugar consumption is approximately twenty-five times greater than in the mid-eighteenth century.[34]

Every one of the drinks that has been considered was at some time promoted as not only enjoyable but also healthy. This was especially the case with newly introduced products, whether the caffeine drinks of the seventeenth century, which were announced as virtual cure-alls, or the soft drinks of the twentieth century, which were advertised as 'brain tonics' or general invigorators. It is as though the purely pleasurable qualities of these substances were insufficient: consumption needed to be justified by the belief that they were beneficial, almost a different type of medicine. From the eighteenth century onwards the healthy body became a subject of intense interest and concern,[35] and medical testimony was sought to buttress the often wild claims of promoters. Alcoholic drinks presented a greater problem since influential doctors like George Cheyne stressed the importance for health of moderation in meat and strong drink, a message of asceticism conveyed by John Wesley and others to a wider community,[36] although brandy and other spirits long continued to be recommended by doctors as restoratives and even supplied in hospitals. In recent times advertisers' claims for the therapeutic properties of drinks have usually been circumspect and non-specific (for example, 'Beer is Best'): modern campaigns concentrate on 'refreshment' themes, thirst-quenching and reviving attributes often linked to sport, activity and leisure pursuits. 'Health' aspects have continued to be promoted in many contemporary drinks such as non-alcoholic beers, decaffeinated coffee, bottled water, 'diet' and 'New Age' soft drinks: the need for beneficial reassurance remains important.

We have seen how in the past drink was intimately associated with work: labourers in the fields were 'given' beer or cider as a spur to effort, the 'inner life of workshops' imposed frequent occasions for alcohol, while heavy manual workers needed to replace lost fluid with large intakes of beer. Drink was also to a marked extent gender-specific. Women at home drank tea, while the small minority who entered public houses usually drank spirits or a heavy wine. As the nature of work has changed in this century away from manual occupations to lighter employment and shorter hours, the former association of drink with work has almost disappeared, but time, means and opportunity for leisure have greatly increased. Drink in its many forms is now more closely linked with leisure than in the past, and while pubs maintain their traditional popularity, the occasions for recreational drinking have been expanded by clubs, holidays, sports, eating out (now 17 per cent of all meals eaten), entertaining and home entertainments. The other great change is that these activities are now largely shared by men and women, and, in particular, the consumption of alcoholic drinks by women is accepted as normal.[37] As independent earners emancipated from Victorian restraints, women now consume alcohol almost as freely as their grandmothers drank tea. Both alcohol and caffeine may be considered essential substances in modern Britain, fulfilling deep social and psychological needs: 'No civilisation', observed Will Durant, 'has found life tolerable without the things that provide at least some brief escape from reality'.[38]

Notes

Introduction

1 The Tea Council Ltd, London, *Annual Report*, 1997, 7. Source: National Drinks Survey. Statistics relate to the United Kingdom population aged 10 and over.

2 Oscar A. Mendelsohn, *Drinking with Pepys*, London, Macmillan, 1963; S.A.E. Strom, *And So To Dine: A Brief Account of the Food and Drink of Mr Pepys*, London, Frederick Books, George Allen and Unwin, 1955. For details of hippocras (hypocras) and similar 'comforting drinks' see Moira Buxton in C. Anne Wilson (ed.), *Liquid Nourishment: Potable Foods and Stimulating Drinks*, Edinburgh University Press, 1993, 70–8.

3 Neil McKendrick, John Brewer and J.H. Plumb, *The Birth of a Consumer Society: The Commercialization of Eighteenth-Century England*, London, Europa Press, 1982, 9.

4 For example, Brian Harrison, *Drink and the Victorians: The Temperance Question in England, 1815–1872*, 2nd edn, Keele University Press, 1994; Gwylmor Prys Williams and George Thompson Brake, *Drink in Great Britain, 1900 to 1979*, London, Edsall, 1980.

5 Josephine A. Spring and David H. Buss, 'Three Centuries of Alcohol in the British Diet', *Nature*, vol. 270, 15 Dec. 1977, 571.

6 Tom Harrison, *The Pub and the People: A Worktown Study by Mass Observation*, London, Victor Gollancz, 1943, 42–3.

7 Louis Lewin, *Phantastica, Narcotic and Stimulating Drugs*, Trans. from 2nd German ed. by D.H.A. Wirth, London, Kegan Paul, Trench, Trubner, 1931, 227–8.

8 Grant McCracken, 'The History of Consumption: A Literature Review and Consumer Guide', *Journal of Consumer Policy*, vol. 10, 1987, 139.

9 K. Polanyi, *The Great Transformation: The Political and Economic Origins of Our Time*, Boston, Mass, Beacon Press, 1957; F. Braudel, *Capitalism and Material Life, 1400–1800*, London, Weidenfeld and Nicolson, 1973.

10 Important recent contributions include John Brewer and Roy Porter (eds), *Consumption and the World of Goods*, London, Routledge, 1993; Jordan Goodman, Paul E. Lovejoy and Andrew Sherratt (eds), *Consuming Habits: Drugs in History and Anthropology*, London, Routledge, 1995; Daniel Miller (ed.), *Acknowledging Consumption: A Review of New Studies*, London, Routledge, 1995.

11 E.W. Gilboy, 'Demand as a Factor in the Industrial Revolution', in A.H. Cole (ed.), *Facts and Factors in Economic History*, Cambridge, Mass., Harvard University Press, 1932, 628.

12 Stephen Mennell, *All Manners of Food: Eating and Taste in England and France from the Middle Ages to the Present*, Oxford, Basil Blackwell, 1985, 6, 15.

13 Mary Douglas (ed.), *Constructive Drinking: Perspectives on Drink from Anthropology*, Cambridge University Press, 1987, 4.

14 Ibid., 7–8.

1 Water

1 Alev Lytle Croutier, *Taking The Waters: Spirit, Art, Sensuality*, New York, Abbeville Press, 1992, 13–14.
2 Margaret Visser, *The Rituals of Dinner: The Origins, Evolution, Eccentricities and Meaning of Table Manners*, Harmondsworth, Middlesex, Penguin Books, 1993, 110.
3 Ibid., 244–50.
4 Best-known in Britain are the well-dressing ceremonies in Derbyshire villages, floral thanksgivings for pure water.
5 When Greeks and Romans mixed wine with their water they may have instinctively sensed what was only discovered much later – that wine contained sterilizing agents.
6 C. Anne Wilson, *Food and Drink in Britain from the Stone Age to the Nineteenth Century*, Chicago, Academy Publishers, 1991, 369; G. Melvyn Howe, *Man, Environment and Disease in Britain: A Medical Geography*, New York, Harper and Row, 1972, 76.
7 Philip Davies, *Troughs and Drinking Fountains: Fountains of Life*, London, Chatto and Windus, 1989, 2.
8 Phyllis Hembry, *The English Spa, 1560–1815: A Social History*, London, The Athlone Press, 1990, 1.
9 Anne Hardy, 'Water and the Search for Public Health in London in the Eighteenth and Nineteenth Centuries', *Medical History*, vol. 28, Part 3, 1984, 251.
10 Hugh Barty-King, *Water: The Book*, London, Quiller Press, 1992, 36 (the fullest recent account of the history of water supplies).
11 Jean-Pierre Goubert, *The Conquest of Water: The Advent of Health in the Industrial Age*, Trans. by Andrew Wilson, Cambridge, Polity Press, 1989, 2.
12 For details of these works see H.W. Dickinson, *Water Supply of Greater London*, Newcomen Society, Leamington Spa and London, The Courier Press, 1954, chs II and III; J. Jeffery, *The Statutory Water Companies: Their History and Development*, Richmond, Surrey, Michael Collins, 1981, 7–11. The cost of the New River undertaking is estimated at over £29,000.
13 William Blackstone, *Commentaries on the Laws of England*, Oxford, 1766, vol. II, 14; cited W. Scott Tebb, *The Metropolitan Water Supply*, T. Connell and Sons, c.1905, 4. 'The monopoly or vested interest in water is therefore contrary to the principles of English law' (Tebb).
14 Harold J. Laski, W. Ivor Jennings and William A. Robson, *A Century of Municipal Progress, 1835–1935*, London, George Allen and Unwin, 1935, 311–2.
15 J.A. Hassan, 'The Growth and Impact of the British Water Industry in the Nineteenth Century', *Economic History Review*, vol. 38, Part 4, 1985, Table 1, 534.
16 The Chelsea Co. 1723, Southwark Co. 1760, Lambeth Co. 1785, Vauxhall Co. 1805, West Middlesex Co. 1806, East London Co. 1807, Kent Co. 1809, Grand Junction Co. 1811. G. Nahlis, 'London's Water Supply, 1800–1830: The Controversy over Control', MA dissertation, Brunel University, 1990, Table 1, 7.
17 A. Boorde, *A Compendyous Regyment or a Dyetary of Helth*, 1542. Cited Wilson, op. cit., 384.
18 Howe, op. cit., 131.
19 Hembry, op. cit., the best and fullest account of the development of the English spa. Between 1560 and 1815 173 spas opened in England, many of which had only a short existence.
20 For the history of the trade in bottled mineral waters see this volume, Chapter 5, 97–8.

21 Hardy, op. cit., 254–8. Lucas calculated that Thames water contained 16 grains of solid matter per gallon, New River water 14 grains: he believed that both were safe for drinking if allowed to settle.

22 Mrs Charlotte Mason, *The Ladies' Assistant for Regulating and Supplying the Table*, London, J. Walter, 6th edn 1787, 479–84.

23 Hembry, op. cit., 161–2.

24 David Vaisey (ed.), *The Diary of Thomas Turner, 1754–1765*. Quoted Brigid Allen (ed.), *Food: An Oxford Anthology*, Oxford University Press, 1994, 323–4.

25 As in prison diets, where bread and water were part of the punishment, the lowest regime on which life could be supported.

26 Dorothy Hartley, *Water in England*, London, Macdonald, 1964, 192.

27 Peter Brears, *Traditional Food in Yorkshire*, Edinburgh, John Donald, 1987, 136–9.

28 Hartley, op. cit., 200.

29 Edwin Grey, *Cottage Life in a Hertfordshire Village*, Harpenden, Hertfordshire, Harpenden and District Local History Society, 1977, 47–9 (1st edn 1934: the account relates to the 1860s and 1870s).

30 Raphael Samuel (ed.), *Village Life and Labour*, London, Routledge and Kegan Paul, 1975, 142. Piped water did not reach Quarry Hill until just before 1914.

31 George Sturt, *Change in the Village*, London, Caliban Books, 1984, 22 (1st edn 1912: the description relates to the 1880s).

32 Flora Thompson, *Lark Rise to Candleford*, Harmondsworth, Middlesex, Penguin Books, 1976, 22–3.

33 B. Seebohm Rowntree and May Kendall, *How The Labourer Lives: A Study of the Rural Labour Problem*, London, Thomas Nelson, 1917, 331.

34 Barty-King, op. cit., 148, 151.

35 Sir Frederic Morton Eden, *The State of the Poor*, 3 vols, London, Frank Cass, 1966, vol. I, 496–7, 525, 531, 542 (facsimile of 1st edn 1797).

36 B.R. Mitchell and Phyllis Deane, *Abstract of British Historical Statistics*, Cambridge University Press, 1962, Population and Vital Statistics, Table 8, 24.

37 G.M. Saul, 'John Rennie (1761–1821): One of his Contributions to Waterworks Technology', *Transactions of the Newcomen Society*, vol. 59, 1987–8, 3–8. Rennie constructed a 30–inch 'Grand Main' for the Grand Junction Co. in 1812.

38 Report of the Select Committee on the Supply of Water to the Metropolis, (537), v, 1821, 5, 7. Nahlis, op. cit., provides the fullest account of the official enquiries of 1821–8.

39 Hardy, op. cit., 260.

40 W.M. Stern, 'J. Wright, Pamphleteer on the London Water Supply', *Guildhall Miscellany*, Feb. 1953, 31–4.

41 Report of the Commissioners Appointed to Inquire into the State of the Supply of Water in the Metropolis, 21 April 1828. The Commissioners were the eminent engineer Thomas Telford, W.T. Brande, Professor of Chemistry, and P.M. Roget, Professor of Physiology, both at the Royal Institution.

42 Ibid., 9.

43 Ibid., 11.

44 These were discussed by another Select Committee on the Supply of Water to the Metropolis, (567), viii, 1828.

45 I am grateful to G.M. Saul for this reference.

46 Howe, op. cit., 174.

47 F.B. Smith, *The People's Health, 1830–1910*, London, Weidenfeld and Nicolson, 1990, 230–2.

48 Edwin Chadwick, *Report on the Sanitary Condition of the Labouring Population of Great Britain, 1842*, with an Introd. by M.W. Flinn, Edinburgh University Press, 1965, 136.

49 Ibid., 141, 145.
50 Ibid., 138–9.
51 Ibid., 141, 423–4.
52 Royal Commission on the State of Large Towns and Populous Districts. First Report (572), XVII, 1844; Second Report (602), (610), XVIII, 1845.
53 Laski *et al.*, op. cit., 313–14.
54 J.D. Chambers, *Modern Nottingham in the Making*, Nottingham, Nottingham Journal, 1945, 10. The good supply here was largely due to the efforts of the Waterworks' Engineer, Thomas Hawkesley.
55 A butter-tub holding 8 gallons cost 1s, a pork tub (42 gallons) 2s 6d and a wine-pipe (125 gallons) 'for those who wish to be quite comfortable' £1. J.L. and Barbara Hammond, *The Bleak Age*, West Drayton, Middlesex, Pelican Books, 1947, 69.
56 Anthony S. Wohl, *Endangered Lives: Public Health in Victorian Britain*, Cambridge, Massachussetts, Harvard University Press, 1983, 63.
57 Hammond, op. cit., 69.
58 Laski *et al.*, op. cit., 315.
59 Howe, op. cit., 175–7.
60 Smith, op. cit., 231–2.
61 C.S. Peel, *A Hundred Wonderful Years: Social and Domestic Life of a Century, 1820–1920*, London, John Lane, The Bodley Head, 1920, 44.
62 Flora Tristan, *Promenades dans Londres*, ed. F. Bedarida, 1978. Quoted Goubert, op. cit., 252.
63 Henry Mayhew, *London Labour and the London Poor*, vol. I, *The London Street-Folk*, London, Griffin, Bohn, 1861, 194–5.
64 Quoted J.C. Drummond and Anne Wilbraham, *The Englishman's Food: A History of Five Centuries of English Diet*. Revised edn by Dorothy Hollingsworth, London, Jonathan Cape, 1957, 312.
65 Colin Emmins, *Soft Drinks. Their Origins and History*, Princes Risborough, Buckinghamshire, Shire Publications, 1991, 12. See this volume, Chapter 5.
66 Hembry, op. cit., Schedules D and E, 366–7.
67 Arthur Hill Hassall, *Food and its Adulterations, Comprising the Reports of the Analytical Sanitary Commission of 'The Lancet'*, London, Longman, Brown, Green and Longmans, 1855, 73.
68 Brian Harrison, *Drink and the Victorians: The Temperance Question in England, 1815–1872*, revised edn, Staffordshire, Keele University Press, 1994, 38, 292.
69 Jennifer Davies, *The Victorian Kitchen*, London, BBC Books, 1991, 153.
70 Visser, op. cit., 278. Staffe was the author of *Usages du Monde*, Paris, 1899.
71 Hardy, op. cit., 259.
72 Dorothy Hartley, *Water in England*, London, Macdonald, 1964, 199.
73 Andrew Barr, *Drink*, London, Bantam Press, 1995, 58–9.
74 Harrison, op. cit., 292.
75 Quoted Norman Longmate, *The Waterdrinkers: A History of Temperance*, London, Hamish Hamilton, 1968, 150.
76 John Burnett, *Plenty and Want: A Social History of Food in England from 1815 to the Present Day*, 3rd edn, London, Routledge, 1989, chs. 5 and 10.
77 Bill Luckin, *Pollution and Control: A Social History of the Thames in the Nineteenth Century*, 1988. Quoted Colin Ward, 'Not the Last Word on Water', *History Workshop Journal*, vol. 41, 1996, 227.
78 The Metropolis Water Act 1852 therefore predated the first general legislation controlling food quality, the Food Adulteration Act 1860.
79 Smith, op. cit., 218.
80 Alan Kekwick, 'The Soho Epidemic of Cholera', *The Medico-Legal Journal*, vol. XXXIII, Part 4, 1965, 154–7.

81 Sir Arthur Newsholme, *Fifty Years in Public Health*, George Allen and Unwin, 1935, 93–6.

82 Philip Davies, *Troughs and Drinking Fountains*, op. cit. (the fullest account of this movement).

83 J.A. Hassan, 'The Growth and Impact of the British Water Industry in the Nineteenth Century', *Economic History Review*, vol. 38, Part 4, 1985, 532.

84 Ibid., Table 2, 534.

85 Barty-King, op. cit., 117, 133–4, 145–7.

86 Opposition to municipalization in London was led by Percy Blakelock, who established the Water Companies' Association in 1885.

87 For a résumé of the Royal Commission on Water Supply within the Metropolis, 1899–1900, see P. and G. Ford, *A Breviate of Parliamentary Papers, 1900–1916*, Shannon, Irish University Press, 1969, 54–6.

88 Laski *et al.*, op. cit., 316–7; Hassan, op. cit., Table 3, 536.

89 William A. Robson, 'The Public Utility Services', in Laski *et al.*, op. cit., 319.

90 Hassall, op. cit., 85.

91 Letter to *The Times*, 7 July 1855.

92 Britain subsequently avoided the later cholera epidemics that affected France and other Continental contries in 1873, 1884–5 and 1892. Goubert, op. cit., 228.

93 Royal Commission on the Pollution of Rivers, Third Report, (3850), xxxiii, 1867, vol. 1, 11.

94 F.B. Smith, op. cit., 219–20, 95; P.J. Smith, 'The Legislated Control of River Pollution in Victorian Scotland', *Scottish Geographical Magazine*, vol. 98, Part 2, 1982, 66–76.

95 Christopher Hamlin, *A Science of Impurity: Water Analysis in Nineteenth Century Britain*, Berkeley and Los Angeles, University of California Press, 1990, 153–6, 179, 195–6. There was some tension between the rôles and opinions of the two men, since Frankland's reports were frequently much more critical of the companies.

96 Fourth Annual Report of the Local Government Board, 1874–5, (C1328), xlii, 1875, 264–6.

97 Tenth Annual Report of the LGB, 1880–81, (C2982), cxi–cxii, 1881.

98 Twenty-eighth Annual Report of the LGB, 1898–9, (C9444), 1899, cli–clv.

99 Wohl, op. cit., 116.

100 Hamlin, op. cit., 301–3.

101 F.B. Smith, op. cit., 227.

102 B. Seebohm Rowntree, *Poverty: A Study of Town Life*, 4th edn, London, Macmillan, 1902, 187–8.

103 Jeffery, op. cit., 19; Barty-King, op. cit., 150.

104 Hamlin, op. cit., 1.

105 How much of this was drunk cannot be known, but a contemporary estimate of the minimum for drinking of 0.33 gallons per head per day and 0.75 gallons for cooking may be a fair indication. Herman Finer, *Municipal Trading: A Study in Public Administration*, London, George Allen and Unwin, 1941, 376.

106 John Sheail, '"Deadwells". Urban Growth and the Threat to Public Health: An Interwar Perspective', *Social History of Medicine*, vol. 6, Part 3, 1993, 367–84.

107 Barty-King, op. cit., 153.

108 The *East Anglian Daily Times*, 22 August 1995. Quoted Ward, op. cit., 229.

109 Derek Cooper, *The Beverage Report*, London, Routledge and Kegan Paul, 1970, 4.

110 Fred Pearce, *Watershed: The Water Crisis in Britain*, London, Junction Books, 1982, 57, 62.

111 *Food Adulteration and How to Beat It*, The London Food Commission, Unwin, 1988, 132. The maximum admissible level for nitrates is 50 milligrams per

litre: the EC Directive allowed Britain until the end of 1995 to conform. In 1990 ninety-four water supply zones, serving 5.5 million people, contained nitrate concentrations above the maximum at some time in the year.

112 *Drinking Water Quality, 1995*, Report of Thames Water Utilities, 1996, 2, 4. In London chloramine is used instead of chlorine as the residual disinfectant together with small amounts of ammonia: these can be converted naturally into nitrite in the distribution system.

113 There has been long-continued controversy over whether the Camelford incident may be a factor in Alzheimer's disease or in a small cluster of cases of leukaemia among teenagers.

114 Ronald F. Packham and James M. Symons, *Drinking Water: The Plain Facts*, Marlow, Buckinghamshire, Water Research Centre, 1995, 11. In July 1996 a case was brought against South-West Water Utilities alleging that pollution of its supplies caused 400–500 cases of diarrhoea and sickness in South Devon.

115 *Water Supply Companies' Factbook*, 1994/5 edn, The Water Companies Association, 1995. 32 per cent of the total goes for waste disposal, 29 per cent for washing and bathing, 35 per cent for uses outside the house and in leakage.

116 *Tap Water Consumption in England and Wales*, Findings from the 1995 National Survey, Birmingham, MEL Research, 1996, iv, 19. This independent research was commissioned by the Drinking Water Inspectorate, and conducted between February and April 1995.

117 *Public Attitudes to Water and Water Privatization*, The Rubens Institute of Industrial and Environmental Health and Safety, University of Surrey, Sept. 1988, Table 1.

118 Apollinaris was marketed in Britain in the 1870s by George Smith, proprietor of the *Pall Mall Gazette*, and Perrier was developed by St John Harmsworth, younger brother of the founder of the *Daily Mail*. Timothy Green, 'Apostles of Purity', *Smithsonian*, vol. 15, Part 7, 1984, 108–10; Maureen and Timothy Green, *The Good Water Guide*, Rosendale Press, revised edn 1994, 26–7, 68–9. For the early history of bottled waters see Chapter 5 of this volume.

119 It has been suggested that the 'fizz' of sparkling waters and the shapes and labels of bottles make them slightly festive, Visser, op. cit., 248. Carbonated waters were at first more popular, but 'still' waters now account for 60 per cent of the UK market.

120 *Tap Water Consumption in England and Wales*, op. cit., Table 4.3, 23.

2   Milk

1 C. Anne Wilson, *Food and Drink in Britain from the Stone Age to Recent Times*, London, Constable, 1973, 150–2.

2 Alexander Fenton, 'Milk and Milk Products in Scotland: the Role of the Milk Marketing Boards', in Adel P. den Hartog (ed.) *Food Technology, Science and Marketing: European Diet in the Twentieth Century*, East Linton, East Lothian, Tuckwell Press, 1995, 89.

3 Carole Shammas, 'The Eighteenth-Century English Diet and Economic Change', *Explorations in Economic History*, vol. 21, Part 3, 1984, Table 5, 264.

4 J.C. Drummond and Anne Wilbraham, *The Englishman's Food: A History of Five Centuries of English Diet*. Revised ed. by Dorothy Hollingsworth, London, Jonathan Cape, 1957, App. A, 465–7.

5 Shammas, op. cit., 264.

6 G.E. Fussell, *The English Dairy Farmer, 1500–1900*, London, Frank Cass, 1966, 17 et seq., on 18th century breeds and breeders.

7 Ibid., 303–4.

8 Quoted G.E. and K.R. Fussell, *The English Countryman: His Life and Work from Tudor Times to the Victorian Age*, London, Orbis Publishing, 1981, 92.

9 Catherine Geissler and Derek J. Oddy (eds), *Food, Diet and Economic Change Past and Present*, Leicester, Leicester University Press, 1993, Introd. 3 et seq.

10 A. Gibson and T.C. Smout, 'From Meat to Meal: Changes in Diet in Scotland', in Geissler and Oddy, ibid., ch. 2, 10–34.

11 David Davies, *The Case of Labourers in Husbandry, Stated and Considered*, Fairfax, New Jersey, Augustus Kelley, 1977 (reprint of 1st edn 1795), 40.

12 Ibid., App. Collection of Accounts, 131 et seq.

13 D.J. Oddy, 'Food, Drink and Nutrition', in F.M.L. Thompson (ed.), *The Cambridge Social History of Britain, 1750–1950*, 2 vols, Cambridge University Press, 1990, vol. 2, Table 5.2, 269.

14 Ibid., Table 5.5, 274.

15 Shammas, op. cit., Table 3, 260–1.

16 Williamm Cobbett, *Cottage Economy*, London, Peter Davies, 1926, 81–92 (1st edn 1823).

17 Bryan Morgan, *Express Journey, 1864–1964: A Centenary History of the Express Dairy Co. Ltd.*, London, Newman Neame, 1964, 10.

18 Roger Scola, *Feeding the Victorian City: The Food Supply of Manchester, 1770–1870*, ed. W.A. Armstrong and Pauline Scola, Manchester University Press, 1992, 76, 88–9.

19 Henry Mayhew, *London Labour and the London Poor*, vol. 1, *The London Street Folk*, London, Griffin, Bohn, 1861, 191–3. Skimmed milk was also sold on Sundays in public places such as Battersea Fields, Clapham Common and Hampstead Heath.

20 Fussell, op. cit., 311.

21 Morgan, op. cit., 4–38.

22 P.J. Atkins, 'The Retail Milk Trade in London, 1790–1914', *Economic History Review*, vol. 13, Part 4, 1980, Table 3, 527–8.

23 Scola, op. cit., 73.

24 B. Seebohm Rowntree, *Poverty: A Study of Town Life*, 4th edn, London, Macmillan, 1902, 191.

25 Fenton, op. cit., 2.

26 E.H. Whetham, 'The London Milk Trade, 1860–1900', *Economic History Review*, Second Series, 1964, xvii, 370.

27 Small cowkeepers also long survived in heavily Jewish areas of London like Whitechapel, where it was a Kosher requirement that the cow should be milked directly into a vessel and its milk not mixed with other milk.

28 Arthur Baxter, 'Milk-Sellers', in Charles Booth (ed.), *Life and Labour of the People in London*, vol. VII, *Population Classified by Trades*, London, Macmillan, 1896, 174–6. Baxter believed that at least half the dairymen in London were Welsh, the sons and relatives of small Welsh farmers.

29 L. Margaret Barnett, *British Food Policy During the First World War*, Boston, Mass., George Allen and Unwin, 1985, 3.

30 The numbers of cows and heifers in milk or in calf in England grew from 1.46 million in 1871 to 2.11 million in 1911: estimated yields per cow increased from 384 gallons p.a. in the early eighteenth century to 550 gallons in 1908: Fussell, *English Dairy Farmer*, op. cit., 49–51, 328–30.

31 David Taylor, 'The English Dairy Industy, 1860–1930', *Economic History Review*, Second Series, 1976, XXIX, Table 3, 589–91.

32 Alan Jenkins, *Drinka Pinta: The Story of Milk and the Industry that Serves It*, London, Heinemann, 1970, 51.

33 Atkins, 'Retail Milk Trade', op. cit., Table 1, 524.

34 Edith Whetham, 'The London Milk Trade, 1900–1930', in Derek Oddy and Derek Miller (eds), *The Making of the Modern British Diet*, London, Croom Helm, 1976, 70.
35 Farmers supplying London wholesalers usually received 5–6d a gallon in summer and 8–10d in winter: the doubling of the retail price represented collection, transport and distribution costs plus profit. Whetham, ibid., 66.
36 W.E. Bear, 'The Food Supply of Manchester', *Journal of the Royal Agricultural Society*, Third Series, 1897, VIII, 507.
37 Elizabeth Gaskell, *Sylvia's Lovers* (1863), quoted Brigid Allen (ed.), *Food: An Oxford Anthology*, Oxford University Press, 1994, 175.
38 R. Hutchison, 'Report on the Dietaries of Scotch Agricultural Labourers', *Transactions of the Highland and Agricultural Society of Scotland*, vol. II, 1868–9, 25.
39 On changes in diet generally, see John Burnett, *Plenty and Want: A Social History of Food in England from 1815 to the Present Day*, 3rd edn, London, Routledge, 1989. For the diets of agricultural labourers, see chs. 2 and 7.
40 T.C. Barker, D.J. Oddy and John Yudkin, *The Dietary Surveys of Dr Edward Smith, 1862–3*, London, Staples Press, 1970, Table 2, 40.
41 Sixth Report of the Medical Officer of Council on Health, Report by Dr Edward Smith on the Food of the Poorer Labouring Classes, PP. XXVIII, 1864, 251.
42 Drummond and Wilbraham, op. cit., 302–3.
43 Local Government Board, *Report on Condensed Milks, with Special Reference to their Use as Infants' Foods*, 1911, New Series No. 56.
44 Elizabeth Roberts, 'Working Wives and their Families', in Theo Barker and Michael Drake (eds), *Population and Society in Britain, 1850–1980*, London, Batsford, 1982, 156–7. The alleged correlation between infant mortality and mothers' employment is disputed by Carol Dyhouse, 'Working-class mothers and infant mortality in England, 1895–1914', *Journal of Social History*, vol. 12, No. 2, 1978.
45 Ian Buchanan, 'Infant Feeding, Sanitation and Diarrhoea in Colliery Communities, 1880–1911', in Derek J. Oddy and Derek S. Miller (eds), *Diet and Health in Modern Britain*, London, Croom Helm, 1985, 148–78.
46 Lady Bell (Mrs Hugh Bell), *At the Works: A Study of a Manufacturing Town*, New edn 1911, London, Thomas Nelson, 92 et seq.
47 Maud Pember Reeves, *Round About a Pound a Week*, London, Virago Press, 1979, 99–100 (1st edn 1913).
48 B. Seebohm Rowntree and May Kendall, *How the Labourer Lives: A Study of the Rural Labour Problem*, London, Thomas Nelson, 1917, 308 (1st edn 1913).
49 Deborah Dwork, 'The Milk Option. An Aspect of the History of the Infant Welfare Movement in England, 1898–1908', *Medical History*, vol. 31, Part 1, 1987, 51–69.
50 Frederick A. Filby, *A History of Food Adulteration and Analysis*, London, George Allen and Unwin, 1934, 52.
51 P.J. Atkins, 'Sophistication Detected, or the Adulteration of the Milk Supply, 1850–1914', *Social History*, vol. 16, Part 3, 1991, 320–321.
52 On Hassall's work, and on food adulteration generally in the 19th century, see Burnett, *Plenty and Want*, op. cit., chs 5 and 10.
53 Arthur Hill Hassall, *Food and its Adulterations, Comprising the Reports of the Analytical Sanitary Commission of 'The Lancet' for the Years 1851–1854 Inclusive*, London, Longman, Brown, Green and Longmans, 1855, 320, 343.
54 Hassall, ibid., 324–6, citing a report by a surgeon, H. Rugg, *Observations on London Milk*.
55 Select Committee on Adulteration of Food. First Report, 432, VIII, 1855, Qs.5, 759–74. Dr Normandy was the author of *A Commercial Handbook of Chemical Analysis* (1850).

56 Ibid., Third Report, PP. 379, VIII, 1856, Q.396.
57 John Burnett, 'Food Adulteration in Britain in the 19th Century and the Origins of Food Legislation', in *Ernährung und Ernährungslehre im 19. Jahrhundert*, Göttingen, Vandenbreck & Ruprecht, 1976, 117–31.
58 Annual Report of the Local Government Board, 1880/1881, Cmd. 2982, lxxxviii–lxxxix.
59 Annual Report of the Local Government Board, 1898/1899, Cmd. 9444, cxxxiv.
60 Public Health (Milk and Cream) Regulations, 1912.
61 Keith Vernon, 'Pus, Sewage, Beer and Milk: Microbiology in Britain, 1870–1940', *History of Science*, vol. 28, Part 3, 1990, 301.
62 A useful summary of the Royal Commission on the Relations between Human and Animal Tuberculosis is in P. and G. Ford, *A Breviate of Parliamentary Papers, 1900–1916*, Shannon, Irish University Press, 1969, 289–90. The Royal Commission was appointed in 1901 but its Final Report was not issued until 1913.
63 P.J. Atkins, 'White Poison? The Social Consequences of Milk Consumption, 1850–1930', *Social History of Medicine*, vol. 5, Part 2, 1992, 217.
64 Vernon, op. cit., 313.
65 John Burnett, 'The Rise and Decline of School Meals in Britain, 1860–1990', in John Burnett and Derek J. Oddy (eds), *The Origins and Development of Food Policies in Europe*, Leicester University Press, 1994, 55–69.
66 F. Lawson Dodd, *Municipal Milk and Public Health*, Fabian Society Tract No. 122, London, 1905, 3rd reprint, 1914, 16–17.
67 Supplies of milk to catering establishments were rationed and the sale of cream prohibited except on doctors' orders. Sir William H. Beveridge, *British Food Control: Economic and Social History of the World War*, London, Humphrey Milford, 1928, 413.
68 Ibid., 310.
69 On the development of child welfare services see Deborah Dwork, *War is Good for Babies and Other Young Children: A History of the Infant and Child Welfare Movement in England, 1898–1918*, London, Tavistock Press, 1986.
70 L. Margaret Barnett, *British Food Policy During the First World War*, Boston, Mass. George Allen and Unwin, 1985, 149–50. The 1918 Order was adopted by twenty-six Metropolitan Boroughs, fifty-one County Boroughs and eighty-seven other local authorities.
71 Morgan, *Express Journey*, op. cit., 48. The Dairy Supply Co. was the whole-saling subsidiary of Express Dairies. Whetham, *London Milk Trade, 1900–1930* gives the date of formation of United Dairies as 1915: Morgan implies that its flotation as a company was in 1917.
72 Whetham, ibid., 71–2.
73 Viscount Astor and B. Seebohm Rowntree, *British Agriculture: The Principles of Future Policy*, Harmondsworth, Middlesex, Penguin Books, 1939, 85–6.
74 Jenkins, op. cit., 44.
75 Sir John Boyd Orr, *Food and the People*, London, The Pilot Press, 1943, 7–8.
76 British Medical Association, *Report of Committee on Nutrition*, London, BMA, 1933, 19.
77 Boyd Orr, *Food and the People*, op. cit., 20–21.
78 Represented by A. Fenner Brockway, *Hungry England*, London, Victor Gollancz, 1932.
79 'The Milk Marketing Board: 61 Years Serving Dairy Farmers', *Milk Producer*, October 1994, 2.
80 Astor and Rowntree, op. cit., 220.
81 In some local education areas including the LCC children could buy two-thirds of a pint for 1d, and in most authorities children recommended for

free milk received two-thirds daily. Marjorie E. Green, *Nutrition and Local Government: What Your Local Authority Can Do*, London, The Children's Minimum Council, 1938, 13.

82 Sir William Crawford and H. Broadley, *The People's Food*, London, William Heinemann, 1938, 218–19.

83 Ibid., 214.

84 Robert Graves and Alan Hodge, *The Long Weekend: A Social History of Great Britain, 1918–1939*, London, Faber and Faber, 1940, 295–6. One milk bar in Upper Regent Street, the Meadow Milk Bar, was managed by a Mr C. Forte.

85 E.S. Turner, *The Shocking History of Advertising*, London, Michael Joseph, 1952, 204. The BMA asked newspapers to insert an advertisement headed 'Is All Milk Safe To Drink?', which, under pressure, they modified to 'Drink Safe Milk'.

86 *Dairy Facts and Figures, 1957*, Thames Ditton, Surrey, The Federation of UK Milk Marketing Boards, Table 6a, 33.

87 *Report of the Committee on Nutrition*, British Medical Association, London, 1950, 48.

88 R.J. Hammond, *History of the Second World War: Food* (2 vols), London, HMSO and Longmans, Green, vol. 1, The Growth of Policy, 1951, 102.

89 *On the State of the Public Health During Six Years of War*. Report of the Chief Medical Officer of the Ministry of Health, 1939–1945. Ministry of Health, London, HMSO, 1946, 93.

90 Hammond, op. cit., vol. 1, 369.

91 Infant mortality fell from 153/1,000 in 1891–1900 to 62 in 1931–5 and 45 in 1944: maternal mortality fell from 3.1/1,000 in 1939 to 1.9 in 1944. *On the State of the Public Health*, 1946, op. cit., 15, 97.

92 *Domestic Food Consumption and Expenditure. Reports of the National Food Survey Committee*, London, HMSO, for 1950 (1952), Table 26, 37; 1969 (1971), Table 17, 75.

93 Ibid., Report for 1959 (1961), Table 29, 52.

94 Lord Hailsham, House of Lords, 14 July 1960, Hansard, vol. 255, No.104, 327.

95 *Milk Drinking in Schools*, London, National Dairy Council Information Booklet No. 2, 1961, 3–4.

96 Margaret Thatcher, 14 June 1971, Hansard, vol. 819, col. 55.

97 David Garner, 'Education and the Welfare State: the School Meals and Milk Service, 1944–1980', *Journal of Educational Administration and History*, vol. 17, Part 2, 1985, 66.

98 *Nutrition in Schools*, Report of the Working Party on Nutritional Aspects of School Meals, 1975, London, Department of Education and Science, HMSO, 11, 18.

99 In 1974 there were 3,380,000 dairy cattle in the UK: milk yield stood at 880 gallons/cow/year compared with 560 gallons in 1938/9. *Dairy Facts and Figures*, op. cit., 1974, 18, 35.

100 *National Drinks Survey*, Drink Type Shares Within Drinks Market, Nielson Beverage Survey, 1994.

101 Caroline Walker and Geoffrey Cannon, *The Food Scandal*, London, Century Publishing Co., 1985, 231.

102 *Liquid Milk Report, 1992*, London, National Dairy Council, 4–5, 15.

103 *Liquid Milk Report*, op. cit., 1990, 3; 1994, 3.

104 M.M. Raats, R. Shepherd and P. Sparks, 'Attitudes, Obligations and Perceived Control In Predicting Milk Selection', *Appetite*, 1993, vol. 20, Part 3, 240.

105 National Food Survey. *Annual Report on Household Food Consumption and Expenditure*, 1994, London, HMSO, 1995, Table B5, 107.

106 *Liquid Milk Report, 1994*, op. cit., 3, 5.
107 Average doorstep delivery prices in 1995 were 38p a pint compared with 28p in supermarkets.
108 In 1993–4 the UK's milk quota was 14,197,000 tonnes, France's 23,503,000 and Germany's 27,765,000. *Dairy Facts and Figures*, 1993, op. cit., Table 34, 65.

3   Tea

1 Louis Lewin, *Phantastica, Narcotic and Stimulating Drugs*, Trans. from 2nd German edn by D.H.A. Wirth, London, Kegan Paul, Trench, Trubner, 1931, 227–8, 263–4. Authorities differ on the amounts of caffeine in tea, coffee and chocolate between the following upper and lower limits: tea 1.0–4.7 per cent, coffee 0.7–3.0 per cent, cocoa 0.07–0.36 per cent. See Paul E. Lovejoy in *Consuming Habits: Drugs in History and Anthropology*, London and New York, Routledge, 1995, 103 and n.2, 119–20.
2 James Mew and John Ashton, *Drinks of the World*, London, The Leadenhall Press, 1892, 299. Lewin, op. cit., states that *c.* 200 substitutes for tea are known throughout the world.
3 Jordan Goodman, Paul E. Lovejoy and Andrew Sherratt (eds), *Consuming Habits*, op. cit. Introduction by Andrew Sherratt, 5.
4 Jill Jonnes, 'The Tale of Tea', *Smithsonian*, vol. 12 (11), 1982, 100.
5 Giovanni Botero, *Delle cause, della grandezza delle citta*, Milan, 1596, 61. Quoted W. Scott Tebb, *Tea and the Effects of Tea Drinking*, London, Cornell and Sons, 1905, 4.
6 William H. Ukers, *All About Tea*, 2 vols, New York, Tea and Coffee Trade Journal Co., 1935, vol. 1, 23.
7 The Portuguese traded with China from their base at Macao since the sixteenth century, and tea-drinking was established in the Portuguese Court before 1660. In 1662 the English Court poet, Edmund Waller, wrote in praise both of tea and the new Queen – 'The best of Queens and best of herbs', etc. Robin Emmerson, *British Tea Pots and Tea Drinking*, Norfolk Museums Service and HMSO, 1992, 2.
8 John E. Wills Jr, 'European Consumption and Asian Production in the Seventeenth and Eighteenth Centuries', in John Brewer and Roy Porter (eds), *Consumption and the World of Goods*, London and New York, Routledge, 1994, 142.
9 The earliest English silver teapot apparently dates from 1670, when one was presented to the Committee of the East India Company by George, Lord Berkeley. Gervas Huxley, *Talking of Tea*, London, Thames and Hudson, 1956, 91. Silver tea cups, of which the Duchess of Lauderdale bought eighteen in 1672, were, not surprisingly, found too hot to hold, and were soon abandoned in favour of porcelain, imported in the holds of East Indiamen; Emmerson, op. cit., 15. The china was stowed below the tea, partly as ballast and to raise the tea above damage by water: the china was not affected by sea water.
10 Sidney W. Mintz, *Sweetness and Power: The Place of Sugar in Modern History*, New York, Viking Penguin, 1985, Note 8, 241.
11 Andrew Sherratt, 'Alcohol and Its Alternatives', ch. 1 in *Consuming Habits*, op. cit., 13–14.
12 See Norbert Elias, *The Civilising Process: The History of Manners*. Trans. by Edmund Jephcott, Oxford, Basil Blackwell, 1978, (1st German edn 1939). Elias cites many examples from conduct literature of the sixteenth to eighteenth centuries on the use of cutlery, plates, serviettes etc.

13 Sidney W. Mintz, 'The Changing Roles of Food in the Study of Consumption', ch. 13 in *Consumption and the World of Goods*, op. cit., 263.
14 John and Linda Pelzer, 'The Coffee Houses of Augustan London', *History Today*, vol. 32, 1982, 41.
15 This custom was well established by the late seventeenth century. In Congreve's *The Double Dealer*, 1694, it is remarked that 'the ladies have retired to tea and scandal'.
16 Jonnes, op. cit., 101. When buying leaf tea from coffee-houses, ladies had had to wait outside in their sedan chairs and send in a male servant to make the purchase. But the Golden Lyon was not a 'tea parlour' (Jonnes), which implies that liquid tea was served there.
17 David MacPherson, *The History of the European Commerce with India*, London, Longman, Hurst, Rees, Orme and Brown, 1812, 132.
18 Neil McKendrick, John Brewer and J.H. Plumb, *The Birth of a Consumer Society: The Commercialization of Eighteenth-Century England*, London, Europa Pubs., 1982, 9.
19 J. Aikin, *A Description of the Country from Thirty to Forty Miles round Manchester*, 1795, London, J. Stockdale, 187–8.
20 Duncan Forbes, *Some Considerations on the Present State of Scotland*, Edinburgh, W. Sands, A. Murray and J. Cohran, 1794, 7.
21 Jonas Hanway, *Letters on the Importance of the Rising Generation of the Labouring Part of our Fellow-subjects*, 2 vols, London, 1767, quoted Mintz, *Sweetness and Power*, op. cit., 117.
22 James Woodforde, *The Diary of a Country Parson*, 1758–1802, ed. John Beresford, Oxford University Press, The World's Classics, 1949, 123, 203. Woodforde had an annual tea bill of £3 18s in addition to occasional payments to 'Andrews, the Smuggler'.
23 Arthur Young, *The Farmer's Tour through the East of England*, 4 vols, London, W. Strahan, 1771, vol. 2, 180–1.
24 Denys Forrest, *Tea for the British: The Social and Economic History of a Famous Trade*, London, Chatto and Windus, 1973, Appendix II, Table 1, Tea Consumption in Britain, 284. The statistics are based on the East India Co.'s sales, less re-exports.
25 Carole Shammas, *The Pre-Industrial Consumer in England and America*, Oxford, Clarendon Press, 1990, Table 4.4, 83–4. Smuggled tea was also often regarded as superior in quality to that generally available.
26 B.R. Mitchell and Phyllis Deane, *Abstract of British Historical Statistics*, Cambridge University Press, 1962, Overseas Trade 4, Official Values of Principal Imports – England and Wales, 1700–1791, 285–6.
27 Hoh-Cheung Mui and Lorna H. Mui, *Shops and Shopkeeping in Eighteenth-Century England*, Kingston, Canada, 1989, 190–1.
28 Woodruff D. Smith, 'From Coffee house to Parlour: The consumption of coffee, tea and sugar in north-western Europe in the seventeenth and eighteenth centuries', ch. 7 in *Consuming Habits*, op. cit., 152–3. The famous Dutch 'tea-doctor' Cornelis Bontekoe advised drinking up to fifty cups of tea a day.
29 Wolfgang Schivelbusch, *Tastes of Paradise: A Social History of Spices, Stimulants and Intoxicants*, Trans. by David Jacobson, New York, Pantheon Books, 1992, 73, 81–3.
30 E.W. Gilboy, 'Demand as a Factor in the Industrial Revolution', 1932. Cited David Felix, 'De Gustibus Disputandem Est: Changing Consumer Preferences in Economic Growth', *Explorations in Economic History*, vol. 16, 1979, 284.
31 Woodruff D. Smith, 'Complications of the Commonplace: Tea, Sugar and Imperialism', *Journal of Interdisciplinary History*, vol. 23(2), 1992, 263–5. The addition of sugar to tea was apparently still a novelty in Italy in 1705: for

black tea the sugar was placed in the cup first, but for green it was fashionable to place a lump of candied sugar in the mouth first. 'One then drinks the boiling tea over the lump, melting it a little at each mouthful, so that the tea is rendered syrupy as one drinks it.' Letter from Lorenzo Magulotti to Leone Strozzi describing a visit to a Dutch lady recently arrived in Italy. Piero Camporesi, *Exotic Brew: The Art of Living in the Age of Enlightenment*, Trans. by Christopher Woodall, Oxford, Polity Press, 1994, 83–4.

32 G.N. Johnstone, 'The Growth of the Sugar Trade and Refining Industry', in Derek Oddy and Derek Miller (eds) *The Making of the Modern British Diet*, London, Croom Helm, 1976, 59.

33 Ibid., Table, 60, citing Noel Deerr, *The History of Sugar*, 2 vols, London, Chapman and Hall, 1949–50, vol. II, 532.

34 Johnstone, op. cit., Table 4, 62.

35 Marcus Arkin, 'Entrepreneurship and the English East India Company', *Business History*, vol. XXIII (1), 1981, 93.

36 John Burnett, *A History of the Cost of Living*, Aldershot, Hampshire, Gregg Revivals, 1993, 128–9, 133.

37 Shammas, *Pre-Industrial Consumer*, op. cit., 134–5. Nutritionists would regard 3,500–4,000 calories per day as necessary for a man engaged in heavy manual work.

38 Ibid., 136–7.

39 Stephen H. Twining, *The House of Twining, 1706–1956*, London, R. Twining and Co. Ltd., 1956, 16, 19, 24, 38, 47–9.

40 Young, *Farmer's Tour*, op. cit., vol. 4, 352.

41 Sir Frederic Morton Eden, *The State of the Poor*, 3 vols, London, J. Davis, 1797, vol. 1, 496–7.

42 'Toast water', made by infusing a burnt crust, hissing hot, in water, was recommended by a London apothecary, James Sedgwick, in 1725. Mew and Ashton, *Drinks of the World*, op. cit., 352.

43 David Davies, *The Case of Labourers in Husbandry*, London, G.G. and J. Robinson, 1795, 39.

44 In the later eighteenth and early nineteenth centuries most large towns had public gardens where music and entertainments accompanied tea and light refreshments. London's most fashionable garden, Ranelagh, charged 2s 6d admission, but Vauxhall, Marylebone and Cuper's Gardens ranged from 6d upwards; others originated from mineral springs such as Islington, Bermondsey and Bagnigge Wells. Some survived into the mid-nineteenth century, Jack Straw's Castle and The Spaniard's Inn on Hampstead Heath being favourites of Charles Dickens. Edward Hewett and W.F. Axton, *Convivial Dickens: The Drinks of Dickens and his Times*, Athens, Ohio University Press, 1983, 11.

45 Joel Mokyr, 'Is There Still Life in the Pessimist Case? Consumption during the Industrial Revolution, 1790–1850', *Journal of Economic History*, XLVIII, 1988, 76–7, citing Ralph Davis, *The Industrial Revolution and British Overseas Trade*, Leicester University Press, 1979, 45–6.

46 Mokyr, Ibid., 78.

47 David Felix, 'De Gustibus Disputandem Est: Changing Consumer Preferences in Economic Growth', *Explorations in Economic History*, 1979, vol. 16, 285, note 34.

48 William Neild, 'Comparative Statement of the Income and Expenditure of Certain Families of the Working Class in Manchester and Dukinfield in the Years 1836 and 1841', *Journal of the Statistical Society of London*, vol. IV, 1841, 320–34. For a full account of the Neild budgets, see John Burnett, *Plenty and Want: A Social History of Food in England from 1815 to the Present Day*, 3rd edn, London, Routledge, 1989, 56–9.

49 Frederick Engels, 'The Condition of the Working-Class in England', in *Karl Marx and Frederick Engels on Britain*, Moscow, Foreign Languages Publishing House, 1953, 107.

50 Twining, op. cit., 111, 114.

51 Edward Smith, *Practical Dietaries for Families, Schools and the Labouring Classes*, London, Henry S. King, 1875 edn, 99.

52 Leone Levi, *Wages and Earnings of the Working Classes. Report to Sir Arthur Bass, MP*, London, John Murray, 1885, Workman's Budget, 1857 and 1884, 34.

53 The 'invention' of afternoon tea is usually credited to the 7th Duchess of Bedford (1788–1861). It probably began in the 1840s, but was still described as a novelty by Fanny Kemble on a visit to Belvoir Castle in 1862. Emmerson, op. cit., 26.

54 It appears that in the eighteenth century milk or cream was poured in first to prevent cracking or discoloration of the fine china by very hot liquid. But the debate about the polite order of tea and milk has continued to the present, fostered by Nancy Mitford's claim in *Noblesse Oblige* that milk in first ('MIF') was 'non-U'. Jane Garney, 'Tea-Time in Britain', *British Heritage*, vol. 8(3), 1987, 56.

55 Emmerson, op. cit., 23.

56 Philippa Levine, 'The Humanising Influences of Five O'Clock Tea', *Victorian Studies*, vol. 33(2), 1990, 306.

57 Report from the Select Committee of the Houses of Lords and Commons on the Affairs of the East India Company, 1830. Reprinted in *The Edinburgh Review*, No. CIV, Jan. 1831, 289.

58 For example, C. Northcote Parkinson, *Trade in the Eastern Seas, 1793–1813*, Cambridge University Press, 1937.

59 Hoh-Cheung Mui and Lorna H. Mui, *The Management of Monopoly: A Study of the English East India Company's Conduct of the Tea Trade, 1783–1833*, Vancouver, University of British Columbia Press, 1984.

60 Ibid., 3.

61 Ibid., 131.

62 Robert Fortune, *Two Visits to the Tea Countries of China and the British Tea Plantations in the Himalaya*, 3rd edn, London, 1853, vol. II, 69–71. Fortune estimated that at least half a pound of Prussian blue and gypsum was used in the glazing of 100 lb of green tea.

63 Frederick Accum, *A Treatise on Adulterations of Food and Culinary Poisons*, London, Longman, Hurst, Rees, Orme and Brown, 1820, 239–240.

64 Arthur Hill Hassall, *Food and its Adulterations, Comprising the Reports of the Analytical Sanitary Commission of 'The Lancet'*, London, Longman, Brown, Green and Longmans, 1855, VII.

65 Annual Reports of the Local Government Board, 1876–1914: Quarterly Reports of Public Analysts, Statistics of Tea Adulteration. From 1875 tea imports continued to be examined by the Customs Department and adulterated consignments destroyed: tea was therefore now subject to a double check.

66 Sir Percival Griffiths, *The History of the Indian Tea Industry*, London, Weidenfeld and Nicolson, 1967, 661 (the fullest account).

67 The best general account is by Peter Mathias, *Retailing Revolution: A History of Multiple Retailing in the Food Trades based on the Allied Suppliers Group of Companies*, London, Longmans, 1967.

68 Denys Forrest, *Tea for the British: The Social and Economic History of a Famous Trade*, London, Chatto and Windus, 1973, 131–2.

69 Ibid., 133–4.

70 John Burnett, *Plenty and Want: A Social History of Food in England from 1815 to the Present Day*, 3rd edn, London, Routledge, 1989, 125–6, 225–6. The most

recent of many histories of the co-operative movement is Johnston Birchall, *Co-op: The People's Business*, Manchester University Press, 1994.

71 Alec Waugh, *The Lipton Story: A Centennial Biography*, New York, Doubleday, 1950.

72 The Home and Colonial was founded by a solicitor, William Capel Slaughter, in 1885 on the cornerstones of tea and Van den Bergh's margarine: in 1900 it had over 100 shops and 4,000 agencies. The Maypole Dairy Co. grew from a Birmingham provision store to 185 branches by 1898.

73 David Wainwright, *Brooke Bond: A Hundred Years*, London, Newman Neame, Pergamon Group, 1969.

74 Kenneth Williams, *The Story of Ty·Phoo and the Birmingham Tea Industry*, London, Quiller Press, 1990.

75 William Cobbett, *Cottage Economy*, London, Peter Davies, 1926, 14, 19, 20.

76 Leone Levi, *Wages and Earnings of the Working Classes*, London, John Murray, 1885, 59–60.

77 At a Charity Tea in the 1880s, 80 poor children consumed 14 lb of sugar to 1½ lb of tea, an average of 3 oz per child. Sarah Freeman, *Mutton and Oysters: The Victorians and their Food*, London, Victor Gollancz, 1989, 224–5. Freeman's calculation of 6 oz of sugar per child appears wrong.

78 Mintz, op. cit., 149.

79 Arnold Palmer, *Movable Feasts*, Oxford University Press, 1952, footnote to 80.

80 Perilla Kinchin, *Tea and Taste: The Glasgow Tea Rooms, 1875–1975*, Wendlebury, Oxon, White Cockade, 1991, 27. Glasgow's tea rooms were boosted by the Great Exhibition there in 1888. From the 1890s many purpose-built tea rooms appeared, the most famous Kate Cranston's The Willow Tea Rooms (1903) designed by Charles Rennie Mackintosh.

81 D.J. Richardson, 'J. Lyons and Co. Ltd., Caterers and Food Manufacturers, 1894–1939', in *The Making of the Modern British Diet*, op. cit., 161–72.

82 Board of Trade, Memoranda, Statistical Tables and Charts, Cmd. 1761, 1903, 210–12, 231.

83 Forrest, op. cit., 201–3.

84 Williams, op. cit., 67.

85 In 1918 the average price of tea stood at 2s 9½d a pound. A.R. Prest and A.A. Adams, *Consumers' Expenditure in the United Kingdom, 1900–1919*, Cambridge University Press, 1954, Table 40, 69. Working-class earnings had generally kept up with, or exceeded, the wartime price rises.

86 Forrest, op. cit., 212–14. Wholesale prices of 'clean common' tea returned to 1s 1½d–1s 5d a pound after 1933.

87 In 1945, when the government prohibited health claims for tea, Brooke Bond renamed their blend 'Pre-Gestie', subsequently abbreviated to 'PG'.

88 Richard Stone, *The Measurement of Consumers' Expenditure and Behaviour in the UK, 1920–1938*, 2 vols, Cambridge University Press, 1954, vol. 1, Table 50, 151.

89 Sir William Crawford and H. Broadley, *The People's Food*, London, William Heinemann, 1938, 275.

90 Ibid., 81.

91 Quoted Wainwright, op. cit., 39.

92 Lord Woolton, *Tea on Service*, London, The Tea Centre, 1947, 75.

93 *Domestic Food Consumption and Expenditure, 1950. Report of the National Food Survey Committee*, London, HMSO, 1952. Supplement. Food Expenditure by Urban Working-Class Households, 1940–1949, Table 4, 119.

94 Geoffrey C. Warren (ed.), *The Foods We Eat*, London, Cassell, 1958, 27.

95 *Household Food Consumption and Expenditure, 1991. Annual Report of the National Food Survey Committee*, London, HMSO, 1992, Table B6, 79.

96 Ibid., Table 2.21, 20.

97 The Tea Council, Annual Report for 1992, 3.
98 Forrest, op. cit., 250–1.
99 The Tea Council, 1992, op. cit., 8.
100 Jonathan Margolis, 'Defining the British to a tea', *Sunday Times*, 25 September 1994.
101 The Tea Council, 1992, op. cit., 8.
102 The best-known television advertisement for tea, the 'PG' chimpanzees, first appeared in 1956, reputedly inspired by the chimpanzees' tea parties at the London Zoo.
103 *While there is Tea there is Hope*, Report by the Tea Council, Feb. 1998, citing research by Professor Vincent Marks, Dean of Medicine, University of Surrey, Professor David Booth, Food Psychologist, Birmingham University and Luci Daniels, Dietician.

4   Coffee

1 Louis Lewin, *Phantastica, Narcotic and Stimulating Drugs*, Trans. from 2nd German edition by D.H.A. Wirth, London, Kegan Paul, Trench, Trubner, 1931, 227–8.
2 Sidney W. Mintz, 'The changing roles of food in the study of consumption' in John Brewer and Roy Porter (eds), *Consumption and the World of Goods*, London, Routledge, 1994, 268.
3 Peter Albrecht, 'Coffee-drinking as a Symbol of Social Change in Continental Europe in the Seventeenth and Eighteenth Centuries', *Studies in Eighteenth Century Culture*, vol. 18, 1988, 91.
4 Bryan S. Turner, *The Body and Society: Explorations in Social Theory*, Oxford, Basil Blackwell, 1984, 168, quoting R. Burton, *The Anatomy of Melancholy* (1927 edn), 160.
5 Turner, ibid., 77–8. Much of Cheyne's advice was popularized in John Wesley's *Primitive Physick, or an Easy and Natural Method of Curing Most Diseases* (1752). Wesley wrote that it was from Cheyne that he had learned 'to eat sparingly and drink water'.
6 Roy Porter, 'Consumption: Disease of the Consumer Society?', in *Consumption and the World of Goods*, op. cit., 69.
7 Piero Camporesi, *Exotic Brew: The Art of Living in the Age of Enlightenment*, Trans. by Christopher Woodall, Oxford, Polity Press, 1994, 47.
8 Pasqua Rosée's handbill for coffee. 'Made and Sold in St Michael's Alley in Cornhill at the Signe of his own Head.' Quoted James Mew and John Ashton, *Drinks of the World*, London, The Leadenhall Press, 1892, 307–9.
9 For details, see Woodruff D. Smith, 'From Coffeehouse to Parlour: The Consumption of Coffee, Tea and Sugar in North-Western Europe in the Seventeenth and Eighteenth Centuries', in Jordan Goodman, Paul E. Lovejoy and Andrew Sherratt (eds), *Consuming Habits: Drugs in History and Anthropology*, London, Routledge, 1995, 152–3.
10 Mary Douglas (ed.), *Constructive Drinking: Perspectives on Drink from Anthropology*, Cambridge University Press, 1987, 83.
11 The Tea Council. Annual Report for 1992, London, 1992, 7.
12 Claudia Roden, *Coffee*, Harmondsworth, Middlesex, Penguin Books, 1981, 19.
13 Gordon Wrigley, *Coffee*, Harlow, Essex, Longman Scientific and Technical, 1988, 6.
14 Daniela U. Ball (ed.), *Coffee in the Context of European Drinking Habits*, Zurich, Johann Jacobs Museum, 1991, Introd., 17.
15 Richard Valpy French, *Nineteen Centuries of Drink in England: A History*, London, Longmans, Green, 1884, 215.

16 Edward Forbes Robinson, *The Early History of Coffee Houses in England*, London, Kegan Paul, Trench and Trubner, 1893, 45.

17 The Angel Inn stood on the site of the present Examination Schools in High Street, Oxford, until closed in 1866. The first coffee-house in Western Europe was probably opened in Venice in 1647, followed by Paris in 1668, Marseilles 1671, Hamburg 1677, Vienna 1685; other early houses began in Amsterdam and The Hague. Albrecht, op. cit., 93–4.

18 Heinrich Eduard Jacob, *The Saga of Coffee: The Biography of an Economic Product*, Transl. by E. and C. Paul, London, George Allen and Unwin, 1935, 128.

19 Robinson, op. cit., 97.

20 Simon Houfe, 'Meer Cocksparrows', *Country Life*, 31 August 1995, 58. The Tuke family of York, coffee-house owners, also laid the foundations of the city's chocolate industry.

21 Quoted in Norman Kolpas, *Coffee*, London, John Murray, 1979, 38.

22 Cited Robinson, op. cit., 166.

23 Mew and Ashton, op. cit., 309, citing Hatton, *A New View of London* (1708).

24 Bryant Lillywhite, *London Coffee Houses: A Reference Book of Coffee Houses of the Seventeenth, Eighteenth and Nineteenth Centuries*, London, George Allen and Unwin, 1963.

25 Mew and Ashton, op. cit., 311–312.

26 John E. Wills Jr, 'European Consumption and Asian Production in the Seventeenth and Eighteenth Centuries', in *Consumption and the World of Goods*, op. cit., 141–2.

27 The legend runs that Franz George Kolschitzky, who acted as a spy for the Austrian army defending Vienna against the Turks in 1683, was rewarded with sacks of coffee left by the invaders and permission to open the first coffee-house: finding that his customers disliked the strong Turkish coffee with a heavy sediment, he strained it and added milk and honey or sugar, so establishing the popularity of Viennese coffee. Literary references on the introduction of sugar to tea, coffee and chocolate are discussed by Jordan Goodman, 'Excitantia, or How Enlightenment Europe took to Soft Drugs', in *Consuming Habits*, op. cit., 132 and refs 61, 62.

28 Thomas Garway's handbill of 1657 advertising his coffee, tea and chocolate. Prices for tea ranged from 16s to 50s a pound. Mills for grinding coffee were sold by Nicholas Brook in St Tulies Street at the high price of 40–45s. Mew and Ashton, op. cit., 258–9.

29 Jacob, op. cit., 142.

30 Clyve Jones, 'The London Life of a Peer in the Reign of Anne: A Case Study from Lord Ossulston's Diary', *The London Journal*, vol. 16, no.2, 1991, 148. Ossulston's favourite was The British Coffee House in Pall Mall; he also used White's, the Greacian and The King's Head. It is clear that these also provided dinners and suppers in private rooms, wines and punch.

31 Alison Olson, 'Coffee House Lobbying', *History Today*, vol. 41, 1991, 35–41.

32 Quoted John and Linda Pelzer, 'The Coffee Houses of Augustan London', *History Today*, vol. 32, 1982, 40–4. A similar complaint about noise and gaming is made in James Douglas, *A Description and History of the Coffee Tree*, London, T. Woodward, 1727, Supplement, 14.

33 A contributory factor in the decline of the London coffee-houses was the proposal of their proprietors in 1729 to publish the *Coffee-House Gazette* with the monopoly of supplying news in the capital, a proposal quickly killed by ridicule and the opposition of the press. Aytoun Ellis, *The Penny Universities: A History of the Coffee-Houses*, London, Secker and Warburg, 1956, 223–5.

34 Ibid., ch.14, 'Coffee-Houses in the Country', 192–222.

35 Alexander Fenton, 'Coffee-drinking in Scotland in the 17th–19th centuries', in Daniela U. Ball (ed.), *Coffee in the Context of European Drinking Habits*, Zurich, Johann Jacobs Museum, 1991, 95.

36 William Maitland, *The History and Survey of London from its Foundation to the Present Time*, London, 1739, 682–3. Quoted John Brewer, 'Credit, Clubs and Independence', in Neil McKendrick, John Brewer and J.H. Plumb, *The Birth of a Consumer Society: The Commercialization of Eighteenth-Century England*, London, Europa Publications, 1982, 203.

37 Brewer, ibid., 226. Public subscriptions for the relief of poverty and the support of local charities were common features of the later eighteenth century.

38 See this volume Chapter 3, 53–54, for the extent of smuggled tea in the eighteenth century.

39 A.H. John, 'Agricultural Productivity and Economic Growth in England', in E.L. Jones (ed.), *Agriculture and Economic Growth in England, 1650–1815*, London, Methuen, 1967, 172–193.

40 Bruce P. Lenman, 'The English and Dutch East India Companies and the Birth of Consumerism in the Augustan World', *Eighteenth Century Life*, vol. 14, Part 1, 1990, 57, citing K.N. Chaudhuri, *The Trading World of Asia and the English East India Company, 1660–1760*, Cambridge University Press, 1978, 359–362. In 1724 coffee represented nearly 21 per cent of the value of the Company's imports, but from then down to 1750 only between 5 per cent and 7 per cent.

41 Lenman, ibid., 56.

42 Lorna Weatherill, *Consumer Behaviour and Material Culture in Britain, 1660–1760*, London, Routledge, 1988, 28, 62, 64.

43 Carole Shammas, 'Changes in English and Anglo-American Consumption from 1550 to 1800', in *Consumption and the World of Goods*, op. cit., Table 9.1, 179.

44 William Massie, *Reasons Humbly Offered against Laying any Further Tax upon Malt and Beer*, London, 1760. Cited Carole Shammas, 'The Eighteenth-Century English Diet and Economic Change', *Explorations in Economic History*, vol. 21, Part 3, 1984, 266.

45 Stephen H. Twining, *The House of Twining, 1706–1956*, London, R. Twining and Co. Ltd., 1956, 15–16, 24.

46 David Davies, *The Case of Labourers in Husbandry Stated and Considered, 1795*. Repub. Fairfield, New Jersey, Augustus M. Kelley, 1977.

47 Camporesi, op. cit., 48.

48 John Beresford (ed.), *The Diary of a Country Parson, 1758–1802*, Oxford, The World's Classics, 1949, 69, 99, 210–12, 304.

49 Tea lacked the viscosity and absorptive qualities of coffee-soup, but hard bread, crusts, bannocks or biscuits dipped in tea was a near equivalent.

50 Heidi Witzig and Jacob Tanner, 'Kaffeekonsum von Frauen im 19. Jahrhundert', in *Coffee in the Context of European Drinking Habits*, op. cit., 153–69.

51 John E. Wills Jr, *Consumption and the World of Goods*, op. cit., 143.

52 Wrigley, op. cit., 530.

53 B.R. Mitchell and Phyllis Deane, *Abstract of British Historical Statistics*, Cambridge University Press, 1962, 355.

54 See this volume, Chapter 3, 52.

55 William H. Ukers, *All About Tea*, 2 vols, New York, Tea and Coffee Trade Publishing, 1935, vol. 1, 67.

56 Simon Smith, *Accounting for Taste: British Coffee Consumption in Historical Perspective*, University of York, Economics Discussion Papers No.94/14, 1994, 27–8.

57 N. Deerr, *The History of Sugar*, 2 vols, London, Chapman and Hall, 1949–50, vol. 2, 1950, 532.

58 Frederick A. Filby, *A History of Food Adulteration and Analysis*, London, George Allen and Unwin, 1934, 60, 61, 241.

59 Mitchell and Deane, op. cit., 355–7. The peak of coffee consumption was in 1847, at 1.34 lb per head per year, but tea had by then grown to 1.66 lb.

60 Statistical Abstract for the United Kingdom in each year from 1840 to 1853. *Quarterly Review*, No. CCII, 1854, Art. VIII, 609–611.

61 Wrigley, op. cit., 48–9. Brazil enjoyed cheap labour as slavery continued there until 1888.

62 Twining, op. cit., 111, 114.

63 William Neild, 'Comparative Statement of the Income and Expenditure of Certain Families of the Working Classes in Manchester and Dukinfield in the Years 1836 and 1841', *Journal of the Statistical Society of London*, vol. IV, 1841, 322 et seq.

64 Roger Scola, *Feeding the Victorian City: The Food Supply of Manchester, 1770–1870*, Manchester University Press, 1992, Tables 9.1 and 9.5, 206, 215.

65 S.R. Bosanquet, *The Rights of the Poor and Christian Almsgiving Vindicated*, London, J. Burns, 1841.

66 Mrs Cobden Unwin (ed.), *The Hungry Forties: Life under the Bread Tax*, London, T. Fisher Unwin, 1905. Letter from 'AJM', 34.

67 Fenton, op. cit., 97, citing I. Levitt and T.C. Smout, *The State of the Scottish Working-Class in 1843*, Edinburgh, 1979, 26, 36. Among Scottish farmworkers in the 1880s, breakfast was still porridge, which might be supplemented by a cup of tea, but in many families tea was only for Sunday morning, 'the day o' the lang lie an' the tay breakfast', T.C. Smout and Sydney Wood, *Scottish Voices, 1745–1960*, London, Collins, 1990, 18.

68 Smout and Wood, ibid., 130–1.

69 Dr Edward Smith, *Sixth Report of the Medical Officer of the Privy Council on the Food of the Poorer Labouring Classes*, Cmd. 3416, PP. XXVIII, 1864, 253.

70 Lillywhite, op. cit., 26.

71 G.R. Porter, *The Progress of the Nation in its Various Social and Economical Relations*, London, John Murray, new edn, 1847, 558.

72 'A Cup of Coffee', *Household Words*, 1852, 566.

73 The temperance movement was begun in Scotland by John Dunlop in 1829 and spread to England shortly afterwards. Temperance coffee-houses and temperance hotels opened in Glasgow and Edinburgh in the 1840s.

74 Iain McCalman, 'Ultra-Radicalism and Convivial Debating Clubs in London, 1795–1838', *English Historical Review*, vol. 102, 1987, 329–30.

75 Henry Mayhew, *London Labour and the London Poor: The Condition and Earnings of Those that Will Work, Cannot Work and Will Not Work*, London, Charles Griffin, 1861, 191–195.

76 The consumption statistics quoted here are for the United Kingdom, then including the whole of Ireland.

77 John Mitchell, *A Treatise on the Falsifications of Food, and the Chemical Means Employed to Detect Them*, London, Bailliere, 1848.

78 A.H. Hassall, *Food and its Adulterations, Comprising the Reports of the Analytical Sanitary Commission of 'The Lancet' for the years 1851 to 1854*. London, Longman, Brown, Green and Longmans, 1855, IX–XI.

79 Select Committee on Adulterations of Food, Drinks and Drugs. First Report, with Minutes of Evidence, 432, VIII, 1855. Evidence of Robert Dundas Thomson, Qs.1207–1213. In 1845 the Manchester Coffee Roasting Company, a co-operative founded in 1823 to supply member-retailers at advantageous terms, decided to install a 'granulating machine' to prepare chicory. Scola, op. cit., 212, 268.

80 A.R. Prest and A.A. Adams, *Consumers' Expenditure in the United Kingdom, 1900–1919*, Cambridge University Press, 1954, 71.

81 Board of Trade, *Memoranda, Statistical Tables and Charts*, Cmd. 1761, 1903, 214.

82 C.G. Warnford Lock (ed.), *Coffee: Its Culture and Commerce*, London, E. and F.N. Spon, 1888, 218. In 1882 Britain consumed 285,000 cwt of coffee and 100,000 cwt of chicory, both now paying the same duty of 1½d a pound, ibid., 223

83 Annual Report of the Local Government Board for 1884/5, Cmd. 4515, CV–CVI.

84 Ibid. Report for 1898/9, Cmd. 9444, CXXXIII–CXXXVI.

85 Eliza Acton, *Modern Cookery*, London, Longman, 1859, 587.

86 Cited Sarah Freeman, *Mutton and Oysters: The Victorians and their Food*, London, Victor Gollancz, 1989, 90.

87 D.J. Richardson, 'J. Lyons and Co. Ltd.: Caterers and Food Manufacturers, 1884 to 1939', in Derek Oddy and Derek Miller (eds), *The Making of the Modern British Diet*, London, Croom Helm, 1976, 163, citing *The Coffee Tavern Guide*, 1884.

88 Robert Thorne, 'The Public House Reform Movement, 1892–1914', in Derek Oddy and Derek S. Miller (eds), *Diet and Health in Modern Britain*, London, Croom Helm, 1985, 239.

89 Kenneth Williams, *The Story of Ty·Phoo and the Birmingham Tea Industry*, London, Quiller Press, 1990, 17.

90 Thorne, op. cit., 242.

91 Mitchell and Deane, op. cit., 357.

92 Prest and Adams, op. cit., 69–70.

93 Ibid., 70.

94 Roden, op. cit., 76.

95 Mitchell and Deane, op. cit., 358.

96 In 1920 the average price of coffee was 36.3d per lb and of medium quality tea 34.5d: in 1938 prices were respectively 26.9d and 27.5d. Richard Stone, *Measurement of Consumers' Expenditure and Behaviour in the UK, 1920–1938*, Cambridge University Press, 1954, Table 50, 151.

97 Kolpas, op. cit., 130.

98 Sir William Crawford and H. Broadley, *The People's Food*, London, William Heinemann, 1938, 278, 280.

99 Twining, op. cit., 81–2. Coffee's popularity was increased by the large numbers of American forces in Britain who were supplied with 25 million pounds of the new instant 'Nescafé', some of which found its way to British consumers. Wrigley, op. cit., 512.

100 *Domestic Food Consumption and Expenditure. Annual Report of the National Food Survey Committee*, London, HMSO, 1952. Supplement on Food Expenditure by Urban Working-Class Households, 1940–1949, Appendix B, 127.

101 The best account of the espresso bar is in Edward Bramah, *Tea and Coffee: A Modern View of Three Hundred Years of Tradition*, London, Hutchinson, 1972, ch. 5, 'The Boom in Coffee Bars', 67 et seq. The initial boom began to fade in the 1960s as proprietors found selling food more profitable and turned their bars into cafés and restaurants. Christopher Driver, *The British At Table, 1940–1980*, London, Chatto and Windus, 1983, 63.

102 Geoffrey C. Warren (ed.), *The Foods We Eat*, London, Cassell, 1958, 75.

103 *Domestic Food Consumption and Expenditure. Annual Reports of the National Food Survey Committee*, 1950 (1952, 105), 1959 (1961, 126), 1969 (1971, 51), 1991 (1992, 10), 1993 (1994, 10).

104 D. Elliston Allen, *British Tastes: An Enquiry into the Likes and Dislikes of the Regional Consumer*, London, Hutchinson, 1968, 87.

105 Cited Derek Cooper, *The Beverage Report*, London, Routledge and Kegan Paul, 1970, 37.

106 *The Changing Structure of Meals in Britain: Special Report*, Taylor Nelson Research Ltd, London, 1988, 24, 32, 51 (cited by kind permission of Taylor Nelson Ltd).

107 G. Heald, 'Trends in Eating Out', in Richard Cottrell (ed.), *Nutrition in Catering*, Carnforth, Lancashire, The Parthenon Publishing Group, 1987, 85.

108 *Social Trends 21*, London, HMSO, 1991, Table 10.21, 180.

109 A hundred years earlier, in 1875, Dr Edward Smith advised readers that 'the simplest and cheapest pot [for making coffee] is the cafetière, in universal use in France'. Edward Smith, *Practical Dietary for Families, Schools and the Labouring Classes*, London, Henry S. King, 1875, 109.

110 The UK stands 17th in the world league of per capita coffee consumers, comparable with Greece and Australia, but drinking only one-fifth as much as Finland and half as much as the US. *The Coffee Story*, International Coffee Organization, London, Coffee Information Centre, n.d. [*c*. 1992], Table 4, 4.

111 International Coffee Organization, Coffee Information Centre, London, Factsheet S.05.

112 *National Drinks Survey*, Drink Type Shares Within Total Drinks Market, 1993. I am grateful to the Tea Council, London, for this information.

113 The Tea Council, Annual Report, 1992, London, 6–7.

5 Soft drinks

1 Roland Barthes, 'Toward a Psychosociology of Contemporary Food Consumption', ch. 11 in *Food and Drink in History: Selections from the Annales*, vol. 5, Robert Forster and Orest Ranum (eds), Baltimore and London, Johns Hopkins University Press, 1979, 172.

2 Brian Inglis, *Fringe Medicine*, London, Faber and Faber, 1964, 67–8.

3 See generally, Roy Porter, *Health for Sale: Quackery in England, 1660–1850*, Manchester University Press, 1989. The idea that 'the people know best' died hard, especially among radical groups. J.F.C. Harrison has noted that many former Chartists turned to fringe medicine. Herbalists eventually sought professional status and attempted to control standards by establishing a National Institute of Medical Herbalists in 1864 (Inglis, op. cit., 68).

4 C.S. Leyel, *Elixirs of Life*, Culpeper House Herbals, London, Faber and Faber, 1948, 14. Leyel lists eighty Nutritious Herbs, fifty-two Tonic Herbs, and twenty-two Bitter Herbs.

5 *The Widdowes Treasure* (1595) and *The Good Housewife's Jewell* (1596), cited James Mew and John Ashton, *Drinks of the World*, London, The Leadenhall Press, 1892, 179.

6 *Receipt Book of Ann Blencowe* (1694), cited M.F.K. Fisher, *A Cordiall Water*, London, The Hogarth Press, Chatto and Windus, 1983, 59, 67.

7 Eliza Smith, *The Compleat Housewife, or Accomplished Gentlewoman's Companion*, Facsimile of 16th edn, 1758, London, Studio Editions, 1994, 255 et seq. Smith included a number of older folk medicines such as Snail Water (500 snails) and Cock Water (for consumption). She died in 1732, having worked as cook in wealthy households for 30 years.

8 See Porter, op. cit., 107 et passim for numerous allegedly medicinal cordials and elixirs.

9 Robert Wells, *Pleasant Drinks: Effervescing Mixtures, Syrups, Cordials, Home-made Wines, etc.*, Manchester, Abel Heywood and Sons, n.d. [*c*. 1900].

10 David Wainwright, *Stone's Ginger Wine: Fortunes of a Family Firm, 1740–1990*, London, Quiller Press, 1990. The Original Green Ginger Wine was manufactured by Bishop and Pell at the Finsbury Distillery and retailed by Stones under an early 'own label' arrangement. In the late 1980s production in Britain stood at 500,000 gallons a year.

11 J.C. Drummond and Anne Wilbraham, *The Englishman's Food: A History of Five Centuries of English Diet*. Revised edn by Dorothy Hollingsworth, London, Jonathan Cape, 1957, 23, 109–11.

12 Alexis Soyer, *A Shilling Cookery for the People*, London, George Routledge, 1855. 'A Series of New and Cheap Drinks', 170.

13 Lemonade is mentioned in a Restoration play, *The Parson's Wedding* (1663), and orangeade was first sampled by Samuel Pepys about the same time. Colin Emmins, *Soft Drinks: Their Origins and History*, Princes Risborough, Buckinghamshire, Shire Books, 1991, 7.

14 Douglas A. Simmons, *Schweppes: The First 200 Years*, London, Springwood Books, 1983, 40.

15 Francesco Leonardi, *Apicio moderno ossia l'arte del credenziere*, Rome, 1807, quoted Piero Camporesi, *Exotic Brew: The Art of Living in the Age of Enlightenment*, Trans. by Christopher Woodall, Oxford, Polity Press, 1994, 71, 83.

16 Drummond and Wilbraham, op. cit., 133–45, contains a full account of the medical history and literature of scurvy.

17 R. Elwyn Hughes, 'The Rise and Fall of the Antiscorbutics: Some Notes on the Traditional Cures for "Land Scurvy"', *Medical History* (GB), vol. 34, Part 1, 1990, 52–64.

18 For example, J. Woodall, *The Surgeon's Mate, or Military and Domestique Surgery*, London, Bourne, 1639; J. Lind, *A Treatise on the Scurvy*, 1753, ed. by C.P. Stewart and D. Guthrie, Edinburgh University Press, 1953. Woodall was Surgeon to the East India Company and Lind Senior Physician at the Royal (Naval) Hospital, Haslam.

19 J. Watt, E.J. Freeman and W.F. Bynum (eds), *Starving Sailors: The Influence of Nutrition Upon Naval and Maritime History*, London, National Maritime Museum, 1981, 31. The daily ration was equivalent to six whiskies, and the rum content was gradually reduced until abolished in 1970.

20 Ibid., 51.

21 The lime juice controversy is discussed in *Starving Sailors*, op. cit., 151 et seq., and in James Watt, 'The Influence of Nutrition Upon Achievement in Maritime History', in Catherine Geissler and Derek J. Oddy (eds), *Food, Diet and Economic Change Past and Present*, Leicester University Press, 1993, 75 et seq.

22 J. Fairley, J. Gillon, C. McMaster and M. Moss, *Chambers Scottish Drink Book: Whisky, Beer, Wine and Soft Drinks*, Edinburgh, W. and R. Chambers, 1990, 22.

23 The 'small beer' of low alcoholic strength that resulted from a second or third brewing of malt and hops is properly discussed in the chapter on beer.

24 Peter Brears, *Traditional Food in Yorkshire*, Edinburgh, John Donald Publishers, 1987, 133.

25 *Chambers Scottish Drink Book*, op. cit., 24. The fourth hole on the Old Course at St Andrews is named Ginger Beer after Old Daw's ginger beer stall, which was a feature there early in this century.

26 Mew and Ashton, op. cit., 325–9. The recipes are quoted from *The Mineral Water Maker's Manual* (1866).

27 Brears, op. cit., 134.

28 Jennifer Davies, *The Victorian Kitchen*, London, BBC Books, 1991, 156.

29 The best account of the development of spas is Phyllis Hembry, *The English Spa, 1560–1815: A Social History*, London, The Athlone Press, 1990. Others include Kathleen Denbigh, *A Hundred British Spas: A Pictorial History*, Spa Publications,

1981; Alev Lytle Croutier, *Taking the Waters*, New York and London, Abbeville Press, 1992; A.B. Granville, *The Spas of England and Principal Sea-Bathing Places*, 2 vols, 1st edn, 1841. Repub. Bath, Adams and Dart, 1971.

30 Neil McKendrick, John Brewer and J.H. Plumb, *The Birth of a Consumer Society: The Commercialization of Eighteenth-Century England*, London, Europa Publications, 1982, 283–4.

31 Sylvia McIntyre, 'The Mineral Water Trade in the Eighteenth Century', *Journal of British Transport History*, New Series, II, Feb. 1973, 1.

32 Ibid., 8.

33 Ibid., Table 4, 16.

34 The early history of analysis of natural mineral waters is described in William Kirkby, *The Evolution of Artificial Mineral Waters*, Manchester, Jewsbury and Brown, 1902.

35 R. Harold Morgan, *Beverage Manufacture (Non-Alcoholic)*, London, Attwood, 1938, 11.

36 Simmons, op. cit., 11–27. In addition to Schweppes, a number of larger manufacturers existed in the early nineteenth century, including Pitt and Norrish, who were manufacturing ginger beer in 1790, Austin Thwaites of Dublin (1799) and John G. Webb (1819) (Morgan, op. cit., 12).

37 Ibid., 42.

38 Kirkby, op. cit., 82–3, 101.

39 Henry Mayhew, *London Labour and the London Poor*, vol. 1, *The London Street-Folk*, London, Griffin, Bohn, 1861, 186–9.

40 J. Thomson and Adolphe Smith, *Street Life in London*, first published in monthly parts, 1877–8, by Sampson Low. Reprinted Wakefield, Yorkshire, EP Publishing, 1973, 19, 73.

41 Kirkby, op. cit., Appendix of photographs of Jewsbury and Brown's factory, Manchester.

42 John Doxat (ed.), *The Indispensable Drinks Book*, London, Macdonald, 1982, 195. Codd's mineral water became well-known as 'Codd's Wallop'.

43 Brian Harrison, *Drink and the Victorians: The Temperance Question in England, 1815–1872*, London, Faber and Faber, 1971, Table 6, 312 and 301.

44 Charles Booth (ed.), *Life and Labour of the People in London*, vol. VII, *Population Classified by Trades*, London, Macmillan, 1896, 128–32.

45 Chambers, op. cit., 24.

46 Robert Roberts, *The Classic Slum: Salford Life in the First Quarter of the Century*, Manchester University Press, 1971, 93. Roberts' father seldom drank less than 4 quarts of beer (8 pints) a day.

47 J.E. Panton, *From Kitchen to Garrett: Hints for Young Householders*, London, Ward and Downey, 1888, 25.

48 Peter Roger Mountjoy, 'Thomas Bywater Smithies, editor of The British Workman', *Victorian Periodicals Review*, vol. 18, Part 2, 1985, 47–8.

49 Norman Longmate, *The Waterdrinkers: A History of Temperance*, London, Hamish Hamilton, 1968, 74–5, 210, 235.

50 Harrison, op. cit., 301.

51 B.R. Mitchell and Phyllis Deane, *Abstract of British Historical Statistics*, Cambridge University Press, 1962, 356–7.

52 G.N. Johnstone, 'The Growth of the Sugar Trade and Refining Industry', in Derek Oddy and Derek Miller (eds), *The Making of the Modern British Diet*, London, Croom Helm, 1976, Tables II and V, 61, 63. Retail prices of sugar fell from 7d a pound in the 1840s to 2d at the end of the century.

53 Angeliki Torode, 'Trends in Fruit Consumption', in T.C. Barker, J.C. McKenzie and John Yudkin (eds), *Our Changing Fare: Two Hundred Years of British Food Habits*, London, Macgibbon and Kee, 1966, 119–30.

54 A.R. Prest and A.A. Adams, *Consumers' Expenditure in the United Kingdom, 1900–1919*, Cambridge University Press, 1954, Table 52, 84. The statistics include imports and exports, which were not significant at this period and roughly balance at around 1 million gallons p.a.

55 Ibid., Table 47, 75.

56 Ibid., Table 58, 88. The likelihood is that the 1870 figure is an overestimate.

57 Jasper Guy Woodroof and G. Frank Phillips, *Beverages: Carbonated and Noncarbonated*, Westport, Connecticut, AVI Publishing Co., Revised edn 1981, 4.

58 Mark Pendergrast, *For God, Country and Coca-Cola: The Unauthorized History of the World's Most Popular Soft Drink*, London, Orion Books, 1994, 16.

59 Information on the history of American soft drinks is drawn mainly from Pendergrast, ibid. Lawrence Dietz, *Soda Pop: The History, Advertising, Art and Memorabilia of Soft Drinks in America*, New York, Simon and Schuster, 1973; E.J. Kahn Jnr, *The Big Drink: An Unofficial History of Coca-Cola*, London, Max Reinhardt, 1960.

60 Diana and Geoffrey Hindley, *Advertising in Victorian Britain*, London, Wayland Publishers, 1972, 111.

61 For the indigenous uses and properties of coca and kola see Jordan Goodman, Paul E. Lovejoy and Andrew Sherratt (eds), *Consuming Habits: Drugs in History and Anthropology*, London, Routledge, 1995, chs. 2 and 5.

62 Pendergrast, op. cit., 33.

63 Stanley C. Hollander and Richard Germain, *Was there a Pepsi Generation before Pepsi Discovered It? Youth-Based Segmentation in Marketing*, Chicago, Illinois, NTC Business Books, 1992, 38. Of the many rivals and imitations of Coca-Cola, the most successful, Pepsi-Cola, was created by a N. Carolina pharmacist, Caleb Bradham, in 1898.

64 Simmons, op. cit., 45–6. Other British manufacturers made 'Kola Champagne' and 'Kola Tonic' in the 1880s.

65 *Chambers Scottish Drink Book*, op. cit., 24–7. Iron Brew was renamed 'Irn-Bru' in 1946: in the late 1980s it was drunk by 44 per cent of those who bought soft drinks in Scotland.

66 Sue Nichols, *Vimto: The Story of a Soft Drink*, Preston, Lancashire, Carnegie Publishing, 1994. An excellent history of the drink, replete with advertisements.

67 Morgan, op. cit., 14.

68 Prest and Adams, op. cit., Table 52, 84. The duty was removed in August, 1924.

69 Simmons, op. cit., 62.

70 Richard Stone, *Measurement of Consumers' Expenditure and Behaviour in the United Kingdom, 1920–1938*, vol. I, Cambridge University Press, 1954. The statistics quoted in my text amalgamate Table 53, 160 (Soft drinks) and Table 68, 188 (Table waters). Stone based his estimates on the Censuses of Production 1924, 1930 and 1935, extrapolating earlier and later years.

71 The retail price of sugar fell from $11\frac{1}{2}$d a pound in 1920 to $2\frac{1}{2}$d a pound in 1931 and remained at this level until 1938. Stone, op. cit., 137.

72 Pendergrast, op. cit., 171.

73 Hollander and Germain, op. cit., 39.

74 J.A.R. Pimlott, *The Englishman's Holiday: A Social History*, London, Faber and Faber, 1947, 214–5.

75 Nichols, op. cit. More non-specific still, an advertisement of the 1920s, 'It is Vimto. Vimto is it', several decades before Coca-Cola's slogan. Vimto also adopted 'the new knowledge of nutrition' in its advertising, e.g. Christmas 1929, 'Not only delicious, but good for you too because it is rich in the vitamins that you need so badly in wintry weather'.

76 Sir William Crawford and H. Broadley, *The People's Food*, London, William Heinemann, 1938, 46, 73.

77 Nichols, op. cit., 9, Simmons, op. cit., 77–81, Dietz, op. cit., 161, Doxat, op. cit., 193. Unlike Churchill, General Eisenhower was a confirmed Coca-Cola drinker.

78 Ministry of Health, *On the State of the Public Health During Six Years of War*, Report of the Chief Medical Officer of the Ministry of Health, London, HMSO, 1946, 92–3.

79 James P. Johnston, *A Hundred Years Eating: Food, Drink and the Daily Diet in Britain since the Late Nineteenth Century*, Dublin, Gill and Macmillan, 1977, 124.

80 Geoffrey C. Warren, *The Foods We Eat: A Survey of Meals etc. by the Market Research Division of W.S. Crawford Ltd*, London, Cassell, 1958, 29, 47, 75, 123, 153.

81 *Domestic Food Consumption and Expenditure, 1959*, Annual Report of the National Food Survey Committee, London, HMSO, 1961, Appendix B, Table 1, 107.

82 *Family Expenditure Survey*, Report for 1957–9, London, HMSO, 1961, Table 3, 17.

83 *Family Expenditure Survey*, Report for 1965, London, HMSO, 1966, Table 1, 25.

84 Derek Cooper, *The Beverage Report*, London, Routledge and Kegan Paul, 1970, 49.

85 K.T.H. Farrer, *A Guide to Food Additives and Contaminants*, Carnforth, Lancashire, Parthenon Publishing Group, 1987, 74.

86 *The ABC of the Manufacture of Soft Drinks*, London, Stevenson and Howell, 9th edn, n.d. [*c.* 1964].

87 Cooper, op. cit., 55.

88 *National Drinks Survey*. Information supplied by the Tea Council, London. 1995: statistics from the Annual Report of the Tea Council, 1995.

89 *Soft Drinks Industry Report, 1995*, Chelmsford, Essex, Britvic Soft Drinks Ltd., 3.

90 *Soft Drinks Industry Report, 1996*, Chelmsford, Essex, Britvic Soft Drinks Ltd., 1–3.

91 *Family Spending*, Report on the 1994/5 Family Expenditure Survey, Central Statistical Office, London, HMSO, 1995, Table 1.3, 20–1. The FES does not include expenditure records of children under the age of 16, many of whom buy soft drinks from pocket money: family expenditure on soft drinks is therefore likely to be seriously under-recorded.

92 *Household Food Consumption and Expenditure*. National Food Survey, 1994, London, HMSO, 1995, Tables 2.10, 9, 2.12, 11, 2.13, 12. In 1994 soft drinks brought home averaged 1,680 ml per head per week (2¾ pints).

93 *Report on Snacks and Light Meals*, London, Taylor Nelson Research Ltd, 1986, 34; *The Changing Structure of Meals in Britain*, Taylor Nelson Research Ltd, 1988, 24, 51.

94 Carol Williams and Patricia Ward, *School Meals*, Report of a survey of parents' attitude to the school meals service, etc. Consumers' Association, May, 1993, 9.

95 G. Heald, 'Trends in Eating Out', in Richard Cottrell (ed.), *Nutrition in Catering: The Impact of Nutrition and Health Concepts on Catering Practice*, Carnforth, Lancashire, The Parthenon Publishing Group, 1987, 85.

96 The Coca-Cola Co., *Annual Report, 1995*, 3–4.

97 The former Chancellor of the Exchequer, Nigel Lawson, gave up alcohol as part of a successful slimming diet. 'Except during meal times (when I drank water) whenever I felt like a drink I used to have either black coffee without sugar or an ice-cold diet cola drink … In the past, I had never trusted the

latter ... It was amazing how soon it became addictive, in a perfectly controlled way.' *The Great Deflation, Sunday Times* News Review, 2 June 1996, 2.

98 *Soft Drinks Industry Report, 1993*, Chelmsford, Essex, Britvic Soft Drinks Ltd, 2.

99 UK consumption of bottled water, 1995, 9 litres per person per year: France 110 litres, Germany 94 litres. To be described as 'natural mineral water' it must be bottled on the site of the spring or well: the only permitted processes are filtration and, if a sparkling version is required, carbonation. 60 per cent of consumption is now of still water. *Bottled Water: The Facts,* The Natural Mineral Water Association, n.d. [*c.* 1994].

100 *Soft Drinks for Adults*, Market Overview, 1995/6. Coca-Cola and Schweppes Bourges Ltd. It is estimated that 12.4 per cent of adults aged 25–34 are now teetotal.

101 Robin Young, 'New Age elixirs restore sparkle to drinks trade', *The Times*, 22 April 1995, 8.

102 'Dangers of drink'. *Guardian Education*, 16 January 1996, Resources, 13. Campaigners are anxious that 'alcopops' be removed from 'soft' drinks displays in supermarkets, and restrictions on their sale to under-18s are currently being reviewed.

103 Maurice Hanssen and Jill Marsden, *E for Additives: The Complete 'E' Number Guide*, Wellingborough, Northants, Thorsons Publishers, 1985. These include four colours (E102, 110, 123, 153), eleven preservatives (E200, 210, 211, 214, 216, 218, 220, 223, 270, 290, 300) and eight emulsifiers and stabilizers (E330, 331b, 333, 334, 335, 338, 400, 412) besides sweeteners and flavours, which may be natural or artificial.

104 Caroline Walker and Geoffrey Cannon, *The Food Scandal*, London, Century Publishing, 1985, 12–13, 227, 272.

105 *The National Diet and Nutrition Survey: Children Aged 1½–4½ Years*, vol. 1, 1995. Report by Gillian Smithers, Economic and Social Research Council Data Archive Bulletin, No. 61, January 1996, 9–10.

106 Ibid., vol. 2, *Report of the Dental Survey*, 1995, 11.

6   Beer

1 For example, Peter Mathias, *The Brewing Industry in England, 1700–1830*, Cambridge University Press, 1959; J. Vaizey, *The Brewing Industry, 1886–1951: An Economic Study*, London, Isaac Pitman and Sons, 1960; E.M. Sigsworth, *The Brewing Trade during the Industrial Revolution: The Case of Yorkshire*, York, St Anthony's Press, 1967; Ian Donnachie, *A History of the Brewing Industry in Scotland*, Edinburgh, John Donald, 1979; T.R. Gourvish and R.G. Wilson, *The British Brewing Industry, 1830–1980*, Cambridge University Press, 1994. Many of the larger breweries have also published their own histories.

2 For example, Norman Longmate, *The Waterdrinkers: A History of Temperance*, London, Hamish Hamilton, 1968; Brian Harrison, *Drink and the Victorians: The Temperance Question in England, 1815–1872*, 1st edn London, Faber and Faber, 1971, New edn Keele University Press, 1994; A.E. Dingle, *The Campaign for Prohibition in Victorian England: The United Kingdom Alliance, 1872–1895*, New Brunswick, New Jersey, USA, Rutgers University Press, 1980; Lilian Lewis Shiman, *Crusade Against Drink in Victorian England*, London, Macmillan, 1988.

3 Reay Tannahill, *Food in History*, Harmondsworth, Middlesex, Penguin Books, revised edn 1988, 48–9. It has even been suggested that cereals were first cultivated for brewing rather than bread, though this seems unlikely: see Jordan Goodman, Paul E. Lovejoy and Andrew Sherratt, *Consuming Habits: Drugs in History and Anthropology*, London, Routledge, 1995, 24–5.

4 C. Anne Wilson, *Food and Drink in Britain: From the Stone Age to the Nineteenth Century*, Chicago, Academy Publishers, 1991, 368.

5 Bobby Freeman, *First Catch Your Peacock*, Ceredigion, Wales, Y. Lolfa, revised edn 1996, 250.

6 Beer was brewed from malted barley, wheat or oats or a mixture of these. Its strength depended on the quantity of fermentable material used: 'small beer' for everyday use was the product of the second or third 'mashing' of the malt after the stronger wort had been extracted. Medieval beers therefore ranged from less than 2 per cent alcohol up to 8–10 per cent.

7 James Mew and John Ashton, *Drinks of the World*, London, The Leadenhall Press, 1892, 207. The word 'ale,' of Saxon origin, denoted a feast or merrymaking before being applied to the drink itself. Richard Valpy French, *Nineteen Centuries of Drink in England: A History*, London, Longmans, Green, 1884, 81.

8 When barley was from 1s 8d to 2s the quarter or wheat from 3s to 3s 4d, town brewers were to sell 2 gallons of beer for 1d, country brewers 3–4 gallons for 1d.

9 John Bickerdyke, *The Curiosities of Ale and Beer*, London, The Leadenhall Press, 1886, 6.

10 C. Anne Wilson, op. cit., 375.

11 Mathias, op. cit., XVII.

12 Paul Hentzner, *A Journey into England* (1598). Quoted J.C. Drummond and Anne Wilbraham, *The Englishman's Food: A History of Five Centuries of English Diet*. Revised edn by Dorothy Hollingsworth, London, Jonathan Cape, 1957, 44.

13 William Harrison, *A Description of England* (1577). Cited Drummond and Wilbrahim, ibid., 32–3.

14 Bickerdyke, op. cit., 274.

15 Carole Shammas, *The Pre-Industrial Consumer in England and America*, Oxford University Press, 1990, 35.

16 Mathias, op. cit., 5–6.

17 Many of these towns had access to a wider market by sea or navigable river. Burton ale was known in London by at least 1630: C. Anne Wilson, op. cit., 385.

18 H.A. Monckton, *A History of English Ale and Beer*, London, The Bodley Head, 1966, Appendix D, 219.

19 Drummond and Wilbraham, op. cit., 114, Appendix A, 465.

20 A. Gibson and T.C. Smout, 'From Meat to Meal: Changes in Diet in Scotland', in Catherine Geissler and Derek J. Oddy (eds), *Food, Diet and Economic Change Past and Present*, Leicester University Press, 1993, 16.

21 Monckton, op. cit., Appendix B, 203.

22 Josephine A. Spring and David H. Buss, 'Three Centuries of Alcohol in the British Diet', *Nature*, vol. 270, 15 December 1977, 567. They estimate that in the 1690s beer would have provided 150 mg of calcium per day of the recommended intake of 500 mg, 133 mg of magnesium of 300, 0.83 mg of riboflavin of 1.7 and 15.7 mg of nicotinic acid of the recommended 18 mg. Table 4, 570.

23 Monckton, op. cit., 219. He estimates that public brewers contributed the following proportions of total output – 1700–1709 35 per cent, 1750–59 37.4 per cent, 1790–99 46 per cent.

24 Stephen Dowell, *History of Taxation and Taxes*, 1888, vol. IV, 63.

25 James Woodforde, *The Diary of a Country Parson, 1758–1802*, ed. John Beresford, Oxford University Press, 1978, 388.

26 David Davies, *The Case of Labourers in Husbandry, Stated and Considered* (1795). Facsimile edn, Fairfield, New Jersey, USA, Augustus M. Kelley, 1977, 11.

27 Ibid., 12.

28 Ibid., 38, 65. A malt tax was first imposed in 1697 at 6½d per bushel: in 1760 it stood at 9d, in 1780 at 1s 4¼d and in 1802 at 2s 5d. Monckton, op. cit., 204.

29 Details of Yorkshire home-brewing and drinking customs are in Peter Brears, *Traditional Food in Yorkshire*, Edinburgh, John Donald Publishers, 1987, chs. 12, 14, 15.

30 Sir Frederic Morton Eden, *The State of the Poor* (3 vols, 1797). Facsimile edn, London, Frank Cass, 1966, vol. I, 547.

31 Gibson and Smout, op. cit., 16.

32 Mathias, op. cit., 25–6.

33 Ibid., Table 37, 543.

34 Fredrick Accum, *A Treatise on Adulterations of Food and Culinary Poisons*, London, Longman, Hurst, Rees, Orme and Brown, 1820, 198.

35 In 1760 a quarter of malt was used to brew 2¼–2¾ barrels, by 1800 3–3½ barrels. Mathias, op. cit., 17.

36 Monckton, op. cit., Appendix D, 220–1.

37 T.S. Ashton, 'Changes in Standards of Comfort in Eighteenth-Century England', *The Raleigh Lecture on History. Proceedings of the British Academy*, vol. XLI, 1955, 185.

38 Estimated from Spring and Buss, op. cit., Fig.1, 568.

39 Benjamin Franklin, *Autobiography*, William N. Otto (ed.), Boston, Mass. 1928, 55–6.

40 Eden, op. cit., vol. II, Parochial Reports, 10, 12, 23, 297, 309, 423, 571, 577; vol. III, 754.

41 Ibid., vol. I, 534–5.

42 Carole Shammas, 'The Eighteenth-Century English Diet and Economic Change', *Explorations in Economic History*, vol. 21, Part 3, 1984, Table 1, 257.

43 S. and B. Webb, *The History of Liquor Licensing in England, Principally from 1700 to 1830*, London, Longmans Green, 1903, note to 80–81.

44 Eden, op. cit., vol. I, 545.

45 A network of radical clubs met in the Spencean taverns in Bethnal Green, Soho, Spitalfields and Finsbury as well as in Birmingham and other towns. Iain McCalman, 'Ultra-Radicalism and Convivial Drinking Clubs in London, 1795–1838,' *English Historical Review*, vol. 102, 1987, 309–33.

46 Board of Agriculture, *The Agricultural State of the Kingdom, 1816*, Repub. Bath, Somerset, Adams and Dart, 1970, 95.

47 Davies, op. cit., 118.

48 Brears, op. cit., 125. Home brewing survived better in the industrial belt of the W. Riding. At Pudsey in the 1820s brewing was on a co-operative basis, and brewing equipment was always being carried round the streets.

49 W.R. Lambert, *Drink and Sobriety in Victorian Wales, c. 1820–1895*, Cardiff University Press, 1983, 8.

50 John Baxter, 'The Organisation of the Brewing Industry'. Unpublished Ph.D. Thesis, University of London, 1944; George B. Wilson, *Alcohol and the Nation*, London, Nicholson and Watson, 1940, Table, 56.

51 Report of the Committee upon . . . the State of the Police of the Metropolis, 1817. Reprint of Reports from Select Committees on the Laws relating to the Sale of Beer, 1817–1850 (292), XXXVII, 1852–3, 7.

52 Royal Commission on the Liquor Licensing Laws, vol. IX, C.9076, XXXV, 1899, Q.22, 242.

53 Thirteenth Report of the Commissioners of Inland Revenue, 1870, 44.

54 Report of the Select Committee on the Sale of Beer, (416), XV, 1833, 7.

55 The derivation was probably the same as that of 'jerry-building', i.e. temporary, flimsy, insecure (from 'jury-mast'). Other, less explicable nicknames were 'Tom and Jerry shops' and 'Tiddlywinks.'

56 Many witnesses to the Royal Commission on the Poor Laws in 1834 blamed beershops as a cause of the Swing Riots, 1830–31.

57 Report of the Select Committee on Public Houses, etc. (367), XIV, 1854, IX.

58 Keith Vernon, 'Pus, Sewage, Beer and Milk: Microbiology in Britain, 1870–1940', *History of Science*, vol. 28, Part 3, 1990, 307–8.

59 John Doxat (ed.), *The Indispensable Drinks Book*, London, Macdonald, 1982, 123–4. Lager was brewed by a different system of bottom-fermentation whereas British beers were top-fermented.

60 For full details of beer adulteration see my thesis 'The History of Food Adulteration in Britain in the Nineteenth Century, with special reference to Bread, Tea and Beer'. University of London Ph.D. thesis, 1958, 377–468. Only a brief account is given in the present chapter.

61 For the period before 1800, see Frederick A. Filby, *A History of Food Adulteration and Analysis*, London, George Allen and Unwin, 1934, 105–27.

62 Accum, op. cit., 173–4.

63 Samuel Child, Brewer, *Every Man his own Brewer: A Practical Treatise*, etc., 1820. First published in 1790, Child's book went through twelve editions in the first half of the nineteenth century.

64 Select Committee on Adulteration of Food, etc. Second Report (480), VIII, 1855, Q.2142 et seq.

65 Ibid., First Report (432), VIII, 1855, Q.1073 et seq.

66 Select Committee on Public Houses etc., 1854, op. cit., Q.6523 et seq.

67 Wentworth Lascelles Scott, 'Food Adulteration and the Legislative Enactments Relating Thereto', *Journal of the Royal Society of Arts*, vol. XXIII, 1875, 433 et seq. Cocculus Indicus was rarely used in quantities sufficient to cause immediate death, but it was a cumulative poison, which could cause serious damage to health over time.

68 Quarterly Reports of Public Analysts to the Local Government Board, 1877–1914: Burnett, thesis op. cit., Table 20, App. XXXV–XXXVI.

69 Royal Commission on the Liquor Licensing Laws, vol. I, Cmd. 8355, XXXIV, 1897, App. 4, 445.

70 Report of the Departmental Committee on Beer Materials, 1899, 9–15.

71 Royal Commission on Arsenical Poisoning from the Consumption of Beer, Cmd. 692, IX – Cmd. 1845, IX, 1901–4.

72 Pamela Horn, *The Rural World, 1780–1850: Social Change in the English Countryside*, London, Hutchinson, 1980, 29–30.

73 Nigel E. Agar, *The Bedfordshire Farm Worker in the Nineteenth Century*, Bedfordshire Historical Record Society, vol. 60, 1981, 113.

74 Raphael Samuel (ed.), *Village Life and Labour*, London, Routledge and Kegan Paul, 1975, 42–3.

75 B. Seebohm Rowntree and May Kendall, *How the Labourer Lives: A Study of the Rural Labour Problem*, London, Thomas Nelson, 1917, 66, 104.

76 Flora Thompson, *Lark Rise to Candleford*, Harmondsworth, Middlesex, Penguin Books, 1976, 62–4.

77 Samuel, op. cit., 198 and note to Plate 14. Those who frequented the Mason's Arms were said to be 'a little school . . . everyone shared' (cf. the loving cup at Oxford college feasts).

78 B. Seebohm Rowntree, *Poverty: A Study of Town Life*, London, Macmillan, 4th edn, 1902, 144–5.

79 Harrison, op. cit., 41.

80 E.P. Thompson, *The Making of the English Working Class*, Harmondsworth, Middlesex, Penguin Books, 1980, 448.

81 A Journeyman Engineer (Thomas Wright), *Some Habits and Customs of the Working Classes* (1867). Reprint, New York, Augustus M. Kelley, 1967, 114–25.

82 Charles Booth, *Life and Labour of the People in London*, Final Volume, Notes on Social Influences, London, Macmillan, 1902, 73.

83 John Dunlop, *The Philosophy of Artificial and Compulsory Drinking Usages in Great Britain and Ireland*, Houlston and Stoneman, 1839. Quoted Longmate, op. cit., 20. See also Wright, op. cit., ch. 6, 'On the Inner Life of Workshops'.

84 The consumption statistics often quoted are those of G.B. Wilson, *Alcohol and the Nation*, op. cit., Table 1, 331–3, but this is a discontinuous series covering England and Wales 1800–29 and the United Kingdom 1830–1914. It therefore distorts the true picture by indicating a large fall from 28.4 gallons per head in 1824–9 to 22 gallons in 1830 when Scotland and Ireland were included.

85 Joel Mokyr, 'Is there still life in the pessimist case? Consumption during the Industrial Revolution, 1790–1850', *Journal of Economic History*, vol. 48, 1988, 78, 91. Mokyr's statement that beer consumption fell by a third between 1800 and 1850 is presumably based on Wilson's conflation of the two sets of statistics (above).

86 Joseph Rowntree and Arthur Sherwell, *The Temperance Problem and Social Reform*, London, Hodder and Stoughton, 3rd edn, 1899, 5–6.

87 Gourvish and Wilson, op. cit., 35.

88 Booth, op. cit., 74.

89 Quoted G.B. Wilson, op. cit., 241–2.

90 Report of the Committee . . . on the Present Appropriation of Wages. 51st Meeting of the British Association for the Advancement of Science, 1881, 276 et seq.

91 B.S. Rowntree, op. cit., 142–3.

92 A.E. Dingle, 'Drink and Working-Class Living Standards in Britain, 1870–1914', in Derek J. Oddy and Derek S. Miller (eds), *The Making of the Modern British Diet*, Croom Helm, 1976, 120.

93 Lady Bell (Mrs Hugh Bell), *At the Works: A Study of a Manufacturing Town*, London, Thomas Nelson, revised edn 1911, 342.

94 Rowntree and Sherwell, op. cit., 439.

95 Booth, op. cit., 70.

96 Rowntree and Sherwell, op. cit., 458–61.

97 Ibid., 475–6.

98 William F. Bynum, 'Chronic Alcoholism in the First Half of the Nineteenth Century', *Bulletin of the History of Medicine*, vol. 42, 1968, 141–3. Psychiatrists at this period believed that between a fifth and a half of mental diseases were due to alcoholism.

99 Roy M. Macleod, 'The Edge of Hope: Social Policy and Chronic Alcoholism, 1870–1900', *Journal of the History of Medicine*, vol. 22, Part 3, 1967, 215–45.

100 Peter Bailey, *Leisure and Class in Victorian England: Rational Recreation and the Contest for Control, 1830–1885*, London, Methuen, 1987, 29.

101 Lambert, op. cit., 42–3.

102 Report from the Select Committee on Drunkenness, (559), VIII, 1834, 5.

103 Rowntree, *Poverty*, op. cit., 315, 324.

104 Booth, op. cit., 59.

105 Ibid., 62–4. Grocers' licenses to sell alcohol were granted in 1861 and were not under magistrates' control until 1902.

106 Lord Rosebery, 1902. Quoted David Wright and Cathy Chorniawry, 'Women and Drink in Edwardian England', *Historical Papers (Canada)*, 1985, 124.

107 Report of the Inter-Departmental Committee on Physical Deterioration, vol. I, Cd. 2175, 1904, 40, XXXII.

108 Bailey, op. cit., 117.

109 Alan Crawford and Robert Thorne, *Birmingham Pubs, 1890–1939*, University of Birmingham Centre for Urban and Regional Studies, 1975.

110 Robert Thorne, 'The Movement for Public House Reform, 1892–1914', in Derek J. Oddy and Derek S. Miller (eds), *Diet and Health in Modern Britain*, Croom Helm, 1985.

111 Henry Carter, *The Control of the Liquor Trade in Britain: A contribution to National Efficiency during the Great War, 1915–1918*, London, Longmans, Green, 2nd edn, 1919, VIII. Carter was a member of the Central Control Board established in 1915.

112 Ibid., X.

113 Full details of wartime beer policies are in G.B. Wilson, ch. 13, Gourvish and R.G. Wilson, 317–36 and Carter, op. cit.

114 G.B. Wilson, op. cit., 58–9.

115 Convictions for drunkenness in the Carlisle area fell from 33 per week in January 1916 to 4 a week at the end of 1917. Carter, op. cit., ch. IX, 209–33.

116 Richard Stone, *The Measurement of Consumers' Expenditure and Behaviour in the United Kingdom, 1920–1938*, Cambridge University Press, 1954, vol. 1, 182.

117 Gwylmor Prys Williams and George Thompson Brake, *Drink in Great Britain, 1900–1979*, London, Edsall, 1980, Table 19, 363.

118 Sir Hubert Llewellyn Smith (ed.), *The New Survey of London Life and Labour*, London, P.S. King, 1935, vol. IX, *Life and Leisure*, ch. 9, 267. Other estimates put the proportions higher – 10–20 per cent of men and 20–40 per cent of women.

119 Ibid., 245–54.

120 B. Seebohm Rowntree, *Poverty and Progress: A Second Social Survey of York*, London, Longmans, Green, 1941, 124, 353–69. (The survey data were gathered in 1936.)

121 Tom Harrisson, *The Pub and the People: A Worktown Study by Mass Observation*, London, Victor Gollancz, 1943.

122 John Burnett, *A Social History of Housing, 1815–1985*, 2nd edn, London, Routledge, 1986, chs. 8, 9.

123 G.B. Wilson, op. cit., 245–50.

124 Quoted B. Seebohm Rowntree and G.R. Lavers, *English Life and Leisure: A Social Study*, London, Longmans, Green, 1951, 188.

125 Henry Carter, *The Nation Surveys the Drink Problem: A Review of the Report of the Royal Commission on Licensing*, London, The Temperance Council of the Christian Churches, 1933.

126 Rowntree and Lavers, op. cit., 179–81.

127 Maurice Gorham and H.McG. Dunnett, *Inside the Pub*, London, The Architectural Press, 1950, 36–40, 114–21.

128 Gourvish and Wilson, op. cit., 357. Exceptions to the zoning scheme were allowed for some national brands of beer, e.g. Bass, Guinness, Whitbread.

129 Ibid., 452.

130 *Family Spending, Report on the 1994/5 Family Expenditure Survey*, London, HMSO, 1995, Tables 6.1 and 7.2, 102, 117.

131 *Social Trends, 23*, London, HMSO, 1993, Table 7.19, 103.

132 *The Drink Pocket Book, 1997*, Henley-on-Thames, Oxfordshire, NTC Publications in Association with Stats M.R., 1996, 63.

133 *Beer and Pub Facts*, Brewers and Licensed Retailers Association, n.d. [*c.* 1996].

134 *Alcohol and the Young*, Report of a Joint Working Party of the Royal College of Physicians and the British Paediatric Association, London, Royal College of Physicians, 1995, 30–1.

135 *The Drink Pocket Book*, op. cit., 63.

7   Wine

1 Robert Farrar Capon, *The Supper of the Lamb*, 1970, quoted Paul Levy (ed.), *The Penguin Book of Food and Drink*, London, Viking, Penguin Books, 1996, 174.
2 Andrew Sherratt, 'Alcohol and its Alternatives: Symbol and Substance in Pre-Industrial Cultures', in Jordan Goodman, Paul E. Lovejoy and Andrew Sherratt (eds), *Consuming Habits: Drugs in History and Anthropology*, London, Routledge, 1995, 18, 38 ref. 42.
3 For details of these, see Margaret Visser, *The Rituals of Dinner: The Origins, Evolution, Eccentricities and Meaning of Table Manners*, London, Penguin Books, 1993, 255–62.
4 Roland Barthes, *Mythologies*, 1972, quoted Simon Rae (ed.), *The Faber Book of Drink, Drinkers and Drinking*, London, Faber and Faber, 1991, 6.
5 In later Protestant churches the wine and wafer merely symbolized the 'real presence' of Christ, though the act of communion still joined communicants in the fellowship of the church.
6 Teetotal reformers developed the 'two wines' theory that Biblical wines were non-intoxicating: in *The Temperance Bible Commentary* (1868) Revd Dawson Burns and Dr Frederick Lees rewrote 493 references in ways favourable to total abstinence. Apart from the semantic difficulties, a major problem was that grape juice tends to ferment naturally, and it was not until 1863 that a Manchester teetotaller, Frank Wright, succeeded in developing a non-fermenting grape juice. See Norman Longmate, *The Waterdrinkers: A History of Temperance*, London, Hamish Hamilton, 1968, 184–91.
7 Richard Rudgley, *Essential Substances: A Cultural History of Intoxicants in Society*, New York, Kodanska International, 1993, 32.
8 Andrew Sherratt, 'Alcohol and its Alternatives', in *Consuming Habits*, op. cit., 18–19.
9 Richard Valpy French, *Nineteen Centuries of Drink in England*, London, Longmans, Green, 1884, 5.
10 Patrick Galliou, 'Days of Wine and Roses? Early Armorica and the Atlantic Wine Trade', in Sarah Macready and F.H. Thompson (eds), *Cross-Channel Trade between Gaul and Britain in the Pre-Roman Iron Age*, Society of Antiquaries of London, 1984, 24–36; Paul Arthur, 'Roman Amphorae from Canterbury', *Britannica*, vol. 17, 1986, 239–58.
11 On the history of English wine production generally, see Hugh Barty-King, *A Tradition of English Wine: The Story of Two Thousand Years of English Wine made from English Grapes*, Oxford Illustrated Press, 1977.
12 A.D. Francis, *The Wine Trade*, London, A. and C. Black, 1972, 9.
13 Charles Petrie, 'Politics and Wine', *Quarterly Review*, 93, 1953, 454.
14 Sidney W. Mintz, *Sweetness and Power: The Place of Sugar in Modern History*, New York, Viking Penguin, 1985, 124. See Mintz generally for the importance of sugar in English foods and drinks.
15 Moira Buxton, 'Hypocras, Caudels, Possets and other Comforting Drinks', in C. Anne Wilson (ed.), *Liquid Nourishment, Potable Foods and Stimulating Drinks*, Edinburgh University Press, 1993, 70–1.
16 An incomplete census of inns and taverns in England and Wales taken in 1577 showed 1,631 inns and 329 taverns, compared with 14,202 alehouses, which were not licensed to sell wine. H.A. Monckton, *A History of English Ale and Beer*, London, The Bodley Head, 1966, 101–2.
17 H. Warner Allen, *The Romance of Wine*, London, Ernest Benn, 1931, 139.
18 Cyrus Redding, *A History and Description of Modern Wines*, London, Henry G. Bohn, 3rd edn 1851, 24.
19 Quoted French, op. cit., 151.

20 Oliver Knox, *Croft, A Journey of Confidence*, London, Collins, 1978. Croft merchants began to reside in and trade from Oporto on the Douro in 1678.

21 Francis, op. cit., 65.

22 Champagne was mentioned in a play of 1668 by Etherage, *She Would If She Could*, and was being imported by the Earl of Bedford in 1665: by the 1670s special glasses for champagne, claret, brandy and sack were being made by Ravenscroft: Francis, op. cit., 69–70. Although champagne was much less charged with carbonic acid gas than today, its bottling at this time only became possible as cork began to replace wood or leather as stoppers.

23 On Pepys's drinking habits see Oscar A. Mendelsohn, *Drinking with Pepys*, London, Macmillan, 1963; S.A.E. Strom, *And So To Dine*, London, Frederick Books, 1955.

24 For details of legislation against smuggling, see André L. Simon, *Bottlescrew Days: Wine Drinking in England during the Eighteenth Century*, London, Duckworth, 1926, ch. 3, 81–105. Simon suggests that in the reign of Queen Anne when the duty on French wines was 3s a quart, best-quality smuggled French claret sold at 3–4s a gallon, 81.

25 Ralph Davis, 'The English Wine Trade in the Eighteenth and Nineteenth Centuries', *Annales Cisalpines d'Histoire Sociale*, 1972, Part 3, 95–6.

26 B.R. Mitchell and Phyllis Deane, *Abstract of British Historical Statistics*, Cambridge University Press, 1962, 5.

27 Davis, op. cit., 88–9.

28 For details of the Methuen negotiations, see Francis, op. cit., 120–3. (John Methuen was the English minister in Lisbon.)

29 George B. Wilson, *Alcohol and the Nation*, London, Nicholson and Watson, 1940, 34–5.

30 For example, Cyrus Redding. 'By this Treaty Englishmen were subsequently compelled to drink the fiery adulterations of an interested wine company . . . Our taste for port wine was forced upon us by our rulers, really out of jealousy towards France. There is no necessity to search for any other reason why port wine was so generally drunk in England.' Redding, op. cit., 235, 237.

31 Simon, op. cit., XII.

32 French, op. cit., 301–2.

33 Thomas B. Gilmore, 'James Boswell's Drinking', *Eighteenth Century Studies*, vol. 24, Part 3, 1991, 337–57. Gilmore believes that Boswell was an alcoholic.

34 Frederick A. Filby, *A History of Food Adulteration and Analysis*, London, George Allen and Unwin, 1934, 133–4.

35 Eliza Smith, *The Compleat Housewife*, London, Studio Editions, 1994. Facsimile of 16th edition, 1758, 236–51.

36 Richard P. Wedeen, *Poison in the Pot: The Legacy of Lead*, Southern Illinois University Press, 1984, 21, 75–82, 191. It is claimed that lead in alcoholic drinks increases the uric acid in the blood, which causes gout.

37 John Hardy, *The Retail Compounder and Publicans Friend, c.* 1794. Cited J.C. Drummond and Anne Wilbraham, *The Englishman's Food: A History of Five Centuries of English Diet.* Revised edn by Dorothy Hollingsworth, London, Jonathan Cape, 1957, 201.

38 Wilson, op. cit., Table 1, 331–3. In the period 1885–97 wine consumption in France ranged between 20.2 and 29.5 gallons per person per year, in Spain 16.2 and 19.6 and in Italy 14.7 and 21.5. Joseph Rowntree and Arthur Sherwell, *The Temperance Problem and Social Reform*, London, Hodder and Stoughton, 3rd edn 1899, Table, 429.

39 Ibid., 3.

40 G.R. Porter, *The Progress of the Nation*, London, John Murray, new edn, 1847, 570.

41 Filby, op. cit., 137–8, citing John Davies, *The Innkeeper's and Butler's Guide* (1805) and R. Westney, *The Wine and Spirit Dealer's and Consumer's Vade Mecum* (1817).

42 Fredrick Accum, *A Treatise on Adulterations of Food and Culinary Poisons*, London, Longman, Hurst, Rees, Orme and Brown, 1820, 95–107.

43 Warner Allen, op. cit., 136.

44 Redding, op. cit., 245.

45 Porter, op. cit., 570.

46 Wilson, op. cit., 38–9, which quotes Gladstone's Budget speech of 1860 at length.

47 Francis, op. cit., 309.

48 Gladstone's policy of free trade in wine was naturally opposed by the teetotal movement and by many brewers: the Conservative Marquis of Salisbury gibed that Gladstone's 'specific for the cure of intemperance . . . was . . . of a somewhat recondite and subtle character – namely, allowing brandy to be sold by grocers.'

49 Alec Waugh, *Merchants of Wine: A Centenary Account of the Fortunes of the House of Gilbey*, London, Cassell, 1957.

50 Asa Briggs, *Wine for Sale: Victoria Wine and the Liquor Trade, 1860–1984*, University of Chicago Press, 1985.

51 *Yates Brothers Wine Lodges Ltd., 1884–1984*. Privately printed by Yates Bros Wine Lodges Ltd, Bolton, Lancashire, 1984. The first acquisition was 'The Angel', High Street, Oldham, and most of the Wine Lodges were concentrated in the North and the Midlands: several restaurants and hotels later joined the chain.

52 Reports of Public Analysts in Annual Reports of the Local Government Board. Ninth Report, 1879–80, C2681, cxv; Tenth Report, 1880–81, C2982, lxxxvii; Fourteenth Report, 1884–5, C4515, cvii; Twentieth Report, 1890–91, C6460, clvi.

53 For details, see Briggs, op. cit., 59.

54 Cited Rowntree and Sherwell, op. cit., 10. A.R. Prest and A.A. Adams suggest a higher total expenditure on wine of £13.5 million in 1880, but give no breakdown. *Consumers' Expenditure in the United Kingdom, 1900–1919*, Cambridge University Press, 1954, Table 53, 85.

55 Dr Robert Druitt, MRCP, *A Report on Cheap Wine* (1865), reviewed and extensively quoted by Moray McLaren in a centenary appreciation, *Pure Wine, or In Vino Sanitas*, Edinburgh, Alastair Campbell, 1965.

56 Charles Booth, *Life and Labour of the People in London*, Final Volume, Notes on Social Influences and Conclusion, London, Macmillan, 1902, 61.

57 Ian Maclean, 'The Wine Cellar in the Nineteenth Century', *The Queen's College Record*, vol. 9, 1993, 23–8. At 3s 6d a bottle, port was the cheapest wine in the cellar up to 1914: the average consumption of Fellows in mid-century was two-thirds of a bottle a night, plus occasional 'treats' and their own purchases.

58 Cited James Mew and John Ashton, *Drinks of the World*, London, The Leadenhall Press, 1895, 55–6.

59 G. Colmore, 'A Budget at £800 a year', *Cornhill Magazine*, New Series, vol. X, Jan–Jun, 1901, 795–7. The annual housekeeping expenses for two adults and two maids totalled £208.

60 Prest and Adams, op. cit., Table 51, 83, for statistics 1900–19.

61 André L. Simon, *A Concise Encyclopaedia of Gastronomy*, Section VIII, Wine, Beer, Spirits etc., London, The Wine and Food Society, 1946, 52.

62 Richard Stone, *The Measurement of Consumers' Expenditure and Behaviour in the UK, 1920–1938*, 2 vols, Cambridge University Press, 1954, vol. I, Table 71, 189.

63 The Colwyn Report. Report of the Committee on National Debt and Taxation, App. X (1926). Cited Sir Hubert Llewellyn Smith (ed.), *The New Survey of London Life and Labour*, vol. IX, Life and Leisure, London, P.S. King and Son, 1935, 247–9, 264.

64 Sir William Broadley and H. Crawford, *The People's Food*, London, William Heinemann, 1938, 72.

65 Tom Harrisson, *The Pub and the People: A Worktown Study by Mass Observation*, London, Victor Gollancz, 1943, 48. The survey was conducted in Bolton in 1938.

66 Waugh, op. cit., 96.

67 Gwylmor Prys Williams and George Thompson Brake, *Drink in Great Britain, 1900–1979*, London, Edsall, 1980, Table 11.5, 380; Table 111.3, 383.

68 *Family Expenditure Survey, Report for 1957–9*, London, HMSO, 1961, Table 4, 25.

69 *Family Spending. Report for 1994–5*, London, HMSO, 1995, Table 6.1, 102. The average household expenditure on wines was £2.63 a week, in the highest-earning decile £8.11. Table 1.3, 20.

70 Williams and Brake, op. cit., 203.

71 *The Drink Pocket Book, 1997*, Henley-on-Thames, Oxfordshire, NTC Publications in Association with Stats M.R., 1996, 80, 104 and 106. 'Made' (British) wines held 16.4 per cent of the total wine market in 1995, two-thirds of which were of low strength (less than 5.5 per cent alcohol).

72 E.A. Maury, *Wine is the best Medicine*, London, Souvenir Press, 1976, 34–5: Stephen Braun, *Buzz: The Science and Lore of Alcohol and Caffeine*, Oxford University Press, 1996, 62–6. In the making of white wine the skins are removed before fermentation, so losing much of this claimed benefit.

73 The principal cider counties were Devon, Worcestershire, Herefordshire, Somerset and Gloucestershire, but in some periods production was also extensive in Kent, Norfolk and Monmouthshire.

74 R.K. French, *The History and Virtues of Cyder*, London, Robert Hale, 1982, 5–6. Cf. W.E. Minchinton, 'The British Cider Industry Since 1870', *Westminster Bank Review*, Nov. 1975, 55.

75 For contemporary opinions see Stuart Davies, 'Vinetum Britannicum: Cider and Perry in the Seventeenth Century', in C. Anne Wilson (ed.), *Liquid Nourishment: Potable Foods and Stimulating Drinks*, Edinburgh University Press, 1993, 79–105.

76 Josephine A. Spring and David H. Buss, 'Three Centuries of Alcohol in the British Diet', *Nature*, vol. 270, 1977, 568.

77 French, op. cit., 17.

78 Henry Gunning, *Reminiscences of the University, Town and County of Cambridge from 1780* (1854), quoted Pamela Horn, *The Rural World, 1780–1850*, London, Hutchinson, 1980, 16. (The reference is to Herefordshire.)

79 The analytical chemist, Brande, estimated that cyder could contain up to 9.87 per cent of alcohol.

80 Walter Minchinton, 'Cider and Folklore', *Folk Life*, vol. XIII, 1975, 66–79.

81 Quoted Francis George Heath, *The English Peasantry*, London, Frederick Warne, 1874, 99–100.

82 E.F. Bulmer, *Early Days of Cider Making*, The Hereford Times, n.d. [c. 1920], 3–26.

83 Prest and Adams, op. cit., Tables 50, 56, 81–6.

84 Stone, op. cit., Tables 68, 71, 72, 188–9.

85 Current statistics from *The Drink Pocket Book*, 1997, op. cit., 16, 18, 71–8.

8 Spirits

1 John Doxat (ed.), *The Indispensable Drinks Book*, London, Macdonald, 1982, 75. Frederick A. Filby, *A History of Food Adulteration and Analysis*, London, George Allen and Unwin, 1934, 153.

2 C. Anne Wilson, 'Water of Life: Its Beginnings and Early History', in C. Anne Wilson (ed.), *Liquid Nourishment: Potable Foods and Stimulating Drinks*, Edinburgh University Press, 1993, 142 et seq. (The fullest modern account.)

3 Jean-Charles Sournia, *A History of Alcoholism*, Oxford, Basil Blackwell, 1990, 17.

4 Eliza Smith, *The Compleat Housewife*, Facsimile of the 1758 edn, London, Studio Editions, 1994, 'All Sorts of Cordial Waters', 255 et seq.

5 Wilson, op. cit., 158.

6 R. Scott-Moncrieff, 'Note on the Early use of Aqua Vitae in Scotland', *Proceedings of the Society of Antiquaries of Scotland*, vol. 50, 1916, 257–66; R.J.S. McDowall, *The Whiskies of Scotland*, London, John Murray, 1967, 3.

7 J.C. Drummond and Anne Wilbraham, *The Englishman's Food: A History of Five Centuries of English Diet*. Revised edn by Dorothy Hollingsworth, London, Jonathan Cape, 1957, 115.

8 A.D. Francis, *The Wine Trade*, London, A. and C. Black, 1972, 74.

9 Filby, op. cit., 157–8.

10 H.A. Monckton, *A History of English Ale and Beer*, London, The Bodley Head, 1966, App. B, 203.

11 Annual production of beer in the United Kingdom fell from a peak of 23,056,000 barrels in 1689 to a low of 14,186,000 barrels in 1699. Monckton, ibid., App. D, 219–20.

12 B.R. Mitchell and Phyllis Deane, *Abstract of British Historical Statistics*, Cambridge University Press, 1962, 254.

13 W.I.H. Lecky, *England in the Eighteenth Century* (1879), vol. 1, 479, quoted Richard Valpy French, *Nineteen Centuries of Drink in England: A History*, London, Longman, Green, 1884, 271.

14 M.D. George, *London Life in the Eighteenth Century*, Kegan Paul, 1925, 51.

15 There were said to be 1,500 distillers in London in the 1730s, of whom 100 had equipment worth £100 or more. Peter Clark, 'The "Mother Gin" Controversy in the Early Eighteenth Century', *Trans. of the Royal Historical Society*, 5th Series, vol. 38, 1988, 64.

16 A.L. Simon, *Drink* (1948), quoted Monckton, op. cit., 142.

17 For a general account of changes in the standard of living in the period, see my *History of the Cost of Living*, Penguin Books, 1969, repub. Aldershot, Hampshire, Gregg Revivals, 1993, 128 et seq.

18 Clark, op. cit., 70–1.

19 The events of 1736 are fully described in James Watney, *Mother's Ruin: A History of Gin*, London, Peter Owen, 1976, 26–38: this includes the strange story of Captain Dudley Bradstreet's 'automatic cat' gin dispenser. George Rudé argues that the main causes of the riots of 1736 were the Gin Act and the substitution of cheap Irish labour for English workers rather than Jacobite agitation. '"Mother Gin" and the London Riots of 1736', in George Rudé (ed.), *Paris and London in the Eighteenth Century: Studies in Popular Protest*, New York, Viking Press, 1971, 201–21.

20 T.G. Coffey, 'Beer Street, Gin Lane: Some Views of Eighteenth Century Drinking', *Quarterly Journal of Studies on Alcohol*, vol. 27, 1966, 669–92.

21 André L. Simon, *Bottlescrew Days*, London, Duckworth, 1926, 28.

22 Ralph Davis, 'The English Wine Trade in the Eighteenth and Nineteenth Centuries', *Annales Cisalpines d'Histoire Sociale*, 1972, Part 3, 94.

23 Richard P. Wedeen, *Poison in the Pot: The Legacy of Lead*, Carbondale, Southern Illinois University Press, 1984, 45–6, 97, 99.

24 Statistical Abstract of Scotland, 1796, quoted C. Anne Wilson, *Food and Drink in Britain: From the Stone Age to the Nineteenth Century*, Chicago, Academy Chicago Publishers, 1991, 402.

25 T.C. Smout and Sydney Wood, *Scottish Voices, 1745–1960*, London, Fontana Press, 1991, 148, 152.

26 Elizabeth Grant of Rothiemurchus, *Memoirs of a Highland Lady, 1798–1827* (1898), quoted Michael Moss, 'Whisky', in *Chambers Scottish Drink Book*, Edinburgh, W. and R. Chambers, 1990, 95.

27 Mitchell and Deane, op. cit., 255–7.

28 George B. Wilson, *Alcohol and the Nation*, London, Nicholson and Watson, 1940, 18–19.

29 This argument is developed persuasively by A.E. Dingle, 'Drink and Working-Class Living Standards in Britain, 1870–1914', in Derek Oddy and Derek Miller (eds), *The Making of the Modern British Diet*, London, Croom Helm, 1976, 117–34. Total tobacco expenditure grew from £13.5 million in 1870 to £42 million in 1914.

30 Report of the Committee of the British Association on the Present Appropriation of Wages, 1882. Cited Joseph Rowntree and Arthur Sherwell, *The Temperance Problem and Social Reform*, 3rd edn, London, Hodder and Stoughton, 1899, 10. Working-class expenditure on spirits was calculated at £30 million p.a. of the total of £40 million.

31 Rowntree and Sherwell, ibid., 5–6, 58–9.

32 Charles Booth, *Life and Labour of the People in London*, Final Volume, Notes on Social Influences and Conclusion, London, Macmillan, 1902, 61–4.

33 These were contemporary expressions. See Edward Hewett and W.F. Axton, *Convivial Dickens: The Drinks of Dickens and his Times*, Athens, Ohio, Ohio University Press, 1983, 90.

34 G.B. Wilson, op. cit., Table 3, 337–9. As gin was sold at 40° under proof, the quantities consumed were considerably greater than these statistics: Wilson, 21.

35 G.R. Porter, *The Progress of the Nation*, London, John Murray, new edn, 1847, 567–8.

36 G.B. Wilson, op. cit., Table 9, 354–5.

37 Doxat, op. cit., 98.

38 Michael Moss, 'Whisky', in *Chambers Scottish Drink Book*, op. cit., 98.

39 T.M. Devine, 'The Rise and Fall of Illicit Whisky-Making in Northern Scotland *c.* 1780–1840', *Scottish Historical Review*, vol. 54, 1975, 155–77.

40 R.B. Weir, 'Distilling and Agriculture, 1870–1939', *Agricultural History Review*, vol. 32 (1), 1984, 50–4.

41 Sir Archibald Geike, *Scottish Reminiscences* (1904), quoted *Scottish Voices*, op. cit., 151.

42 Asa Briggs, *Wine for Sale: Victoria Wine and the Liquor Trade, 1860–1984*, University of Chicago Press, 1985, 84.

43 Weir, op. cit., 51–3.

44 G.B. Wilson, op. cit., Table 4, 341–2.

45 Fredrick Accum, *A Treatise on Adulterations of Food and Culinary Poisons*, London, Longman, Hurst, Rees, Orme and Brown, 1820, 271–2, 282.

46 Dilution of spirits was detectable by the hydrometer invented by Clarke in 1725, but this required elaborate adjustments, and more practical instruments were made by Dicas, Sykes and others into the early nineteenth century. Filby, op. cit., 164–70.

47 Arthur Hill Hassall, *Food and its Adulterations, Comprising the Reports of the Analytical Sanitary Commission of 'The Lancet'*, London, Longman, Brown, Green and Longmans, 1855, 642–5.

48 Select Committee on Adulteration of Food, etc. First Report with Minutes of Evidence, (432), 1855, 70–1.

49 Annual Reports of the Local Government Board: Reports of Public Analysts for 1879–80 (1880), cx; 1881–2 (1882), cvi; 1883–4 (1884), cxii; 1890–91 (1891), cliii.

50 Sournia, op. cit., 23.

51 John Burnett, 'The Rise and Decline of School Meals in Britain, 1860–1990', in John Burnett and Derek J. Oddy (eds), *The Origins and Development of Food Policies in Europe*, Leicester University Press, 1994, 60–2. The statistics of medical rejection related to the period 1894–1902, and included volunteers for the S. African War (1899–1902).

52 G.B. Wilson, op. cit., Table 1, 333.

53 Henry Carter, *The Control of the Drink Trade in Britain: A Contribution to National Efficiency During the Great War, 1915–1918*, London, Longmans, Green, 1919, 60–6. (The fullest account of wartime controls.) Warehousing reduced the amount of intoxicating fusel oils present in newly distilled spirit.

54 G.B. Wilson, op. cit., 194.

55 Gwylmor Prys Williams and George Thompson Brake, *Drink in Great Britain, 1900–1979*, London, Edsall, 1980, Table 1.11, 354; Table 1.20, 375; Table 1.21, 376.

56 Carter, op. cit. Preface by Lord D'Abernon, X-XI.

57 G.B. Wilson, op. cit., 157–8.

58 The average price per pint of proof spirits was 15.3s in 1920 and 16.2s in 1938. The fall in expenditure on spirits in the UK from £124.3 million to £63.4 million reflects the decline in consumption. Richard Stone, *The Measurement of Consumers' Expenditure and Behaviour in the UK, 1920–1938*, 2 vols, Cambridge University Press, 1954, vol. 1, Tables 71 and 72, 189.

59 Weir, op. cit., Table 4, 59.

60 James B. Jefferys, *The Distribution of Consumer Goods*, 1950, 242–52, cited Stone, op. cit., 176.

61 The word 'cocktail' is apparently derived from the French 'coquetel', a mixed wine cup made for centuries in Bordeaux: it was carried to America by Lafayette's officers who joined the revolutionaries in 1779. Many 'juleps', 'slings', 'cobblers' and other mixed drinks were developed in America in the first half of the nineteenth century. Watney, op. cit., 92–9.

62 Alec Waugh, *Merchants of Wine: A Centenary Account of the House of Gilbey*, London, Cassell, 1957, 86. Waugh himself gave a better-attended cocktail party in 1925.

63 Stone, op. cit., Table 68, 188.

64 Sir Hubert Llewellyn Smith, *The New Survey of London Life and Labour*, vol. IX, *Life and Leisure*, P.S. King and Son, 1935, 247–8.

65 Tom Harrisson, *The Pub and the People: A Worktown Study by Mass Observation*, London, Victor Gollancz, 1943, 48–51.

66 Quoted McDowall, op. cit., 6.

67 Moss, op. cit., 105–8. In 1947 output was further reduced to 25 per cent of that of 1939.

68 Watney, op. cit., 114–15.

69 Williams and Brake, op. cit., Table 11.5, 380.

70 UK beer consumption (population aged over 15) 1970 29.5 gallons p.a., 1979 34.0 (peak), 1995 27.2. *The Drink Pocket Book, 1997*, Henley-on-Thames, Oxfordshire, NTC Publications in Association with Stats M.R., 1996, 44.

71 Rowntree and Sherwell, op. cit., 9–10. The national drink bill in 1898 was £154 million, of which two-thirds was estimated to be working-class expenditure, or 6s 5d per family per week of an average wage of 35s.

72 *Family Spending*, Report on the 1994/5 Family Expenditure Survey, London, Central Statistical Office, 1995. Table 1.2, 16; Table 1.3, 20; Table 5.3, 88; Table 6.1, 102.

73 Ibid., Table 7.2, 117.

74 *The Drink Pocket Book*, op. cit., 136.

Conspectus

1 H.A. Monckton, *A History of English Ale and Beer*, London, The Bodley Head, 1966, App. D, 219–20. Statistics are for the United Kingdom and include estimated private brewing.

2 Josephine A. Spring and David H. Buss, 'Three Centuries of Alcohol in the British Diet', *Nature*, vol. 270, 15 December 1977, 567. National beer consumption was officially recorded from 1684.

3 For the early history of chocolate see Wolfgang Schivelbusch, *Tastes of Paradise: A Social History of Spices, Stimulants and Intoxicants*, Trans. by David Jacobson, New York, Pantheon Books, 1992, ch. 3, 85 et seq.; Sophie D. Coe and Michael D. Coe, *The True History of Chocolate*, London, Thames and Hudson, 1996. Cacao contains only trace elements of caffeine but mainly theobromine, which has a mildly stimulating effect on the nervous system.

4 Carole Shammas, *The Pre-Industrial Consumer in England and America*, Oxford University Press, 1990, 259, 293–8.

5 See my *History of the Cost of Living*, Aldershot, Hampshire, Gregg Revivals, 1993, 131 et seq. On the Phelps Brown index of the cost of a standard 'basket' of consumables (1500 = 100), a fall from 671 points in 1700 to 599 in 1749 was followed by a steady rise to 824 in 1780–9 and steeper increases to 1,148 in 1799 and 1,567 in 1800. Table, 199.

6 B.R. Mitchell and Phyllis Deane, *Abstract of British Historical Statistics*, Cambridge University Press, 1962, Table 6, 355.

7 George B. Wilson, *Alcohol and the Nation*, London, Nicholson and Watson, 1940, App. F, Table 1, 331–2.

8 Mitchell and Deane, op. cit., Table 6, 355–6.

9 See generally, David Felix, 'De Gustibus Disputandem Est. Changing Consumer Preferences in Economic Growth', *Explorations in Economic History*, 16, 1979; Joel Mokyr, 'Is there still life in the pessimist case? Consumption during the Industrial Revolution, 1790–1850', *Journal of Economic History*, XLVIII, 1988.

10 Wilson, op. cit., 332.

11 T. Othick, 'The Cocoa and Chocolate Industry in the Nineteenth Century', in Derek Oddy and Derek Miller (eds), *The Making of the Modern British Diet*, London, Croom Helm, 1976, Table 2, 78.

12 Helen M. Pollard, 'A Liquid Diet', in C. Anne Wilson (ed.), *Liquid Nourishment: Potable Foods and Stimulating Drinks*, Edinburgh University Press, 1990, 43 et seq.

13 Brewers and Licensed Retailers Association, Statistical Report 1996, Table A1.

14 Gwylmor Prys Williams and George Thompson Brake, *Drink in Great Britain, 1900 to 1979*, London, Edsall, 1980, Table 1.1, 345; Table 2.5, 380.

15 Wilson, op. cit., 308.

16 Spring and Buss, op. cit., 571.

17 Statistics for 1965–95 calculated from Brewers and Licensed Retailers, op. cit., Table D3; for 1876 from Joseph Rowntree and Arthur Sherwell, *The Temperance Problem and Social Reform*, 3rd edn, London, Hodder and Stoughton, 1899, 4. Their statistics are given in 'proof spirits', which at the time represented 50 per cent absolute alcohol: they have therefore been halved in my calculation.

18 *The Drink Pocket Book, 1997*, Henley-on-Thames, Oxfordshire, NTC Publications in Association with Stats M.R., 1996, 159. These statistics relate to 1994.

19 Paul Glennie, 'Consumption within Historical Studies', in Daniel Miller (ed.), *Acknowledging Consumption: A Review of New Studies*, London, Routledge, 1995, 177.

20 *Family Spending, Report on the 1994/5 Family Expenditure Survey*, HMSO, 1995, Table 6.1, 102.

21 Catherine Geissler and Derek J. Oddy (eds), *Food, Diet and Economic Change Past and Present*, Leicester University Press, 1993, 3.

22 David Davies, *The Case of Labourers in Husbandry*, Fairfield, New Jersey, Augustus M. Kelley, 1977 (facsimile of 1st edn, 1795), 39.

23 Carole Shammas, 'The Eighteenth-Century English Diet and Economic Change', *Explorations in Economic History*, 21 (Part 3), 1984, 258.

24 Roman Sandgruber, 'Kaffeesuppe und "kleiner Brauner"', in Daniela U. Ball (ed.), *Coffee in the Context of European Drinking Habits*, Zurich, Johann Jacobs Museum, 1991, 53–68.

25 Vernon D. Wickizer, *Coffee, Tea and Cocoa: An Economic and Political Analysis*, California, Stanford University Press, 1951, 391.

26 Wilson, op. cit., 197.

27 Francis McKee, 'The Popularisation of Milk as a Beverage during the 1930s', in David F. Smith (ed.), *Nutrition in Britain: Science, Scientists and Politics in the Twentieth Century*, London, Routledge, 1997, 123–39.

28 Ben Fine, 'From Political Economy to Consumption', in Daniel Miller (ed.), *Acknowledging Consumption*, op. cit., 144.

29 Norbert Elias, *The History of Manners: The Civilising Process, vol. 1*, Trans. by Edmund Jephcott, Oxford, Basil Blackwell, 1978, 60.

30 Stephen Braun, *Buzz: The Science and Lore of Alcohol and Caffeine*, Oxford University Press, 1996, 140.

31 Woodruff D. Smith, 'Complications of the Commonplace: Tea, Sugar and Imperialism', *Journal of Interdisciplinary History*, 23(2), 1992, 267 et seq.

32 Sidney W. Mintz, *Sweetness and Power: The Place of Sugar in Modern History*, New York, Viking Penguin, 1985.

33 The Tea Council, Annual Report 1992, 8.

34 John Yudkin, 'The Need for Change', in John Yudkin and J.C. McKenzie (eds), *Changing Food Habits*, London, MacGibbon and Kee, 1964, 19.

35 Roy Porter, *Health For Sale: Quackery in England, 1660–1850*, Manchester University Press, 1989.

36 Bryan S. Turner, *The Body and Society: Explorations in Social Theory*, Oxford, Basil Blackwell, 1984.

37 In 1995 19 per cent of adult women were reported as never drinking alcohol compared with 12 per cent of men. Regular table wine drinkers were almost equally male and female, while a higher proportion of women than men were regular drinkers of gin, vodka, white rum and brandy. *The Drink Pocket Book, 1997*, op. cit., 24, 106, 136.

38 Quoted William Emboden, Foreword to Richard Rudgley, *Essential Substances: A Cultural History of Intoxicants in Society*, New York, Kodanska International, 1994, viii–ix.

Select bibliography

This list includes only the more important works used. The place of publication is London unless otherwise stated.

Books and chapters in books

Accum, F. *A Treatise on Adulterations of Food and Culinary Poisons*, Longman, Hurst, Rees, Orme and Brown, 1820.

Acton, E. *Modern Cookery*, Longman, 1859.

Agar, N.E. *The Bedfordshire Farm Worker in the Nineteenth Century*, Bedfordshire Historical Record Society, vol. 60, 1981.

Allen, B. (ed.) *Food: An Oxford Anthology*, Oxford, Oxford University Press, 1994.

Allen, D.E. *British Tastes: An Enquiry into the Likes and Dislikes of the Regional Consumer*, Hutchinson, 1968.

Allen, H.W. *The Romance of Wine*, Ernest Benn, 1931.

Astor, Viscount and Rowntree, B.S. *British Agriculture: The Principles of Future Policy*, Harmondsworth, Middlesex, Penguin Books, 1939.

Bailey, P. *Leisure and Class in Victorian England: Rational Recreation and the Contest for Control, 1830–1885*, Methuen, 1987.

Ball, D.U. (ed.) *Coffee in the Context of European Drinking Habits*, Zurich, Johann Jacobs Museum, 1991.

Barker, T. and Drake, M. (eds) *Population and Society in Britain, 1850–1980*, Batsford, 1982.

Barker, T.C., Oddy, D.J. and Yudkin, J. *The Dietary Surveys of Dr Edward Smith, 1862–3*, Staples Press, 1970.

Barnett, L.M. *British Food Policy During the First World War*, Boston, Massachussetts, George Allen and Unwin, 1985.

Barr, A. *Drink*, Bantam Press, 1995.

Barthes, R. 'Toward a psychosociology of contemporary food consumption' in R. Forster and O. Ranum (eds) *Food and Drink in History: Selections from the Annales*, vol. 5, Baltimore and London, Johns Hopkins University Press, 1979.

Barty-King, H. *A Tradition of English Wine: The Story of Two Thousand Years of English Wine made from English Grapes*, Oxford, Oxford Illustrated Press, 1977.

—— *Water: The Book*, Quiller Press, 1992.

Baxter, A. 'Milk-sellers', in C. Booth (ed.) *Life and Labour of the People in London*, vol. VII, *Population Classified by Trades*, Macmillan, 1896.

Bell, H. Lady (Mrs. H. Bell) *At the Works: A Study of a Manufacturing Town*, New edn, Thomas Nelson, 1911.

Beresford, J. (ed.) *The Diary of a Country Parson, 1758–1802*, Oxford, The World's Classics, 1949.

Beveridge, Sir W.H. *British Food Control: Economic and Social History of the World War*, Humphrey Milford, 1928.

Bickerdyke, J. *The Curiosities of Ale and Beer*, The Leadenhall Press, 1886.

Birchall, J. *Co-op: The People's Business*, Manchester, Manchester University Press, 1994.

Booth, C. (ed.) *Life and Labour of the People in London*, vol. VII, *Population Classified by Trades*, Macmillan, 1896.

Bramah, E. *Tea and Coffee: A Modern View of Three Hundred Years of Tradition*, Hutchinson, 1972.

Braudel, F. *Capitalism and Material Life, 1400–1800*, Weidenfeld and Nicolson, 1973.

Braun, S. *Buzz: The Science and Lore of Alcohol and Caffeine*, Oxford, Oxford University Press, 1996.

Brears, P. *Traditional Food in Yorkshire*, Edinburgh, John Donald, 1987.

Brewer, J. and Porter, R. (eds) *Consumption and the World of Goods*, London and New York, Routledge, 1994.

Briggs, A. *Wine for Sale: Victoria Wine and the Liquor Trade, 1860–1984*, Chicago, University of Chicago Press, 1985.

Buchanan, I. 'Infant feeding, sanitation and diarrhoea in colliery communities, 1880–1911', in D.J. Oddy and D.S. Miller (eds) *Diet and Health in Modern Britain*, Croom Helm, 1985.

Bulmer, E.F. *Early Days of Cider Making*, Hereford, The Hereford Times, n.d. [*c*. 1920].

Burnett, J. *A History of the Cost of Living*, Penguin Books, 1969, repub. Aldershot, Hampshire, Gregg Revivals, 1993.

—— 'Food adulteration in Britain in the 19th century and the origins of food legislation', in E. Heischkel-Artelt (ed.) *Ernährung und Ernährungslehre im 19. Jahrhundert*, Göttingen, Germany, Vandenbreck & Ruprecht, 1976.

—— *A Social History of Housing, 1815–1985*, 2nd edn, Routledge, 1986.

—— *Plenty and Want: A Social History of Food in England from 1815 to the Present Day*, 3rd edn, Routledge, 1989.

—— 'The rise and decline of school meals in Britain, 1860–1990', in J. Burnett and D.J. Oddy (eds) *Origins and Development of Food Policies in Europe*, Leicester, Leicester University Press, 1994.

Buxton, M. 'Hypocras, caudels, possets and other comforting drinks', in C.A. Wilson (ed.) *Liquid Nourishment; Potable Foods and Stimulating Drinks*, Edinburgh, Edinburgh University Press, 1993.

Camporesi, P. *Exotic Brew: The Art of Living in the Age of Enlightenment*, trans. Woodall, C., Oxford, Polity Press, 1994.

Carter, H. *The Control of the Liquor Trade in Britain: A Contribution to National Efficiency during the Great War, 1915–1918*, 2nd edn, Longmans, Green, 1919.

—— *The Nation Surveys the Drink Problem: A Review of the Report of the Royal Commission on Licensing*, The Temperance Council of the Christian Churches, 1933.

Chadwick, E. *Report on the Sanitary Condition of the Labouring Population of Great Britain, 1842*, with an Introduction by Flinn, M.W., Edinburgh, Edinburgh University Press, 1965.

Chambers, J.D. *Modern Nottingham in the Making*, Nottingham, Nottingham Journal, 1945.

Chaudhuri, K.N. *The Trading World of Asia and the English East India Company, 1660–1760*, Cambridge, Cambridge University Press, 1978.

Cobbett, W. *Cottage Economy*, Peter Davies, 1926.

Coe, S.D. and Coe, M.D. *The True History of Chocolate*, Thames and Hudson, 1996.

Cooper, D. *The Beverage Report*, Routledge and Kegan Paul, 1970.

Cottrell, R. (ed.) *Nutrition in Catering*, Carnforth, Lancashire, The Parthenon Publishing Group, 1987.

Crawford, A. and Thorne, R. *Birmingham Pubs, 1890–1939*, Birmingham, University of Birmingham Centre for Urban and Regional Studies, 1975.

Crawford, Sir W. and Broadley, H. *The People's Food*, William Heinemann, 1938.

Croutier, A.L. *Taking the Waters: Spirit, Art, Sensuality*, New York, Abbeville Press, 1992.

Davies, D. *The Case of Labourers in Husbandry*, G.G. and J. Robinson, 1795, repub. Fairfield, New Jersey, Augustus M. Kelley, 1977.

Davies, J. *The Victorian Kitchen*, BBC Books, 1991.

Davies, P. *Troughs and Drinking Fountains: Fountains of Life*, Chatto and Windus, 1989.

Davies, S. 'Vinetum Britannicum. Cider and perry in the seventeenth century', in C.A. Wilson (ed.) *Liquid Nourishment; Potable Foods and Stimulating Drinks*, Edinburgh, Edinburgh University Press, 1993.

Davis, R. *The Industrial Revolution and British Overseas Trade*, Leicester, Leicester University Press, 1979.

Deerr, N. *The History of Sugar*, Chapman and Hall, 1949–50.

Denbigh, K. *A Hundred British Spas: A Pictorial History*, Spa Publications, 1981.

Dickinson, H.W. *Water Supply of Greater London*, Newcomen Society, Leamington Spa and London, The Courier Press, 1954.

Dietz, L. *Soda Pop: The History, Advertising, Art and Memorabilia of Soft Drinks in America*, New York, Simon and Schuster, 1973.

Dingle, A.E. 'Drink and working-class living standards in Britain, 1870–1914', in D.J. Oddy and D.S. Miller (eds) *The Making of the Modern British Diet*, Croom Helm, 1976.

—— The *Campaign for Prohibition in Victorian England: The United Kingdom Alliance, 1872–1895*, New Brunswick, New Jersey, Rutgers University Press, 1980.

Donnachie, I. *A History of the Brewing Industry in Scotland*, Edinburgh, John Donald, 1979.

Douglas, M. (ed.) *Constructive Drinking: Perspectives on Drink from Anthropology*, Cambridge, Cambridge University Press, 1987.

Doxat, J. (ed.) *The Indispensable Drinks Book*, Macdonald, 1982.

Driver, C. *The British at Table, 1940–1980*, Chatto and Windus, 1983.

Drummond, J.C. and Wilbraham A. *The Englishman's Food: A History of Five Centuries of English Diet*, Revised edn by Hollingsworth, D., Jonathan Cape, 1957.

Dunlop, J. *The Philosophy of Artificial and Compulsory Drinking Usages in Great Britain and Ireland*, Houlston and Stoneman, 1839.

Dwork, D. *War is Good for Babies and Other Young Children: A History of the Infant and Child Welfare Movement in England, 1898–1918*, Tavistock Press, 1986.

Eden, Sir F.M. *The State of the Poor*, Facsimile of 1st edn, 1797, 3 vols, Frank Cass, 1966.

Elias, N. *The Civilising Process: The History of Manners*, trans. Jephcott, E., Oxford, Basil Blackwell, 1978. (1st German edn 1939.)

Ellis, A. *The Penny Universities: A History of the Coffee Houses*, Secker and Warburg, 1956.

Emmerson, R. *British Tea Pots and Tea Drinking*, Norfolk Museums Service, HMSO, 1992.

Emmins, C. *Soft Drinks: Their Origins and History*, Princes Risborough, Buckinghamshire, Shire Publications, 1991.

Fairley, J., Gillon, J., McMaster, C. and Moss, M. *Chambers Scottish Drink Book: Whisky, Beer, Wine and Soft Drinks*, Edinburgh, Chambers, 1990.

Farrer, K.T.H. *A Guide to Food Additives and Contaminants*, Carnforth, Lancashire, Parthenon Publishing Group, 1987.

Fenton, A. 'Coffee-drinking in Scotland in the 17th–19th centuries', in D.U. Ball (ed.) *Coffee in the Context of European Drinking Habits*, Zurich, Johann Jacobs Museum, 1991.

—— 'Milk and milk products in Scotland: the role of the Milk Marketing Boards', in A.P. den Hartog (ed.) *Food Technology, Science and Marketing: European Diet in the Twentieth Century*, East Linton, East Lothian, Tuckwell Press, 1995.

Filby, F.A. *A History of Food Adulteration and Analysis*, George Allen and Unwin, 1934.

Fine, B. 'From political economy to consumption', in D. Miller (ed.) *Acknowledging Consumption. A Review of New Studies*, Routledge, 1995.

Finer, H. *Municipal Trading: A Study in Public Administration*, George Allen and Unwin, 1941.

Fisher, M.F.K. *A Cordiall Water*, The Hogarth Press, Chatto and Windus, 1983.

Forrest, D. *Tea for the British: The Social and Economic History of a Famous Trade*, Chatto and Windus, 1973.

Forster, R. and Ranum, O. (eds) *Food and Drink in History: Selections from the Annales*, vol. 5, Baltimore and London, Johns Hopkins University Press, 1979.

Francis, A.D. *The Wine Trade*, A. and C. Black, 1972.

Freeman, B. *First Catch Your Peacock*, Revised edn, Ceredigion, Wales, Y. Lolfa, 1996.

Freeman, S. *Mutton and Oysters: The Victorians and their Food*, Victor Gollancz, 1989.

French, R.K. *The History and Virtues of Cyder*, Robert Hale, 1982.

French, R.V. *Nineteen Centuries of Drink in England: A History*, Longmans, Green, 1884.

Fussell, G.E. *The English Dairy Farmer, 1500–1900*, Frank Cass, 1966.

Fussell, G.E. and Fussell, K.R. *The English Countryman. His Life and Work from Tudor Times to the Victorian Age*, Orbis Publishing, 1981.

Geissler, C. and Oddy, D.J. (eds) *Food, Diet and Economic Change Past and Present*, Leicester, Leicester University Press, 1993.

George, M.D. *London Life in the Eighteenth Century*, Kegan, Paul, 1925.

Gibson, A. and Smout, T.C. 'From meat to meal: changes in diet in Scotland', in C. Geissler and D.J. Oddy (eds) *Food, Diet and Economic Change Past and Present*, Leicester, Leicester University Press, 1993.

Gilboy, E.W. 'Demand as a factor in the Industrial Revolution', in A.H. Cole (ed.) *Facts and Factors in Economic History*, Cambridge, Massachussetts, Harvard University Press, 1932.

Glennie, P. 'Consumption within historical studies', in D. Miller (ed.) *Acknowledging Consumption: A Review of New Studies*, Routledge, 1995.

Goodman, J. 'Excitantia, or how Enlightenment Europe took to soft drugs', in J. Goodman, P.E. Lovejoy and A. Sherratt (eds) *Consuming Habits: Drugs in History and Anthropology*, Routledge, 1995.

Goodman, J., Lovejoy, P.E. and Sherratt, A. (eds) *Consuming Habits, Drugs in History and Anthropology*, London and New York, Routledge, 1995.

Gorham, M. and Dunnett, H.McG. *Inside the Pub*, The Architectural Press, 1950.

Goubert, J-P. *The Conquest of Water: The Advent of Health in the Industrial Age*, trans. by Wilson, A., Cambridge, Polity Press, 1989.

Gourvish, T.R. and Wilson, R.G. *The British Brewing Industry, 1830–1980*, Cambridge, Cambridge University Press, 1994.

Granville, A.B. *The Spas of England and Principal Sea-Bathing Places*, 2 vols, 1st edn 1841, repub. Bath, Adams and Dart, 1971.

Green, M. and T. *The Good Water Guide*, Revised edn, Rosendale Press, 1994.

Griffiths, Sir P. *The History of the Indian Tea Industry*, Weidenfeld and Nicolson, 1967.

Hamlin, C. *A Science of Impurity: Water Analysis in Nineteenth Century Britain*, Berkeley and Los Angeles, University of California Press, 1990.

Hammond, J.L. and B. *The Bleak Age*, West Drayton, Middlesex, Pelican Books, 1947.

Hammond, R.J. *History of the Second World War: Food* (2 vols), vol. 1, *The Growth of Policy*, HMSO and Longman, Green, 1951.

Harrison, B. *Drink and the Victorians: The Temperance Question in England, 1815–1872*, Revised edn, Staffordshire, Keele University Press, 1994.

Harrisson, T. *The Pub and the People: A Worktown Study by Mass Observation*, Victor Gollancz, 1943.

Hartley, D. *Water in England*, Macdonald, 1964.

Hartog, A.P. den (ed.) *Food Technology, Science and Marketing: European Diet in the Twentieth Century*, East Linton, East Lothian, Tuckwell Press, 1995.

Hassall, A.H. *Food and its Adulterations, Comprising the Reports of the Analytical Sanitary Commission of 'The Lancet'*, Longman, Brown, Green and Longmans, 1855.

Heald, G. 'Trends in eating out', in R. Cottrell (ed.) *Nutrition in Catering*, Carnforth, Lancashire, The Parthenon Publishing Group, 1987.

Hembry, P. *The English Spa, 1560–1815: A Social History*, The Athlone Press, 1990.

Hewett, E. and Axton, W.F. *Convivial Dickens: The Drinks of Dickens and his Times*, Ohio, Ohio University Press, 1983.

Hindley, D. and G. *Advertising in Victorian Britain*, Wayland Publishers, 1972.

Hollander, S.C. and Germain, R. *Was there a Pepsi Generation before Pepsi Discovered It? Youth-Based Segmentation in Marketing*, Chicago, Illinois, NTC Business Books, 1992.

Horn, P. *The Rural World, 1780–1850: Social Change in the English Countryside*, Hutchinson, 1980.

Howe, G.M. *Man, Environment and Disease in Britain: A Medical Geography*, New York, Harper and Row, 1972.

Huxley, G. *Talking of Tea*, Thames and Hudson, 1956.

Inglis, B. *Fringe Medicine*, Faber and Faber, 1964.

Jacob, H.E. *The Saga of Coffee: The Biography of an Economic Product*, Trans. by Paul, E. and C., George Allen and Unwin, 1935.

Jeffery, J. *The Statutory Water Companies: Their History and Development*, Richmond, Surrey, Michael Collins, 1981.

Jenkins, A. *Drinka Pinta: The Story of Milk and the Industry that Serves It*, Heinemann, 1970.

John, A.H. 'Agricultural productivity and economic growth in England', in E.L. Jones (ed.) *Agriculture and Economic Growth in England, 1650–1815*, Methuen, 1967.

Johnston, J.P. *A Hundred Years Eating: Food, Drink and the Daily Diet in Britain since the Late Nineteenth Century*, Dublin, Gill and Macmillan, 1977.

Johnstone, G.N. 'The growth of the sugar trade and refining industry', in D.J. Oddy and D.S. Miller (eds) *The Making of the Modern British Diet*, Croom Helm, 1976.

Kahn, E.J. Jnr *The Big Drink: An Unofficial History of Coca-Cola*, London, Max Reinhardt, 1960.

Kinchin, P. *Tea and Taste: The Glasgow Tea Rooms, 1875–1975*, Wendlebury, Oxon, White Cockade, 1991.

Kirkby, W. *The Evolution of Artificial Mineral Waters*, Manchester, Jewsbury and Brown, 1902.

Knox, O. *Croft, A Journey of Confidence*, Collins, 1978.

Kolpas, N. *Coffee*, John Murray, 1979.

Lambert, W.R. *Drink and Sobriety in Victorian Wales, c. 1820–1895*, Cardiff, Cardiff University Press, 1983.

Laski, H.J., Jennings, W.I. and Robson, W.A. *A Century of Municipal Progress, 1835–1935*, George Allen and Unwin, 1935.

Levi, L. *Wages and Earnings of the Working Classes: Report to Sir Arthur Bass, M.P.*, John Murray, 1885.

Levy, P. (ed.) *The Penguin Book of Food and Drink*, Viking, Penguin Books, 1996.

Lewin, L. *Phantastica: Narcotic and Stimulating Drugs*, trans. from 2nd German edn by Wirth, D.H.A., Kegan Paul, Trench, Trubner, 1931.

Leyel, C.S. *Elixirs of Life*, Culpeper House Herbals, Faber and Faber, 1948.

Lillywhite, B. *London Coffee Houses: A Reference Book of Coffee Houses of the Seventeenth, Eighteenth and Nineteenth Centuries*, George Allen and Unwin, 1963.

Lock, C.G.W. (ed.) *Coffee: Its Culture and Commerce*, E. and F.N. Spon, 1888.

Longmate, N. *The Waterdrinkers: A History of Temperance*, Hamish Hamilton, 1968.

Luckin, B. *Pollution and Control: A Social History of the Thames in the Nineteenth Century*, Bristol, Hilger, 1988.

McDowall, R.J.S. *The Whiskies of Scotland*, John Murray, 1967.

McKee, F. 'The popularisation of milk as a beverage during the 1930s', in D.F. Smith (ed.) *Nutrition in Britain: Science, Scientists and Politics in the Twentieth Century*, Routledge, 1997.

McKendrick, N., Brewer, J. and Plumb, J.H. *The Birth of a Consumer Society: The Commercialization of Eighteenth-Century England*, Europa Publications, 1982.

McLaren, M. *Pure Wine, or In Vino Sanitas*, Edinburgh, Alastair Campbell, 1965.

MacPherson, D. *The History of the European Commerce with India*, Longman, Hurst, Rees, Orme and Brown, 1812.

Mathias, P. *The Brewing Industry in England, 1700–1830*, Cambridge, Cambridge University Press, 1959.

—— *Retailing Revolution: A History of Multiple Retailing in the Food Trades based on the Allied Suppliers Group of Companies*, Longmans, 1967.

Maury, E.A. *Wine is the Best Medicine*, Souvenir Press, 1976.

Mayhew, H. *London Labour and the London Poor*, vol. I, *The London Street Folk*, Griffin, Bohn, 1861.

Mendelsohn, O.A. *Drinking with Pepys*, Macmillan, 1963.

Mennell, S. *All Manners of Food: Eating and Taste in England and France from the Middle Ages to the Present*, Oxford, Basil Blackwell, 1985.

Mew, J. and Ashton, J. *Drinks of the World*, The Leadenhall Press, 1892.

Miller, D. (ed.) *Acknowledging Consumption: A Review of New Studies*, Routledge, 1995.

Mintz, S.W. *Sweetness and Power: The Place of Sugar in Modern History*, New York, Viking Penguin Inc., 1985.

―――― 'The changing roles of food in the study of consumption', in J. Brewer and R. Porter (eds) *Consumption and the World of Goods*, London and New York, Routledge, 1994.

Mitchell, B.R. and Deane, P. *Abstract of British Historical Statistics*, Cambridge, Cambridge University Press, 1962.

Mitchell, J. *A Treatise on the Falsifications of Food, and the Chemical Means Employed to Detect Them*, Bailliere, 1848.

Monckton, H.A. *A History of English Ale and Beer*, The Bodley Head, 1966.

Morgan, B. *Express Journey, 1864–1964: A Centenary History of the Express Dairy Co. Ltd.*, Newman Neame, 1964.

Morgan, R.H. *Beverage Manufacture (Non-Alcoholic)*, Attwood, 1938.

Mui, H-C. and L.H. *The Management of Monopoly: A Study of the English East India Company's Conduct of the Tea Trade, 1783–1833*, Vancouver, University of British Columbia Press, 1984.

―――― *Shops and Shopkeeping in Eighteenth-Century England*, McGill-Queen's University Press, Kingston, Canada, 1989.

Nichols, S. *Vimto: The Story of a Soft Drink*, Preston, Lancashire, Carnegie Publishing, 1994.

NTC Publications, *The Drink Pocket Book*, in Association with Stats M.R., Henley-on-Thames, Oxfordshire, 1996.

Oddy, D.J. 'Food, drink and nutrition', in F.M.L. Thompson (ed.) *The Cambridge Social History of Britain, 1750–1950*, vol. 2, Cambridge, Cambridge University Press, 1990.

Oddy, D.J. and Miller, D.S. (eds) *The Making of the Modern British Diet*, Croom Helm, 1976.

―――― *Diet and Health in Modern Britain*, Croom Helm, 1985.

Orr, J.B. *Food, Health and Income*, Macmillan, 1936.

―――― *Food and the People*, The Pilot Press, 1943.

Othick, T. 'The cocoa and chocolate industry in the nineteenth century', in D.J. Oddy and D. S. Miller (eds) *The Making of the Modern British Diet*, Croom Helm, 1976.

Packham, R.F. and Symons, J.M. *Drinking Water: The Plain Facts*, Marlow, Buckinghamshire, Water Research Centre, 1995.

Palmer, A. *Movable Feasts*, Oxford, Oxford University Press, 1952.

Parkinson, C.N. *Trade in the Eastern Seas, 1793–1813*, Cambridge, Cambridge University Press, 1937.

Pearce, F. *Watershed: The Water Crisis in Britain*, Junction Books, 1982.

Pendergrast, M. *For God, Country and Coca-Cola: The Unauthorized History of the World's Most Popular Soft Drink*, Orion Books, 1994.

Pimlott, J.A.R. *The Englishman's Holiday: A Social History*, Faber and Faber, 1947.

Polanyi, K. *The Great Transformation: The Political and Economic Origins of Our Time*, Boston, Massachusetts, Beacon Press, 1957.

Pollard, H.M. 'A liquid diet', in C.A. Wilson (ed.) *Liquid Nourishment: Potable Foods and Stimulating Drinks*, Edinburgh, Edinburgh University Press, 1993.

Porter, G.R. *The Progress of the Nation in its Various Social and Economical Relations*, New edn, John Murray, 1847.

Porter, R. *Health for Sale: Quackery in England, 1660–1850*, Manchester, Manchester University Press, 1989.

Prest, A.R. and Adams, A.A. *Consumers' Expenditure in the United Kingdom, 1900–1919*, Cambridge, Cambridge University Press, 1954.

Rae, S. (ed.) *The Faber Book of Drink, Drinkers and Drinking*, Faber and Faber, 1991.

Redding, C. *A History and Description of Modern Wines*, 3rd edn, Henry G. Bohn, 1851.

Reeves, M.P. *Round About a Pound a Week*, Virago Press, 1979.

Renner, H.D. *The Origin of Food Habits*, Faber and Faber, 1944.

Richardson, D.J. 'J. Lyons Ltd., caterers and food manufacturers, 1894–1939', in D.J. Oddy and D.S. Miller (eds), *The Making of the Modern British Diet*, Croom Helm, 1976.

Roberts, E. 'Working wives and their families', in T. Barker and M. Drake (eds) *Population and Society in Britain, 1850–1980*, Batsford, 1982.

Roberts, R. *The Classic Slum: Salford Life in the First Quarter of the Century*, Manchester, Manchester University Press, 1971.

Robinson, E.F. *The Early History of Coffee Houses in England*, Kegan Paul, Trench and Trubner, 1893.

Robson, W.A. 'The public utility services', in H.J. Laski, W.I. Jennings and W.A. Robson *A Century of Municipal Progress, 1835–1935*, George Allen and Unwin, 1935.

Roden, C. *Coffee*, Harlow, Essex, Longman Scientific and Technical, 1988.

Rowntree, B.S. *Poverty: A Study of Town Life*, 4th edn, Macmillan, 1902.

—— *Poverty and Progress: A Second Social Survey of York*, Longmans, Green, 1941.

Rowntree, B.S. and Kendall, M. *How the Labourer Lives: A Study of the Rural Labour Problem*, Thomas Nelson, 1917.

Rowntree, B.S. and Lavers, G.R. *English Life and Leisure: A Social Study*, Longmans, Green, 1951.

Rowntree, J. and Sherwell, A. *The Temperance Problem and Social Reform*, 3rd edn, Hodder and Stoughton, 1899.

Rudé, G. '"Mother Gin" and the London riots of 1736', in G. Rudé (ed.) *Paris and London in the Eighteenth Century: Studies in Popular Protest*, New York, Viking Press, 1971.

Rudgley, R. *Essential Substances: A Cultural History of Intoxicants in Society*, New York, Kodanska International, 1993.

Schivelbusch, W. *Tastes of Paradise: A Social History of Spices, Stimulants and Intoxicants*, trans. Jacobson, D. New York, Pantheon Books, 1992.

Scola, R. *Feeding the Victorian City: The Food Supply of Manchester*, Manchester, Manchester University Press, 1992.

Shammas, C. *The Pre-Industrial Consumer in England and America*, Oxford, Clarendon Press, 1990.

—— 'Changes in English and Anglo-American consumption from 1550 to 1800', in J. Brewer and R. Porter (eds) *Consumption and the World of Goods*, Routledge, 1994.

Shiman, L.L. *Crusade Against Drink in Victorian England*, Macmillan, 1988.

Sigsworth, E.M. *The Brewing Trade during the Industrial Revolution: The Case of Yorkshire*, York, St Anthony's Press, 1967.

Simmons, D.A. *Schweppes: The First 200 Years*, Springwood Books, 1983.

Simon, A.L. *Bottlescrew Days: Wine Drinking in England during the Eighteenth Century*, Duckworth, 1926.

—— *A Concise Encyclopaedia of Gastronomy*, Section VIII, *Wine, Beer, Spirits etc.*, The Wine and Food Society, 1946.

Smith, Ed. *Practical Dietaries for Families, Schools and the Labouring Classes*, Henry S. King, 1875 edn.

Smith, El. *The Compleat Housewife, or Accomplished Gentlewoman's Companion*, Facsimile of 16th edn, 1758, Studio Editions Ltd, 1994.

Smith, F.B. *The People's Health, 1830–1910*, Weidenfeld and Nicolson, 1990.

Smith, Sir H.L. (ed.) *The New Survey of London Life and Labour*, vol. IX, *Life and Leisure*, P.S. King, 1935.

Smith, S. *Accounting for Taste: British Coffee Consumption in Historical Perspective*, York, University of York, Economics Discussion Papers No.94/14, 1994.

Smith, W.D. 'From coffee house to parlour: the consumption of coffee, tea and sugar in north-western Europe in the seventeenth and eighteenth centuries', in J. Goodman *et al. Consuming Habits: Drugs in History and Anthropology*, London and New York, Routledge, 1995.

Smout, T.C. and Wood, S. *Scottish Voices, 1745–1960*, Fontana Press, 1991.

Sournia, J.-C. *A History of Alcoholism*, Oxford, Basil Blackwell, 1990.

Stone, R. *The Measurement of Consumers' Expenditure and Behaviour in the UK, 1920–1938*, 2 vols, Cambridge, Cambridge University Press, 1954.

Strom, S.A.E. *And So To Dine*, Frederick Books, 1955.

Tannahill, R. *Food in History*, Revised edn, Harmondsworth, Middlesex, Penguin Books, 1988.

Tebb, W.S. *Tea and the Effects of Tea Drinking*, London, Cornell and Sons, 1905.

—— *The Metropolitan Water Supply*, London, T. Cornell, n.d. [*c*. 1905].

Thompson, E.P. *The Making of the English Working Class*, Harmondsworth, Middlesex, Penguin Books, 1980.

Thompson, F. *Lark Rise to Candleford*, Harmondsworth, Middlesex, Penguin Books, 1976.

Thorne, R. 'The public house reform movement, 1892–1914', in D.J. Oddy and D.S. Miller (eds) *Diet and Health in Modern Britain*, Croom Helm, 1985.

Torode, A. 'Trends in fruit consumption', in T.C. Barker, J.C. McKenzie and J. Yudkin (eds) *Our Changing Fare: Two Hundred Years of British Food Habits*, Macgibbon and Kee, 1966.

Turner, B.S. *The Body and Society: Explorations in Social Theory*, Oxford, Basil Blackwell, 1984.

Turner, E.S. *The Shocking History of Advertising*, Michael Joseph, 1952.

Twining, S.H. *The House of Twining, 1706–1956*, R. Twining and Co. Ltd, 1956.

Ukers, W.H. *All About Tea*, 2 vols, New York, Tea and Coffee Trade Journal Co., 1935.

Unwin, Mrs.C. (ed.) *The Hungry Forties: Life under the Bread Tax*, T. Fisher Unwin, 1905.

Vaizey, J. *The Brewing Industry, 1886–1951: An Economic Study*, Isaac Pitman and Sons, 1960.

Visser, M. *The Rituals of Dinner: The Origins, Evolution, Eccentricities and Meaning of Table Manners*, Penguin Books, 1993.

Wainwright, D. *Brooke Bond: A Hundred Years*, Newman Neame, Pergamon Group, 1969.

—— *Stone's Ginger Wine: Fortunes of a Family Firm, 1740–1990*, Quiller Press, 1990.

Walker, C. and Cannon, G. *The Food Scandal*, Century Publishing, 1985.

Warren, G.C. (ed.) *The Foods We Eat*, Cassell, 1958.

Watney, J. *Mother's Ruin: A History of Gin*, Peter Owen, 1976.

Watt, J. 'The influence of nutrition upon achievement in maritime history', in C. Geissler and D.J. Oddy (eds), *Food, Diet and Economic Change Past and Present*, Leicester, Leicester University Press, 1993.

Watt, J., Freeman, E.J. and Bynum, W.F. (eds) *Starving Sailors: The Influence of Nutrition Upon Naval and Maritime History*, National Maritime Museum, 1981.

Waugh, A. *The Lipton Story: A Centennial Biography*, New York, Doubleday, 1950.

—— *Merchants of Wine: A Centenary Account of the Fortunes of the House of Gilbey*, Cassell, 1957.

Weatherill, L. *Consumer Behaviour and Material Culture in Britain, 1660–1760*, Routledge, 1988.

Webb, S. and B. *The History of Liquor Licensing in England, Principally from 1700 to 1830*, Longman Green, 1903.

Wedeen, R.P. *Poison in the Pot: The Legacy of Lead*, Carbondale, Southern Illinois University Press, 1984.

Wells, R. *Pleasant Drinks: Effervescing Mixtures, Syrups, Cordials, Home-made Wines, etc.*, Manchester, Abel Heywood and Sons, n.d. [*c.* 1900].

Whetham, E. 'The London milk trade, 1900–1930', in D.J. Oddy and D.S. Miller (eds) *The Making of the Modern British Diet*, Croom Helm, 1976.

Wickizer, V.D. *Coffee, Tea and Cocoa: An Economic and Political Analysis*, California, Stanford University Press, 1951.

Williams, G.P. and Brake, G.T. *Drink in Great Britain, 1900–1979*, Edsall, 1980.

Williams, K. *The Story of Ty·Phoo and the Birmingham Tea Industry*, Quiller Press, 1990.

Wills, J.E. Jr. 'European consumption and Asian production in the seventeenth and eighteenth centuries', in J. Brewer and R. Porter (eds) *Consumption and the World of Goods*, London and New York, Routledge, 1994.

Wilson, C.A. *Food and Drink in Britain: From the Stone Age to the Nineteenth Century*, Chicago, Academy Publishers, 1991.

—— (ed.) *Liquid Nourishment: Potable Foods and Stimulating Drinks*, Edinburgh, Edinburgh University Press, 1993.

Wilson, G.B. *Alcohol and the Nation*, Nicholson and Watson, 1940.

Wohl, A.S. *Endangered Lives: Public Health in Victorian Britain*, Cambridge, Massachussetts, Harvard University Press, 1983.

Woodroof, J.G. and Phillips, G.F. *Beverages: Carbonated and Noncarbonated*, Revised edn, Westport, Connecticut, AVI Publishing, 1981.

Woolton, Lord, in *Tea on Service*, The Tea Centre, 1947.

Wright, T. (A Journeyman Engineer) *Some Habits and Customs of the Working Classes*, (1867), reprint New York, Augustus M. Kelley, 1967.

Wrigley, G. *Coffee*, Harlow, Essex, Longman Scientific and Technical, 1988.

Yates Brothers Wine Lodges Ltd., 1884–1984, privately printed by Yates Bros Wine Lodges Ltd, Bolton, Lancashire, 1984.

Yudkin, J. 'The need for change', in J. Yudkin and J.C. McKenzie (eds) *Changing Food Habits*, Macgibbon and Kee, 1964.

Articles in journals

Albrecht, P. 'Coffee-drinking as a symbol of social change in Continental Europe in the seventeenth and eighteenth centuries', *Studies in Eighteenth Century Culture*, **18**, 1988.

Arkin, M. 'Entrepreneurship and the English East India Company', *Business History*, **XXIII**(1) 1981.

Ashton, T.S. 'Changes in standards of comfort in eighteenth-century England', *The Raleigh Lecture on History, Proceedings of the British Academy*, **XLI**, 1955.

Atkins, P.J. 'The retail milk trade in London, 1790–1914', *Economic History Review*, Second Series, **XXXIII**(4), 1980.

—— 'Sophistication detected, or the adulteration of the milk supply, 1850–1914', *Social History*, **16**(3), 1991.

—— 'White poison? The social consequences of milk consumption, 1850–1930', *Social History of Medicine*, **5**(2), 1992.

Bear, W.E. 'The food supply of Manchester', *Journal of the Royal Agricultural Society*, 3rd Series, **VIII**, 1897.

Bynum, W.F. 'Chronic alcoholism in the first half of the nineteenth century', *Bulletin of the History of Medicine*, **42**, 1968.

Clark, P. 'The "Mother Gin" controversy in the early eighteenth century', *Transactions of the Royal Historical Society*, 5th Series, **38**, 1988.

Coffey, T.G. 'Beer Street, Gin Lane: some views of eighteenth century drinking', *Quarterly Journal of Studies on Alcohol*, **27**, 1966.

Colmore, G. 'A budget at £800 a year', *Cornhill Magazine*, New Series, **X**, 1901.

Davis, R. 'The English wine trade in the eighteenth and nineteenth centuries', *Annales Cisalpines d'Histoire Sociale*, **3**, 1972.

Devine, T.M. 'The rise and fall of illicit whisky-making in northern Scotland *c.* 1780–1840', *Scottish Historical Review*, **54**, 1975.

Dwork, D. 'The milk option: An aspect of the history of the infant welfare movement in England, 1898–1908', *Medical History*, **31**(1), 1987.

Dyhouse, C. 'Working-class mothers and infant mortality in England, 1895–1914', *Journal of Social History*, **12**(2), 1978.

Felix, D. 'De gustibus disputandum est: changing consumer preferences in economic growth', *Explorations in Economic History*, **16**, 1979.

Garner, D. 'Education and the Welfare State: the school meals and milk service, 1944–1980', *Journal of Educational Administration and History*, **17**(2), 1985.

Garney, J. 'Tea-time in Britain', *British Heritage*, **8**(3), 1987.

Gilmore, T.B. 'James Boswell's drinking', *Eighteenth Century Studies*, **24**(3), 1991.

Green, T. 'Apostles of purity', *Smithsonian*, **15**(7), 1984.

Hardy, A. 'Water and the search for public health in London in the eighteenth and nineteenth centuries', *Medical History*, **28**(3), 1984.

Hassan, J.A. 'The growth and impact of the British water industry in the nineteenth century', *Economic History Review*, **38**(4), 1985.

Hughes, R.E. 'The rise and fall of the antiscorbutics: some notes on the traditional cures for "land scurvy"', *Medical History*, (GB), **34**(1), 1990.

Hutchison, R. 'Report on the dietaries of Scotch agricultural labourers', *Transactions of the Highland and Agricultural Society of Scotland*, **II**, 1868–9.

Jones, C. 'The London life of a peer in the reign of Anne: a case study from Lord Ossulston's diary', *The London Journal*, **16**(2), 1991.

Jonnes, J. 'The tale of tea', *Smithsonian*, **12**(11), 1982.

Kekwick, A. 'The Soho epidemic of cholera', *The Medico-Legal Journal*, **XXXIII**(4), 1965.

Lenman, B.P. 'The English and Dutch East India Companies and the birth of consumerism in the Augustan world', *Eighteenth Century Life*, **14**(1), 1990.

Levine, P. 'The humanising influences of five o'clock tea', *Victorian Studies*, **33**(2), 1990.

McCalman, I. 'Ultra-radicalism and convivial debating clubs in London, 1795–1838', *English Historical Review*, **102**, 1987.

McCracken, G. 'The history of consumption: a literature review and consumer guide', *Journal of Consumer Policy*, **10**, 1987.

McIntyre, S. 'The mineral water trade in the eighteenth century', *Journal of British Transport History*, New Series, **II**, 1973.

Maclean, I 'The wine cellar in the nineteenth century', *The Queen's College Record*, **9**, 1993.

Macleod, R.M. 'The edge of hope. Social policy and chronic alcoholism, 1870–1900', *Journal of the History of Medicine*, **22**(3), 1967.

Milk Producer, 'The Milk Marketing Board. 61 years serving dairy farmers', Oct. 1994.

Minchinton, W. 'Cider and folklore', *Folk Life*, **XIII**, 1975.

—— 'The British cider industry since 1870', *Westminster Bank Review*, Nov. 1975.

Mokyr, J. 'Is there still life in the pessimist case? Consumption during the Industrial Revolution, 1790–1850', *Journal of Economic History*, **XLVIII**, 1988.

Neild, W. 'Comparative statement of the income and expenditure of certain families of the working class in Manchester and Dukinfield in the years 1836 and 1841', *Journal of the Statistical Society of London*, **IV**, 1841.

Olson, A. 'Coffee house lobbying', *History Today*, **41**, 1991.

Pelzer, J. and L. 'The coffee houses of Augustan London', *History Today*, **32**, 1982.

Petrie, C. 'Politics and wine', *Quarterly Review*, **93**, 1953.

Quarterly Review, 'Statistical abstract for the United Kingdom in each year from 1840 to 1853', **CCII**, Art. VIII, 1854.

Saul, G.M. 'John Rennie (1761–1821): one of his contributions to waterworks technology', *Transactions of the Newcomen Society*, **59**, 1987–8.

Scott, W.L. 'Food adulteration and the legislative enactments relating thereto', *Journal of the Royal Society of Arts*, **XXIII**, 1875.

Scott-Moncrieff, R. 'Note on the early use of aqua vitae in Scotland', *Proceedings of the Society of Antiquaries of Scotland*, **50**, 1916.

Shammas, C. 'The eighteenth-century English diet and economic change', *Explorations in Economic History*, **21**(3), 1984.

Sheail, J. '"Deadwells": Urban growth and the threat to public health: an inter-war perspective', *Social History of Medicine*, **6**(3), 1993.

Smith, P.J. 'The legislated control of river pollution in Victorian Scotland', *Scottish Geographical Magazine*, **98**(2), 1982.

Smith, W.D. 'Complications of the commonplace: tea, sugar and imperialism', *Journal of Interdisciplinary History*, **23**(2), 1992.

Spring, J.A. and Buss, D.H. 'Three centuries of alcohol in the British diet', *Nature*, **270**, 1977.

Stern, W.M. 'J. Wright, pamphleteer on the London water supply', *Guildhall Miscellany*, Feb. 1953.

Taylor, D. 'The English dairy industry, 1860–1930', *Economic History Review*, Second Series, **XXIX**, 1976.

Vernon, K. 'Pus, sewage, beer and milk: microbiology in Britain, 1870–1940', *History of Science*, **28**(3), 1990.

Ward, C. 'Not the last word on water', *History Workshop Journal*, **41**, 1996.

Weir, R.B. 'Distilling and agriculture, 1870–1939', *Agricultural History Review*, **32**(1), 1984.

Whetham, E.H. 'The London milk trade, 1860–1900', *Economic History Review*, Second Series, **XVII**, 1964.

Wright, D. and Chorniawry, C. 'Women and drink in Edwardian England', *Historical Papers* (Canada), 1985.

Official publications

PP = Parliamentary Papers
RC = Royal Commission
SC = Select Committee

1821	Report of the *SC on the Supply of Water to the Metropolis* (537), v.
1828	Report of the *SC on the Supply of Water to the Metropolis* (567), viii.
1833	Report of the *SC on the Sale of Beer* (416), XV.
1834	Report from the *SC on Drunkenness* (559), VIII.
1844	*RC on the State of Large Towns and Populous Districts*. First Report (572), XVII.
1845	Second Report (602), (610), XVIII.
1852–3	*Sale of Beer*. Reprint of Reports from SCs on the Laws relating to the Sale of Beer, 1817–1850 (292), XXXVII.
1854	Report of the *SC on Public Houses*, etc. (367), XIV.
1855	*SC on Adulteration of Food*, First Report (432), VIII.
1855	Second Report (480), VIII
1856	Third Report (379), VIII
1864	Smith, Dr E. *Sixth Report of the Medical Officer of the Privy Council on the Food of the Poorer Labouring Classes*, (3416), XXVIII.
1867	*RC on the Pollution of Rivers*, Third Report (3850), xxxiii, vol. 1.
1875–1914	*Annual Reports of the Local Government Board*, containing *Reports and Statistics of the Public Analysts*.
1897	*RC on the Liquor Licensing Laws*, vol. I (8355), XXXIV.
1899	*RC on the Liquor Licensing Laws*, vol. IX (9076), XXXV.
1901–4	*RC on Arsenical Poisoning from the Consumption of Beer* (692), IX – (1845), IX.
1903	*Board of Trade, Memoranda, Statistical Tables and Charts*, (1761).
1904	*Report of the Inter-Departmental Committee on Physical Deterioration*, vol. I (2175), XXXII.
1911	Local Government Board, *Report on Condensed Milks, with Special Reference to their Use as Infants' Foods*, New Series No. 56.
1946	*On the State of the Public Health During Six Years of War*. Report of the Chief Medical Officer of the Ministry of Health, 1939–45, Ministry of Health, London, HMSO.
1952–95	*Domestic Food Consumption and Expenditure. Reports of the National Food Survey Committee*, London, HMSO.

1961–95   *Family Expenditure Survey*, Annual Reports, London, HMSO.
1991   *Social Trends 21*, London, HMSO.

Other publications

1881   *Report of the Committee ... on the Present Appropriation of Wages.* 51st
           Meeting of the British Association for the Advancement of Science.
1905   Dodd, F.L. *Municipal Milk and Public Health*, Fabian Society Tract
           No. 122.
1933   *Report of the Committee on Nutrition*, British Medical Association,
           London, BMA.
1950   *Report of the Committee on Nutrition*, British Medical Association,
           London, BMA.
1957, 1974,
1993   *Dairy Facts and Figures*, Thames Ditton, Surrey, The Federation of
           UK Milk Marketing Boards.
1961   *Milk Drinking in Schools*, London, National Dairy Council
           Information Booklet No. 2.
1975   *Nutrition in Schools*, Report of the Working Party on Nutritional
           Aspects of School Meals, London, Department of Education and
           Science, HMSO.
1983   *Report on Snacks and Light Meals*, Taylor Nelson Research Ltd
1988   *The Changing Structure of Meals in Britain: Special Report*, Taylor Nelson
           Research Ltd
1990–4   *Liquid Milk*, Annual Reports, National Dairy Council.
1992–8   The Tea Council, Annual Reports.
1993   *School Meals*, Report of a survey of parents' attitude to the school
           meals service, etc., Consumers' Association.
1993–6   *Soft Drinks Industry Reports*, Chelmsford, Essex, Britvic Soft Drinks
           Ltd
1995   *Alcohol and the Young*, Report of a Joint Working Party of the Royal
           College of Physicians and the British Paediatric Association, Royal
           College of Physicians.
1995   *Water Supply Companies' Factbook*, The Water Companies Association.
1995   *Annual Report*, The Coca-Cola Co.
1995   *The National Diet and Nutrition Survey: Children Aged 1½–4½ Years*, vol.
           1, Report by Gillian Smithers, Economic and Social Research
           Council Data Archive Bulletin No. 61.
1995–6   *Soft Drinks for Adults*, Market Overview, Coca-Cola and Schweppes
           Bourges Ltd
1996   *Drinking Water Quality, 1995*, Report of Thames Water Utilities.
1996   *Tap Water Consumption in England and Wales*, Findings from the 1995
           National Survey, Birmingham, MEL Research.

Index